Weber, Habermas, and Transformations of the European State
Constitutional, Social, and Supranational Democracy

This book critically engages Jürgen Habermas's comprehensive vision of constitutional democracy in the European Union. John P. McCormick draws on the writings of Max Weber (and Habermas's own critique of them) to confront the difficulty of theorizing progressive politics during moments of radical state transformation. Both theorists anachronistically employ normative and empirical categories drawn from earlier historical epochs to analyze contemporary structural transformations: Weber evaluated the emergence of the *Sozialstaat* with antedated categories derived from nineteenth-century and premodern historical examples, while Habermas understands the EU almost exclusively in terms of the liberal (*Rechtsstaat*) and welfare state (*Sozialstaat*) paradigms. Largely forsaking the focus on structural transformation that characterized his early work, Habermas conceptualizes the EU as a territorially expanded nation-state, a continental polity to which he believes his discourse theory of law and democracy can be applied unproblematically. McCormick demonstrates the deficiencies of such an approach and outlines a more appropriate normative-empirical model, the supranational *Sektoralstaat*, for evaluating prospects for constitutional and social democracy in the EU.

John P. McCormick is professor of political science at the University of Chicago. He has received several fellowships, grants, and awards, including a Fulbright to the Center for European Law and Politics at the University of Bremen, Germany, and a Monnet at the European University Institute in Florence, Italy. Professor McCormick is the author of *Carl Schmitt's Critique of Liberalism: Against Politics as Technology* (Cambridge, 1997) and the editor of *Confronting Mass Democracy and Industrial Technology: German Political and Social Thought from Nietzsche to Habermas* (2002). He has published numerous articles on twentieth-century continental legal-political theory and Renaissance political and constitutional thought in scholarly journals such as the *American Political Science Review* (1992, 1999, 2001, 2006) and *Political Theory* (1994, 1998, 2001, 2003, 2006).

Weber, Habermas, and Transformations of the European State

Constitutional, Social, and Supranational Democracy

JOHN P. McCORMICK
University of Chicago

CAMBRIDGE
UNIVERSITY PRESS

CAMBRIDGE UNIVERSITY PRESS
Cambridge, New York, Melbourne, Madrid, Cape Town, Singapore, São Paulo

Cambridge University Press
32 Avenue of the Americas, New York, NY 10013-2473, USA

www.cambridge.org
Information on this title: www.cambridge.org/9780521811408

First published 2007

Printed in the United States of America

A catalog record for this publication is available from the British Library.

Library of Congress Cataloging in Publication Data

McCormick, John P., 1966–
Weber, Habermas, and transformations of the European state : constitutional, social, and
supranational democracy / John P. McCormick.
    p.   cm.
Includes bibliographical references and index.
ISBN-13: 978-0-521-81140-8 (hardback)
1. European Union.   2. Democracy – European Union countries.   3. Constitutional
history – European Union countries.   4. Social integration – European Union
countries.   5. Weber, Max, 1864–1920.   6. Habermas, Jürgen.   I. Title.
JN30.M384   2007
341.242′2–dc22   2006023303

ISBN   978-0-521-81140-8 hardback

For Kay and Angie,
In loving memory

Contents

Acknowledgments

This project began during my graduate studies in the mid-1990s while attending a seminar on Max Weber's sociology of law conducted by Stephen Holmes and Richard Posner in the Law School at the University of Chicago. At the time, I was also engaged in constant and vigorous conversation with Neil Brenner over Jürgen Habermas's social and political theory. In this milieu, I began to ponder the adequacy of Weber's account of the transformation from the liberal state to the welfare state and the role of law within this transition, and to reconsider Habermas's attempt to make up for the deficiencies of Weber's narrative in his own theoretical project. Furthermore, I ventured to ask whether Habermas's framework stood up to the demands of the present situation in which the welfare state was transforming under supranational or global imperatives and pressures. In graduate school, my thoughts on these issues were also deeply influenced by courses and conversations with Robert Pippin, Moishe Postone, Lloyd Rudolph, and Susanne Hoeber Rudolph, as well as by intellectual exchange and enduring friendship with Dan Carpenter.

These ideas continued to develop as I spent successive years as a post-doctoral Fellow at institutions devoted to the study of the legal dimensions of European integration: the Centers for Social Policy (ZeS) and European Legal Policy (ZERP) at the University of Bremen, Germany, and the Departments of Law and Political-Social Science at the European University Institute in Florence, Italy. I thank the faculty and staff of both venues for their support, in particular Christian Joerges, an intellectual-institutional pillar at both universities: Christian supported the project from the start and invited me back to Florence on numerous occasions to present parts of it and participate in seminars and conferences relevant to its concerns. I had the opportunity to write and redraft large portions of the manuscript while a Research Fellow at the Remarque Institute, New York University, in 2001. I thank Tony Judt and Jair Kessler for their considerable generosity and hospitality. A Mellon-Morse Junior Faculty Fellowship awarded by Yale University made possible my leave during 2001–2, and the Division of the Social Sciences at the University of Chicago supported a faculty sabbatical in 2005–6, during which I completed the book.

Earlier versions of sections and chapters of the book have appeared in the following publications, each of which I thank for granting reprint permission: *Political Theory*, *American Political Science Review*, *Modern Law Review*, *European Journal of Political Theory*, *Yale Journal of Law and the Humanities*, and the *Canadian Journal of Law and Jurisprudence*. Lewis Bateman, my editor at Cambridge University Press, has been patient, understanding, constructive, and inspirational throughout the composition and production process. Louise Calabro and Helen Greenberg provided diligent and detailed production and copyediting work, while Don Reneau expertly prepared the index, and B. J. Carrick carefully proofread the manuscript.

The manuscript and parts that comprise it have gone through many changes over the years. At crucial points in the book's development Seyla Benhabib, Steven Smith, Rogers Smith, and Bruce Western offered constructive criticisms that prompted me to refocus it in more fruitful ways. The following have read significant parts of the manuscript and generously offered their comments or criticisms: Bruce Ackerman, David Cameron, Cathy Cohen, Maeve Cooke, David Dyzenhaus, Arthur Jacobson, Stephan Leibfried, Steven Lukes, John Mearsheimer, Don Moon, Jan Müller, Gianfranco Poggi, Ulrich Preuß, Bill Scheuerman, Philippe Schmitter, Ian Shapiro, Steven Skowronek, Peggy Somers, Yasemin Soysal, Camil Ungureanu, Stephen White, Richard Wolin, and the late Iris Marion Young. Cynthia Burns, Loren Goldman, Michele Kennedy, and Justin Zaremby provided invaluable research assistance. Gia Pascarelli patiently endured many of the disappointments, disruptions, and relocations experienced while I researched and composed the book. I'm deeply grateful for all the affection, support, and especially wit that she so graciously and generously shared with me during those many years.

This book is dedicated to the memory of my grandmothers, Catherine and Angelina, who played an immeasurable role in my rearing and education. They are, in a strange but significant sense, coauthors of the book and all the things I do.

JPM
Chicago, Illinois
1 February 2007

Abbreviations

Max Weber

SL "Economy and Social Norms" and "Sociology of Law" in *Economy and Society: An Outline of Interpretive Sociology*, Guenther Roth and Claus Wittich, eds., 2 vols. (Berkeley: University of California Press, 1978), 311–38 and 641–899.

RS "Die Wirtschaft und die gesellschaftlichen Ordnungen" and "Rechtssoziologie" in *Wirtschaft und Gesellschaft: Grundriss der Verstehenden Soziologie* (Tübingen: Mohr [Siebeck], 1922), 181–98 and 387–513.

Jürgen Habermas

STPS *The Structural Transformation of the Public Sphere: An Inquiry into a Category of Bourgeois Society* (1962), trans. Thomas Burger with Frederick Lawrence (Cambridge, MA: MIT Press, 1989).

LC *Legitimation Crisis* (1973), trans. Thomas McCarthy (Boston: Beacon Press, 1975).

TCA1 *The Theory of Communicative Action, Vol. 1: Reason and the Rationalization of Society* (1981), trans. Thomas McCarthy (Boston: Beacon Press, 1984).

TCA2 *The Theory of Communicative Action, Vol. 2: Lifeworld and System: A Critique of Functionalist Reason* (1981), trans. Thomas McCarthy (Boston: Beacon Press, 1987).

LM   "Law and Morality," trans. Kenneth Baynes, in S. M. McMurrin, ed., *The Tanner Lectures on Human Values, Vol. 8* (Salt Lake City: University of Utah Press, 1988), 217–79.

BFN   *Between Facts and Norms: Contributions to a Discourse Theory of Law and Democracy* (1992), trans. William Rehg (Cambridge, MA: MIT Press, 1996).

FG   *Faktizität und Geltung: Beiträge zur Diskurstheorie des Rechts und des demokratischen Rechtsstaats* (Frankfurt a.M.: Suhrkamp, 1992).

IO   *The Inclusion of the Other: Studies in Political Theory*, Ciaran Cronin and Pablo de Grieff, eds. (Cambridge, MA: MIT Press, 1998).

PC   *The Postnational Constellation: Political Essays*, Max Pensky, ed. (Cambridge, MA: MIT Press, 2001).

NLR   "The European Nation-State and the Pressures of Globalization," *New Left Review* 235 (1999), 46–59.

DEU   "Beyond the Nation-State?: On Some Consequences of Economic Globalization," in E. O. Eriksen and J. E. Fossum, eds., *Democracy in the European Union: Integration Through Deliberation?* (London: Routledge, 2000), 29–41.

RSC   "Warum braucht Europa eine Verfassung?" in Habermas, *Zeit der Übergänge* (Frankfurt a.M.: Suhrkamp, 2001), 104–29 ["So, Why Does Europe Need a Constitution?" trans. Michelle Everson (www.iue.it/RSC/EU/Reform02.pdf)].

Weber, Habermas, and Transformations of the European State
Constitutional, Social, and Supranational Democracy

I

Introduction

Theorizing Modern Transformations of Law and Democracy

Social scientists today attempt to formulate categories that illuminate evolving supranational developments and emerging international institutions associated with globalization, most concretely the European Union (EU).[1] Simultaneously, many political theorists refine a normative model of democracy legitimated by deliberative practices and instituted through legal-constitutional procedures.[2] This study combines and contributes to

---

[1] In an ever-growing literature on European integration, the following works are generally concerned with the issue of democracy in the EU: Andrew Moravcsik, *The Choice for Europe: Social Purpose and State Power from Messina to Maastricht* (Ithaca, NY: Cornell University Press, 1998); Neil MacCormick, *Questioning Sovereignty: Law, State, and Nation in the European Commonwealth* (Oxford: Oxford University Press, 1999); J. H. H. Weiler, *The Constitution of Europe: "Do the New Clothes Have an Emperor?" and Other Essays* (Cambridge: Cambridge University Press, 1999); Fritz Scharpf, *Governing in Europe: Effective and Democratic?* (Oxford: Oxford University Press, 1999); G. F. Mancini, *Democracy and Constitutionalism in the European Union* (Oxford: Hart, 2000); Philippe C. Schmitter, *How to Democratize the European Union... And Why Bother?* (Lanham, MD: Rowman & Littlefield, 2000); Larry Siedentop, *Democracy in Europe* (New York: Columbia University Press, 2001); Karen J. Alter, *Establishing the Supremacy of European Law: The Making of an International Rule of Law in Europe* (Oxford: Oxford University Press, 2001); and Klaus Eder and Bernhard Giesen, eds., *European Citizenship: National Legacies and Transnational Projects* (Oxford: Oxford University Press, 2001).

[2] Out of another vast literature, consult Seyla Benhabib and Fred R. Dallmayr, eds., *The Communicative Ethics Controversy* (Cambridge, MA: MIT Press, 1990); James S. Fishkin, *Democracy and Deliberation: New Directions for Democratic Reform* (New Haven, CT: Yale University Press, 1993); Bruce A. Ackerman, *Social Justice in the Liberal State* (New Haven, CT: Yale University Press, 1993); James Bohman, *Public Deliberation: Pluralism, Complexity and Democracy* (Cambridge, MA: MIT Press, 1996); Amy Gutmann and Dennis Thompson, *Democracy and Disagreement* (Cambridge, MA: Harvard Belknap Press, 1996); James Bohman and William Rehg, eds., *Deliberative Democracy: Essays*

these efforts by asking how democracy and the rule of law may be secured
and advanced in supranational institutions such as the EU during the
dawning century. However, I venture an answer to this question in an
apparently indirect and ostensibly anachronistic manner: the book revisits two of the *last century's* most powerful normative-empirical analyses
of European state transformations: specifically, Max Weber's sociology
of law and Jürgen Habermas's discourse theory of law and democracy. I
demonstrate how these theorists' strengths and shortcomings contribute
to a more sophisticated theoretical engagement with the current situation
of law and democracy as the European state transforms as a result of
globalization and the integration process.

Part of my task is to show that Weber's "Sociology of Law"³ is much
less of an encyclopedia of legal categories or a history of legal development in the West than many scholars commonly suppose. Weber's SL is
first and foremost an intense confrontation with what was a transformation of state and society in Weber's own time: specifically, the transition
from the nineteenth-century liberal state, or *Rechtsstaat*, to the admin-
istrative/welfare state, or *Sozialstaat*, of the twentieth century.⁴ Despite
the incomparable breadth of Weber's analysis, his study underestimates
the progressive possibilities for the rule of law and substantive democracy in the emerging *Sozialstaat*. I trace this shortcoming to historical

on *Reason and Politics* (Cambridge, MA: MIT Press, 1997); Jon Elster, ed., *Deliberative
Democracy* (Cambridge: Cambridge University Press, 1998); and Stephen Macedo, ed.,
Deliberative Politics: Essays on Democracy and Disagreement (Oxford: Oxford University
Press, 1999).

³ I refer to the following sections of Weber's *Economy and Society* as the "Sociology of
Law" and combine them for citation purposes under the abbreviation SL in the text:
Weber, "Economy and Social Norms" and "Sociology of Law" in *Economy and Society:
An Outline of Interpretive Sociology* (c. 1920), Guenther Roth and Claus Wittich, eds.,
2 vols. (Berkeley: University of California Press, 1978), 311–38 and 641–899.

⁴ Generally I use the German term "*Sozialstaat*" – literally, "social state" – rather than the
alternatives ("welfare state," "regulatory state," "administrative state") because it captures both crucial aspects of state–society interaction inherent in the model: the egalitarian
redistributive *and* capital-friendly regulatory aspects of the social, economic, and political
configuration. I occasionally use the term "administrative/welfare state," as previously,
since it seems most appropriate if more cumbersome than "*Sozialstaat*." On European
state development generally, see Charles Tilly, *Coercion, Capital, and European States, AD
990–1992* (Oxford: Blackwell, 1992); on the European *Sozialstaat* more specifically, see
Peter Baldwin, *The Politics of Social Solidarity: Class Bases of the European Welfare State,
1875–1975* (Cambridge: Cambridge University Press 1992); and on its emergence in the
U.S. context, see Stephen Skowronek, *Building a New American State: The Expansion of
National Administrative Capacities, 1877–1920* (Cambridge: Cambridge University Press
1982).

assumptions that compel Weber to associate the *Sozialstaat* with characteristics of premodern patrimonial authority. Weber's comparison of these two political examples is not a straightforward deployment of Weber's famous "ideal types," through which similar social phenomena from different historical contexts might be better understood. Rather, I suggest that it is in fact a desperate and ideological misrecognition of a dauntingly novel historical development that threatens Weber's social scientific categories, as well as the normative worldview that he purported to keep separate from them.

In light of this analysis of Weber, I interrogate Habermas's attempt to rectify the historical and normative deficiencies of Weber's efforts in his own theoretical-empirical projects: in particular, Habermas's more differentiated historical analysis of the rise of both the liberal and welfare states in *Public Sphere*[5] and his later formulation of the legal and democratic potential of communication within the postwar *Sozialstaat* in works like *Communicative Action* and *Between Facts and Norms*.[6] However, I argue that Habermas ultimately repeats Weber's historical missteps, especially in recent attempts to apply his discourse model of law and democracy to supranational developments in the EU. In essays and book chapters contained in *The Inclusion of the Other* and *The Postnational Constellation*,[7] and in several important pieces published after them, Habermas interprets the EU as an emerging constitutional-social democracy in a way that directly repudiates his earlier fine-grained sociohistorical analyses of the *Rechtsstaat*'s emergence and its subsequent transformation into the *Sozialstaat*.

Habermas often ascribes to the development of supranational institutions like the EU a historical logic continuous with previous state transformations. In other words, he understands these developments as largely

[5] Habermas, *The Structural Transformation of the Public Sphere: An Inquiry into a Category of Bourgeois Society* (1962), trans. Thomas Burger with Frederick Lawrence (Cambridge, MA: MIT Press, 1989), hereafter STPS.

[6] Habermas, *The Theory of Communicative Action, Vol. 1: Reason and the Rationalization of Society* (1981), trans. Thomas McCarthy (Boston: Beacon Press, 1984), hereafter TCA1; *The Theory of Communicative Action, Vol. 2: Lifeworld and System: A Critique of Functionalist Reason* (1981), trans. Thomas McCarthy (Boston: Beacon Press, 1987), hereafter TCA2; *Between Facts and Norms: Contributions to a Discourse Theory of Law and Democracy* (1992), trans. William Rehg (Cambridge, MA: MIT Press, 1996), hereafter BFN.

[7] Habermas, *The Inclusion of the Other: Studies in Political Theory*, Ciaran Cronin and Pablo de Grieff, eds. (Cambridge, MA: MIT Press, 1998), and *The Postnational Constellation: Political Essays*, Max Pensky, ed. (Cambridge, MA: MIT Press, 2001).

repeating or further expanding the rise of the nation-state, rather than as signaling a qualitative change within the history of the latter. I argue that the development of the EU, according to strictures of Habermas's own critical-theoretical methodology, necessitates the consideration of historical rupture and institutional innovation. Habermas makes some gestures in this direction, but they prove insufficient to ensure that normative aspirations from the *Sozialstaat* configuration can be carried over to the new configuration presently emerging in Europe – one that I call a supranational "*Sektoralstaat*." Rather than entertain, articulate, and confront the possibility of a new structural configuration, Habermas stubbornly holds out the hope of adapting the *Sozialstaat* – reconstructed according to his normative specifications, to be sure – to the structural transformation presently entailed by European integration.

Just as Weber misapprehended the progressive possibilities of the *Sozialstaat* by evaluating it through antedated categories drawn from premodern cases, Habermas now potentially mislocates the progressive possibilities of the EU by imposing upon its historical development evaluative categories largely derived without qualification from an earlier era. What facilitates this "uncritical" or "ideological" theoretical move that Habermas, preeminent heir to the Frankfurt tradition of critical theory, would have sought at all costs to avoid in his early work? Midway through his career, Habermas turns from a theory of historical change focused on transitions of discrete epochs in modernity (e.g., absolutist, mercantilist, liberal and state-capitalist historical configurations) to a transhistorical evolutionary model where important social change is understood largely in terms of a tradition–modernity dichotomy. Moreover, rather than political economy, Habermas has come to rely extensively on Weberian notions of secularization and value pluralism to explain the mechanisms of historical change. As I point out, this move is only marginally problematic so long as Habermas theorized the *Sozialstaat* as a quasi-permanent sociopolitical arrangement – one whose overall structure as opposed to discontinuous history indicates the way to secure normative aspirations. But, as I explain later in this chapter and demonstrate throughout this book, successful normative-empirical analysis of the transition from sovereign European *Sozialstaat*s to an integrated European *Sektoralstaat* requires attention to intramodern historical change associated with transformations in political economy and sociopolitical aspirations related to such transformations.

In short, Habermas attempts to retain the normative goals of his mature transhistorical work (those associated with the *Sozialstaat* legitimated by the discourse theory of law) in circumstances that hearken back to his

more historically specific earlier efforts (circumstances of structural transformation). He moves from a model that theorized multiple structural
transformations within modernity – indeed, due to the various commodification dynamics unique to capitalist societies, one that understood such
transformations to be possible *only* in modernity – to a model that, like
Weber's, prioritizes the traditional-to-modern transition in worldviews
as the single or primary transformation within modernity.[8] While Weber
would not fully accept the normative challenge of the structural transformation toward the *Sozialstaat*, and so interpreted it as a reversion to a
more primitive and authoritarian social form such as medieval patrimonialism, Habermas insists that his theoretically reconstructed *Sozialstaat*
is an appropriate normative-empirical model for the new circumstances
associated with European integration (even if, as we will see, he sometimes
comes very close to describing it in terms of a structural transformation).

Therefore, I suggest that *both* theorists posit the *past* – one more distant, the other more recent – as the *future* in ultimately unreflective ways.
Habermas's discourse theory of law and democracy impressively corrects
the normative myopia of Weber's legal analysis of the *Sozialstaat*. But
Habermas's project itself proves particularly susceptible to Weber's historical astigmatism as he attempts to reconcile it with supranational developments in our own time. As I explain in the next section, my critique
has implications for both (1) the project of critical theory today and (2)
the attempt to advance democracy in the contemporary supranational,
historical constellation.[9] My analysis is relevant in these regards because,

---

[8] For a serious interrogation of the "modernity" issue that is suspicious of most treatments
of the concept, whether deployed in evolutionary *or* historically specific strategies, see
Bernard Yack, *The Fetishism of Modernities: Epochal Self-Consciousness in Contemporary Social and Political Thought* (South Bend, IN: Notre Dame University Press, 1998).

[9] A work influential on this study that combines normative concerns, empirical sophisti-
cation, and historical sensitivity in the analysis of earlier supranational developments is
Karl Polanyi, *The Great Transformation: The Political and Economic Origins of Our
Time* (1944), fore. Joseph E. Stiglitz, intro. Fred L. Block (Boston: Beacon Press, 2001).
For multidisciplinary approaches to globalization today, see David Held, *Democracy and
the Global Order: From the Modern State to Cosmopolitan Governance* (Stanford, CA:
Stanford University Press, 1995); Paul Hirst and G. Thompson, *Globalisation in Ques-
tion: The International Economy and the Possibilities of Governance* (Cambridge: Polity
Press, 1996); Susan Strange, *The Retreat of the State: The Diffusion of Power in the World
Economy* (Cambridge: Cambridge University Press, 1996); Saskia Sassen, *Globalization
and Its Discontents* (New York: New Press, 1996); and Arjun Appadurai, *Modernity
at Large: Cultural Dimensions of Globalization* (Minneapolis: University of Minnesota
Press, 1996). For liberal perspectives on globalization, see John Rawls, *The Law of Peo-
ples: With the Idea of Public Reason Revisited* (Cambridge, MA: Harvard University
Press, 1999), and the following review of it: Charles Beitz, "Rawls's Law of Peoples,"
Ethics 110 (July 2000), 670–5.

on the one hand, Habermas still remains expressly committed to a critical project of social research that contributes to emancipatory political practice and, on the other, progressive engagements with globalization today tend to rely on undertheorized presuppositions about the history of the modern state rather than on fully articulated theories of historical change.

1. Critical Theory and Structural Transformations

The theory of historical change expressed by Habermas's work of the 1970s and 1980s has two dimensions: on the one hand, he describes a social evolutionary process of improving communicative capacities, grounded in transhistorical human learning processes, and he repeatedly invokes the transition from traditional (or premodern) to posttraditional or modern social forms. Here I would like to sketch briefly the extent to which this constitutes a dramatic departure from the Hegelian–Marxist orientation of critical theory, arguably best exhibited by the young Habermas's *Public Sphere* book. As I will show in Chapter 2, this departure is sufficiently serious to undermine some of the normative potentials for mutual understanding that Habermas considers immanent to advanced capitalist – that is, *Sozialstaat* – societies and also, as I show in Chapters 5 and 6, sufficiently serious to jeopardize his efforts to account for state transformation in a supranational historical constellation today.

Contrary to the view of many commentators on the Frankfurt School, Western Marxism, and critical theory, the decisive "standing Hegel on his head" adopted by the later Marx, the early Lukács, the Frankfurt Institute for Social Research, and the young Habermas was not the prioritization of a "material base" associated with orthodox Marxism and, concomitant with it, a labor-centric notion of historical change throughout human history.[10] Although often incapable of resisting the temptation to revert

---

[10] Notwithstanding differences with my own interpretation of this tradition, consult the following important studies of it: Martin Jay, *The Dialectical Imagination: A History of the Frankfurt School and the Institute of Social Research, 1923–1950* (Boston: Little, Brown, 1973); David Held, *Introduction to Critical Theory: Horkheimer to Habermas* (Berkeley: University of California Press, 1980); Raymond Geuss, *The Idea of a Critical Theory: Habermas and the Frankfurt School* (Cambridge: Cambridge University Press, 1981); Richard Wolin, *The Terms of Cultural Criticism: The Frankfurt School, Existentialism, Poststructuralism* (New York: Columbia University Press, 1992); Rolf Wiggershaus, *The Frankfurt School: Its History, Theories, and Political Significance*, ed. Thomas McCarthy, trans. Michael Robertson (Cambridge, MA: MIT Press, 1994); and in a broader philosophical context, Michael Rosen, *On Voluntary Servitude: False Consciousness and the Theory of Ideology* (Cambridge, MA: Harvard University Press, 1996).

to such orthodox-materialist positions, in another spirit entirely, critical theory reconstructed Hegelian dialectics and philosophy of history by deemphasizing (and sometimes even jettisoning) the transhistorical periodizations that Hegel posited (both crudely and brilliantly) across human time to illustrate consciousness's coming to know itself.[11]

Rather, the critical as opposed to dogmatic aspects of Marx, Lukács, and the Frankfurt scholars accentuate changes *within* modernity itself, changes facilitated by dynamics unleashed by the specifics of modern society – not only the strictly economic dimensions of free labor and universal exchange but also the sociocultural dimensions of civil society and the state.[12] Such a critical theory identifies the interactions among and changing forms of these sites as more appropriate contexts in which to realize the quasi-Kantian notions of human consciousness and norms of autonomy that Hegel himself situated in a linear and ideational transepochal theodicy.[13] Nevertheless, the significance of the intramodern as opposed to transhistorical orientation of critical theory is still very much "Hegelian": after all, for Hegel, the *transition* between epochs was crucial for exhibiting the conflicts between and eventual *Aufhebung*

[11] See G. W. F. Hegel, *Phenomenology of Spirit*, trans. A. V. Miller, fore. J. N. Findlay (Oxford: Oxford University Press, 1979), and Hegel, *Introduction to the Philosophy of History*, trans. Leo Rauch (New York: Hackett, 1997).

[12] See Karl Marx, *Capital: A Critique of Political Economy, Vol. 1*, trans. Ben Fowkes (London: Vintage, 1976), and Georg Lukács, *History and Class Consciousness*, trans. Rodney Livingstone (Cambridge, MA: MIT Press, 1988). Moishe Postone distinguishes the historically specific and subjectively social aspects of *Capital* from the crudely transhistorical and materially objective characteristics of Marx's earlier work in *Time, Labor and Social Domination: A Reinterpretation of Marx's Critical Theory* (New York: Cambridge University Press, 1993). Andrew Feenberg, in *Lukács, Marx, and the Sources of Critical Theory* (Oxford: Oxford University Press, 1986), separates the commodity-focused and nondeterminist moments of *History and Class Consciousness* from the logic that culminates at the book's climax with Lukács's anointing of the proletariat as a world-historical subject. Seyla Benhabib convincingly traces back the labor-centric and materially evolutionary – and thus socially undifferentiated and politically authoritarian – aspects of Hegelian Marxism to Hegel himself, but also highlights important moments throughout this tradition where the reality of, and prospect for further, human intersubjectivity is discovered, elaborated, and promoted: see Benhabib, *Critique, Norm, and Utopia: A Study of the Foundations of Critical Theory* (New York: Columbia University Press, 1986).

[13] Although this description may be an unfair exaggeration of Hegel's philosophy of history, see Michael Rosen, *Hegel's Dialectic and Its Criticism* (Cambridge: Cambridge University Press, 1985), 23–54; Steven B. Smith, *Hegel's Critique of Liberalism: Rights in Context* (Chicago: University of Chicago Press, 1989), 168–79; Robert B. Pippin, *Idealism as Modernism: Hegelian Variations* (Cambridge: Cambridge University Press, 1997), 17–18, 418; and Alan Patten, *Hegel's Theory of Freedom* (Oxford: Oxford University Press, 1999), 163–200.

of different modes of consciousness, much more so than simple *contrasts* between discrete, already superseded, and eventually superseding epochs.[14]

Yet, in the English-language literature on the Frankfurt School of the 1970s and 1980s, the excesses of the "philosophy of history" associated with attention to structural-historical change was perhaps overemphasized because Habermasian critical theory had wagered that modern history had reached something like a final or only minutely changing form in "late" or "advanced" capitalism. In this literature the philosophy of history was often assimilated to the "philosophy of the subject" or the "philosophy of consciousness" – both of which became dirty terms associated with the authoritarian theory and practice of Orthodox Marxism and Soviet-style state socialism. Consequently, the centrality of historical change within modernity to the critical theoretical method was often neglected, replaced by Habermas's fairly linear evolutionary communicative theory that explained little about the actual historical past and portended even less about the future.[15] But growing popular and academic awareness of globalization in recent years has put history and structural-historical change back on the table, as contemporary critical theorists are beginning to realize.[16]

---

[14] As Charles Taylor explains, the dialectical *process* itself yields knowledge, not just paradigmatic or epochal *contrasts* that result from it: "What could not be expressed in external existence is expressed in the movement by which these existents come to be and pass away. The 'distortion' which external reality imposed on Spirit's message is corrected by its necessary demise. Spirit never comes to one unchanging expression which says it all, but in the play of affirmation and denial it manifests what it is." See Taylor, *Hegel and Modern Society* (Cambridge: Cambridge University Press, 1979), 56. Cf. also Rosen, *Hegel's Dialectic and Its Criticism*, 55–90.

[15] Benhabib upholds the place of "the transfigurative" and not merely "reformist" impulses of critical theory; the former is open to new normative aspirations in new historical circumstances, and is not just concerned with comparing present reality to its own ideals, as is the latter. But she is far more critical of the foreclosure of this transfigurative potential by Hegel's and Marx's labor centrism and macrohistorical "transsubjectivity" than she is of Habermas's social evolutionism, which, as she concedes, serves to reify the present as future. See Benhabib, *Critique, Norm, and Utopia*, 13, 60–1, 114, 142, 276–7. In Chapter 2, I will also push more forcefully the criticisms of Habermas's increasingly unreflective philosophy of history set forth by, e.g., Thomas McCarthy's *The Critical Theory of Jürgen Habermas* (Cambridge, MA: MIT Press, 1978) and Axel Honneth's *Critique of Power: Reflective Stages in a Critical Social Theory* (1985), trans. Kenneth Baynes (Cambridge, MA: MIT Press, 1991).

[16] See Held, *Democracy and the Global Order*; Nancy Fraser, *Justice Interruptus: Critical Reflections on the "Postsocialist" Condition* (London: Routledge, 1996); and Seyla Benhabib, *The Claims of Culture: Equality and Diversity in the Global Era* (Princeton, NJ: Princeton University Press, 2002).

We will observe in Chapter 5 Habermas's attempt to adapt his theory to these new developments, more specifically his equivocations on the extent to which they signal a new structural transformation, if a transformation at all. The question will be whether, in his analysis of the EU, Habermas is able to free himself from the static historical paradigm that he adopted to better facilitate deliberative-juridical emancipation *within* a *Sozialstaat* model in works like TCA and BFN. Moreover, I ask in Chapter 6 whether Habermas's paradigm is appropriate to the *Sektoralstaat* model of governance emerging in the EU. The *Sektoralstaat* model accentuates deliberation among interested parties in microspheres of transnational policymaking, but also insulates those spheres from public and governmental oversight and regulation through which the *Sozialstaat* attempted to guarantee the equity of negotiation, if not always deliberation for all participants affected.

As Habermas himself argues, those *Sozialstaat* guarantees were sanctioned by universal principles institutionalized in constitutional orders and protected, albeit imperfectly, by practices of judicial review. Notwithstanding recurring cycles of excitement over a European constitution[17] and pervasive assumptions concerning the prowess of the EU's European Court of Justice (ECJ), these institutions are markedly less powerful at the Union level than they were in the *Sozialstaat*, and are likely to remain so for structural reasons I will address. In addition, the *Sektoralstaat* that the EU is becoming will likely permit individual member states to opt in or out of different policy sectors, thus grouping themselves into multiple "policy Europes" within the polity. Different assemblages of EU member states would constitute separate energy, defense, trade, communications, welfare, environment, and other subpolities.[18] This means that the EU will be a "Union" that tolerates – in de jure and not just de facto

---

[17] See the proclamation of the EU Charter of Fundamental Rights (Nice, 7 December 2000) (O.J. 2000, C 346/1 of 18 December 2000) and the European Council's Laeken Declaration (14–15 December 2001) on a constitutional convention, which convened in March 2002 (europeanconvention.eu.int/plen sess.asp?lang=EN). Cf. also Richard Bellamy and Dario Castiglione, "Between Cosmopolis and Community: Three Models of Rights and Democracy within the European Union," in *Reimagining Political Community: Studies in Cosmopolitan Democracy*, D. Archibugi, D. Held, and M. Köhler, eds. (Oxford: Polity Press, 1998); "The Normative Challenge of a European Polity: Cosmopolitan and Communitarian Models Compared, Criticized and Combined," in *Democracy and the EU*, Andreas Follesdal and Peter Koslowski, eds. (Berlin: Springer, 1998); and " 'A Republic, If You Can Keep It': The Democratic Deficit and the Constitution of Europe," (manuscript, University of Manchester, 1999).

[18] This eventuality is most explicitly predicted and advocated in Scharpf, *Governing in Europe*; and Schmitter, *How to Democratize the European Union*.

manner – greater disparities of material welfare, economic liberty, and social protection among its component parts than any federal state permitted in the *Sozialstaat* era. As we will see, these characteristics of the European *Sektoralstaat* pose greater problems for Habermas's model of discursively noncoercive and egalitarian law and policy formation than his analysis of the EU suggests.

Returning to the significance of Habermas's earlier work: besides sensitivity to intramodern historical change, another advantage that his *Public Sphere* maintains over previous works of critical theory is the book's sensitivity to the indispensable place of law throughout each epoch of modernity. Habermas accentuates the emancipatory advance heralded by the *Rechtsstaat* (particularly the unprecedented potential for publicly institutionalizing discursively produced mutual understanding), the ideological and structural limitations inherent in it (such as its socially exclusionary and economically inegalitarian features), and the possibilities and pathologies immanent in the transformation from the *Rechtsstaat* into the *Sozialstaat* (on the one hand, the widening of participation and the material improvement of larger segments of society and, on the other, a devastating potential for political stultification and technocratic unaccountability). As opposed to Weber, who delineated all the normative advantages of the *Rechtsstaat* in ostensibly objective-descriptive terms in SL and yet erupted into utter panic over the ramifications of its supercession by the *Sozialstaat*, Habermas was willing to acknowledge the accomplishments and social improvements offered by the latter model – even if they could be maximized fully only through the legally facilitated and publicity-inducing reforms that he proposes toward the conclusion of STPS. In fact, as we will see, it is precisely the character of the transformation between the two configurations that points up the emancipatory possibilities of the *Sozialstaat* for the young Habermas.

Thus, while earlier critical theorists largely underestimated the progressive potential of social integration through law,[19] and while Weber

---

[19] On the original Hegelian formulation of the *Rechtsstaat*, see Smith, *Hegel's Critique of Liberalism*, 140, 145–8, as well as the essays contained in *Hegel and Legal Theory*, eds. Drucilla Cornell, Michel Rosenfeld, and David G. Carlson (New York: Routledge, 1991). Marx notoriously belittles law as "bourgeois form," and note Lukács's rather casual dismissal of law in the "Legality and Illegality" essay included in *History and Class Consciousness*, 256–71. Of course, Franz Neumann and Otto Kirchheimer were Frankfurt critical theorists especially attuned to transformations of modern law. See Franz L. Neumann and Otto Kirchheimer, *The Rule of Law Under Siege: Selected Essays*,

was willing or able to identify only one modern incarnation of law in modernity as normatively advantageous,[20] in STPS Habermas carefully focuses on transformations of legal arrangements during intramodern social change so as to illustrate the gains and losses, possibilities and constraints, and aspirations and strategies offered by the interaction of consciousness and political economy across different modern epochs. By contrast, the transhistorical social evolutionism and historically blunt premodern–modern opposition deployed by Habermas to account for social change in later work approximates a reversion to a kind of traditional, overly speculative Hegelianism still in thrall to Kant.[21] It was, after all, Hegel's faithfulness to Kant's theory of autonomy that sent him searching for ways to escape the abstract formalism and practical urealizability of that theory in the course of human history and, somewhat uncritically, in the institutions of his own day.[22] What Marx, Lukács, the pre-fatalistic

ed. W. E. Scheuerman (Berkeley: University of California Press, 1996). But their rather Weberian lament over the demise of *Rechtsstaat* formal law and the rise of *Sozialstaat* material law renders them less perspicacious analysts than the young Habermas. Despite these limitations, see the excellent study by William E. Scheuerman, *Between the Norm and the Exception: The Frankfurt School and the Rule of Law* (Cambridge, MA: MIT Press, 1994).

[20] See Joan Tronto, "Law and Modernity: The Significance of Max Weber's Sociology of Law," *Texas Law Review* 63 (1984), 554–65.

[21] On the important albeit ultimately incomplete advances of Hegelian over Kantian normative analysis, see Benhabib, *Critique, Norm, and Utopia*, 71–80, 89–92; Rosen, *Hegel's Dialectic and Its Criticisms*, 115–20; Benhabib, *Situating the Self: Gender, Community, and Postmodernism in Contemporary Ethics* (London: Routledge, 1992), 23–67; and Patten, *Hegel's Theory of Freedom*, 82–102. On Habermas's place in this dilemma, see Kenneth Baynes, *The Normative Grounds of Social Criticism: Kant, Rawls, and Habermas* (Albany: State University of New York Press, 1991).

[22] Pippin, for instance, argues: "Hegel clearly accepts a modern, essentially Kantian criterion for evaluating the worth of actions. To act freely is to act rightly, and to act rightly is to act in a way consistent with the will of all, or to act universally, and to act in some sense with this intention as a reason. But, in an argument indebted to his general idealist position, he does not believe that we can formulate the content of such a universal law except by reference to the history of ethical institutions, the history of what we have come to regard as counting as universal, as what all others would or could accept as a maxim." See Pippin, *Modernism as a Philosophical Problem: On the Dissatisfactions of European High Culture* (Oxford: Basil Blackwell, 1991), 72; cf. also Patten, *Hegel's Theory of Freedom*, 43–81. In the next chapter, I show that Habermas's theory of history reverts to this Kantian Hegelianism and away from Hegelian Marxism in precisely Pippin's terms: "Hegel believes he can describe a general 'process,' a development, in a community's emerging self-consciousness about such criteria that can account for the periodic breakdown of such consensus and the emergence of a new self-understanding. In a word, Hegel is an idealist; he believes that communities are the way they are basically because of how they understand themselves and what they value, and these criteria and values are the way they are because of the determinate insufficiencies of prior attempts at self-understanding

Frankfurt scholars, and the young Habermas added to this orientation was a better sense of how ideals of autonomy might be realized through attention to transformations of capitalist society, if not wholly reduced to their economic aspects. This is not an easy task, and despite being, to my mind, the work that comes closest to carrying it out successfully, *Public Sphere* is hardly seamless or fully successful in carrying this out, as we will see.[23] Nevertheless, I want to ask whether Habermas had cast his analytical net so wide historically in post–*Public Sphere* work – that is, in attempting to account for communicative capacities throughout all human time – that he actually let slip through the stretched pores of his analysis the details of recent developments that make communicative and legally facilitated democracy still viable. But, as I will explain, Habermas is not alone in this regard.

2. Critical Theory and the Supranational Constellation

Notwithstanding claims to understand recent developments associated with globalization and European integration as something like "things-in-themselves" that can be apprehended objectively through empirical methods, and therefore about which normative prescriptions can be fashioned fairly easily, the contemporary literature on European integration

and self-legitimation." See Pippin, *Modernism as a Philosophical Problem*, 69. However, see Pippin's criticisms of Habermas's misreadings of Hegel in *Idealism as Modernism*, 159–74, and Rosen's in *Hegel's Dialectic and Its Criticisms*, 35–40. Kant himself engaged in the stark epochal contrast that I criticize in the work of Habermas: "What Is Enlightenment?" posits something of a fairly sharp pre-Enlightenment–Enlightenment historical opposition. See Immanuel Kant, *Political Writings*, trans. H. B. Nisbet, ed. Hans Reiss (Cambridge: Cambridge University Press, 1999).

[23] The excesses entailed by hasty and insufficiently reflective attempts to locate the decisive contemporary institutions or social subject that might seize and exploit a moment of radical social change for purportedly emancipatory ends are well elaborated in many criticisms of critical theory. Nevertheless, I will aver that such criticism ought not to force critical theorists to accept too readily prevailing liberal philosophies of history, most notably expressed in either naive linear conceptions of "progress" or a kind of resignation to the purported incommensurable value standpoints of modernity that potentially retard collective efforts to affect social change: the latter perspective is articulately expressed in contemporary liberal theory by Stephen Holmes, *Passions and Constraint: On the Theory of Liberal Democracy* (Chicago: University of Chicago Press, 1995); Charles Larmore, *Patterns of Moral Complexity* (Cambridge: Cambridge University Press, 1987); and J. Donald Moon, *Constructing Community: Moral Pluralism and Tragic Conflicts* (Princeton, NJ: Princeton University Press, 1993). Stephen White tests the extent to which Habermas's theories are susceptible to this as well as poststructuralist "incommensurable value" critiques in *The Recent Work of Jürgen Habermas: Reason, Justice and Modernity* (Cambridge: Cambridge University Press, 1990).

seems haunted by categories derived from previous epochs. As I show in Chapter 6, like Habermas, much research on the EU replays the Weberian theoretical-historical move described in the previous section. When challenged by the reality of the vast changes of the state order today, theoretically informed researchers have a tendency to reach back for categories formulated through the analysis of previous periods and impose them on the new situation. In other words, many scholars tend to evaluate empirical evidence through their own historical preconceptions.[24] For instance, so-called Euroskeptics tend to view European integration as merely the new way that the European state system – the pinnacle for institutionalizing rationalist politics – manages itself. By contrast, supranationalists often view the EU as an emerging constitutional-federal *Sozialstaat*, sometimes even suggesting that its development is a step in the historical unfolding of universal humanitarian progress, perhaps culminating in a global federation of other such regions.

Especially in scholarly debates over the status of EU law, the power of the ECJ, and the future of the European Parliament (EP), the EU is cast generally as either a treaty organization among states or a federal state writ large – both of which are theoretical categorizations derived from earlier historical models, those of the nineteenth and twentieth centuries, respectively.[25] It is difficult to make sense of these starkly contradictory approaches, given the different empirical data, theoretical frameworks, and normative goals enlisted by the respective scholars. Yet, any reliable assessment of "democracy in the EU" would need to reconcile the workable aspects of these accounts and dispense with the outmoded ones. In Chapter 6, I attempt to highlight the potentially anachronistic historical logics of each set of recent studies and accentuate what is historically viable in their prescriptions for the future of democracy in Europe. Specifically, I sketch out the *Sektoralstaat* model of supranational governance, which I believe captures EU policymaking as it is evolving presently, and then prescribe some institutional recommendations,

---

[24] On the generally unacknowledged interaction between intellectual constructions and empirical reality in the study of international affairs, see Alexander Wendt, *Social Theory of International Politics* (Cambridge: Cambridge University Press, 1999).

[25] Note how the EU is treated as a treaty arrangement of states or an emerging constitutional statelike entity by, respectively, Geoffrey Garrett, R. Daniel Keleman, and Heiner Schulz, "The European Court of Justice, National Governments, and Legal Integration in the European Union," *International Organizations* 52 (Winter 1998), 149–76; and Alec Stone Sweet and Thomas L. Brunell, "Constructing a Supranational Constitution: Dispute Resolution and Governance in the European Community," *American Political Science Review* 92 (March 1998), 63–82.

reminiscent of those launched by the young Habermas in *Public Sphere*, such that it might conform with standards of constitutional-social democracy today.

My examination of Weber's and Habermas's respective encounters with the *Sozialstaat*, and my own reflections on the emerging *Sektoralstaat*, suggest that the task for social scientists concerned with the preservation and extension of democratic principles and practices in a supranational historical era is to explore the role of law in social transformations in a way that is not crippled by either faulty historical presuppositions or less-than-fully-refined abstract categories. This is precisely what Weber and Habermas attempted during the emergence and consolidation of the twentieth-century *Sozialstaat*, and what Habermas still attempts in the midst of the emergence of what he identifies as the "postnational constellation" today. Law, in particular, seems to persist as the appropriate gauge with which to measure the quality and extent of change, as well as the possibilities for progressive politics during such moments.[26] Attention to the law has been the most effective way of grasping the several transformations of state, society, and economy in the modern epoch despite the differences among the discrete eras contained within it. It might be argued that in the contemporary literatures on globalization and the EU, approaches that trace changes in international and interstate *law* yield more concrete answers about the present and more plausible prognoses concerning the future of supranational polities than those focused on *markets* and *state* power. Yet, as mentioned, even these heroic efforts are hampered by the seemingly inevitable indeterminacy that accompanies observation of and predictions concerning a qualitatively changing historical reality.

Nevertheless, if the law has been a constant key to the understanding of qualitative structural change in the various periods of modernity, then previous attempts to analyze it may have relevance for contemporary efforts to apprehend social change. Hence my focus on both Weber's

---

[26] As Christian Joerges provocatively claimed in "Taking the Law Seriously: On Political Science and the Role of Law in the Process of European Integration," *European Law Journal* 2, no. 1 (1996), 105, and more recently: law in European integration acts "as a sort of sensitive seismograph, set close to the conflicts, yielding rich, even if often encoded, messages from 'reality'." Joerges, "'Deliberative Supranationalism' – Two Defences," *European Law Journal* 8, no. 1 (2002), 133–51 at 37. Joerges's thinking is also consonant with the aims of this study in the way that he traces "the law's potential to stabilise the deliberative quality of political processes and thus contribute to the legitimacy of transnational governance" (137).

legal sociology, which engaged the transformation of the nineteenth-century *Rechtsstaat* to the twentieth-century *Sozialstaat*, and Habermas's empirically informed philosophy of law that largely rectifies the deficiencies of Weber's account of law, state, and society in the post–World War II era. On the one hand, as a result of their ideological-historical "reading back" of present developments through categories derived from previous eras, their works are indispensable maps of the pitfalls to be avoided when conducting such an analysis of law, democracy, and social change. On the other, the continuities within their analyses of the transformations to and from the *Sozialstaat* provide insight into where the goals of deliberative, constitutional, and social democracy might be pursued more fruitfully in supranational strategies and institutions. After all, I argue ultimately that Habermas's discourse-theoretical model of law and democracy *does* have viability at a supranational level, not through a direct transposition of *Sozialstaat* institutions, but rather by adaptation to the specifics of the *Sektoralstaat* reality of European governance today. As Habermas's STPS showed, goals of liberty and equality could be achieved communicatively in the *Sozialstaat*, but not via the identical institutional mechanisms that characterized the *Rechtsstaat*.

The difficulties that Weber and Habermas encounter while trying to apprehend a changing historical circumstance – in particular their grasping at categories and logics more appropriate to earlier epochs – are still prevalent today. I will suggest that these ideological impulses must be overcome, not only for more effective realization of normative goals, but for the accurate understanding of the contemporary historical moment. In this sense, the project revives, resignifies, and reconstructs a mode of analysis that has fallen into near-universal disrepute, especially since the events of 1989: the philosophy of history.[27]

---

[27] Based on the preceding remarks and the analysis that ensues in this work, I would more cumbersomely qualify this phrase and the method that it describes as a "critical Hegelian philosophy of history." On the philosophy of history more generally, see Alan Donagan, *Philosophy of History* (New York: Macmillan, 1965); George H. Nadel, *Studies in the Philosophy of History* (New York: Harper & Row, 1965); Raymond Martin, *The Past within Us: An Empirical Approach to Philosophy of History* (Princeton, NJ: Princeton University Press 1989); Patrick Gardiner, ed., *Philosophy of History* (Oxford: Oxford University Press, 1990); Agnes Heller, *Philosophy of History in Fragments* (Oxford: Basil Blackwell, 1993); Jean Hyppolite, *Introduction to Hegel's Philosophy of History*, trans. Bond Harris and J. B. Spurlock (Gainesville: University Press of Florida, 1996); W. H. Walsh, *An Introduction to the Philosophy of History* (New York: Books International, 1998); and William H. Dray, *Philosophy of History* (Upper Saddle River, NJ: Prentice Hall, 1998).

3. Chapter Outline

Rather than proceeding chronologically, that is, by starting with a discussion of Weber's sociology of law, I begin by establishing matters more conceptually. Thus, Chapter 2 explores the complicated relationship between the respective projects of Weber and Habermas, with a particular emphasis on the problematic of law and democracy during structural transformations of the state. In many ways, Habermas's career has been a simultaneous carrying-forward and corrective of Weber's early-twentieth-century project. Indeed, this chapter shows that Habermas's work responds to Weber's in a more profound way than the literature often recognizes and perhaps even more than Habermas himself admits.[28] While Habermas understood himself to be undertaking, after Lukács, the second major appropriation of Weber's theory of rationalization in the history of Western Marxism, my focus on *law* will show that Habermas's is the *only* major such appropriation of normative significance of that tradition – or perhaps anywhere else.

Weber famously hedged his bet on the possibility of democratic progress in an era of increasing rationalization and bureaucratization: on the one hand, he emphasized the rationally legal rule of law and, on the other, a charismatic authority inaccessible to critical rationality. Many have blamed the latter, potentially explosive viewpoint for accelerating, if not causing, the collapse of Germany's first attempt at constitutionally bound social democracy, the Weimar Republic.[29] But, of course, Weimar's collapse was only the worst case of many scenarios portended by the structural transformation of the *Rechtsstaat*.[30] Habermas's work

---

[28] Notwithstanding this observation, Habermas's reconstruction of Weber's rationalization thesis has been treated with great sensitivity in the Anglo-American literature from, quite early on, Richard J. Bernstein, *The Restructuring of Social and Political Theory* (Philadelphia: University of Pennsylvania Press, 1976) to, more recently, George E. McCarthy, *Objectivity and the Silence of Reason: Weber, Habermas, and the Methodological Disputes in German Sociology* (Piscataway, NJ: Transaction, 2001).

[29] See Detlev Peukert, *The Weimar Republic: The Crisis of Classical Modernity*, trans. Richard Deveson (New York: Hill and Wang, 1992); Mary Nolan, *Visions of Modernity: Fordism and Economic Reform in the Weimar Republic* (Oxford: Oxford University Press, 1994); and Young-Sun Hong, *Welfare, Modernity, and the Weimar State, 1919–1933* (Princeton, NJ: Princeton University Press, 1998). Consult the review of the latter by Michael Geyer in the *Journal of Modern History* 72, no. 3 (September 2000) 832–4.

[30] See Bernhard Schlink and Arthur Jacobson, eds., *Weimar: A Jurisprudence of Crisis* (Berkeley: University of California Press, 2000); David Dyzenhaus, *Legality and Legitimacy: Carl Schmitt, Hans Kelsen and Hermann Heller in Weimar* (Oxford: Oxford University Press, 1997); and Peter C. Caldwell, *Popular Sovereignty and the Crisis of German Constitutional Law: The Theory and Practice of Weimar Constitutionalism* (Durham, NC: Duke University Press, 1997).

has always been stalked by this collapse and the subsequent turn of events in Germany and Europe.[31] Not only did he take up Weber's problematic in his own theoretical project, but Habermas tried to open more hopeful possibilities for democracy within a rationalized society and through a bureaucratized state than Weber's theory of law could afford. In Habermas's *Sozialstaat* model, communication generated in society, embedded in constitutional institutions, and facilitated by private law renders public policy both rationally moral and popularly accountable.

After explicating Habermas's immanent critique of Weber's theory of legal legitimacy – one that demonstrates that Weber presupposes consensual agreement institutionalized in modern constitutional-legal frameworks – I turn to the historical dimensions of Habermas's work. Along the lines described previously, I examine Habermas's historical account of the rise of the *Sozialstaat* in *Public Sphere* and his elaboration of the discourse-based possibilities for freedom and egalitarianism within such a regime in TCA. At certain junctures, *Public Sphere* is just as pessimistic as Weber's writings in emphasizing the oppressive tendencies of the *Sozialstaat*, but it highlights the emancipatory potentials unrealized in that configuration that might be tapped through practical political reforms. However, I suggest that Habermas's mature works, such as TCA, which refine these reforms in a more intersubjective model of human action, begin to take on many of the attributes of Weber's secularization philosophy of history. This creeping Weberianism may merely raise questions for Habermas's *Sozialstaat* model but, more seriously, it may prove crippling on theoretical-historical grounds for his later work on state transformations associated with the EU and globalization. In the next chapter, I show how the misapplication of anachronistic sociopolitical categories that will plague Habermas's recent writings on constitutionalism in the EU was prefigured in Weber's writings on law in the *Sozialstaat* from the early twentieth century.

Thus, I more precisely establish the relationship of Weber's SL to the sociolegal transformation of his own time in Chapter 3, showing that Weber turns his attention to the legal aspects of premodern patrimonial authoritarianism in direct response to phenomena associated with the

---

[31] See Habermas, "Law and Morality," trans. Kenneth Baynes in S. M. McMurrin, ed. *The Tanner Lectures on Human Values, Vol. 8* (Salt Lake City: University of Utah Press, 1988), 217–79, especially 233; Habermas, *The New Conservatism: Cultural Criticism and the Historians' Debate*, trans. Shierry Weber Nicholsen, intro. Richard Wolin (Cambridge, MA: MIT Press, 1989); and Wolin, "Working Through the Past: Habermas and the German Historians Debate," in Wolin, *Labyrinths: Explorations in the Critical History of Ideas* (Amherst: University of Massachusetts Press, 1995), 83–102.

rise of the *Sozialstaat*. As a result of this historical orientation, in his more abstractly analytic and normatively prescriptive moments, Weber asserts that *Sozialstaat* law is a contradiction in terms. Law is supposed to separate the state from society except under conditions finely specified by constitutional rules. According to Weber, the "deformalized" law of the *Sozialstaat* purportedly facilitates intervention that becomes as excessive as the authority of the premodern patrimonial lord because of the muddled, unlimited, and arbitrary way that it is exercised. Weber operationalizes this analysis of law and the *Sozialstaat* in his writings on the nascent Weimar Republic – a legally instituted, if ill-fated, *Sozialstaat* – after World War I. This analysis sheds new light on old issues in Weber studies: Weber paints himself into the uncomfortable corner of supposing that if law is the derationalized equivalent of a patrimonial command, and parliament is the inefficient and overly bureaucratized conduit of popular will, then perhaps a charismatic, plebiscitarily elected president will more effectively and faithfully express the will of the people.

In light of Habermas's critique of Weber explicated in the previous chapter, I will question Weber's conclusions concerning law and the *Sozialstaat* on both historical and empirical grounds. Weber is unconvincing historically because his critical standards are derived from a distant and pejoratively depicted past – that is, the functionally undifferentiated and politically unlimited authority of the patrimonial lord. His account is empirically unsatisfying because the widespread lack of access to courts, as well as the reluctance of courts to engage in socioeconomic jurisdictions, in many respects facilitated a greater level of lawlessness under the *Rechtsstaat* than would be the case in the *Sozialstaat*. The lawlessness of an absent state, or a state restrained by the power of socioeconomic elites, could be *guiltier* of injustice than one that attempts, however imperfectly, to ameliorate injustice and manage risk within society. Weber underestimates the indeterminacy, arbitrariness, and lawlessness that actually obtained under the supposedly discrete, consistent, and liberty-protecting ideal type of the *Rechtsstaat*. The sphere of law in the *Sozialstaat*, rather than confirming the rise of antilegal authoritarian practices, in many respects signifies an extension and deepening of legality within newly industrial societies. As a result of fixed categories drawn from his skewed historical preconceptions, Weber never raises this issue in juridical terms, but only in a manner *external* to legal analysis such that he cannot – in accord with his own left-liberal policy preferences – restrain his own powerfully pernicious contribution to the neo-conservative critique of the *Sozialstaat* on both sides of the Atlantic.

Chapter 4 is devoted to Habermas's final elaboration of how the law facilitates and institutionalizes democratic communication in BFN. Ultimately, Habermas proposes a "reflexive" theory of law that opts between *Rechtsstaat*-style formal law and *Sozialstaat*-style deformalized law depending on certain criteria, including the input of those most directly affected by a policy. Attempting to elude the legal either/or posed by Weber, Habermas's reflexive approach intends to make available the best qualities of each of these models: crudely, the freedom-preserving quality of nineteenth-century formal law and the equality-ensuring quality of twentieth-century deformalized or "material" law. Habermas suggests that the *Sozialstaat* does not eliminate formal strategies of lawmaking; they remain viable sociojuridical options. However, he insists that the decision to deploy either strategy must be left open to discussion within the public sphere and through government institutions. The ramifications of the respective "hands-off" or "assertive" quality of each legal strategy must become part of public policy language and debates. Deliberating publics and administrative officials need to discuss openly which kind of law is more appropriate in particular circumstances: on the one hand, law that leaves more power in the hands of social actors, thereby risking intensifying asymmetries of power or, on the other, more direct government intervention risking the conversion of citizens into clients.

Chapter 5 deals with Habermas's application of the discourse-theoretical model of law and democracy to the supranational level of the EU. Habermas conceives of the EU as a postnational vehicle to preserve and further pursue the liberal and social democratic achievements of the European nation-state, while at the same time shedding the excesses of the domestically and externally directed xenophobia to which the nation-state has too often resorted. In his estimation, the EU might facilitate the self-government and economic equality necessary for human autonomy without the inclination toward discrimination, war, and even genocide that inevitably destroys that autonomy. I argue that while Habermas's normative flank is well covered, his analysis of the EU abandons precisely the kind of sensitivity to historical change that set his work apart from that of conventional normative theorists in the past: rather than fully confronting the serious possibility that the *Sozialstaat* is undergoing a structural transformation, Habermas chooses to pose this change in mere spatial terms; that is, the structure of the *Sozialstaat* remains largely the same in his analysis, and is merely extended up to and expanded territorially across the continental level. Moreover, I show that, in his analysis of the problems raised by globalization and potentially solved by the EU, Habermas interprets the political economy and the historical development of the nation-state in ways that contravene his earlier analysis of the development of the state, and so – according to Habermas's own theoretical standards – jeopardizes the very efficacy of his normative vision. Specifically, by overestimating the accomplishments of the *Sozialstaat* and minimizing the traumatic nature of previous transformations of the nation-state, Habermas exaggerates the feasibility of a kind of perfected state at the European level.

In particular, Habermas's reflexive theory of law seems vulnerable in the present transformation to the supranational *Sektoralstaat*. Each paradigm of law combined by Habermas in the reflexive theory – formal and material – emerged out of particular historical situations whose contemporary relevance and status must be demonstrated rather than assumed. I argue that in its abstract categorization, Habermas's reflexive theory betrays a historical myopia reminiscent of Weber: two paradigms of law appropriate to the past are imposed somewhat mechanically upon the present. Based on the way that each of these earlier paradigms emerged out of, at the time, new historical configurations, it seems unlikely that some combination of, or selection between, two previous ones will adequately address a new one. The *Rechtsstaat* model presupposed a unity or coherence of legal form, and the *Sozialstaat* model presupposed a unity or coherence of policy-making and policy-affecting publics. As I explain subsequently and in later chapters, neither assumption holds under *Sektoralstaat* conditions.

Habermas's EU analysis emphasizes transnational public spheres and a continental civil society that author law through the institutional processes of the EU, reconstructed along the lines of a traditional separation of powers arrangement. But his analysis does not account for the fact that "comitological" or "infranational" policymaking within the EU *Sektoralstaat* does *not* conform with processes of statute formation in either the *Rechtsstaat* or *Sozialstaat* models. Therefore, the micro-policy-making publics of the EU may not be the normative-empirical equivalents of the public spheres that initiate lawmaking in Habermas's *Sozialstaat* model, not least of all because the micropublics of EU governance are not bound by constitutional norms.[32] Habermas's enthusiastic plea for a European

---

[32] Consult the debate between Christian Joerges and Rainer Schmalz-Brun over the compatibility of infranationalism/comitology with principles of deliberative and constitutional democracy: Joerges and Jürgen Neyer, "From Intergovernmental Bargaining to Deliberative Political Processes: The Constitutionalization of Comitology,"

constitution does not take comitological policymaking into account, nor does it address the likelihood of structurally segregated macropolicy sectors – multiple policy Europes – within the EU. Put simply, throughout his analyses of the new Europe, Habermas does not ask the following historical questions: Is a novel kind of law, already discernible in EU policymaking, being generated by new empirical circumstances for the state? Is this novel juridical reality reflected vertically vis-à-vis local, regional, and continental levels of adjudication and horizontally vis-à-vis multiplying policy spheres? Can this new kind of law be explained and engaged by a mere reconfiguration of categories drawn from past state paradigms, as is Habermas's reflexive theory of law and his prescriptions regarding European constitutionalism?

Chapter 6 situates Habermas's analysis of the EU within normative-empirical debates over European integration. Among intergovernmentalists, supranationalists, and theorists I will associate with the term *Sektoralstaat*, Habermas is most closely affiliated with the supranationalists. While the supranational approach has demonstrated successfully the historically unprecedented extent of constitutional-legal integration among the member states in the EU,[33] this literature perhaps overestimated the extent to which legal-constitutional integration would "spill over" into political and social integration, that is, to fairly uniform modes of policy formation and generally high levels of social protection throughout the EU.[34] Certainly, Habermas and the supranationalists are right to

---

European Law Journal 3 (1997) 273–99; Joerges and Michelle Everson, "Challenging the Bureaucratic Challenge," in E. O. Eriksen and J. E. Fossum, eds., *Democracy in the European Union: Integration through Deliberation* (London: Routledge, 2000), 164–88; Joerges, "Interactive Adjudication in the Europeanisation Process?: A Demanding Perspective and a Modest Example," *European Review of Private Law* 8, no. 1 (2000), 1–16; Rainer Schmalz-Bruns, "Grenzerfahrungen und Grenzüberschreitungen: Demokratie im integrierten Europa?" in B. Kohler-Koch, ed., *Regieren in entgrenzten Räumen* (Stuttgart: Westdeutscher, 1998), 369–80; Schmalz-Bruns, "Deliberativer Supranationalismus," *Zeitschrift für Internationale Beziehungen* 6 (1999), 185–242; Schmalz-Bruns, "Demokratisierung der Europäischen Union oder Europäisierung der Demokratie?: Das Projekt Europa in herrschaftskritischer Perspektive," paper presented at the conference on the "Arbeitskreis Europäische Integration" of the Deutsche Vereinigung für Politische Wissenschaft über "Macht und Herrschaft in der EU," September 30–October 1, 1999, in Bremen.

33 See the following landmark articles from the early 1990s: those collected in Weiler, *The Constitution of Europe*; and Anne-Marie Burley and Walter Mattli, "Europe Before the Court: A Political Theory of Legal Integration," *International Organization* 47 (Winter 1993), 41–76.

34 A fact intimated by some, if not fully conceded by all, of the adherents of this position today: see, e.g., Weiler's late 1990s essays in *The Constitution of Europe*.

resist the sometimes-overreaching counterarguments of the more state-centrist, intergovernmentalist analysts of the EU concerning the impossibility of a supranational social democracy in Europe.[35] But he and the supranationalists do not fully confront the evidence suggesting that the emerging European polity will institutionally resemble neither the constitutional-federal state of their aspirations nor the treaty-organization model insisted upon by the intergovernmentalists. As the latter assert, the EU will *not* develop into a supranational constitutional, federal, social democracy any time soon, but *not* for the reasons that they set forth.

Alternately, the *Sektoralstaat* model that I derive from associational, comitological, and infranational approaches to the EU[36] conceives of European policymaking and institutional arrangements in the following way: the parties concerned in a particular policy sphere (consumers, producers, distributors, servicers, experts, scholars, etc.) discuss and set the regulations appropriate to that sphere, facilitated by committee arrangements under the authority of the European Commission. Because the actors are not per se economic adversaries, and since the goal of the policymaking process is efficient outcomes, the proceedings take on a more discursively free and "common goals" quality than industrial relations under *Sozialstaat* arrangements. Moreover, while the *Sektoralstaat* model obviously bears some similarity to, for instance, previous "corporatist"

---

[35] See Geoffrey Garrett, R. Daniel Keleman, and Heiner Schulz, "The European Court of Justice, National Governments, and Legal Integration in the European Union," *International Organizations* 52 (Winter 1998), 149–76; and Andrew Moravcsik, *The Choice for Europe*; although the latter provides for more ECJ autonomy in certain spheres than the former, as do the following, more traditional state-centrists: Robert Keohane and Stanley Hoffmann, "Conclusions: Community Politics and Institutional Change," in William Wallace, ed., *The Dynamics of European Integration* (London: Pinter, 1990), 261–82.

[36] In this effort, I will draw upon the very different approaches of Scharpf, *Governing in Europe*; Schmitter, *How to Democratize the European Union*; Christian Joerges, "Bureaucratic Nightmare, Technocratic Regime and the Dream of Good Transnational Governance," in Joerges and Ellen Vos, eds., *EU Committees: Social Regulation, Law and Politics* (Oxford: Hart Publishing, 1999), 3–17; Joerges and Jürgen Neyer, "From Intergovernmental Bargaining to Deliberative Political Processes: The Constitutionalization of Comitology," *European Law Journal* 3 (1997), 273–99; Charles F. Sabel and Joshua Cohen, "Directly-Deliberative Polyarchy," *European Law Journal* 3 (1997), 313–42; Sabel and Cohen, "Sovereignty and Solidarity in the EU: A Working Paper Where We Face Some Facts," paper presented at the Legal Theory Workshop, Yale University, April 11, 2002; Giandomenico Majone, *Regulating Europe* (London: Routledge, 1996); Svein S. Andersen and Thomas R. Burns, "The European Union and the Erosion of Parliamentary Democracy: A Study of Post-Parliamentary Governance," in Svein S. Andersen and Kjell A. Eliassen, eds., *The European Union: How Democratic Is It?* (London: Sage, 1995); and Andersen and Burns, *Societal Decision-Making: Democratic Challenges to State Technocracy* (Hampshire, U.K.: Dartmouth, 1992).

models of policy making,[37] it differs from them in two important respects: (1) it involves micropolicy spheres as well as large-scale economic sectors, and it includes many more than three major actors (capital, labor, and state) in discussions and bargaining over policies; and (2) specific subsets of EU member states participate in different macropolicy spheres such that there is no such thing as a common or general "European" policy throughout the EU across major sectors of the economy. Therefore, whatever the extent of the segmentation that may have been criticized in the industrial and economic relations of the *Sozialstaat*, the *Sektoralstaat* will be even more fundamentally fragmented by the increased number of smaller policy-making spheres, the more rigid boundaries between macropolicy alignments, and the lack of an overarching political enforcement mechanism holding the different pieces together or at least serving as quasi-objective monitor of them.

In certain ways, the *Sektoralstaat* model conforms with important principles that Habermas set out in TCA and BFN – specifically, the requirement that those most affected by policies participate discursively in their formulation. However, this model is incompletely Habermasian to the extent that it falls short of other requirements, such as the generality and neutrality of law, the necessity of general material welfare, and the requirement that such principles be secured by or institutionalized in constitutions. For instance, the *Sektoralstaat* (1) dismisses or at the very least downgrades the participation or "say" of those *less* affected but still *concretely* affected by a policy; (2) virtually abandons participation of or sanctioning by the polity at large through either constitutional or statutory law; and (3) tolerates different levels of social protection and redistribution throughout what, in this case, is somewhat ironically named the "Union." For these reasons, the *Sektoralstaat* emerging in Europe raises the issue of dissonance between the functioning of multifarious policy subgroups and the rights and interests of the larger public in a way perhaps never before observed in European democratic theory and practice. They highlight the way in which participation, egalitarianism and accountability, and the feasibility of their legal facilitation will be the mission of democratic theory in Europe in the new century.

---

[37] See Howard J. Wiarda, *Corporatism and Comparative Politics: The Other Great Ism* (Armonk, NY: M. E. Sharpe, 1996); Wolfgang Streeck and Philippe C. Schmitter, eds., *Private Interest Government: Beyond Market and State* (London: Sage, 1985); and Coen N. Teulings and Joop Hartog, *Corporatism or Competition?: Labour Contracts, Institutions and Wage Structures in International Comparison* (Cambridge: Cambridge University Press, 1998).

In Chapter 7 I elaborate a historical and normative model of law and democracy in Europe that learns from the historical shortcomings of Weber and Habermas and attempts to render the normative vision of Habermas more applicable to a supranational scenario, specifically the practices and institutions that I identify with the *Sektoralstaat*. I begin by resuming and reintegrating my criticisms of Weber and Habermas: despite quite brilliantly discerning law's function as the vehicle of mass democracy, Weber's analysis of the emerging *Sozialstaat* was hampered by historical presuppositions not appropriate to his object of investigation. Weber's incessant imposition of categories developed to describe patrimonial authority upon the new legal-political configuration forced him to miscast and underestimate the more democratic and fully lawful dimensions of the transformation unfolding before him. For his part, Habermas's deliberative model of constitutional-social democracy in the EU is guilty of the kinds of historical prejudices that hampered Weber's efforts in the earlier socio-legal transformation. Habermas draws upon categories too intimately tied to the emergence of the nation-state and then the *Sozialstaat* in his nevertheless impressive formulation of an empirically informed, normative vision of the new Europe. While Habermas "reaches back" to more recent pasts and does so in the service of a more sanguine view of the compatibility of law and democracy than did Weber, Habermas's project nevertheless fails to capture the full novelty of the *Sektoralstaat* order that the EU is increasingly more likely to become.

I do not spring this critique on Weber and Habermas arbitrarily; that is, I do not hold them to standards to which they themselves never aspired. After all, both Weber and Habermas abandon the historically sensitive tools that they themselves deployed in the analysis of earlier periods (e.g., *The Protestant Ethic* and *Public Sphere*, respectively) at precisely the moment when they are confronted with the necessity of accounting for radical change in their immediate present. I suggest that the ramifications of this flight from the present into the past are potentially dire: it would imply, on the one hand, that empirical reality never can be apprehended faithfully during moments of dramatic historical change and, on the other, that attempts to pursue progressive political agendas in the midst of such moments and on the basis of such analyses will inevitably be misdirected and ineffectual.

4. Law, Democracy, and State Transformation Today

As the fin de siecle era fades and is remembered less in terms of postcommunism and more in terms of globalization, it becomes apparent that historical presuppositions are decisive for diagnoses of the present and prognoses concerning the future. The collapse of communism discredited the philosophical integration of social scientific and historical analysis – unfortunately, the efforts of Hegel, Marx, and Lukács, as well as those of Lenin and Stalin. Yet, whether we like it or not, conceptions of history – presently repressed, dismissed, or ignored – need to be "brought back in" if researchers are to evaluate soberly speculation about the future that runs rampant in the social sciences and cultural studies today. Observers of contemporary developments may conceive of the global future in terms of perpetual democratic peace, neo-liberal–conservative capitalist nightmare, global civil war of identity groups, and so on. Some might assert that the EU will become a federal state or that it will remain a treaty agreement among sovereign states. However, more often than not, these conclusions are drawn on the basis of something other than empirical facts alone; obviously, the latter are filtered through normative preferences and, less obviously, through assumptions about historical development.

This book explores the proposition that lack of self-consciousness concerning history encourages social scientific misdiagnoses of the present that then feed back into material reality, deleteriously affecting the future. This suggests that social scientists ought to revive and refine their notions of history. By revisiting Weber's analysis of the *Sozialstaat* and interrogating Habermas's model of European democracy in light of the *Sektoralstaat* model of European integration, I hope to forge an account of normative possibilities in the midst of a contemporary crisis that remotely approximates Habermas's *Public Sphere* from a previous one.

I harbor no illusions about outpacing Minerva's owl or even preempting its flight by offering insights into a sociopolitical configuration like the *Sektoralstaat* before its full consolidation. In one sense, such a goal would entail a seemingly impossible standpoint poised historically in advance of present circumstances. After all, the two greatest works inspiring the task at hand were composed well after the social structures, political institutions, and moral consciousness of their import had already been established. Hegel's *Philosophy of Right*[38] was composed after the main aspects of the *Rechtsstaat* were consolidated, even if the work proved exceedingly precocious in its timing; and Habermas published *Public Sphere* two or three full generations after the structures of the *Sozialstaat* had become discernible. These are not works of "predictive" social science in the strictest sense, but they may be the most empirically grounded

---

[38] G. W. F. Hegel's *Elements of the Philosophy of Right*, trans. H. B. Nisbet, ed. Allen Wood (Cambridge: Cambridge University Press, 1991).

"philosophies of history" ever composed. Moreover, both works trace historical transformations whose possible outcomes were apparent to contemporary social actors and remained well within their range of control. As I will explain at length, this fact alone should make us less anxious than is the mature, and especially post-1989, Habermas, about the "excesses" of a critical philosophy of history.

2

The Historical Logic(s) of Habermas's Critique of Weber's "Sociology of Law"

Max Weber's "Sociology of Law"[1] holds a peculiar place in German history and legal philosophy.[2] Systematically, it is the most elaborate and influential analysis of the possibility of realizing political legitimacy through legal procedures. But, historically, SL is often read as a testament to the failure or impossibility of liberal democracy's ability to secure substantive legitimacy through the law. Weber suggested that rational-legal authority is legitimate because subjects comply with the law on the basis of its rationality or logical consistency, best exemplified by parliamentary government. This form of legitimacy is superior to traditional authority, which is undergirded by force of habit, or charismatic authority, which is based on ecstatic devotion, or any form of authority that is supported by the mere threat of violent sanction.[3] However, in his practical political writings from roughly the same era, Weber ascribed superior democratic legitimacy to a directly elected president over the legislature in the

---

[1] In this chapter, I refer to the following sections of Weber's *Economy and Society* as the "Sociology of Law" and combine them for citation purposes under the abbreviation SL in the text: Weber, "Types of Legitimate Domination," "Economy and Social Norms," and "Sociology of Law" in *Economy and Society: An Outline of Interpretive Sociology* (c. 1920), Guenther Roth and Claus Wittich, eds., 2 vols. (Berkeley: University of California Press, 1978), 212–23, 311–38, 641–899.

[2] See Ulrich K. Preuß, "Die Weimarer Republik – ein Laboratorium für verfassungsrechtliches Denken," in Andreas Gödel, Dirk van Laak, and Ingeborg Villinger, eds., *Metamorphosen des Politischen: Grundfragen der politischen Einheitsbildung seit den zwanziger Jahren* (Berlin: Akademie Verlag, 1995), 182–96.

[3] See Weber, "The Profession and Vocation of Politics" (1919), in Weber, *Political Writings*, Peter Lassman and Ronald Speirs, eds. (Cambridge: Cambridge University Press, 1994), 309–69, and SL, 212–301.

emerging Weimar Republic.[4] According to some scholars, Weber's theoretical underspecification of rational-legal legitimacy, his skeptical practical prescriptions concerning parliament and law, and the subsequent
consequences for Germany's first attempt at constitutional democracy
are not coincidentally related.[5] I will offer my own account of the relationship of Weber's sociology of law and the Weimar context of a fragile
constitutional-social democracy in the next chapter.

In this chapter I provide an overview of Jürgen Habermas's critique of
Weber, which raises the problems of legal legitimacy and historical change
that will guide us throughout the book. Habermas engages Weber's SL
in virtually every one of his major works, just as surely as the historical disaster of the collapse of Weimar hovers over the totality of his
intellectual efforts.[6] My reconstruction of Habermas's critique of Weber
focuses on four themes: (1) the undertheorized relationship of legality
and legitimacy in SL; (2) the moral presuppositions supporting Weber's
purportedly positivist theory of modern law; (3) Weber's inability to justify rationally the place of law in the emerging administrative/welfare
state or *Sozialstaat*; and (4) the presumptions about the history of modern rationalization underlying *all* of these deficiencies of Weber's legal
sociology.[7] Ultimately, however, I criticize Habermas for falling prey to a

[4] See Weber, "Parliament and Government in Germany Under a New Political Order"
(1918), in *Political Writings*, 130–271. Hans Kelsen was the leading exponent of the view
that legislative ascendancy was necessary for a robust rule of law at the time; see Kelsen,
Vom Wesen und Wert der Demokratie ([1920] Aalen: Scientia, 1981). For a contemporary
account of this position, see Jeremy Waldron, *The Dignity of Legislation* (Cambridge:
Cambridge University Press, 1999).

[5] See Jacob Peter Mayer, *Max Weber and German Politics: A Study in Political Sociology*
(London: Faber & Faber, 1944); Wolfgang Mommsen, *Max Weber and German Politics,
1890–1920*, trans. Michael S. Steinberg (Chicago: University of Chicago Press, 1984); and,
more sympathetically, Karl Loewenstein, *Max Weber's Political Ideas in the Perspectives
of Our Time* (Cambridge, MA: University of Massachusetts Press, 1965).

[6] On the relationship of Habermas's social scientific mission to Weber's theoretical framework, see Thomas McCarthy, *The Critical Theory of Jürgen Habermas* (Cambridge, MA:
MIT Press, 1978), 140–6; and Stephen K. White, *The Recent Work of Jürgen Habermas: Reason, Justice and Modernity* (Cambridge: Cambridge University Press, 1990),
92–102. The Weimar legacy is perhaps most palpable in Habermas, *The New Conservatism: Cultural Criticism and the Historians' Debate*, trans. Shierry Weber Nicholsen,
intro. Richard Wolin (Cambridge, MA: MIT Press, 1989); and Wolin, "Working Through
the Past: Habermas and the German Historians' Debate," in Wolin, *Labyrinths: Explorations in the Critical History of Ideas* (Amherst: University of Massachusetts Press, 1995),
83–102.

[7] See Habermas, *The Structural Transformation of the Public Sphere: An Inquiry into a
Category of Bourgeois Society* (1962), trans. Thomas Burger with Frederick Lawrence
(Cambridge, MA: MIT Press, 1989), hereafter STPS; *Legitimation Crisis* (1973), trans.

shortcoming reminiscent of the last element of his critique of Weber; more specifically, I insist that Habermas progressively adopts a neo-Weberian theory of history that renders his normative prescriptions potentially inefficacious.

As Habermas's work develops over his career, he more seriously subscribes to a conception of modern history, one that shares the "secularization" assumptions of Weber's Protestant ethic thesis, even as Habermas ever more explicitly and intensely criticizes the master's theories of legal and societal rationalization. Habermas turns away from the historically specific attempt to embed progressive normative possibilities within the contradictions of political economy exposed by moments of dramatic structural transformation within modernity. Instead he adopts a social evolutionism focused on the "history of the species" that (a) privileges ideas over the specific structures that both constrain and make possible their realization, (b) underestimates socioeconomic change within modernity that makes normative aspirations and progressive action possible, and (c) encourages a secularization or emerging value-pluralism explanation of change within modernity that points just as likely to the same uncritically pessimistic moral developments that Habermas associates with Weber as it does to the supposedly better-conceptualized optimistic developments that Habermas himself champions.

I argue that this infiltration of Habermas's theory by Weber's historical categorizations endangers Habermas's effort to criticize and reconstruct Weber's legal sociology, particularly when grounding it in subsequent moments of historical change. This will become clearer in later chapters, where I suggest that these historical oversights and misinterpretations jeopardize Habermas's own efforts to theorize the progressive possibility of law in circumstances of radical social change such as the rise of the *Sozialstaat* and, more pressingly, the contemporary transformation typified by supranational, legal-political integration in Europe.

Thomas McCarthy (Boston: Beacon Press, 1975), hereafter LC; *The Theory of Communicative Action, Vol. 1: Reason and the Rationalization of Society* (1981), trans. Thomas McCarthy (Boston: Beacon Press, 1984), hereafter TCA1; *The Theory of Communicative Action, Vol. 2: Lifeworld and System: A Critique of Functionalist Reason* (1981), trans. Thomas McCarthy (Boston: Beacon Press, 1987), hereafter TCA2; "Law and Morality," trans. Kenneth Baynes, in S. M. McMurrin, ed., *The Tanner Lectures on Human Values, Vol. 8* (Salt Lake City: University of Utah Press, 1988), 217–79, hereafter LM; *Between Facts and Norms: Contributions to a Discourse Theory of Law and Democracy* (1992), trans. William Rehg (Cambridge, MA: MIT Press, 1996), hereafter BFN.

1. The Fragility of Legal-Rational Legitimacy

Habermas often asserts that the status of legal-rational authority as a type of legitimacy is jeopardized by Weber's reliance on an insufficiently substantiated notion of "belief" (e.g., LC 98).[8] Weber's legal-rational authority requires subjects to *believe* in its legality, that is, in formally correct procedures for creating and applying law. In LC, Habermas worries that the belief in legitimacy consequently shrinks to a belief in legality – in effect, that it amounts to nothing more than the appeal to the legal manner in which a decision comes about (LC 98). Of course, any policy outcome, even the most horrible that one might imagine, can be generated through procedural means; and the simple acknowledgment or recognition of these procedures by a particular body of subjects does not legitimize them in any rational sense. This scenario approximates just another arbitrary appeal to authority if the procedure itself is not *legitimized*, that is, justified rationally (LC 98). Habermas suggests that a step toward the legitimization of such procedures is supplied by modern constitutionalism, which potentially institutionalizes rational consensus within legal procedures (LC 98). I return to this claim later.

Weber demonstrated that charismatic and traditional types of legitimate authority have motivational substance all their own – respectively, ecstatic and conventional motivations. People may obey authority due to the weight of tradition or the allure of a leader/prophet. Habermas argues in TCA1 that legal-rational authority tends to collapse into one of the other two forms of legitimacy in Weber's account because law possesses only a formally procedural shell and no practical-moral substance of its own (TCA1 265). He indicates that simple "belief" is an inappropriate motivational grounding for rational-legal domination: a static belief in an already existing order conforms more closely to the model of traditional

[8] "Belief" is the element most explicitly linked to normative *substance* in Weber's SL. In the economy and law sections, Weber describes two valences of legal validity that pertain to rational *formalism*, both of which are seemingly devoid of "content": (1) legal validity in the textual sense is the normative meaning attributed to a verbal pattern having the form of a legal proposition with correct logic; (2) empirical validity is based on the probability that people will obey the law (SL 311). The first assumes that the jurist "believes" that logical consistency is possible; the second assumes that people obey the law because they "believe" in it. This could be a belief in its morality, its correctness, or its status as force-backed norms. Therefore, neither definition makes any explicit judgments as to the relative moral substance of the law because Weber's self-professed sociological point of view requires only the perspective of "legal technology" (SL 717). Habermas associates popular belief with formal correctness in Weber and excavates more serious normative expectations from the less explicit levels of SL.

authority, and if followers believe in a charismatic leader, then law is relatively unnecessary as a mode of political organization. In this light, Weberian legality does not seem to be a form of legitimacy at all.

These criticisms suggest that Weber is wrong to claim that legal-rational authority is independent of the other types of legitimate authority and, consequently, that it cannot sustain liberal democratic regimes without the auxiliary support of some traditional or charismatic elements. The pervasiveness of nostalgia for the Kaissereich and a longing for a charismatic *Führer* that plagued Weimar constitutional democracy would seem to bear this out. But the various incarnations of Habermas's critique of Weber's SL do not conclude on this ungenerous and pessimistic note: Habermas proceeds to show that Weber's notion of legal-rational legitimacy actually gestures toward moral-practical rationality or even presupposes an infrastructure shot through with the moral elements in modern societies (e.g., BFN 67). Hence, according to Habermas, once reconstructed, Weber's theory can still serve as a theoretical guideline to rational-legal legitimacy in liberal democratic regimes

2. Moral Underpinnings of Formal Law

In *Public Sphere*, Habermas closely follows Weber's account of the progressive advantages of rationality in the late eighteenth and early nineteenth century bourgeois form of law. But Habermas is much more forthcoming about the morally relevant characteristics of bourgeois formal law than Weber ever was: Habermas notes that the generality and abstractness of legal norms celebrated by Weber in SL conformed with rational and egalitarian social practices, and hence were not reducible to empty formalism or proceduralism; rather, they were "imbued with life" in this historical context (STPS 54). Habermas emphasizes that it is not merely the formal rationality of the law, as such, that renders it normatively advantageous but rather the facilitation of substantive morality provided by this proceduralism that does so: more specifically, the public practice of critical debate in which the better argument prevailed led to public opinion that was substantively rational. The substantive rationality generated by these practices reflexively reinforced the formally legal institutions that enabled public will and opinion formation and served to render political power morally accountable to the public.

Habermas's subsequent engagements with Weber aim to show that the sociologist himself, despite his positivist machismo, assumes that the moral substance underlies the formal proceduralism of modern law.

In TCA1, Habermas focuses on SL, as well as on passages excluded from *Economy and Society*, to confirm that Weber presumes the centrality of consensual agreement in the development of modern law. Habermas shows that Weber slips conceptually between value-rational and purposive-rational action as determining factors in the development of law (TCA1 255). In particular, Weber ultimately appeals to *consensually interactive* aspects of the nineteenth-century bourgeois formal law to cast in relief aspects of the organization-dominated administrative/welfare state or *Sozialstaat* (TCA1 255). Such a move is out of sync with the superficial level of the SL, where Weber celebrates the *Rechtsstaat* model for abstractly formal, *not* any consensually moral, characteristics.[9] Habermas also shows that in little-known passages from Weber's methodological writings he invokes the category of "consensual action" to accompany "purposive-rational action" (TCA1 210). Thus, Weber attributes to modern legal arrangements a moral substance derived from rational consensus that establishes the framework for the pursuit of self-interest through instrumental action in a market society. Many accounts of the rise of modern law economistically assume, as does Weber at his most cynical, that instrumental rationality provides the constitutional framework for its own practice.

Later in the LM, Habermas reconstructs more conceptually the moral presuppositions of Weber's legal sociology and without resort to apocryphal texts. Habermas examines the three aspects of rationality that Weber attributes to the bourgeois formal law: (a) the rule-rationality that ensures the predictability required for behavior orientation in the planning of long-term enterprises; (b) its capacity to accommodate the rational pursuit of self-defined interests and goals by individuals; and (c) the imitation of the scientific method in the formulation of complex legal codes by juridical experts (LM 223–4). Habermas argues that each of the three aspects of formal rationality is supported by a moral assumption

---

[9] Sven Eliaeson rightly points out that "Weber hardly uses the word *Rechtsstaat* [because] the word itself has natural-law connotations" and "normative associations." See Eliaeson, "Constitutional Caesarism: Weber's Politics in Their German Context," in Stephen Turner, ed., *The Cambridge Companion to Weber* (Cambridge: Cambridge University Press, 2000), 137, 139. But because Weber emphasizes precisely those aspects of the bourgeois formal law that fall under the descriptive category of the *Rechtsstaat*, I use the term with reference to his work. In fact, as Habermas and I both show, since Weber reluctantly ascribed a *normative status* to the ensemble of principles and practices that make up the *Rechtsstaat*, if not one affiliated with natural law, it is especially appropriate to do so.

that actually supplies law with legitimating force in Weber's thought: (a) A decidedly moral outlook determines precisely what outcome is "predictably" guaranteed by rules: the predictability of limitations on liberty and property guaranteed by formal law is a *value* that often competes with other values such as the equal distribution of opportunities and outcomes – and often competes with these other values even in the high-laissez-faire nineteenth century (LM 225). Predictability does not exist apart from a normative perspective on what goals or circumstances ought to be rendered calculable and consistent.

(b) The abstract and general components of formal rationality can exacerbate political illegitimacy rather than ensure legitimacy when they inhibit full access to law by those subject to it (LM 225–6). After all, Habermas suggests, equality, as much as liberty, is a moral value associated with the facilitation of individual choice in the nineteenth-century context, since such individualism presumes equality before the law (LM 226). To be rationally coherent, the bourgeois formal law cannot, without seriously compromising itself, sacrifice equality to liberty by serving social exclusion in the name of "generality and abstractness." More broadly, according to Habermas, the formal aspects of law are subordinate to the moral principles that they help to secure: "abstract and general laws can be justified as rational only in the light of morally substantive principles" (LM 226). Relatedly, (c) the systematic organization of law as a hierarchy of intricate rules does not in and of itself supply the intersubjectively derived meaning among legal subjects that is necessary for legitimacy (LM 226). Habermas reminds us that scientific techniques do not lend the law any more meaning or truth content than do the classifications and methodology of the natural sciences in their context. On the contrary, the example helps to demonstrate that meaning can only be supplied socially in a consensually rational fashion.

Habermas acknowledges that Weber's model of legality may superficially conform to strict formal rationality, but he indicates the practical-moral bases *assumed* by the model such that it constitutes a theory of *substantive legitimacy*. Habermas provides a nineteenth-century example to bear this out: from the perspective of workers engaged in class struggles and the development of the labor movement, bourgeois formal law certainly was not legitimate in any substantive way (LM 224). As he remarks in LC regarding the social bases underlying the *Rechtsstaat*: the unplanned, anarchic, quasi-natural aspects of the unlimited economic development of productive forces in liberal capitalism are potentially incompatible with a communicative ethics "which requires not only generality of norms but [also] a discursively attained consensus about the generalizability of the normatively proscribed interests" (LC 23). Economic chaos and gross inequality severely threaten communicatively generated legitimacy even if they are facilitated "rationally" in formal terms.

This example brings us to the third element of Habermas's critique of Weber: he charges that Weber so steadfastly adheres to his formally rational model of law that he underestimates the necessity and potential coherence of the so-called deformalized or materialized law associated with the *Sozialstaat*, a type of law that developed in response to the demand for legitimacy salient in the aforementioned example of class struggle. Once the relationship between formally rational procedures and morally practical consensus is reconstructed appropriately, law associated with the administrative/welfare state need not be interpreted, as Weber did and neo-conservatives continue to do so, as a death of law per se (cf. LM 233–4). Habermas argues, "the legitimacy of legality can be found in the procedural rationality built into the democratic legislative process" (LM 237). But he cautions that "as soon as abstract and general norms that rule out all indeterminacies no longer serve as the prototypical form of regulation in the welfare state, we are left without a mechanism for transmitting any stipulated rationality of legislative procedures to the procedures of adjudication and administration" (LM 237). The task is to fashion such mechanisms for the *Sozialstaat*, and not, *pace* Weber and neo-conservatives, to return to formal law. I will show in subsequent chapters how Habermas undertakes this task himself; here I continue to focus on his criticisms of Weber's failure to do so, and their methodological and historical ramifications.

3. The Possibility of Rationally Coherent *Sozialstaat* Law

Habermas has never tried to downplay the serious ramifications of the deformalized or materialized law that Weber criticizes in SL. From *Public Sphere* through BFN, he is quite forthright about the threat to judicial accountability, legal generality, and juridical coherence posed by *Sozialstaat* law and the problem of clientalization posed by the social policies instituted through it.[10] In general, the difference between the semantic

---

[10] Seyla Benhabib detects a distinct change of focus from the merely "paradoxical" to the dangerously "disintegrative" aspects of the *Sozialstaat* in Habermas's *Observations on "Spiritual Situation of the Age"* (1979), trans. Andrew Buchwalter (Cambridge, MA:

forms of law in the respective *Rechtsstaat* and *Sozialstaat* models indicates the gist of the problem. Legal precepts in the former are structured as conditional statements: if social circumstance *x* occurs, then state action *y* ensues. The very form of the law keeps the state out of society, except under the specific conditions where the law deems it appropriate a priori. In the *Sozialstaat* model, legal statements tend to be mere assertions: simply *y*, if you will. The state is empowered to achieve certain goals without the same time frame and task specification inherent in *Rechtsstaat* law. Subsequent statements qualifying these legal commands only further encumber statute composition and encourage further administrative and judicial discretion. Moreover, citizens constantly, rather than only intermittently, experience the functioning of state activity raising the specter of ineluctable bureaucratic domination.

In the LM, Habermas identifies several policy-specific types of deformalization of law that have become even more problematic since Weber's time: the emergence of (a) what he calls here "reflexive law" that institutionalizes arbitration proceedings where conflicting parties settle affairs themselves, thereby making legal agreements relatively autonomous of general criticizability; (b) "marginalization" that exacerbates gaps in the law through increasingly experimental and goal-oriented regulation; (c) "functionalism" whereby normative views are subordinated to bureaucratic imperatives or market pressures; and (d) increasing turnover of parliamentary coalitions whose legislation of varying moral standpoints potentially undermines the basis of legal validity (LM 231–2). According to Habermas, these developments pose a challenge to the status of law in the *Sozialstaat* but do not necessarily rule out its proper functioning completely.

In *Public Sphere*, Habermas describes these kinds of problems by relying not only on Weber, but more specifically, extensively, and rather alarmingly, Nazi-cum-neo-conservative jurists enamored of Weber's critique of *Sozialstaat* law – Helmut Schelsky, Ernst Forsthoff, Carl Schmitt, and so on. Throughout the work, Habermas seriously entertains and sometimes appears to agree with their diagnoses of the pathological law-facilitated and law-destroying "stateification of society" associated with

---

MIT Press, 1984). See Benhabib, *Critique, Norm, and Utopia: A Study of the Foundations of Critical Theory* (New York: Columbia University Press, 1986), 248, 393, n. 46. Stephen K. White identifies a similar shift on the extent to which the pathologies of capitalism under the *Sozialstaat* can be addressed in the transition from LC to TCA. See White, *The Recent Work of Jürgen Habermas*, 118–19.

legal deformalization.[11] However, at a crucial juncture in the book, Habermas turns the tables on these nefarious critics by demonstrating that *more*, not less, *Sozialstaat* law is the answer to the pathologies of the welfare state, *not* a return to bourgeois formal law and the necessarily anarchic and coercive social results that would ensue from its reinstitutionalization. Rather, the crisis of the *Sozialstaat* requires a reconstructed normative understanding and more widely public justification of welfare/administrative state substantive law (STPS 208–10).

Habermas asserts that the public sphere, which has declined with the eclipse of the *Rechtsstaat*, can reassume "functions of political critique and control, beyond mere participation in political compromises" (STPS 208). But to do so, the public sphere must itself be "radically subjected to the requirements of publicity" (STPS 208). Along these lines, he suggests that the public sphere in the *Sozialstaat* can be protected from "reactionary misdirection" only if publicity is "extended to institutions that until now have lived off the publicity of the other institutions rather than being themselves subject to the public's supervision: primarily to parties but also to politically influential mass media and special-interest associations under public law" (STPS 209). In other words, the inner structures of media organizations, businesses, labor unions, and other associations must be reorganized to allow critical publicity – the rational criticism of their particular memberships as well as the general public (STPS 210). But Habermas insists that this reform can only be effective and not result in arbitrarily intrusive outcomes if it is facilitated *legally* (STPS 210).

In this way, moral-practical reason would permeate the various components of the *Sozialstaat*'s structure and compensate for the latter's undermining of the social consensus that formal law had institutionalized in the *Rechtsstaat* era. Legally facilitated policies of redistribution, regulation, accountability, and public debate, while apparently *exacerbating* the destructive unruliness of *Sozialstaat* practices in Weberianly influenced neo-conservative accounts, according to Habermas's reform proposal can

---

[11] Of course, not only conservative thinkers voice these concerns. See the work of theorists affiliated with Habermas's own Frankfurt tradition of critical theory: Franz Neumann and Otto Kirchheimer, *The Rule of Law Under Siege: Selected Essays*, William E. Scheuerman, ed. (Berkeley: University of California Press, 1996). Curiously, Habermas does not rely on the thought of these scholars, perhaps because he recognized in the hyperformal prescriptions of their mature work a de facto capitulation to the neo-conservatism that he himself critiques immanently in STPS and other works. Scheuerman's own revival of their thought is unintentionally susceptible to similar charges: see Scheuerman, *Between the Norm and the Exception: The Frankfurt School and the Rule of Law* (Cambridge, MA.: MIT Press, 1994); and my review of the work in *History of Political Thought* XVII, no. 4 (Winter 1997), 32–41.

actually reinfuse them with moral-practical reason. Habermas insists that moral-practical justification and institutionalization are more important than the pristine, elegant, and discrete formalism associated with the *Rechtsstaat* model. Beautiful statutes do not make a just society. He insists that if one focuses on the moral-practical necessities of legitimacy in the contemporary state–society configuration rather than the formal qualities of law that – ultimately unsuccessfully – attempted to guarantee legitimacy in a nineteenth-century scenario of unfettered capitalism, a participatory *Sozialstaat* is potentially *more* legitimate than an exclusionary *Rechtsstaat*.

Habermas expounds on this point of view in TCA2, where he charges that Weber is insufficiently attentive to the legitimation necessities of legally facilitated capitalism. Weber collapses societal rationalization generally with capitalist modernization specifically, and, further, did not sufficiently emphasize the pathological side effects of the capitalist class structure undergirding the *Rechtsstaat* (TCA2 303). Thus, the necessity/potential of moral-practical rationality associated with societal rationalization is subsumed under the abstractly formal qualities of market rationality, especially as it is affiliated with bourgeois law. Habermas attributes what we will observe in the next chapter to be Weber's panic over the rise of *Sozialstaat* law to Weber's failure at balancing: on the one hand, the pathologies of class inequality accompanying unregulated capitalism against, on the other, the pathologies of alienating rationalization accompanying an expanding administrative apparatus. Both legitimation problems are recognized by Weber but remain unintegrated in his theory: as we will observe, SL betrays Weber's anguish over both the need for economic regulation/redistribution and the threat posed by the *Sozialstaat* to the efficacy of law and bourgeois conceptions of freedom. According to Habermas, as a result of tensions in Weber's notion of rationality, Weber is more concerned with the threat posed by rather than the necessity for regulation/redistribution (TCA2 304).

For Weber, the class problem, in particular, stretches the legitimation capacity of modernity: workers blindly support "legal ideologies" that undermine legal formalism and thereby expose the fact that "legal domination rests on a formalism that is weak in legitimation and subjectively difficult to bear" (TCA2 324). Habermas shows how Weber understands modernity in terms of heightened expectations and demands, especially concerning "unsatisfied needs for material justice" that cannot be met because of the intransigence of different institutions that reflect a mutually incommensurable plurality of values (TCA2 324). This further delegitimizes those institutions and sends people looking for "false prophets" (TCA2 324). But in this context, Habermas suggests that Weber was well aware that his "heroic nihilism," associated with his own vaunted "value skepticism," could not facilitate broad social integration (TCA2 324).

Nevertheless, Habermas asserts that Weber could not accept the fact – presupposed by his own legal sociology – that, for instance, constitutions embody the capacity for mutual understanding associated with cultural reproduction more than they merely reflect strategic imperatives toward conflict resolution or compromise that may never fully foster legitimation.[12] Habermas asserts, "if we look at the self-understanding expressed in the basic principles of democratic constitutions, modern societies assert the primacy of a lifeworld in relation to the subsystems separated out of institutional orders" (TCA2 345). Modern lifeworlds, as opposed to their premodern counterparts, reflect "communicatively achieved understanding" rather than "normatively ascribed agreement" (TCA1 340). Lifeworld beliefs, which are no longer consigned to "taken-for-granted background assumptions" and so become contested aspirations, can be instantiated in legal institutions that then direct the systemic apparatuses of material production and social coordination (TCA1 335).[13] From this

---

[12] Russell Hardin detects a similar consensus that is institutionalized in modern constitutions, although he associates it with the coordination of the mutual advantage of politically salient groups in a given society rather than mutual understanding that is the product of a rationalizing lifeworld. See Hardin, *Liberalism, Constitutionalism, and Democracy* (Oxford: Oxford University Press, 2000). Like Habermas, whom Hardin treats rather gingerly (151), Hardin suggests that consensus emerges rather spontaneously in the constitutionalization process: the relevant interests seem to fall into place once participants recognize that they gain more from cooperation than from defection. But, as opposed to Habermas, for Hardin, interests are rather static, and perceptions of them are changeable only under the most dramatic circumstances (286). As powerful in its precision and simplicity as Hardin's theory is, it could be pushed on Habermasian grounds to explain why the class compromise of social democracy was sustainable over decades when the theory suggests that such regulation and redistribution are almost impossible to guarantee constitutionally (277). Moreover, Hardin argues that the coordination of accurately perceived interests is fairly impervious to normative claims in constitution making. Yet, in his discussion of the U.S. Constitutional Convention of 1787, why does Hardin make note of the significant effect of the absence of a "formidable orator" such as Patrick Henry (104)? Habermas would no doubt argue that deliberation, persuasion, and mutual understanding play a greater role in the theory than Hardin himself acknowledges.

[13] I will postpone an elaborate discussion of Habermas's system–lifeworld distinction until Chapter 4. Here let me note that in TCA, Habermas describes the modern lifeworld as decentered, hence capable of further rationalization, and differentiated into instrumental-technical, moral-pragmatic, and aesthetic-expressive spheres. In this chapter, I am dealing with Habermas's attempt to distinguish the second from the first sphere, which many theorists, most notably Weber, often collapse. I deal with the third sphere hardly at all. In

standpoint, the legally facilitated regulatory and redistributive policies of the *Sozialstaat* are *not* irrational when evaluated in terms of legitimation necessities – first and foremost, the need for citizens to participate effectively in lawmaking. Again, this participation cannot be realized under conditions of economic chaos and/or gross inequality even if the prevailing semantics and practices of law are formally rational.

However, in TCA2, Habermas concedes that *Sozialstaat* juridification engenders problems, particularly clientalization, that are not side effects of generally well-functioning institutions but rather are qualitatively new pathologies characteristic of a novel sociopolitical configuration (TCA2 364). In this light, *Sozialstaat* law, which, through compensatory social policies, is supposed to better facilitate participation than did the *Rechtsstaat*, actually undercuts participation by politically stultifying citizens. But Habermas cautions against taking this critique too far, with the result that substantive participation is abandoned as a normative goal in contemporary circumstances simply because certain aspects of the *Sozialstaat* stymie efforts to attain it:

> From the legal standpoint . . . one might presume that the structure of bourgeois formal law becomes dilemmatic precisely when [legal] means are no longer used to negatively demarcate areas of private discretion, but are supposed to provide positive guarantees of membership and participation in institutions and benefits. . . . However, such arguments cannot be used to deduce aspects of taking away freedom from the very *form* of participatory rights, but only from the bureaucratic ways and means of their *implementation*. (TCA2 364)

Habermas faces up to the significant problems posed by the implementation of *Sozialstaat* law, particularly the latter's tendency to regulate and "normalize" spheres of life not already adapted to the functioning of state administration.[14] While the already semipublic organizations of labor and capital might be regulated without sociologically pathological

any case, note Axel Honneth's criticisms of Habermas's tendency to reify the opposition of lifeworld and system, as well as that of money and power over more concretely personal or social agents in the systemic realm. See Honneth, *Critique of Power: Reflective Stages in a Critical Social Theory* (1985), trans. Kenneth Baynes (Cambridge, MA: MIT Press, 1991), chaps. 8 and 9. On the gendered aspects of the distinction, see Nancy Fraser, *Unruly Practices: Power, Discourse, and Gender in Contemporary Social Theory* (Minneapolis: University of Minnesota Press, 1989).

14 Stephen White describes Habermas's position this way: "pathologies specific to contemporary capitalism arise as the media of money and power increasingly infiltrate spheres of social life in which traditions and knowledge are transferred, in which normative bonds are intersubjectively established, and in which responsible persons are formed." See White, *The Recent Work of Jürgen Habermas*, 112.

results, there are other social domains in which attempts to ameliorate market excesses *deform* rather than *facilitate* communicative potentials:

Social-welfare law, through which social compensation is implemented, differs from, for instance, the laws governing collective bargaining, through which freedom of association becomes effective, in one important respect: measures of social-welfare law (as a rule, compensatory payments) do not, like collective wage and salary agreements, intervene in an area that is *already* formally organized. Rather, they regulate exigencies that, as lifeworld situations, belong to a communicatively structured area of action. (TCA2 367)

Habermas argues that *Sozialstaat* law functioning as a *medium*, as described in the second part of the quote, provides a clear path through which the system may colonize the lifeworld. The danger is that it may do so more effectively than *Sozialstaat* law functioning as an *institution*, as described in the first part of the quote, translates the communicative practices and moral-practical rationality of the lifeworld into systemic imperatives. The first form of *Sozialstaat* law is destructive; the second, constructive. But neither aspect of law can be dispensed with if the *Sozialstaat* is to be both legitimate and effective – after all, as Habermas avers, "*legal institutions* that guarantee social compensation become effective only through *social-welfare law used as a medium*" (TCA2 367).

Habermas insists that despite its systemic (mis)functionings, *Sozialstaat* law can and must be justified in moral-practical terms because its functioning as a medium structures communicative as well as instrumental action. It supports the moral fiber of society, not merely strategic behavior within it:

Law as a medium...remains bound up with law as an institution. By legal institutions I mean legal norms that cannot be sufficiently legitimized through a positivistic reference to procedure. Typical of these are the bases of constitutional law, the principles of criminal law and penal procedure, and all regulation of punishable offenses close to morality (e.g., murder, abortion, rape, etc.). As soon as the validity of these norms is questioned in everyday practice, the reference to their legality no longer suffices. They need substantive justification, because they belong to the legitimate orders of the lifeworld itself and, together with informal norms of conduct, form the background of communicative action. (TCA2 365)

In other words, law may serve as a temporary placeholder for subtantive rational discussion but not as a permanent or fictional substitute for it. Law not only facilitates conflict resolution but also institutionalizes consensually held positions – institutionalizations that may be changed when consensus has been challenged by verifiable validity claims. But the problem of accommodating dissensus is neither, *pace* Weber, a threat to the overall legitimacy of legal institutions nor, *pace* systems theorists, a disruption of systemic operations. Law as medium in the *Sozialstaat* allows for constant revisions of background assumptions and alterations of the institutions that sustain them.

Habermas uses family and education policies in TCA2 to make his argument concrete, just as he will invoke the status of women in the welfare state to the same effect in BFN. These spheres show how *Sozialstaat* law affects people as a medium and not as an institution, that is, it pathologically affects their ability to participate in the justification of the policies or regulation affecting them; it also disrupts their capacity to communicate among themselves (TCA2 368–9). As Seyla Benhabib points out with respect to this example, social policy can only facilitate communication, not substitute for it, and indeed often degrades it:

Through processes of regulation and intervention, the lifeworld context is subject to monetary and legal measures. But the communicative structures of the lifeworld can fulfill the functions of cultural reproduction, social integration, and socialization when individuals themselves can generate motives and reasons for action via argumentative processes. There can be no "administrative production of meaning," for meaning and motives can only be recreated through the power of conviction as experienced by participants themselves.[15]

Regarding the problem inherent in the contrast between the *Rechtsstaat* and *Sozialstaat* mentioned earlier, law is most effective when it facilitates state action called for by society itself, when it responds to social conditions in only the most general sense of "equal opportunity," "fairness," and so on, and not when law is generated by the state itself. Habermas implies that to achieve this more "grassroots" invitation to state-legal intervention, discussion of legal institutionalization and mediatization must become part of the lifeworld. Only then is *Sozialstaat* law actually requisitioned by the lifeworld as opposed to acting as a colonizing agent of it.

It is not until BFN, however, that Habermas more specifically prescribes, as he did at the conclusion of *Public Sphere*, a way to alleviate quasi-Weberian anxieties over *Sozialstaat* law and render it both progressive and coherent. He still adheres to the idea that the public and semipublic institutions and arrangements of liberal democracies should be opened to general debate and participation. However, in BFN, Habermas

---

[15] Benhabib, *Critique, Norm and Utopia*, 249.

gives this strategy a less socially holistic and homogeneous character, and deploys at a fundamental level a more interpersonally rather than interassociatively based model of communication.[16] An important new element in Habermas's prescriptions in BFN is his proposal for a "reflexive" theory of law that opts between *Rechtsstaat*-style formal law and *Sozialstaat*-style deformalized law, depending on certain criteria (BFN 393). This choice should be part of public, legislative, and judicial discourse such that the costs and benefits of alternate strategies of achieving social goals can be made explicit, and not remain the exclusive preserve of bureaucratic elites who colonize the lifeworld, even if with the best of intentions.

Attempting to elude the legal either/or posed by Weber, Habermas's reflexive approach intends to make available the best qualities of each of the two models: crudely, the freedom-preserving quality of nineteenth-century formal law and the equality-ensuring quality of twentieth-century deformalized or materialized law (BFN 220, 224). Habermas shows how the *Sozialstaat* does not permanently eliminate formal strategies of law-making, but rather leaves them available as viable options to use alongside deformalized or materialized methods. But the decision to deploy either strategy must be left open to discussion within government institutions and public spheres (now discussed in the plural rather than the singular). The ramifications of the respective "hands-off" or "assertive" quality of each legal paradigm must become part of public policy language and debates so that deliberating publics and administrative officials can discuss which kind of law is more appropriate in particular circumstances: on the one hand, formal law that leaves more power in the hands of social actors themselves, thereby risking an intensification of semiprivate asymmetries of power, or, on the other, more direct government intervention that risks converting citizens into mere clients.

As I will argue in Chapter 4, when I more fully explicate Habermas's solution to the Weberianly posed problem of law and democracy, his proposal in BFN seems like a compromise, not only between types of law that Weber considered to be incommensurable, but also between the spirits of two distinct historical epochs. The final sections of this chapter engage the issue of history in Habermas's critique of Weber's legal sociology and in Habermas's own critical methodology.

---

[16] See Habermas's perhaps excessively apologetic and overdrawn distinction along these lines: "Further Reflections on the Public Sphere," in Craig Calhoun, ed. *Habermas and the Public Sphere* (Cambridge, MA: MIT Press, 1992), 421–61.

4. Secularization, Commodification, and History

Anyone concerned with the extent of Weber's influence on Habermas and the depth of the latter's critique of the former cannot help but be struck by this fact: in Habermas's account of modern European history in *Public Sphere*, the Protestantization-cum-secularization thesis for which Weber is most famous is virtually nonexistent. In fact, Weber's *The Protestant Ethic* is not even cited in the work.[17] Habermas's discussion of the history of the public sphere in the West from classical Greece through the Middle Ages and then in successive periods of modernity is centered on legal distinctions of public and private and on juridical definitions of *res publica* expressed in Roman law (STPS 4). The bourgeois public sphere seems furthered to no significant degree by secularization processes, understood in Weberian terms. In Habermas's account, the rise of the bourgeois public sphere is largely economically driven, with economics described in secular terms: Habermas notes that in the seventeenth and eighteenth centuries, new modes of sharing information and facilitating interaction resulted from a new kind of "traffic in commodities" (STPS 16).

To this extent, then, commodification, not a change in or loss of religious belief, makes rational criticism possible and necessary in Habermas's account: "The private people for whom the cultural product became available *as a commodity* profaned it inasmuch as they had to determine its meaning on their own (by way of rational communication with one another), verbalize it, and thus state explicitly what precisely in its implicitness for so long could assert its authority" (STPS 37, emphasis added). The emergence of the bourgeois public sphere cannot be reduced to a dissipation of belief, or a collapse in the consensus that the latter supposedly ensured, but rather must be attributed to a qualitative change in the production, distribution, and experience of commodities. As Marx suggested, the quantitatively rational and sensually felt experience of commodities is only possible in a society of universally free labor and general exchange. On this basis, Habermas argues that the development of a political public sphere between civil society and the state required the "social precondition" of a "liberalized" market that "made affairs in the sphere of social reproduction as much as possible a matter of private people left to themselves and so finally completed the privatization of civil society" (STPS 74). If one must speak in terms more crude than those resorted to

---

[17] Weber, *The Protestant Ethic and the Spirit of Capitalism* (1905/1919), trans. Peter Baehr and Gordon Wells (New York: Penguin, 2002).

by either Weber or Habermas: for the author of the *The Protestant Ethic*, religious reformation facilitates the rise of capitalism; for the Habermas of STPS, the case is the reverse.

Given that the sources of the transformation to modernity are different for Weber and Habermas, it is not surprising to find that the respective authors' understanding of historical continuity and discontinuity should differ as well. Very early in *Public Sphere*, Habermas engages in a historical contrast seemingly reminiscent of Weber's SL: as we will see, Weber describes the entwinement of public and private in the Middle Ages so as to emphasize the importance of their separation in the *Rechtsstaat* model and the danger of their apparent re-merging under the *Sozialstaat* (e.g., SL 643–4). But Habermas's point is somewhat more subtle: he notes that, indeed, public and private were not formally separated in medieval practice, as they were to some extent in ancient and assuredly in certain modern arrangements (STPS 5). But Habermas refuses to impose this conceptual distinction too forcefully on the medieval situation, where, he intimates, it simply may not be appropriate at all. Thus, Habermas does *not* conceptualize the private realm – so important to his definition of the bourgeois public sphere as a collection of private persons coming together to discuss what is publicly relevant – as something that was "bound" to the medieval manor and then subsequently "freed" from it with the emergence of capitalist modernity. Habermas suggests that what constitutes the "private" in medieval and modern social forms are simply qualitatively different phenomena.

This fine-grained distinction signals Habermas's attempt in *Public Sphere* to avoid the large-scale transhistoricizations and simplified periodizations that often characterize Weber's SL, as well as other works. On the contrary, in accord with Habermas's understanding of critical theory, *Public Sphere* attempts to explicate more specific periodizations in delimiting social change, because only the details of *discrete* socioeconomic configurations suggest the specific emancipatory political potentials immanent to them – immanent emancipatory potentials that can be reconstructed historically and prescribed within contemporary circumstances.[18] Therefore, rather than rely on a premodern–modern

---

[18] Benhabib describes the moribund state in which critical theory was left by thinkers such as T. W. Adorno and Max Horkheimer before Habermas took up its revival. By giving up the attempt to ground normative prescriptions in the contradictions exhibited by a particular historical status of capitalism, Frankfurt critical theory situated the critic in the following untenable position: "The critical theorist must either speak in the name of a future utopian vision to which he alone has access, or he must play the role of memory and

sociopolitical contrast to highlight normative achievements and potentials in modernity, throughout *Public Sphere* Habermas relies on a more refined absolutist–mercantilist–laissez-faire–Fordist periodization of European history from the eighteenth through the twentieth century.

Thus, unlike Weber, who observes in the rise of the *Sozialstaat* a return of feudalism, the Habermas of STPS, despite some ambiguous terminology, recognizes in the *Sozialstaat* emerging at the turn of the century a new social form, even if it exhibits characteristics similar to those in previous ones: as Habermas notes, in the development of the administrative/welfare state, "a policy of 'neo-mercantilism' went hand in hand with a kind of 'refeudalization' of society" (STPS 142). According to Habermas, the *Sozialstaat* is reminiscent of two previously distinct sociopolitical formations, feudal patrimonialism and modern mercantilism, while, as we will see in the next chapter, Weber understood it primarily in terms of refeudalization as such. Habermas's use of terms like "refeudalization" may be an indication of his immanent critique of the Nazi-cum-neo-conservative critics mentioned above earlier, among whom this characterization of the *Sozialstaat* was very popular.[19] In any case, it is important to point out that, contra these neo-conservative critics, Habermas shows that the state intervention characteristic of the *Sozialstaat*, in and of itself, is *not* a new phenomenon in modernity, since mercantilism had previously pursued similar policies. He convincingly demonstrates how state-interventionist mercantilism facilitated the era of laissez-faire that was to follow it as a different stage (STPS 17–19, 24, 57). Rather, Habermas shows that another phenomenon accompanying the *Sozialstaat*, namely, the "societalization" of public authority – which entails the complicity of the very agents of capital allied with these neo-conservative critics – is, in fact, quite new. Therefore, the interaction between processes of stateification and societalization is what constitutes the *Sozialstaat* as a new social formation in *Public Sphere*.

conscience in a culture that has eliminated its own past. Neither this utopian vision nor retrospective remembrance are [sic] based upon norms and values derived from the self-understanding of this culture and social structure. The standpoint of the critic transcends the present and juxtaposes to the existent what ought to be or what could have been had the past not been betrayed" (Benhabib, *Critique, Norm and Utopia*, 180).

[19] Carl Schmitt made this case most dramatically in "Ethic of State and the Pluralistic State," trans. David Dyzenhaus, in Chantal Mouffe, ed., *The Challenge of Carl Schmitt* (London: Verso, 1999), 195–209; but F. A. Hayek, whose debt to the Schmitt school goes too often unacknowledged, made it most famous in *The Road to Serfdom* (Chicago: University of Chicago Press, 1994). See William E. Scheuerman, "The Unholy Alliance of Carl Schmitt and Friedrich A. Hayek," *Constellations* 4, no. 2 (October 1997), 172–88.

Clearly, Habermas does not completely ignore historical continuity in this early work. *Public Sphere* may be famous for emphasizing the wholesale, qualitative, structural transformation entailed by the supercession of the *Rechtsstaat* by the *Sozialstaat*. But when Habermas makes the case for practices within the latter configuration that might serve the same emancipatory function as the bourgeois public sphere in the former, he emphasizes continuity in the normative aspirations associated with the two models. Habermas states quite explicitly that "the transformation of the liberal constitutional state in the direction of a state committed to social rights . . . is characterized by continuity rather than by a break with the liberal traditions" (STPS 224). This seems to imply that emancipatory ideals have remained the same throughout the transformation even as the social structures that necessarily condition them have changed.

When Habermas describes the transformation of the bourgeois public sphere with the emergence of the *Sozialstaat*, he uses terms such as "decomposition" and phrases that describe tendencies toward "collapse" (STPS 4). Statements like these imply a qualitative transformation, as does the following description: the nineteenth-century market commodified products by making them readily available but *not* readily consumed psychologically (thereby leaving space for rational criticism), while the *Sozialstaat* entails the more ominous development that "culture became a commodity not only in form but also in content" (such that it is swallowed rather than questioned) (STPS 166). The consumption of, not participation in, discussion that makes for acclamatory consent and benevolent passivity sounds like a definitive difference between the two configurations (STPS 198–200). In Habermas's historical and social scientific descriptions of the transformation in *Public Sphere*, the rupture seems definitive; in his normative evaluations of it, there appears to be quite a bit of continuity.

Especially in the later parts of *Public Sphere*, Habermas proceeds in a manner accentuating normative continuity despite his empirical evidence that depicts the transformation as a qualitative break: for instance, according to Habermas, the *Sozialstaat* had to move beyond the "negative determinations" of liberal rights in order to achieve "justice" already aspired to in the *Rechtsstaat* model (STPS 224). But this raises the following Hegelian–Marxian question still appropriate to the methodological commitment of this early work: to what extent are particular normative aspirations strictly bound to specific historical configurations and not transposable to subsequent ones? The effort to sort out continuity and disruption is necessary if the critical theory that Habermas practices in

Public Sphere is to apprehend a historical situation and the normative potentials concomitant with it in a fruitful manner. In short, therefore, Habermas has a tendency in the work to describe the *crises* accompanying transformation in terms of qualitative change, but then to describe the *solution* to them in terms of significant continuity. If this remained a healthy tension in his work, it still might yield perspicacious results in later writings. But I will suggest that Habermas moves to a theory of history that, while gesturing to change, relies upon presuppositions of continuity, presuppositions that make it difficult if not impossible to discern socially specific normative possibilities. He seems to hold up not just normative aspirations, but also *social structures themselves* in works such as TCA and BFN.

Thus, despite a clear departure from the secularization thesis that dominates Weber's work, Habermas's treatment of modernity and engagement with Weber's SL in *Public Sphere* exhibits a tension between historical continuity and disrupture. As I will suggest in the next section, one could say that the failures to resolve continuity and disrupture, and to specify the normative implications thereof, haunt Habermas's work, as if like a ghost, throughout his whole career. In later works, Habermas moves to an approach even less sensitive to change *within* modernity in favor of one focused on the transformation *to* modernity – works that perhaps not coincidentally criticize "philosophies of history" associated with Hegel (cf. TCA2 332, 378–9, 382, 397; LM 237). I will cite this as the cause of Habermas's deemphasis of structural disrupture in his mature social and political theory. Since the issue of historical change is central to the endeavor, this has important ramifications for Habermas's critique and reconstruction of Weber.

In TCA1, Habermas focuses on Weber's two alternate descriptions of the rise of rationalization in the West – on the one hand, the account associated with the Protestant ethic and, on the other, the one associated with the rise of modern law (TCA1 166ff). He consistently suggests that Weber's analysis unnecessarily allows the secularization of purposive rational behavior characteristic of the former – eventually embodied in the instrumental rationality associated with the market and the state – to be identified with rationality as such.[20] By doing so, Habermas asserts, in

---

[20] McCarthy deftly explains Habermas's reconstruction of Weber's categories of purposive-rational and strategic action and points to certain theoretical inconsistencies that result from the effort. See McCarthy, *The Critical Theory of Jürgen Habermas*, 24–5; 390, n. 23 and 31.

a manner that will now be familiar to the reader, that Weber neglects the normative consensus that, arrived at through moral-practical rationality, inheres in and can be further extended by modern law (TCA1 190–2, 198, 219–20). In Volume II, the dark side of the secularization thesis becomes clearer as Habermas links Weber's ostensibly empty legal legitimacy to his nihilistic social and political tendencies:

> Weber drew these consequences not only for himself, as a social scientist; he thought that they also set the premises for the actions of citizens involved in the legitimation process. In their eyes, a political order not amenable to normative justification, a struggle for political power carried out only in the name of subjective gods and demons, had to appear in the end wanting legitimation. A political system that *no longer* had at its disposal the binding power of *religious-metaphysical worldviews* was threatened by the *withdrawal of legitimation*. (TCA2 324, emphasis added)

According to Habermas, Weber is so seduced by his own account of a secularized instrumental rationality that he ignores ways in which values or preferences are formulated contextually or interpersonally; as such, these preferences have no practical or substantive rational content or grounding in Weber's theory (TCA1 171). Habermas points out that Weber did not consider the extent to which law might have rationalized the West independently of – that is, without the methodical outlook and existential-cum-social unbrotherliness associated with – the Protestant ethic. While no doubt partially the outcome of the religious civil wars, as well as the policies of absolutism, the *Rechtsstaat*, in principle, develops more or less independently of this religious ethic. Thus, its moral force should persist beyond the dissipation of religious motivations famously lamented by Weber and therefore should be immune to the melancholia of the secularization thesis. However, in the course of this discussion, it is clear that Habermas takes on the either/or historical categorizations reminiscent of Weber's studies of religion and political writings: Habermas persistently uses categories such as conventional/postconventional, traditional/modern, and so on, suggesting that the crucial "structural transformation" that one should consider is modernization, as such, rather than the changes *within* modernity (TCA1 198–9, 254). Largely absent from Habermas's own historical descriptions in TCA are the more differentiated periodizations of modernity laid out in *Public Sphere* – whatever tensions, as mentioned above, that may have plagued it as a theory of historical change.

For instance, toward the conclusion of TCA1, Habermas criticizes Weber's understanding of what *drives* history, but nevertheless clearly accepts Weber's historical *categories*: "In Weber's view . . . the transition to modernity is characterized by a differentiation of spheres of value and structures of consciousness that makes possible a certain critical transformation of traditional knowledge in relation to specifically given validity claims" (TCA1 340). As noted earlier, in *Public Sphere*, "transition to modernity" is hardly a category at all; moreover, it is a category that makes little sense to a critical theory attempting to locate emancipatory potential in more historically specific circumstances. Throughout TCA and most subsequent works, Habermas is anxious about succumbing to a "philosophy of history," which he clearly associates with earlier work such as *Public Sphere*. Habermas comes to recognize the problems associated with this approach as economic reductionism, the attribution of a singular consciousness to mass movements or populations, and a teleological interpretation of history. I elaborate on this in the next section.

As a result of this conversion, in the midst of his reconstruction of Weber in TCA, Habermas begs off ideology critique as a methodology: "It is not my intention to pursue a critique of ideology probing the roots of this inconsistency [in Weber's approach]. I am concerned with the immanent reasons for Weber's inability to carry through his theory of rationalization as it is set up" (TCA1 270). Immanent critique here is disengaged from history in a decidedly un-Hegelian manner and is affiliated instead exclusively with a strictly analytical interrogation of Weber's categories. In the next section, I focus on Habermas's changed historical logic with the more narrow goal of exploring its ramifications for law in the following terms: in excavating a substantive moral rationality associated with law from Weber's somewhat reductionist theory of purposive rationalization, does Habermas himself, under the former's influence, occlude historical conditions of emancipation previously associated with his own standards of critical theory?

Excursus: The Transformation of Habermas's Theory of History

But first, I offer some considerations on how and why Habermas adopts this changed historical focus. The most sensitive interpreters of Habermas have explored the status of the philosophy of history in his mature works. Axel Honneth, Thomas McCarthy, and Seyla Benhabib trace the transition from an explicitly philosophical-historical Marxian materialism to a more idealist social-evolutionary theory that purports to escape the constraints posed by a philosophy of history, traditionally conceived.[21] I can

---

[21] See also the following article-length explorations of the issue: Anthony Giddens, "Reason without Revolution?" *Praxis International* 2 (1982), 318–38; Moishe Postone, "History

add nothing fundamental to these analyses, upon which I will draw extensively here.[22] Ultimately, I supplement and extend their efforts by posing
a starker contrast between the philosophy of history as practiced in STPS
(which plays a relatively insignificant role in these critics' interpretations)
and the philosophy of history exhibited in later works such as TCA and
BFN. I believe that the ramifications of the wholesale transformation in
Habermas's historical analysis in these works standing at opposite ends
of his career will become more clear in Chapter 5 when I explicate his
attempt to address a new structural transformation in writings on one
specific subset of globalization: European integration.

McCarthy points out that in Habermas's early work, critical theory was
explicitly dependent on "the idea of a philosophy of history," that is, the
practical reason-derived meaning drawn from the contradiction between
a social situation and its history, and further verified by theoretical-
empirical testing.[23] McCarthy demonstrates how Habermas, in his middle work, becomes impatient with the unitary subject presupposed in
Marxian and neo-Marxian philosophies of history, but does not yet articulate a repudiation but rather a "radicalization" of such approaches: for
Habermas at this point, philosophy of history "must itself become more
historically self-conscious, for the presuppositions of the philosophy of
history are themselves the result of historical development."[24] McCarthy
shows that for Habermas, philosophy of history must become conscious
of its own grounding in particular circumstances; it is not narrowly philosophical but rather a prologue to practice.[25]

It would be impossible to apply these statements to Habermas's post-
1989 works that explicitly and wholeheartedly reject philosophy of history, even as he brings his theoretical apparatus to bear on what is arguably
a new historical epoch. McCarthy confirms this disjuncture between the

---

and Critical Social Theory," *Contemporary Sociology* 19 (1990), 112–15; Jeffrey Alexander, "Beyond the Marxian Dilemma?" in Axel Honneth and Hans Joas, eds., *Communicative Action* (Cambridge, MA: MIT Press, 1991); and Nancy Love, "What's Left of
Marx?" in Stephen K. White, ed., *The Cambridge Companion to Habermas* (Cambridge:
Cambridge University Press, 1995).

[22] In addition, on Habermas's moral-philosophical works written between TCA and BFN
and after the publication of the critical commentaries drawn on here, see White, *The
Recent Work of Jürgen Habermas.*

[23] McCarthy, *The Critical Theory of Jürgen Habermas*, 127, 129; he refers specifically to
Habermas, "Literaturbericht zur philosophischen Diskussion um Marx und den Marx-
ismus," *Philosophische Rundschau* 5, nos. 3–4 (1957), 165–235.

[24] McCarthy, *The Critical Theory of Jürgen Habermas*, 132.

[25] Ibid., 136.

young and mature Habermas when he discusses the relationship between idealist and empiricist moments of Habermas's critical theory. These moments can no longer be mediated in Habermas's recent thought, the latter having become idealist in an almost Rawlsian fashion, and, as we will see, ideals and facts having become so hypostatized in essays on the EU. On the contrary, for the Habermas of the years immediately following *Public Sphere*, ideas are firmly embedded in structural and empirically verifiable reality:

Developments in the spheres of social labor and political domination can themselves bring about a restructuring of worldviews. To be sure, these developments are themselves linguistically mediated; but they are not, as a rule, simply the results of a new way of looking at things. Rather changes in the mode of production or the system of power relations can themselves overturn accepted patterns of interpretation. A reduction of social inquiry to *Sinnverstehen* could be justified only on the idealist assumption that linguistically articulated consciousness determined the material conditions of life. But the objective framework of social action is not exhausted by the dimension of intersubjectively intended and symbolically transmitted meaning. The latter is rather a moment of a complex that however symbolically mediated, is also constrained by the constraints of reality.[26]

Such reality is constituted specifically by the demands of outer nature tending toward technical mastery and of inner nature tending toward forms of repression.

From McCarthy's account, it is clear that between STPS and TCA, Habermas operated with a reconstructed philosophy of history, one that he would later claim to have abandoned. In this philosophy of history, moral-practical possibilities need not be attributed by the omniscient great mind of a theorist in an undifferentiated fashion to a social totality, a new consciousness, or an unsubstantiated telos, but rather must be grounded within the possibilities and constraints of social actors in a properly ascertained historical moment:

While philosophy of history is impossible as a contemplative exercise (that is, as a closed theory of an open future), it is possible as a practical enterprise. As an actor I can project or anticipate a future, which I can also work to bring about. The closure that is impossible in theory is not only possible but necessary in practice. Finally he argues that practical projections of the future need not be arbitrary. They can be made on the basis of an examination of the real determinants of social processes and in the light of an analysis of the real possibilities of development in the present.[27]

[26] Ibid., 184.
[27] Ibid., 186.

Habermas is able to do without this mediation of historically unfolding aspirations and emerging structural constraints as he moves to the more abstract analysis indicated by his adoption of social evolutionism around the publication of LC.[28] The commentators point out that in his social-evolutionary writings Habermas operated with an unacknowledged philosophy of history, even as he claimed to be shedding it, and I hope to show that he operates with a deficient one now that he professes to be completely free of philosophy of history altogether.

McCarthy argues that the social evolutionism characterizing Habermas's post-Marxian period is still a philosophy of history in the sense that it arranges different stages of rationality in a hierarchical pattern and employs hypotheses concerning cognitive capacities, system crises, and social movements "to explain the history of the species as a learning process."[29] Furthermore, McCarthy discusses the predictive or forecasting potential of Habermas's philosophy of history reconstructed in light of social evolutionism, an outlook still not completely distinct from his earlier historical materialism:

> We can only project the future practically, engage ourselves for it politically, and analyze the present in a prospective retrospective from the vantage points opened by practice. Thus, for example, the analysis of existing constellations of power and interest involves a hypothetico-practical moment. . . . Our "provinciality with respect to the future" means that we cannot adopt a purely theoretical attitude toward it; we are forced to anticipate it practically. This places the critical theorist in the role of an advocate for a more human society, with all the situation-dependency, uncertainty and risks that this implies.[30]

But while McCarthy recognizes Habermas's social evolutionism as a historical narrative, he does not pursue the ramifications of its universally transhistorical quality, a quality that his previous reconstructed historical

---

[28] Habermas would later rely even more extensively on social evolutionism in moral-philosophical works such as *Communication and the Evolution of Society* (Cambridge, MA: Beacon Press, 1979), especially, chaps. 3 and 4. See the devastating critique of this aspect of Habermas's project, albeit from a systems-theoretic perspective, by Michael Schmid, "Habermas's Theory of Social Evolution," in J. B. Thompson and David Held, eds., *Habermas: Critical Debates* (Cambridge, MA: MIT Press, 1982).

[29] McCarthy, *The Critical Theory of Jürgen Habermas*, 268–9. In his mature work, besides historical-evolutionary stages, Habermas also focuses on individual cognitive-developmental stages derived from the Piaget–Kohlberg tradition of psychology. For an excellent discussion, see White, *The Recent Work of Jürgen Habermas*, 48–68. See also Robert Pippin's criticisms of Habermas's recourse to both theories of stages for being naturalistic and question-begging with respect to the "superiority" of different stages: Pippin, *Idealism as Modernism: Hegelian Variations* (Cambridge: Cambridge University Press, 1997), 178.

[30] McCarthy, *The Critical Theory of Jürgen Habermas*, 267.

materialism, which took little account of the relationship of consciousness and social structures in epochs before capitalism, did not have. The social evolutionary perspective runs the risk of positing potentially ideological claims to knowledge about previous eras and states of consciousness that a modernity-centered, commodity-based analysis does not. As the sophisticated approach of STPS suggests, Habermas could have turned to a historically specific, transforming-capitalism-enabled theory of communicative progress without engaging in the crude economic determinism that he associates with unreconstructed Marxist philosophies of history.

In *Critique of Power*, Honneth attributes Habermas's mid-career theoretical shift to a rearrangement of Weber's theory of social rationalization: the shift from an historically specific, capitalistically enabled theory of rational criticism, on the one hand, to a transhistorical theory of communicative evolution, on the other:

Purposive-rational action emerges here as the reproductive core of society. Its gradual productive increase results in "new technologies" and "improved strategies" for the control of the environment. In contrast to this, the institutions that normatively regulate social intercourse are so far only passively changed in that they successively reproduce the evolutionary advances of purposive-rationally organized action spheres. Admittedly, Habermas retains this traditional concept for only a short time. He abandons it the moment he no longer conceives the change of socially integrated norms as a passive process but rather traces it back to an active learning process tied to the moral experiences of symbolically mediated interaction. But at this point it is not yet communicative action but purposive-rational action that represents the force propelling social evolution forward. The mechanism of the history of the species is characterized in such a way that "structural modification is necessitated under the pressure of relatively developed productive forces."[31]

At first, communication is wholly dependent on objective structures, but Habermas would invert the relationship once his theory was completely free of conceptual dependence on labor and instead relied upon communication as a socially constitutive practice. Further on, Honneth observes, "by means of the application of the evolutionary scheme that he has taken from historical materialism, he can thus assume that the development of the relations of production comes about as a process of moral emancipation that at every historical stage is again impinged upon by the advances in the development of productive forces."[32] Still further on, however,

---

[31] Honneth, *Critique of Power*, 257, quoting Habermas's *Toward a Rational Society: Student Protest, Science and Politics*, trans. Jeremy Shapiro (Boston: Beacon Press, 1970).
[32] Ibid., 260.

Honneth indicates why Habermas eventually abandons "history" under-stood even in this qualified sense: the later Habermas

opposes not only the Marxist analysis of capitalism and the Weberian concept of rationalization but also Adorno and Horkheimer's diagnosis of history in order to ground his own approach in a critique of the classical theories of social rational-ization. As he had done earlier with respect to Marx and Weber, he now attempts with respect to critical theory to work out the action-theoretic bottlenecks that stand in the ways of the goal of a comprehensive and grounded critique of the one-sided, purposive-rational form of socialization. To this extent, the new work can also be understood as an attempt to give a communicative-theoretic turn to the diagnosis that in the *Dialectic of Enlightenment* took the form of a philosophy of history.[33]

For his part, McCarthy asserts that Habermas can make this change with-out sacrificing advantages of his previous methodology:

The theory of social evolution does not replace the earlier conceptions of critical social theory as historically situated, practically interested reflection on a forma-tive process. Rather it represents a further enrichment of its theoretical basis. In addition to a horizontal account of the structure of nondistortred communicative interaction, critical self-reflection can also draw on a vertical account of the devel-opment of structures of interaction. . . . The theory of social evolution . . . locates historical changes in an evolutionary framework: history, with all its diversity and contingency, takes on the shape of a learning process.[34]

McCarthy describes Habermas's strategy as an attempt to overcompen-sate for a technological determinism in Marxism and in his own earlier work: he notes that unlike technical knowledge and productive capacities that are often theorized in evolutionary terms, moral, political, and social developments are usually regarded as "mere change."[35] But Habermas wants to attribute a learning dimension, a discernible direction, and a specific telos to the history of these phenomena as well.[36] Although sens-ing the risk of an equally untenable ideational determinism, McCarthy is quick to insist that Habermas does not understand evolutionary learning processes as logically necessary or independent of social action.[37]

In *Critique, Norm and Utopia*, Benhabib points out that Habermas revives the crucial evaluative aspect of critical theory precisely through

---

[33] Ibid., 285.

[34] McCarthy, *The Critical Theory of Jürgen Habermas*, 270.

[35] Ibid., 270. But consider White's comparison of the system–lifeworld distinction with Marx's base–superstructure one: White, *The Recent Work of Jürgen Habermas*, 104.

[36] McCarthy, *The Critical Theory of Jürgen Habermas*, 270.

[37] Ibid., 424, n. 66.

his adoption of a more evolutionary notion of history. Habermas abandons the philosophy of history associated with Adorno and Horkheimer – whose own approach to social and historical specificity was not nearly as refined as the one that Habermas practiced in STPS – for a social evolutionism that supposedly is not a philosophy of history. According to Benhabib, as Habermas understands it:

> Unlike transcendental philosophy, reconstructive theorems do not assume that such deep structures [of cognition and action] are ahistorical, non-evolving frameworks. To the contrary, Habermas views such deep structures as patterns of rule competencies, which evolve in the history of the individual and of the species. Although individuals are more often than not unaware of the logic and dynamic of such evolution, they are the agents of such evolution, for it is through learning processes that they acquire such rule competencies.... Social change, he maintains, cannot be observed from the standpoint of the observer alone. There are aspects of social evolution which must be viewed as sequences in a developmental logic and which can be reconstructed internally.[38]

But Benhabib perceives that this evolutionism risks giving an overly ideational dimension to historical change; Habermas continues to acknowledge social structures, but cognitive adaptation seems to motor the process almost autonomously of the former:

> Social innovation occurs through the answers that social agents give to the ever-new problems of their lifeworld. Through institutionalization, the experiences leading to a specific answer set become part of the material and cultural history of society. These previous answers are available to social agents as the legacy of the past; they reproduce their lifeworld by recapitulating these already available answers while creating and seeking new ones. The concept of reproduction of the lifeworld thus presupposes the related notions of a "learning process" as an internally reconstructable sequence meaningful to participants themselves.[39]

Having established this historical model, Benhabib then raises serious questions about it: she points out that Habermas's concept of a legitimation crisis presupposes a motivational crisis exhibited in civic, familial, and vocational decline, and thus, like his Frankfurt School forebears, a certain collapse of bourgeois standards.[40] Yet,

> this argument indicates a particular difficulty in the use of evolutionary-developmental models within a critical social theory. When applied to a macro-level, such arguments carry with them *overtones of a speculative philosophy of*

---

[38] Benhabib, *Critique, Norm and Utopia*, 264.
[39] Ibid., 265.
[40] Ibid., 276.

history. The future projected by the theorist, and which is fundamentally open, is presented as if it were a necessary and "normal" outcome of a course of development. It is only in this light that deviations from the theory can be deemed "regressions." It is presupposed that *we already possess the yardstick by means of which to judge the future....* Neither are we at the end of history, nor can we point to a "normal" course of development in light of which we can judge "regressions" and "deviations." The history of the species is so far unique, sui generis; we have no established model of development to compare with.[41]

Benhabib points to the fact that Habermas's mature work relies on an unacknowledged philosophy of history that in some sense presupposes an end of history, and, although she does not say so explicitly, to that extent it is even more deterministic than the Hegelian–Marxian theory of qualitative social change, one in which the relationship of consciousness and social structures *transforms* rather than merely *extends* or accumulates what already has come to be.[42] Habermas's unacknowledged philosophy of history posits the future as simply a more challenging version of the present and elevates the most desirable normative possibilities inspired by that vision to the status of moral standards by which present realities can be assessed. Unfortunately, as *Public Sphere* demonstrates so masterfully, history, facts, and norms cannot be coordinated so easily. Honneth, Benhabib, and McCarthy detect a philosophy of history in the mature Habermas largely without reference to STPS, the work where he put his early Marxian philosophy of history into practice. And yet Benhabib, in particular, is still able to discern the following without the stark relief effect provided by that book:

Evolutionary theories flatten this horizon of the future by making the future appear like the necessary consequence of the present. To put the objection I am raising to Habermas's reliance on evolutionary theory in a nutshell: if the problem with

---

[41] Ibid., 276–7, emphasis added.

[42] Again, this raises questions regarding philosophical-methodological characterization of Habermas's work: take, for instance, *The Recent Work of Jürgen Habermas*, in which White identifies as "Hegelian–Marxist" those aspects of Habermas's project focused on concrete social pathologies (91). Yet, such efforts could fall very easily into a Weberian, neo-Kantian framework. Without the attention to historical change, and particularly when cast in relief with Habermas's STPS, there is little about his mature work that could be deemed Hegelian–Marxist. In this vein, cf. White's perhaps too abruptly dismissive treatment of Lukács (104) and the fact that qualitative structural transformation within modernity does not even figure in his definition of critical theory (128). White attributes the "quasi-Kantian" aspect of Habermas's project to his focus on rationality and the Hegelian–Marxist aspect, generally, to his grappling with "modernity," writ large (128), or, more specifically, to the "practical guidance" that new social movements provide when criticizing "industrial civilization" (142).

early critical theor[ies] seemed to be that their conception of utopian reason was so esoteric as not to allow embodiment in the present, the difficulty with Habermas's concept is that it seems like such a natural outcome of the present that it is difficult to see what would constitute an emancipatory break with the present if communicative rationality were fulfilled.[43]

Just as Hegel presumed the Prussian monarchical *Rechtsstaat* to approximate an end of history, despite a method that pointed beyond it, does Habermas do the same with respect to a reformed *Sozialstaat*, in spite of the power of his own approach? In Chapter 5, I will confirm these charges by contrasting Habermas's study of the structural transformation of the twentieth century, the rise of the *Sozialstaat* in *Public Sphere*, with his recent attempts to analyze the transformation becoming apparent in the twenty-first century, European integration.

Here, on the basis of my own contrast of *Public Sphere* with later works, and on the basis of the analyses of Habermas's middle period by his most influential interpreters, we may conclude the following: works like LC mark a transition in Habermas's thought from an interepochal analysis of *transformation* to a more intraepochal one of *crisis*. His theory becomes less concerned with dramatic social change within modernity, engaging instead in more wide-scale epochal descriptions that transcend capitalist modernity. Habermas still employs historically specific analysis but now combines the latter with social critique that enlists transhistorical evolutionary categories. It is not clear, however, whether the structural descriptions and normative prescriptions that Habermas derives from this new (un)historical theoretical framework are any less, respectively, deterministic and speculative than the efforts of earlier Marxists and critical theorists.

Yet, in LC, Habermas still seems to call for research that is more historically focused than, for instance, systems theory; he specifically advocates the conduct of research pitched to "a level of analysis at which the *connection* between normative structures and steering problems becomes palpable. I find this level in a historically oriented analysis of social systems, which permits us to ascertain for a given case the range of tolerance within which the goal values of the system might vary without its continued existence being critically endangered" (LC 7). But, consonant with the findings of Habermas's interlocutors mentioned earlier, Habermas asserts that the "boundaries of historical continuity" must be measured against criteria of "social evolution" (LC 7). LC, therefore,

[43] Benhabib, *Critique, Norm and Utopia*, 277.

finds Habermas attempting to decipher continuous versus discontinuous aspects of history, and systemic versus intentional aspects of social change, in a manner very much *unlike* his efforts in *Public Sphere*:

The history of secular knowledge and technology is a history of truth-monitored successes in coming to terms with outer nature. It consists of discontinuous but, in the long run, cumulative processes. To explain the world-historically cumulative character of scientific and technical progress, knowledge of empirical mechanisms is necessary but not sufficient. To understand the development of science and technology, we must also conjecture an inner logic through which a hierarchy of non-reversible sequences is fixed from the outset. (LC 11)

Unlike the historically discrete characterizations of *Public Sphere*, despite gestures to historical discontinuity, Habermas here speaks of a "directional" or "cumulative" process of "social evolution" that takes into account all of world history (LC 11). Moreover, he speaks of history in terms of "the development from myth, through religion, to philosophy and ideology, the demand for discursive redemption of normative-validity claims" (LC 11); and further lays out as stages four social formations: primitive, traditional, capitalist, postcapitalist (LC 17).

In works like LC, Habermas might have been able to ground social evolution *within* capitalist modernity much as he did critical rationality in *Public Sphere*. But because he uses "evolution" in so grossly a species-historical manner, the effort to elucidate a specific program of emancipation is bound to be ultimately unconvincing because, as Benhabib has argued, it is largely foreordained. Habermas defends himself by asserting, "without a theory of social evolution to rely on, principles of organization cannot be grasped abstractly, but only picked out inductively and elaborated with reference to the institutional sphere (kinship system, political system, economic system) that possesses functional primacy for a given stage of development" (LC 18). In other words, contemporary social structures can only be discerned when cast in relief with historically antecedent or subsequent formations; Habermas no longer relies on contradictions immanent to different stages of and exclusive to modernity to identify objective possibilities for and constraints on emancipation.

Thus, despite the fact that he will still make mention of the different possibilities and constraints posed by different eras in the history of capitalism, in post-LC works Habermas treats in a rather cursory manner the qualitative change within modernity that presumably conditions the kind of moral progress that concerns him. To be sure, Habermas raises the issue of change within modernity at the conclusion of a section of

LC on liberal capitalism with the following question: "Has capitalism been fully transformed into a post-capitalist social formation that has overcome the crisis-ridden form of economic growth?" (LC 31). But he neither answers this question nor explores whether it portends the end of historical transformations within modernity altogether. Habermas compounds the problem by starting the chapter on crises in advanced capitalism with the disappointing pronouncement: "I must neglect here the very complex transition from liberal to organized capitalism" (LC 33). At the end of *Public Sphere*, Habermas had implied that normative possibilities could only be located in the transitions among epochs in modernity (STPS 244), and he grounded his prescriptions for reform of the *Sozialstaat* with insights from such a transition. But Habermas does not even cite *Public Sphere* as a plausible guide to answering his question here in *Legitimation Crisis* and in subsequent work.

5. Philosophy of History and the Sociology of Law

How does Habermas's new historical orientation pertain to the specific concerns of this chapter? What is the impact of Habermas's adoption of Weber's secularization account of modernity on the critique of Weber's sociology of law? To put it succinctly, as Habermas's historical scope becomes universally evolutionary and transepochal, his theory of social change within modernity becomes virtually indistinguishable from the secularization thesis. The rather simplified ideas-respond-to-structural-constraints view of history represented by social evolutionism seems to contribute to a privileging of consciousness in his analysis, and Protestant vocationalism becomes irresistibly attractive to Habermas as a normative-cultural standpoint. Moreover, as he proceeds to engage Rawls and Rawlsian issues throughout the 1980s, the secularization perspective that is also central for Rawl's worldview becomes even more dominant in Habermas's work.

Stephen White sums up Habermas's new historical sensibility quite well:

As the corrosiveness of modern consciousness on religion and tradition became increasingly evident, that consciousness began to experience itself as self-alienating. Modern consciousness is marked from this point on by a search for "self-assurance," or a search for some standards, which are both made available by that consciousness and yet can provide some normative guide for it in modern life.[44]

---

[44] See White, *The Recent Work of Jürgen Habermas*, 91.

This is far from the perspective of *Public Sphere*, where social and political actors make "critical-rational" sense out of the social world without being hounded by the anxiety of "meaninglessness." Moreover, this change makes Habermas vulnerable to the problems of normative vacuity that plagued Weber's theory to begin with, thus putting Habermas's historical-normative response to Weber's sociology of law on shaky grounds. The most devastating results of this move will not become clear until we observe Habermas's attempt to confront a novel structural transformation in Chapter 5.

Toward the end of TCA2, Habermas identifies four epochal juridification moments in the history of Western law. This periodization is worthy of his descriptions of successive configurations of political economy in *Public Sphere* and is, on the face of things, even subtler than the twofold *Rechtsstaat–Sozialstaat* dichotomy that governs most of his legal-theoretical analysis. The juridification stages that he identifies are those that successively result in the absolutist/bourgeois state, the nineteenth-century constitutional state (*Rechtsstaat*), the postrevolutionary democratic-constitutional state (*demokratischer Rechtsstaat*), and the twentieth-century democratic welfare state (*soziale und demokratische Rechtsstaat*) (TCA2 357–62). But, as I will show, these periods function in neither his account nor in subsequent work with anything approaching the analytical import of his distinction between "traditional" and "post-traditional" authority in these writings. In fact, this delineation of epochs appears to be something of an ad hoc attempt at historical specificity in a work that has largely abandoned it as a methodological approach.

The periodization mentioned earlier does, however, most forcefully serve to highlight the pathologies of *Sozialstaat* law. In terms that seem rather remote from the same topic in *Public Sphere*, Habermas asserts that the first wave of juridification, the bourgeois state, achieved "emancipation from *premodern* relations of power and dependence" (TCA2 366, emphasis added). Habermas notes that the next three waves increased freedom by making political and economic dynamics subject to democratic control: "The step-by-step development toward the democratic welfare state is directed against those modern relations of power and dependence that arose with the capitalist enterprise [and] the bureaucratic apparatus of domination" (TCA2 366). In these passages, Habermas claims to be considering the development of positive law "historically," that is, by taking into account the relationship of moral consciousness and legal institutions over time: "the epochal juridification waves are, on the one hand, characterized by *new legal institutions*, which are also reflected in the legal consciousness of everyday practice. Only with respect to this second category of juridification do questions of normative evaluation arise" (TCA2 366).

This statement seems to imply that these periods are qualitative transformations of consciousness and institutions, while in the functional or structural realm we witness only a quantitative expansion of what already exists. Therefore, one might conclude that the systemic aspects of modern society are already in place and do not change; rather, this perspective equates historical with the adaptation of consciousness and institutions to the continued expansion of a social form that is already intact. In his most recent work on transformations associated with globalization and European integration, besides holding firm to a secularization account of modernity, we will observe that Habermas remains ambivalent on the question of whether such developments signal only a functional extension of a previous sociopolitical configuration or, on the contrary, the emergence of a qualitatively new one.[45]

There is a significant turn in TCA2 that may be traceable to the revised view of history that Habermas exhibited in LC, one that is perhaps attributable to an infiltration of Habermas's theory by his own object of critique, namely, Weber. In volume II, Habermas seems to change substantially his assessment of the respective statuses of legal and religious rationalization in Weber. In TCA1 the two were separate, alternate accounts of the rise of modernity, the first promising the possibility of reaching understanding, the second portending the loss of such a possibility that leaves in its wake only the war of incommensurable values (the dissipation of belief thesis). For instance, in Volume I, Habermas declares:

Weber explains the institutionalization of purposive-rational economic action first by way of the Protestant vocational culture and subsequently by way of the modern legal system. Because they embody posttraditional legal and moral

---

[45] See Habermas, *The Inclusion of the Other: Studies in Political Theory*, Ciaran Cronin and Pablo de Grieff, eds. (Cambridge, MA: MIT Press, 1998), and *The Postnational Constellation: Political Essays*, Max Pensky, ed. (Cambridge, MA: MIT Press, 2001). In the latter work, Habermas adheres to the secularization thesis as an unproblematic explanation of modernity (135), yet criticizes Weber's more pessimistic "disenchantment" version of it: namely, "the transformation, and dissolution, of holistic religious worldviews" that cannot be compensated for in Weber's account by theoretical or practical reason (138). The legal rationalization account of modernity, more dominant in TCA1, would seem to stand at a much safer distance from the disenchantment thesis than the secularization account that Habermas also adopts.

representations, both of these make possible a societal rationalization in the sense of an expansion of the legitimate orders of purposive-rational action. With them arises a new form of social integration that can satisfy the functional imperatives of the capitalist economy. (TCA1 221)

Further on in TCA1, in the middle of a lament over the lack of a fully systematic treatment of law in Weber's general theory of societal rationalization, Habermas observes, "modern law played a role in the institutionalization of purposive-rational action orientations similar to that played by the Protestant Ethic of the calling" (TCA1 242). In both of these passages, Protestantism and legal rationalism arise separately, serve similar integration functions, but are not attributable to each other. The two phenomena are functionally alike but sociologically distinct. But there is conceptual slippage even in the first passage (TCA1 221): "Protestant vocational culture" is "posttraditional" only to the extent that it has been secularized. But, if it is secular, why should it be termed "Protestant"? More definitively, however, in TCA2, Habermas consistently merges the Protestant ethic with secular developments that did not necessarily have religious origins in the early modern period; and then he further combines both of these with legal rationalization.

In the process of conflating the two motors of rationalization, Habermas attributes to Weber the view that the "vocational ethic" was, "in the early phase, particularly influential among capitalist entrepreneurs and juristically trained expert officials" (TCA2 290). Habermas affiliates a vocational ethic with its Protestant origins throughout the second volume of the work and does not separate it from such an origin in this passage. Hence he starts to collapse a moral outlook associated with Protestantism with the rise of juridical rationalization. But Weber himself seldom, if ever, emphasizes any "protestantization" of modern jurists in SL.[46] Moreover, Habermas never mentioned it in his account of Weber in TCA1 – in fact, he consistently juxtaposed juridical-constitutional and religious-economic

---

[46] See Harold J. Berman and Charles J. Reid, Jr., "Max Weber as Legal Historian," in Turner, ed., *The Cambridge Companion to Weber*, 223–9. Berman and Reid point out and criticize Weber's failure to compare and integrate the findings of his studies of law and his study of the Protestant ethic (223). Moreover, they criticize the neglect of legal history in works like *The Protestant Ethic* and *The City*: they accuse Weber of inappropriately tracing medieval urban and early modern religious developments without reference to "legal concepts and legal values" (232–8). I explore the ramifications of such charges for Weber in the next chapter on SL. Here it is sufficient to note that Weber kept separate what Habermas tends to collapse: Protestant vocationalism and the rationalization of law. See also Assaf Likhovski, "Protestantism and the Rationalization of English Law: A Variation on a Theme by Weber," *Law and Society Review* 33, no. 2 (1999), 365–92.

rationalization.[47] Habermas not only appears to capitulate to Weber in this instance – as he does with respect to the periodizations of modernity – but he capitulates to a *caricature* of Weber: that is, he allows the "Protestant ethic" thesis to creep up on, and swallow whole, plausible alternative explanations of the rise of modern rationalization. Weber's *The Protestant Ethic* notoriously invited readers to understand the ideocentric causal account of modernity in reverse, that is, in a way that privileges the material account. Habermas's tacit adoption of the secularization thesis unwittingly leaves us no choice but to pursue material accounts alone.

Along these lines, Habermas asserts, "Weber investigated the norming of purposive-rational action under both *vocational-ethical* and *legal* aspects" (TCA2 315). Weber lamented the fading of vocational ethics and the reversal of the relationship between law and reason in the *Sozialstaat*. The modern "vocation," reflecting an ethic of conviction, embodies a substantive, not purposive-rational, standpoint even if it furthers purposive rationality in Habermas's account of Weber. But Habermas ignores Weber's *critique* of the ethic of conviction in the *Politik* lecture and the significant extent to which the Protestant ethic and the ethic of conviction remained separate in Weber's account.[48] Habermas charges that "Weber concentrated almost exclusively on the Reformation and some of the sectarian movements emanating from it; he neglected the bourgeois revolution and the mass movements of the 19th century" (TCA2 316).

In truth, Weber explores the bourgeois revolution in terms of natural law theories in SL, even if he does so in a somewhat cursory and dismissive manner (cf. TCA2 319).[49] But, again, the author of *The Protestant Ethic* did not link together the Reformation and law in SL, and Habermas, in TCA1, explicates Weber's legal history of modernity as an *alternative* account to the one focused on the rise of Protestantism. In the first place, if there were a causal link between these two phenomena, then the emergence of secular bourgeois law in non-Protestant Europe would need to be explained. More importantly, Habermas's reprotestantizing of the

---

[47] Similarly, in his most recent writings, Habermas still attributes to Weber an association between Protestantism and "the motivational basis of elites" who supported the new institutions of capitalist modernity. But in *The Protestant Ethic*, Weber analyzes Calvinist Protestantism as a socially general phenomenon, not one that simply affected elite behavior. It seems that Habermas consistently bends the Protestant ethic thesis to explain more than Weber ever asked it to, perhaps so as to fill in the causal vacancies in Habermas's own thesis.

[48] See Weber, "The Profession and Vocation of Politics."

[49] On the underdeveloped quality of Weber's analysis of natural law, see Berman and Reid, "Max Weber as Legal Historian," 227, n. 18.

rationalization of law jeopardizes the categorical coherence and historical accuracy of his reconstruction of Weber's SL.

To this extent then, in TCA2 Habermas reverses important aspects of his method in *Public Sphere* and capitulates to Weber's categories in an ostensible reconstruction of them. In other words, Habermas previously focused on the social bases of historical change rather than the transformation or dissipation of religious worldviews. But unless there is a secular-moral agent of the transformation like the legal institutionalizing of mutual understanding, Habermas's project is in Weberian jeopardy of falling prey to the excesses of the "warring pluriverse of worldviews" thesis. In TCA1, Habermas points out that, according to Weber's own account, modern law "appeared from the start in secularized form" (TCA1 243). But in the passages from Volume II that I discuss in this section, Habermas consistently attributes some religious motivations to its origins, which leaves him susceptible to the pessimistic "dissipation" aspect of the secularization thesis. From this perspective, the diminishing of religious worldviews reduces the possibility of mutual understanding in late capitalism. Therefore, despite claiming to supplant the "secularization hypothesis" focused on "the erosion of ethical attitudes" (TCA2 318), Habermas, here and in subsequent works, reveals himself to have subscribed to it in a not insignificant way:

> With the development of modern societies, the sacred domain has largely disintegrated, or at least has lost its structure-forming significance.... [M]orality and law detach themselves from their religions and metaphysical background. With this *secularization of bourgeois culture*, the cultural value spheres separate off sharply from one another and develop according to standards of their inner logics specific to different validity claims. (TCA2 196)

It would seem as if the traditional/postconventional model of historical periodization that Habermas relies on in his mature works is, despite notable assertions to the contrary, susceptible to similar criticisms often launched against Weber's secularization/warring-gods thesis. If Habermas relies as much as Weber on the secularization thesis and acknowledges the validity of a phenomenon like the dissipation of religious belief, then is not the intransigent amorality that plagues Weber's later work threatening Habermas's as well? Certainly, the either/or periodization of premodernity/modernity that results from Habermas's social evolutionism entails a secularization account of modernity that subsequently crowds out practical-moral, social differentiation, and commodity exchange accounts. TCA2 is replete with contrasts of premodern and modern law that would have been impossible in *Public Sphere*. For instance, Habermas asserts that "in premodern societies, social labor and political domination are still based on first-order institutions that are *merely overlaid and guaranteed by law*; in modern societies, they are replaced by orders of private property and legal domination that appear *directly* in forms of positive law" (TCA2 309). Habermas's point is that law is not abstract and autonomous in premodernity; it does not serve the constitutive function that it does in modernity. My point is that premodernity and modernity may not be appropriate categories of critical theory at all – a fact borne out for this author by the fact that "premodernity," or anything remotely like it, is completely absent from STPS.

Throughout Volume II, despite the gesture to historical stages of juridification, Habermas actually analyzes law *not* in relationship to specific stages of modernity, social differentiation, and market interactions, but almost always in contrast with premodern law:

Modern compulsory law is uncoupled from ethical motives; it functions as a means for demarcating areas of legitimate choice for private legal persons and scopes of legal competence for officeholders (for incumbents of organized power positions generally). In these spheres of action, legal norms replace the prelegal substratum of traditional morals to which previously, in their metainstitutional role, legal norms had reference. The law no longer starts from previously existing structures of communication; it generated forms of commerce and chains of command suited to communication. (TCA2 309–10)

Amid this somewhat crude approach to legal history, Habermas admonishes systems theorists for failing to locate what "causes" modern systems: they should, Habermas avers, "identify the system problems in the feudal society of the high Middle Ages that could not be resolved on the basis of agricultural production regulated by feudal law, handicrafts centered in the cities, local markets, and foreign trade oriented to luxury consumption" (TCA2 313). Habermas suggests that these problems were not exclusive to Europe, but rather, "the fact that they were taken up as *evolutionary challenges*" on that continent was, in the first place, especially European (TCA2 313). But Habermas himself has a similar problem in his account of the rationalization of the lifeworld: this rationalization is meant to serve as the causal motor of modernity, and yet it has no concrete referents beyond the contrast of "sacred" and "secular" authority and of "premodern" and "modern" phenomena.

In his post–*Public Sphere* works, Habermas no longer positively demonstrates the moral bases of legal development: as opposed to providing evidence for the normative function of law in the bourgeois public sphere, he shows that Weber and others *presuppose* the reality of such a basis in their supposedly empiricist theories. Yet, having abandoned a sociologically concrete and historically specific approach in works spanning LC, TCA, and, eventually, BFN, Habermas may have few resources reserved with which to *construct* the normative basis of legal rationalization. The premodern/modern periodization reminiscent of Weber and the secularization thesis seems lacking in the wherewithal to do the job. In other words, Habermas's revised Protestant ethic is no more capable of providing a moral-legal consensus sustained beyond the Reformation than was Weber's. Without reference to discretely specific socioeconomic historical periods within modernity, Habermas no longer commands the means to construct a critical theory of law.

In later works such as the LM, Habermas moves definitively away from a neo-Hegelian, commodity-based framework to a reluctant Weberian model centered on the "pluriverse of values": "To the extent that religious worldviews gave way to a pluralism of privatized gods and demons, and common-law traditions were more and more penetrated, via *usus modernus*, by scholarly law, the tripartite structure of the legal system had to collapse" (LM 262). In *Public Sphere*, Habermas analyzed law as the autonomously secular agent of bourgeois self-rule. In these later works he claims that modern law was, as a result of dissipating religious worldviews, "burdened with the task of filling the gap that the *theologically* administered natural law had left behind and of achieving this on its own, through political legislation" (LM 262, emphasis added).

One is compelled to ask whether the following crudely ahistorical question from these lectures could have been possible in STPS and *even* in TCA: "Can obligating authority still arise from an arbitrarily changeable political law as it had previously from sacred law?" (LM 263). In the next chapter, I demonstrate how Weber's SL relies primarily on the comparison/contrast of modern sociolegal developments with the example of medieval patrimonial authority. By the time of LM, Habermas himself explicitly resorts to the same kind of uncritical historical analysis of law, the very kind that he deliberately tried to avoid in STPS. In statements on the evolution of Western law, Habermas remarks on the origins of the modern rule of law in the changing conditions of the authority of the patrimonial chief: "The role of chieftain, whose leadership ... rested only on his de facto influence and prestige, must significantly change once the concept of morally binding norm is applied to arbitration" (LM 266). For our purposes, the point of this contrast between patrimonialism and the rule of law signals a clear capitulation to Weber, in historical terms, in Habermas's attempt to overcome Weber normatively. If this charge is correct, then Habermas's reconstruction of Weber's legal sociology will be susceptible to the same criticisms as the original object of criticism.

Conclusion

In the works examined in this chapter, Habermas never exclusively confines his critique to the abstractly moral presuppositions of Weber's legal sociology. In keeping with the strictures of critical theory, Habermas seeks to locate the concrete grounds of these abstract presuppositions in historical reality. The rapidly changing historical reality that exposed the categorical deficiencies and swallowed up the normative potentials of Weber's theory was the transition from the *Rechtsstaat* to the *Sozialstaat*. Habermas reconstructs the categories of Weber's legal sociology so as to re-embed them in those circumstances, rendering the *Sozialstaat* more conducive to legally facilitated discursive democracy, as we will see in Chapter 4. But Habermas focuses so closely on reconstructing the normative possibilities of the *Sozialstaat* that he begins to identify modernity as such with this historical configuration and to treat it as something like the final stage of modern history. To this extent, modernity becomes a one-period process for Habermas (notwithstanding his gestures to juridification epochs within it); and history per se takes on a simple two-period character exemplified by traditional–posttraditional and premodern–modern contrasts (*pace* Habermas's adoption of a "history of the species" social evolutionism).

Thus, despite the motivation to locate his critique of Weber concretely in historical and empirical reality, as Habermas's critique of SL becomes more explicit over the course of his career, the theory of social change and modernity in which Habermas grounds the critique becomes more abstract and unspecific. It is almost as if, in order to criticize Weber's theory of law, Habermas must capitulate to Weber's most dominant theory of modernity, one focused on secularization, and he becomes less concerned with changes *within* modernity than with the change *to* modernity. Just because Habermas resists the temptation to respond to these wide-scale changes in a Cassandra-like Weberian manner does not mean that his premises may not lead others to more pessimistic Weberianesque conclusions.

Why does Habermas move to a more abstract and much less differentiated account of history? Perhaps he turns to an either/or, traditional/postconventional framework of modernity because the historically specific one established in *Public Sphere*, one that identifies the practice of rational consensus formation and its institutionalization through law, was *too* concrete and criticizable. Perhaps Habermas found it too difficult to generalize from a case, the bourgeois public sphere, that was so singular and could be shown to have been so drastically overwhelmed in Habermas's own empirical-historical account by the emergence of the *Sozialstaat*. In addition, the model was so closely identified with its concrete practitioners, that is, bourgeois white men, that critics often doubted the work's emancipatory potential.[50] The more abstract theory of "postconventional morality institutionalized through modern law" that Habermas adopts in later works is much less falsifiable and criticizable on conceptual and normative grounds. But it is also a model that, according to Habermas's former standards of critical theory, is too institutionally and sociostructurally imprecise to point to fully worthwhile emancipatory prescriptions. The bourgeois public sphere, despite its limitations, had the advantage of being an actual sociohistorical reality. The abstract model of his later work is, of course, a "reality" as well. But Habermas primarily reconstructs it in "negative" terms by pointing out the fact that its existence is presupposed in Weber's and, later, in systems-theoretic and rational-choice accounts of modernity.[51] Unfortunately, it is especially difficult to derive a guide for reforming political practice or crafting legal institutions from *in absentio* arguments.

But despite these historical deficiencies that were somewhat anticipated in Benhabib's criticisms of Habermas's social evolutionism, as we observed earlier, she shows that Habermas must be credited with reviving the explanatory-diagnostic dimension of critical theory. Benhabib notes how Habermas "sought to restore the link between 'critique' and 'crisis'" that was broken by Adorno's and Horkheimer's pessimistically disengaged

---

[50] See the essays collected in Calhoun, ed. *Habermas and the Public Sphere*, especially those by Benhabib, Nancy Fraser, and Mary Ryan.

[51] Even in his most recent work, Habermas identifies rational choice and systems theories as incomplete Weberianisms: rational choice focuses on the purposive rationality of individual actors and systems theory on the autonomously functional rationality of organizational subsystems. See Habermas, *The Postnational Constellation: Political Essays*, 142. As Jon Elster notes, Weber's sociologies of law and bureaucracy attempted to account for both: see Elster, "Rationality, Economy, and Society," in Turner, ed. *The Cambridge Companion to Weber*, 21–41.

critical theory.[52] In their efforts, critical theory ran the risk of becoming what Marx denounced as "mere criticism."[53] The Habermas of TCA can be said to have re-embedded philosophical reflection in the possibilities and constraints associated with the *Sozialstaat* sociopolitical model. But the issue of whether Habermas's own efforts to apprehend the historical configuration emerging out of recent transformations tend toward mere criticism will be explored more fully in Chapter 5.

[52] Benhabib, *Critique, Norm and Utopia*, 252.
[53] Ibid., 252.

3

The Puzzle of Law, Democracy, and Historical Change in Weber's "Sociology of Law"

During the second decade of the twentieth century, in the midst of a radical transformation of legal reality in Europe and North America, Max Weber drafted the component parts of what would be titled, "The Sociology of Law."[1] For nearly half a century the status and function of law had been changing in a fundamental way, summed up in the following oversimplified manner: law became less of a purportedly discrete safeguard of society against the state and more of a multifaceted state agent of social restructuring. In some instances this restructuring was society-generated, as in the case of social welfare, or state-initiated, as in administrative policy directed at "regulation" of various kinds. This transformation from a state that was bound by the liberal rule of law, or *Rechtsstaat*, to the administrative/welfare state, or *Sozialstaat*, was experienced in particularly dramatic ways in Central Europe. Perhaps as a result, it inspired some of the most sensitive analyses of the relationship of government, society, and the law produced anywhere in industrial societies of the late nineteenth and early twentieth centuries.[2] Moreover, the transformation

---

[1] Max Weber, *Rechtssoziologie* in *Wirtschaft und Gesellschaft: Grundriss der Verstehenden Soziologie* (Tübingen: Mohr [Siebeck], 1922), vol. 2, chap. 7; *Max Weber on Law in Economy and Society*, trans. Edward Shils and Max Rheinstein (Cambridge, MA: Harvard University Press, 1954), hereafter SL. I cite this translation as revised in Weber, *Economy and Society: An Outline of Interpretive Sociology* (1920), ed. Guenther Roth and Claus Wittich, 2 vols. (Berkeley: University of California Press, 1978), 311–38, 641–899. Amended translations correspond with the fifth German edition, published in 1990, edited by Johannes Winckelmann, hereafter RS. On the dating and grouping of different sections of the SL, see Roth's Introduction in *Economy and Society*, lxv.

[2] See Peter C. Caldwell's study of German legal theory in the late Kaiserreich and Weimar periods, *Popular Sovereignty and the Crisis of German Constitutional Law: The Theory*

itself would reach a more catastrophic culmination in Central Europe than anywhere else in the first part of the twentieth century.[3] As stated in the previous chapter, Weber's study of law is certainly emblematic of the high level of legal analysis in the period, and his related political writings of the same time are often associated with the calamity of the era.[4]

This chapter seeks to understand the relationship of Weber's theoretical efforts to the sociolegal transformation of his time in a way that avoids the pitfalls of Habermas's reconstruction of the SL. As we have seen, Habermas brilliantly interrogates the analytic discussion of legal and economic rationality and rational-legal legitimacy found in the work, but often avoids and sometimes misinterprets the historical dimensions of the SL. I hope to correct these deficiencies in this chapter, agreeing with Habermas that a reconstruction of Weber is the appropriate place to begin exploring the relationship of law, democracy, and social change in modernity, but with a sharper focus on change *within* modernity in the conduct of such an analysis. Weber declares that he examines legal phenomena alternately from the standpoint of the sociological observer, the legal subject, and the legal practitioner. I focus on the tensions among approaches less overtly invoked by, and perhaps less than obvious to, Weber himself: the formulation of ahistorical analytical categories, the positing of linear historical development, and the discernment of qualitative epochal change.[5]

---

and Practice of Weimar Constitutionalism (Durham, NC: Duke University Press 1997). See also the indispensable collection of essays from this era, *Weimar: A Jurisprudence of Crisis*, eds. Arthur Jacobson and Bernhard Schlink (Berkeley: University of California Press, 2000).

[3] See, generally, Charles S. Maier, *Recasting Bourgeois Europe: Stabilization in France, Germany, and Italy in the Decade After World War I* (Princeton, NJ: Princeton University Press, 1988); Geoff Eley, *Reshaping the German Right: Radical Nationalism and Political Change After Bismarck* (Ann Arbor: University of Michigan Press, 1991); Gary Herrigel, *Industrial Constructions: The Sources of German Industrial Power* (Cambridge: Cambridge University Press, 1996); David Blackbourn, *The Long 19th Century: A History of Germany, 1780–1918* (Oxford: Oxford University Press, 1997); and Sheri Berman, *The Social Democratic Moment: Ideas and Politics in the Making of Interwar Europe* (Cambridge, MA: Harvard University Press, 1998).

[4] See Jacob Peter Mayer, *Max Weber and German Politics: A Study in Political Sociology* (London: Faber & Faber, 1944); Leo Strauss, *Natural Right and History* (Chicago: University of Chicago Press, 1953); Wolfgang Mommsen, *Max Weber and German Politics, 1890–1920*, trans Michael S. Steinberg (Chicago: University of Chicago Press, 1984); and Karl Loewenstein, *Max Weber's Political Ideas in the Perspectives of Our Time* (Cambridge, MA: University of Massachusetts Press, 1965).

[5] Werner Gephart demonstrates how separate and sometimes contradictory themes and strategies like these are embedded in portions of the text composed at very different times

I want to test the hypothesis that one cannot understand a whole-sale socioeconomic change like the one just described theoretically, let alone intervene in it with the intention of furthering progressive political aims, without delimiting the differences among these types of analysis. Each of these approaches entails a theoretical drawback: purely analytic approaches that subsume contemporary legal phenomena under time-less categories simply may not be able to detect change. Approaches that extrapolate from legal history in a way that postulates future develop-ment on the basis of the past may ultimately project the past *as* the future. Hyper-historically specific approaches that emphasize the novelty of the present moment have considerable difficulty confirming that innovation without appropriate comparison and contrast to other historical config-urations and without recourse to older categories. As we will see in the discussion of BFN in Chapter 4, Habermas attempts such a specification, but does so in a way that is prejudiced by a one-sided reading of Weber and by legal and societal rationalization.

Through a detailed and immanent reading of SL, more attentive to the historical sections of the work than Habermas's efforts, I demonstrate how Weber struggles with these modes of analysis throughout the work such that it is never really clear whether he intends to set out a concep-tual encyclopedia of legal phenomena, a history of law in the West, or an analysis of the emergence of *Sozialstaat* law. Weber often conflates these approaches in a way that fuses the formulation of categories intended to explain the present with presuppositions conditioned by observations of the historical past. More specifically, Weber seems to turn his atten-tion to the legal aspects of premodern patrimonial authoritarianism in response to phenomena associated with the rise of the *Sozialstaat*; subse-quently, he seems compelled to describe this contemporary development in terms derived from his account of the former, that is, in a manner that would seem to be rather anachronistic historically. As I turn to Haber-mas's confrontation with the structural transformation of the European state associated with globalization and European integration, I suggest that had he been more sensitive to these kinds of deficiencies in his recon-struction of Weber in his mature works, he would have been less likely to succumb to them in his latest ones.

and pasted together in the final version of SL. See Gephart, "Max Weber's 'Sociology of Law': From Interpretive Complexity to the Multidimensionality of a Text," paper presented at the Center for Comparative Research, Yale University, 4 March 2002. SL was composed between 1908 and 1920 and appeared in 1922. On the background of the work, see Rheinstein's Introduction to *Max Weber on Law*, xxv–lxxii.

Despite Weber's mitigating qualifications, it becomes increasingly difficult throughout SL to disentangle the categories appropriate to two different historical periods – the Middle Ages and the *Sozialstaat* – and determine which is the quasi-objective standpoint by which the other can be evaluated. Moreover, as a result of this historical orientation, in his more abstract analytical and normatively prescriptive moments, Weber asserts that *Sozialstaat* law is a contradiction in terms. As we know from Habermas's critique of Weber, for the latter, as for the fascist-cum-neo-conservative jurists enamored of him, law is supposed to separate the state from society except under conditions finely specified by legal rules. The "deformalized" or "materialized" law of the *Sozialstaat* purportedly facilitates intervention that becomes as excessive as the authority of the pre-Enlightenment patrimonial lord because of the muddled, unlimited, and arbitrary way that it is promulgated and exercised. Is this conclusion convincing when the criteria used to arrive at it are derived from a historically distant and pejoratively depicted past – that is, the functionally undifferentiated and politically unlimited authority of the patrimonial lord?

Weber died in 1920 before he was able to finalize the manuscript and perhaps better clarify these issues and more convincingly justify his arguments. Familiarity with works that Weber was able to finish and polish in his own lifetime, such as *The Protestant Ethic*, does not lead one to believe that he necessarily would have produced – by contemporary standards – a causally coherent and methodologically rigorous study of law.[6] Notwithstanding the fact, or rather due to the fact, that SL in its extant state approximates something like social scientific free association, it may yield even more profound results than would a more refined version of the work. The unpolished quality of SL provides a glimpse into the mind of Weber, the legally trained social scientist,[7] working

---

[6] Weber, *The Protestant Ethic and the Spirit of Capitalism* (1905/1919), trans. Peter Baehr and Gordon Wells (New York: Penguin, 2002). On the immense difficulties in understanding the causal logic of Weber's most famous work, see Gianfranco Poggi, *Calvinism and the Capitalist Spirit: Weber's Protestant Ethic* (Amherst: University of Massachusetts Press, 1983).

[7] See Karl Engisch, "Max Weber als Rechtsphilosoph und als Rechtssoziologe," in Engisch, B. Pfister, and Johannes Winckelmann, eds., *Max Weber: Gedächtnisscrift der Ludwig-Maximilians-Universität München* (Berlin: Duncker & Humblot, 1966), 67–88; Stephen P. Turner and Regis A. Factor, *Max Weber: Lawyer as Social Thinker* (London: Routledge, 1994); and Harold J. Berman and Charles J. Reid, Jr., "Max Weber as Legal Historian," in Stephen Turner, ed., *The Cambridge Companion to Weber* (Cambridge: Cambridge University Press, 2000), 223–39.

through the dilemmas of law, both generally and under the specific pressures of his own time – that is, mass democratization and transformation of the laissez-faire–liberal state into the administrative/welfare state.[8] I would like to extrapolate conclusions on this basis concerning the formation of social scientific concepts during moments of wholesale historical change in some sense inspired by Weber's greatest interpreter, Habermas, who shared such goals, but in a matter that is nevertheless critical of the latter.[9]

1. The Public–Private Law Distinction and "Modern" Law

One of the lingering questions about SL is whether Weber intended it to be a study of modern law or law per se. The opening section of the work reveals that Weber attempts to set out the defining characteristics of law in different historical periods. But the sociological pressures of Weber's own time spur him to proceed in a less than systematic manner, that is, in neither a strictly chronological nor an explicitly thematic manner. As Weber discusses the modern distinction between public and private law, contemporary threats to this distinction prompt him to analyze a time before that distinction defined legal concerns. As a result, Weber describes the newly emerging context that is blurring the distinction between public and private law in terms of these older "primordial" categories.

The SL proper begins on a fairly topical note: the first section is concerned with what Weber identifies as a specifically contemporary (*heutige*) distinction: public versus private law (SL 641). Weber does not posit as his point of departure an instance in the historical past from which he

---

[8] My approach differs from the following similarly concerned treatments of SL: Anthony Kronman, *Profiles in Legal Theory: Max Weber* (Stanford, CA: Stanford University Press, 1983), and David Kettler and Volker Meja, "Legal Formalism and Disillusioned Realism in Max Weber," *Polity* 18, no. 3 (Spring 1996), 307–31. Kronman is not concerned with the context of legal change that often imposes itself on Weber's text; rather, he chooses to focus on what he understands to be the conceptual unity of the work. Kettler and Meja most articulately address the decisive role of this context of transformation for the arguments of the work, but do so mostly in Weber's own explicit terms. In what follows, I tease out the subtextual references to the rise of the *Sozialstaat* in SL, on the one hand, and confront Weber with alternative accounts of its emergence, on the other.

[9] This essay has benefited from the following articles in the SL literature: Stephen M. Feldman, "An Interpretation of Max Weber's Theory of Law: Metaphysics, Economics, and the Iron Cage of Constitutional Law," *Law & Social Inquiry* 16 (1991), 205–48; David M. Trubek, "Reconstructing Max Weber's Sociology of Law," *Stanford Law Review* 37 (1985), 919–36; and Joan Tronto, "Law and Modernity: The Significance of Max Weber's Sociology of Law," *Texas Law Review* 63 (1984).

might move forward chronologically. Rather, a conceptual–practical distinction from the present provisionally serves as a criterion by which other legal situations can be evaluated. Therefore, at the start of SL, the present serves as the lens through which Weber will view the distant and recent past, as well as the probable future. Weber understands the past in terms of the absence of a differentiation between public and private law, and he projects the immediate future to be a resumed and continued erosion of this distinction.

What characterizes the distinction between public and private law? Weber offers several definitions. He declares that, according to sociological standards, private law concerns the norms that regulate non-state action, even if the state is the agent enforcing these norms (SL 641). On the other hand, public law pertains to norms that regulate state action (SL 641). Weber asserts that the objectives of such state action must be *valid* as a result of "enactment or consensus" (SL 641). He does not mention the validity of the *means* to attain such objectives, nor does he elaborate on the substance of enactment and consensus. "Enactment" suggests a somewhat arbitrary validity: what the state *can* enact is in fact valid. This connotes effectual competence as opposed to competence granted by, to use a word important in other parts of *Economy and Society*, a "legitimate" authority. "Consensus," in this context, does not necessarily mean popular consensus – the acquiescence of those over whom state action is exercised – but, just as likely, merely agreement among those who institute the policy.[10]

Weber then offers a second formulation of the public–private law distinction: public law concerns *rule* norms, while private law concerns *claim* norms (SL 642). Rule norms guide officials as to the conduct of their duties, while claim norms concern the rights of social actors (SL 642).

---

[10] Thus, the emphasis on consensus in this passage does not chase away the cloud of coercion that hovers over Weber's efforts. Elsewhere in SL, Weber evaluates validity in terms of the relative compliance of subjects with the law, as measured empirically and factually (SL 311). This approach is ultimately indifferent to whether compliance with the law is secured through the coercion of subjects to whom it is applied or as a result of the latter's subjective belief in the law. Both are of sociological interest. Weber initially attempts to distinguish the blatantly coercive aspect of this definition from the freely believed-in aspect of it. Yet, he finally collapses the two since he concludes that all law is to some extent based upon force: "The distinction between an order derived from voluntary agreement and one which has been imposed is only relative" (Weber, *Economy and Society*, 37; cf. 214). Of course, we observed in the previous chapter how Habermas fairly convincingly showed the presupposition of consensus in much of Weber's legal-sociological efforts.

Public law may establish certain *political* rights, such as the right to vote. According to Weber, such rights are violable by the state since a simple change in rules can affect and even abolish them. State authority cannot treat inviolable rights, such as property rights, in a functional manner. Weber does not raise the more foundational question of *why* the right to vote would remain within the purview of state rules, while the right to property would seem to have some extrapolital or, more accurately, prepolitical authority. Certainly the European tradition of *Rechtsstaat* tolerates more limited standards of popular political participation than it does obtrusive state infringements on the free use of private property.

But Weber mentions that, of course, private property is not completely inviolable and can be limited under certain circumstances by the state, as long as there are provisions for adequate compensation (SL 642). Weber's quite continental view of the distinction results in the following resolution: an individual who votes has been merely delegated by the rules of the state to perform a state-related function; that individual is a mere reflex of the state's rule-formulation and -abiding. Therefore, a change in the conditions of that exercise of duty does not constitute interference by the state in an inviolable social domain, and, as such, no compensation need be provided for that change. While it would be an exaggeration to think of publicly created rights as completely violable and privately embedded rights as inalienably vested, something of this contrast governs Weber's distinction.[11]

Weber's thinking here presupposes one of the two most important aspects of the nineteenth-century *Rechtsstaat*: the conceptual separation of state and society.[12] The state is permitted to intervene in society only to enforce criminal law or to serve as an arbitrator that resolves tort-related conflicts. Indeed, along these lines, Weber sets out a third contrast between private and public law that defines the former as "coordination" among private actors and the latter as "subordination" of some actors to others within the state hierarchy. Qualifying matters, as he so often does in SL, Weber remarks that not all rules of public law concern "command" but

[11] This passage does not, of course, reflect Weber's more complicated theories of political participation and democracy. In fact, Peter Breiner derives a rather substantive democratic theory from Weber's work in *Max Weber and Democratic Politics* (Ithaca, NY: Cornell University Press, 1995).

[12] In the German context, the "nineteenth-century *Rechtsstaat*" refers to the period from the initial consolidation of the *Kaiserreich* to the onset of the Great War (1867–1914). See Stefan Korioth's introduction to the section, "The Shattering of Methods in Late Wilhelmine Germany," in *Weimar: A Jurisprudence of Crisis*, 43.

also coordination of a different kind: one of the most important functions of such rules is the coordination of various public organs (SL 643).[13]

More interestingly, it is just as Weber discusses subordination – that is, the subordination of some state officials to others in bureaucratic chains of command – that he finally raises the issue of legitimacy in the main section of SL. Here he broaches the means by which the subjects of state organs "create and control those organs" (SL 643). In an almost Platonic manner, Weber raises justice even as he tries to focus exclusively on power: public law in this context concerns the terms according to which subjects allow themselves to be subordinated by the state. This, however, turns out to be a rather narrow definition of legitimacy, as Weber exempts certain forms of authority from legal regulation: he invokes the authority of heads of households (*Hausvaters*) over families and that of bosses over employees as kinds of authority that should not be regulated by public law – at least according to *Rechtsstaat* standards (SL 643). In this context, public law only concerns the maintenance of the state and the pursuit of the state's objective, and leaves private relations of command and subordination to the sphere of private law. In terms discussed in the previous chapter, the second relationship of subordination left exempt from legal amelioration by Weber, that of employers over workers, is precisely what Habermas describes as one of the motivations for the *Sozialstaat*. The first such relationship mentioned by Weber, that of, literally, "the fathers of the house" over wives and children, is one that Habermas's communicatively reconstructed *Sozialstaat* model has been notoriously weak in addressing.[14] As far as Weber is concerned, the use of the first example is particularly noteworthy: for one of the leitmotifs of SL will prove to be the fact that the authority of the patriarchal household master and then the patrimonial monarch was *merged with law* in "traditional arrangements," and that, as shown here, such authority was separated from what is publicly legal in the *Rechtsstaat*.

However, after discussing these relations of subordination in a rather unproblematic manner, Weber observes, perhaps wryly: "of course, the

---

[13] A recent theorization of constitutions as coordination mechanisms that shares commonalities with Weber's account is Russell Hardin, *Liberalism, Constitutionalism, and Democracy* (Oxford: Oxford University Press, 2000).

[14] See Seyla Benhabib, *Critique, Norm, and Utopia: A Study of the Foundations of Critical Theory* (New York: Columbia University Press, 1986), 252, and Nancy Fraser, *Unruly Practices* (Minneapolis: Minnesota University Press, 1989). Consult the qualifications offered by Stephen K. White, *The Recent Work of Jürgen Habermas: Reason, Justice and Modernity* (Cambridge: Cambridge University Press, 1990), 143.

question as to what the particular objectives [of the state] should be is answered in varying ways even today" (SL 643). As he acknowledges later in SL, Weber knows full well that previously fixed notions concerning public law's appropriate domain were being contested as he wrote; state objectives were expanding into precisely those spheres of authority traditionally conceived as sacrosanct, such as the family and the workplace. The emerging *Sozialstaat* of Weber's time was converting areas previously held to be private into issues of public concern and regulating them through public law. Thus, what Weber had been describing from the beginning of SL as the "modern" state is *not* the state of the early-twentieth-century context in which he is writing, but rather the *Rechtsstaat* arrangement of state and society in the high laissez-faire nineteenth century. Weber promotes as the paradigmatic form of modern law – indeed, of law itself, as we will see – the sociolegal configuration of the era that had just been superseded.

Thus, in these opening passages of the main body of SL, Weber has not been describing *contemporary* legal arrangements but rather those of a recent, yet distinctly different, if still modern, past. Here Weber's theory confronts – whether or not he is fully aware of it at this juncture – changes *within* modernity as much as, or more than, the transition *to* modernity generally discussed by Weber scholarship.[15] But does Weber conduct such a historical *Auseinandersetzung* with adequate precision? After all, at the moment that he begins to confront this recent sociolegal transformation, Weber immediately turns to history more broadly and universally for the theoretical and empirical resources with which to understand it. In light of this, an important question is whether the history of "law" serves to provide Weber with a contrast to present legal reality, whether it demonstrates how such a reality emerged continuously over time, or whether it helps to determine and confirm the general legal categories that he develops throughout the work.

We will observe later that when Weber poses a contrast between previous and present sociolegal arrangements, he actually confirms – albeit with qualifications – a similarity between the past and his own historical moment, thus raising questions about the efficacy of such an approach to legal history. It may neither tell us anything reliable about the past under excavation nor supply appropriate categorical or normative insight into

---

[15] On the excesses and limits of this kind of analysis – in which Weber and Weber scholarship have played no small part – see Bernard Yack, *The Fetishism of Modernities: Epochal Self-Consciousness in Contemporary Social and Political Thought* (South Bend, IN: Notre Dame University Press, 1998). On Weber specifically, see Guenther Roth and Wolfgang Schluchter, *Max Weber's Vision of History: Ethics and Methods* (Berkeley: University of California Press, 1979).

the present. Throughout SL, developments associated with the *Sozialstaat* bubble up into Weber's discussions of general legal phenomena or those characteristic of other distinct epochs over the course of legal history – specifically, his discussions of imperium, organizations, rights, status, contracts, and so on. In the following sections, I resume the immanent analysis of SL launched in this section, hopefully better illustrating the mutual influence of past and present on Weber's efforts at legal analysis. But first, it might be helpful to briefly outline the legal ramifications of the *Sozialstaat* as Weber intimates them across SL and elaborates them in its concluding sections. The reader will recall from the previous chapter that Habermas attempted to reconstruct or refute key aspects of Weber's analysis of the *Sozialstaat*. Attention to them here will help us identify and analyze these moments in Weber's work as they unfold in my subsequent interrogation of the narrative of SL.

Weber understands the crisis of *Rechtsstaat* in terms of the contemporary emergence of what he calls "deformalized law," or what is referred to subsequently as "materialized law."[16] The difference between formal and material types of law can be explained somewhat reductively in the following way: in the context of laissez-faire capitalism, where the state to some extent remains distinct from society, the law serves as the general and supposedly neutral rules to be followed by all individuals within society; these rules are set by a state that itself acts only as an umpire. This model presupposes a continental version of the separation of powers, where the legislature takes precedence over the other two branches, especially the government or administration, delegating to them specific tasks and duties. The two "separations" of the *Rechtsstaat* mutually support each other: the state–society separation is maintained by the principle that no substantive laws affecting the life, liberty, or property of citizens can be enacted without the formal functioning of the legislature, which is separate from the administration that executes it.

As mentioned before, formal law also presupposes a formula in which legal statutes are promulgated in conditional "if x, then y" statements; that is, there is no state action without a specific condition or prior action, and hence a particular case, to trigger it. Such laws are addressed generally to individuals and are directed to no particular social group. These

---

[16] Again, as Sven Eliaeson points out, Weber rarely used the word *Rechtsstaat* because he associates natural-law normativism with the term. See Eliaeson, "Constitutional Caesarism: Weber's Politics in Their German Context," in Turner, ed. *The Cambridge Companion to Weber*, 137, 139. However, since Weber describes the bourgeois formal law in the precise terms of the structural characteristics of the *Rechtsstaat*, I deem it appropriate for use in this context.

specifications work to keep the state from intruding arbitrarily in society. However, the obvious flaw in this model, based upon empirical evidence that Weber himself invokes, is that this nonintervention or qualified interventionism allows significant asymmetries of socioeconomic power to remain unaddressed by the state within society. In other words, this model guards against political domination while letting social domination remain unregulated in notable instances: wage slavery, child labor, unlimited work hours, subordination of women, and so on. These constitute the very domains over whose status as jurisdictions of public law Weber equivocated earlier in the text.

Under conditions of increasing intervention in the twentieth century, the *Sozialstaat* takes a more active role in both regulating the economy and addressing issues of social justice. Lawmaking now entails the creation of the very rules by which the state itself plays. State action is no longer exclusively triggered by a particular case but, because of the broad goals that it is meant to achieve, continues in perpetuity. Social actors, constituted more and more corporately rather than individually, determine the guidelines for their own behavior outside of the parliamentary-statutory context and in more ad hoc settings such as arbitration hearings. Legal sentences no longer take the form of conditional statements but rather direct decrees without term limits or specific parameters within which they might be framed and contained. Bargains and agreements take on the force of law without appeal to rational and general principles, but rather the concrete terms of the case and the expediency of the situation.

As a result, the *separations* so characteristic of the *Rechtsstaat* tend to become *entwinements*: the separation of powers is significantly undermined as the legislature grants the executive and judiciary wide discretion to carry out broad social tasks – in short, the tasks of administration and adjudication blur. The separation of state and society dissolves as the state intervenes more substantively into society, and segments of society strike bargains within itself and with organs of the state that have the force of public law. Weber, despite his advocacy of social welfare and state intervention elsewhere, laments these developments – perhaps because of his legal training – as a crisis of law's rationality, accountability, and determinacy.[17]

---

[17] Kathi V. Friedman reconstructs and responds to Weber's conception of law and the *Sozialstaat*, and applies it to post–World War II conditions, in *Legitimation of Social Rights and the Western Welfare State: A Weberian Perspective* (Chapel Hill: University of North Carolina Press, 1982).

2. History as Confirmation/Contestation of Legal Categories

To return to the point in SL where I left off earlier, Weber definitively confirms that he is grappling with a contemporary phenomenon – the merging of public and private law jurisdictions in the administrative/welfare state – when he declares that the "delimitation" of the two spheres is "today not entirely free from difficulty" (SL 643). But rather than explain the socio-legal dimensions of this new state of affairs at this point, Weber turns to "the past," where the public–private law distinction was even *less* clear, if it obtained at all (SL 643). Weber evokes a time before the *Rechtsstaat* when "all law, all jurisdictions, and particularly all powers of exercising authority" were personal privileges and prerogatives of the head of the household, the landlord, or the master of serfs (SL 643). Under these kinds of patrimonialism, what is considered public law in Weber's own time was then the private domain of personal authority.

Weber qualifies this account of patrimonial authority by admitting that it is an "ideal type," never fully actualized in reality (SL 643).[18] But he insists that the description has real historical traction, most obviously in the case of the European Middle Ages (SL 643–4). This ideal-typical configuration allows him to better conceptualize the next law-related institution that he analyzes, government. In contrast to patrimonialism, which is characterized by only loosely limited personal authority, Weber describes government in terms of rules and the absence of social rights. By proceeding in this manner, Weber has moved in only a matter of paragraphs from the *Rechtsstaat*, to the *Sozialstaat*, to patrimonial arrangements, and back to a specific attribute of the modern state. It starts to become clear in these passages that Weber conceives of the *Rechtsstaat* as standing conceptually and historically *between* two opposite legal configurations, which themselves have much in common: quasi-feudal patrimonial and twentieth-century bureaucratic-statist authority.

In the context of the *Rechtsstaat*, Weber situates government, or the executive, within a framework of public institutions that also includes legislation and adjudication (SL 644). Weber observes that government must function legitimately; in other words, it must be authorized to function by

---

[18] On this crucial aspect of Weber's methodology, see Susan J. Hekman, *Weber, the Ideal Type, and Contemporary Social Theory* (South Bend, IN: Notre Dame University Press, 1983). Berman and Reid argue that Weber's use of ideal types led to important insights but also serious distortions of legal history, what they call an "unhistorical use of legal history": see "Max Weber as Legal Historian" in Turner, ed., *The Cambridge Companion to Weber*, 223, 231.

constitutional norms. Weber characterizes this as "positive" legitimacy, whereby government is enabled to act by constitutional prescriptions (SL 644). Government can also be rendered legitimate "negatively" by the restraints imposed by legal rules and the vested "subjective" rights of society, that is, the articulation of the limits that government cannot overstep. Weber notes that these characteristics are as applicable to legislation and adjudication as to government; they too are enabled and constrained by constitutional prescriptions and restrictions. Thus, these cannot be the *defining* characteristics of government.

More specific to government, even more specific than the enforcement of law created by legislatures, is the tendency to pursue its own agenda on the basis of "political, ethical, utilitarian, or some other" concerns (SL 645). Despite being constrained in the ways described previously, government is of a more unitary institutional mind and is subject to fewer internal collegial or procedural restraints than, respectively, legislative or judicial institutions. And much more than these other institutions, Weber remarks that the government views individuals and their interests, in a legal sense, as mere *objects* rather than as bearers of rights.[19] But in his discussion of the *Sozialstaat*, as we will see, government seems to pursue such agendas *not* of its own accord, but in response to demands by labor and democratic organizations, as well as a significant segment of the legal profession. The problem of the *Sozialstaat*, as Weber ultimately explains it, is not unilateral state action but state action directed by democratizing segments of society.

In any case, Weber concedes that this supposedly special characteristic of the government or the administrative branch – the tendency to function according to something other than rules – is, in his day, increasingly characteristic of other branches of the state, particularly the judiciary: "in the modern state there exists a trend to assimilate adjudication to administration formally" (SL 645; RS 389). Judges frequently resort to substantive factors such as ethics and expediency in rendering decisions. Moreover, the rise of the *Sozialstaat* opens institutional options to resolve

---

[19] For a more differentiated, if not much more sanguine, account of the administrative perspective – one that takes better account of the standpoint of the "objects" of state strategies – see James C. Scott, *Seeing Like a State: How Certain Schemes to Improve the Human Condition Have Failed* (New Haven, CT: Yale University Press, 1998). As we have observed and will revisit in the next chapter, this statement by Weber might be said to be one of the inspirations of Habermas's own sociolegal project: forcing the state through law to be more responsive to citizens as interactive subjects and not as manipulable or exploitable objects.

conflicts bureaucratically, as opposed to juridically, in the forms of arbitration and economic hearings and tribunals. Weber perceives this as a crisis because adjudication is, at least conceptually, fundamentally at odds with administration. As he explains later, adjudication rests upon formally general principles and procedures, while administration is based on concrete objectives and the most expedient means to achieve them. In this new situation, judicial officers and institutions engage in the ad hoc resolution of specific conflicts rather than the application of general norms.

Not only are administration and adjudication blurred in the *Sozialstaat*, but so too are administration and legislation. The government makes rules for its own behavior that are not necessarily sanctioned by the legislature. In addition, the government may simply ignore rules that it previously set down for itself or act in many circumstances for which there are no guidelines or precedents at all. Again, this blurring of functions that results from discernible trends within the development of the contemporary state jeopardizes both pillars of the *Rechtsstaat*: the separation of powers and the separation of state and society. Thus, Weber cannot set out the precise characteristics of government that distinguish it (1) from unrestrained patrimonial authority in the past and (2) from the other branches or functions of the *Rechtsstaat*, legislation and adjudication. The former failure is to some extent the result of the latter: if the *Sozialstaat* blurs the tasks of administration, adjudication, and legislation, then government no longer appears as a strictly delimited and restrained type of executive power, but rather one that has much in common with premodern arbitrary and undifferentiated executive power. As I show in the next section, Weber then launches into a more detailed discussion of patrimonial authority, since it is, to his mind, unavoidably reminiscent of his own legal present.

3. Legal History as Contrast/Continuity with the Present

At this point, it is already clear how Weber's SL foreshadows neoconservative and even some leftist characterizations of the welfare state as a quasi-authoritarian form of governance.[20] Weber abruptly jumps

---

[20] See, on the right, Friedrich Hayek, *Law, Liberty, Legislation*, 3 vols. (Chicago: University of Chicago Press, 1978), and on the left, Franz L. Neumann and Otto Kirchheimer, *The Rule of Law Under Siege: Selected Essays*, ed. William Scheuerman (Berkeley: University of California Press, 1996). The infamous jurist Carl Schmitt, in some sense a student of Weber, celebrated and revived the "archaic air" of such authority. See Schmitt, *Political Theology: Four Chapters on the Concept of Sovereignty* (1922), trans. George

back from his discussion of the increasingly arbitrary functioning of *all*
branches of the *Sozialstaat* to remarks on the "primeval," "primitive"
form of administration: the "unlimited" authority of the household patri-
arch (SL 645). I do not mean to suggest that this sudden and, in fact,
rather startling shift in Weber's exposition is an esoteric signal or a proto-
poststructuralist performance meant to alert the reader surreptitiously to
a certain homology between the two separate historical configurations.
While I would not deprive such hermeneutic strategies of their place and
purpose, in this case such approaches would be ridiculous given the unfinished nature of Weber's manuscript. Nevertheless, this unfinished quality
does suggest that on some level Weber was attuned to similarities between
the two different sociopolitical formations that he was not yet able fully
to articulate. He may have been making associations for himself that he
would have purged from the final manuscript.

It should be pointed out that nearly identical shifts occur repeatedly
at similar junctures throughout SL. At first, Weber seems to turn to
the "traditional" past with the intention of only contrasting it, in good
Enlightenment fashion, with the present such that the latter – the modern,
the contemporary – would seem more consistent, uniform, and nonarbi-
trary in relief. But Weber discerns that the *contemporary* is no longer
"modern" in this sense; the contemporary relationship of law, authority,

---

Schwab (Cambridge, MA: MIT Press, 1985), and John P. McCormick, *Carl Schmitt's
Critique of Liberalism: Against Politics as Technology* (Cambridge: Cambridge University Press, 1997). But it should be noted that Weber makes several claims that qualify
any mechanical equating of his formally inclined critique of the *Sozialstaat* with those
of neo-conservatives and authoritarians. Weber's distinction between administration and
legislation rests on a more fundamental one between formal and substantive law. Substantive law involves state interference in the life, liberty, or property of the citizens,
while formal law corresponds to the fact that it is issued by the legislature, irrespective
of its contents. (See the note by editors Roth and Wittich: SL 662, n. 9.) This means
that for Weber, as opposed to Schmitt and Hayek, there are laws that are "substantive,"
which are not automatically decrees or "measures." Measures, in the continental sense,
do not interfere with civil liberties and hence need not be valid in a formal sense, that
is, sanctioned by statute. They are simply "administrative acts" like that which sets the
budget. However, tax and customs provisions must be passed by statute, that is, they
must conform to formal validity (663, n. 9). The other theorists mentioned previously
attempt to hold hostage a social democratic state or liberal welfare state to a notion of
law that can never concretely address the economic needs of a market or an industrial
society. In other words, such a state can never redistribute wealth or regulate prices, as
just two examples, without being charged with lawlessness. As perilously close as Weber
veers to such positions, his definition of law is not so rigidly formal as to level such
charges against the *Sozialstaat* in the manner of Schmitt or Hayek.

and society may have more in common with earlier patrimonial forms of that constellation than with the classically modern *Rechtsstaat* arrangement of those entities that serves as the critical guideline of so much of Weber's analyses.

In this turn to the past, Weber describes the patriarchal authority of the clan leader or tribal chief in the following terms: "those subordinated to his power have no rights against him, and norms regulating his behavior toward them exist only as indirect effects of heteronomous religious checks on his conduct" (SL 645). In case there is any doubt about "the presence of the present" in this depiction of the supposed past, Weber uses contemporary quasi-bureaucratic terms like "arbitration proceedings" to describe the institutional arrangements of patriarchal authority. In this case, the arbitration proceedings at which kinship groups air grievances provide the counterforce to the "theoretically unrestrained" authority of the master (SL 645). Just as the administrative state is functionally unlimited in its ability, yet in reality checked by the semiformal arrangements of arbitration boards, legislative-bureaucratic committees, and, of course, a more administratively inclined court system, the master is checked by the customs of religion and the interactions among kinship groups.

For Weber, who speaks in normative and not just descriptive terms here, the problem is not so much that both kinds of authority are unlimited, but that in such arrangements the limits are "indirect," "heteronomous," and hence irregular and inconsistent. From the standpoint of the classical *Rechtsstaat*, this almost always means arbitrary and unjust as well. The *Rechtsstaat* assumes that such informal methods of limiting authority were susceptible to corruption and inefficacy, and were less reliable than the discrete, legally defined interactions of separated branches of the state and a concomitant separation of the latter from society. Hence, the administrative state would be described by many – without Weber's good-faith if inconsistent attempt at empirical-historical verification – as a return to the "horde," "barbarism," or "serfdom" in many circles whose intellectual categories had been framed by the bourgeois-liberal arrangements of the nineteenth century.[21]

---

[21] On these criticisms of the welfare state, see Renato Cristi, "Hayek and Schmitt on the Rule of Law," *Canadian Journal of Political Science* 17, no. 3 (1984), 521–35; and Bill Scheuerman, "The Unholy Alliance of Carl Schmitt and Friedrich A. Hayek," *Constellations* 4, no. 2 (October 1997). In a more leftist vein, these are the conditions that make possible Adorno's and Horkheimer's immanent critique of the administrative state/society through an ostensible tracing of it back to primitive social forms and Homeric

The other salient aspect of Weber's account of the "primitive" relationship of law and authority that invites comparisons with early-twentieth-century arrangements of that kind is the emphasis on groups. The juridical focus of the *Rechtsstaat* is the individual. With the rise of the *Sozialstaat*, corporate groups, those representing industry, labor, or special interests, become principal juridical subjects. Weber returns to this in his sections on organization, as we will see. Here Weber attributes the emergence of law proper to the increased strength of kinship groups, since the term "law" cannot be applied appropriately to circumstances of completely unchallenged patriarchal authority. With the empowering of groups, injuries are converted into claims that the group pursues on behalf of the offended member of their kin. Subsequently, verdicts are rendered, formalities established, and time frames set – that is, proper judicial procedure emerges (SL 645).

Weber describes this development in terms of functional differentiation: the adjudicative functions of kinship interaction develop out of the administrative functions of the master and his house.[22] According to Weber, the separation of adjudication from administration is a progress *toward* law, whereas the reverse, the regression of adjudication into administration, is a collapse *of* law. In the historical development of Western law, particularly in Roman law, the authoritarian power of the household master is dwarfed by an expanding private law and a public authority more influenced by the latter than the former (SL 645). The master's domain, free of rules, is tamed and circumscribed by the rule-filled sphere of the juridical. The interaction of authority and norms would dominate modern jurisprudence, which finally settled upon an arrangement in the *Rechtsstaat* whereby the government was subservient to the legislature and kept separate from the judiciary.

Weber betrays a tendency toward progressive teleology when he frowns upon developments that deviate from the trajectory of administrative-to-adjudicative dominance. In particular, he describes the patrimonial monarchy as a sociopolitical order where "domestic authority diffused beyond its original sphere into forms of political power, and thereby the administration of justice" (SL 645; RS 389). Anticipating criticisms that

epics – a critique that is too often taken literally and at face value. See T. W. Adorno and Max Horkheimer, *Dialectic of Enlightenment* (1944), trans. John Cummings (London: Verso, 1997).

[22] This approach to law is most fully elaborated in the twentieth-century context by Niklas Luhmann, *A Sociological Theory of Law*, trans. Elizabeth King and Martin Albrow (London: Routledge & Kegan Paul, 1985).

Hannah Arendt would later make famous,[23] Weber seems to lament a situation where domestic concerns infiltrate public ones such that a crisis of legal-institutional determinacy ensues: such a scenario threatened the substance of public discourse and political action for Arendt, while it jeopardizes the distinctions between legislation, adjudication, and government and a bourgeois notion of freedom for Weber (SL 646).

Further, Weber identifies as vaguely feudal the proliferation of judicial decrees or directives in contemporary adjudication, which he earlier observed in primitive society. In the patrimonial monarchy, Weber claims, adjudication becomes administration through the lord's issuing of decrees or commands that are motivated by expediency – in other words, "without fixed forms and at arbitrary times" (SL 646). Historically, Weber generally attempts to keep these categories distinct – that is, he tries not to collapse all that is premodern into the categories of "feudal" or "primitive" – but there is slippage in his account whenever the development of the *Sozialstaat* emerges anywhere in close textual proximity. When Weber compares phenomena from the latter with pre-*Rechtsstaat* ones, he resorts to undifferentiated characterizations of both the premodern and the *Sozialstaat*.

Recall that Habermas was tempted to use terminology associating the *Sozialstaat* with a kind of feudalization in *Public Sphere*.[24] Habermas demonstrates the foreclosing of the progressive possibilities harbored, albeit imperfectly, in the nineteenth-century *Rechtsstaat* and its sociological underpinnings. Habermas identifies the transition to the welfare state of the late nineteenth and early twentieth centuries as a "refeudalization" of society and politics (STPS 141). What Habermas describes as mutual "societalization" of the state and "stateification" of society destroys the condition of possibility of the public sphere and the *Rechtsstaat*, the separation of state and society (STPS 142, 231). Less accountable bodies make policy in place of the nineteenth-century-style parliament that transferred and maintained the rational discussion generated by certain privileged sectors of the populace over the deployment of authority. Habermas shows

---

[23] See *The Portable Arendt*, ed. Peter Baehr (New York: Penguin, 2000). On this aspect of her thought, see Hanna Fenichel Pitkin, *The Attack of the Blob: Hannah Arendt's Concept of the Social* (Chicago: University of Chicago Press, 1998); serious mitigating concerns on this point are raised by Seyla Benhabib's *The Reluctant Modernism of Hannah Arendt* (London: Sage, 1996).

[24] Jürgen Habermas, *The Structural Transformation of the Public Sphere: An Inquiry into a Category of Bourgeois Society* (1962), trans. T. Burger and F. Lawrence (Cambridge, MA: MIT Press 1989), hereafter STPS.

that this role is assumed by, and conducted among, private bureaucracies, special interest groups, political parties, and the bureaucracy (STPS 176). In the *Sozialstaat* popular sanction is still necessitated to maintain legitimacy; thus, these entities make a show of themselves and their "products" to the general public through "publicity work": "In the measure that it is shaped by public relations, the public sphere of civil society again takes on feudal features. The 'suppliers' display a showy pomp before customers ready to follow. Publicity imitates the kind of aura proper to the personal prestige and supernatural authority once bestowed by the kind of publicity involved in representation" (STPS 195). Therefore, public authority takes on the personal trappings of the manorial lord and patrimonial monarch. However, I argued that the more historically specific mode of analysis driving *Public Sphere* militated against Habermas's pushing these conclusions in too crude a fashion. I suggested that it was not until later work that Habermas would be less precise in demarcating historical social formations, and I will show in Chapter 5 that such Weberian moves will take their revenge on him in his recent work.

Perhaps sensing the excesses of his analytical-historical approach in SL, Weber cautions against exaggerating the applicability of the ideal formulations with which he operates here to concrete reality; they never apply, he avers, except in "extreme cases." Ironically, this is precisely how numerous radical critics characterize judicial cases in the *Sozialstaat*: the arbitrariness that results from the fundamental incompatibility between facts and rules, especially in the *Sozialstaat*, purportedly renders all legal cases "exceptions."[25] But Weber insists that a similar situation occurs *wherever* judges dominate proceedings as inquisitors as opposed to mere referees. When the trial procedures and the rules of evidence are dictated by a judge as opposed to preestablished rules and/or the parties themselves, the arrangement is analogous to judgments pronounced by the head of a manorial household. In such arrangements, legal authority is bound to be idiosyncratically personal rather than publicly standardized.

---

[25] Legal theorists of the right and left who agree with this depiction of juridical reality and do not necessarily think of it as a bad thing are, respectively, Schmitt and the lawyers associated with the Critical Legal Studies (CLS) movement; see Schmitt, *Political Theology*, and *Legality and Legitimacy* (1932), trans. Jeffrey Seitzer; intro. John P. McCormick (Durham, NC: Duke University Press, 2004); and the CLS compendium, *Critical Legal Studies*, ed. James Boyle (New York: New York University Press, 1994). On the similarities and differences between these legal approaches, see John P. McCormick, "Three Ways of Thinking 'Critically' about the Law," *American Political Science Review* 93, no. 2 (June 1999), 413–28.

According to Weber, the conflation of quasi-private and quasi-public authority does not result in the unmitigated colonization of the former by the latter, as, for instance, Arendt's work might later suggest. Rather, Weber observes how, conversely, administration also takes on characteristics of adjudication when "domestic authority diffuses into extra-household spheres" (SL 646; RS 390). Weber lists as explicit examples of this phenomenon the adjudicative-administrative tasks taken up by modern parliaments. In this almost seamless textual transition from the patrimonial monarchy to the *Sozialstaat*, Weber again emphasizes the informal and quasi-personal arrangements common to both, as opposed to the consistent and formal channels supposedly established by the nineteenth-century *Rechtsstaat*:

> The distinction between "administrative" and "private" law becomes fluid where the official actions of the organs of official bodies assume the form of agreements between individuals. This is the case when officials in the course of their duties make contractual arrangements for the exchange of goods or services either with members of the organization or with other individuals. Frequently such relationships are withdrawn from the norms of private law, are arranged in some way different from the general legal norms as to substance or as to the mode of enforcement, and are thus declared to belong to the sphere of administration. (SL 646)

The more substantive regulation of contracts between labor and capital by state institutions that become parties to the agreement is but one example of this development.[26]

4. Legal Limits on Power: Separation and Application

Again, Weber cannot be associated too readily with conservative or radical critics of the welfare state. To be sure, it may not be as easy to distinguish his positions from theirs in the manner that was possible for the Habermas of *Public Sphere* in the previous chapter. Nevertheless, the case must be made. Weber notes that the blurring of administrative and private law does not necessarily entail either the wholesale disappearance of bourgeois rights or the uncontrolled expansion of social rights (SL 646). Rights, especially economic rights, are not only appropriate to the scenario of a trial where rules are applied to a case; they also can be compatible with arbitration or other kinds of hearings. Weber appeals to Roman law, which upheld rights in both kinds of cases. Thus, according to Weber's

---

[26] See Philip Selznick, *Law, Society and Industrial Justice* (New Brunswick, NJ: Transaction Books, 1980).

logic, the *Sozialstaat can* be compatible with discrete rights if this was so in Roman private law: the latter could protect rights even when judgments were rendered through magisterial discretion as opposed to a judge deciding in accordance with legal rules. Roman law continually serves as the early historical instance of rational law throughout SL; it shadows the *Rechtsstaat* in the way that patrimonial authority shadows Weber's descriptions of the *Sozialstaat*. Here it illustrates that the *Rechtsstaat* need not be the only "rational" way of securing rights. But this passage is an exception in SL and is at odds with what Weber suggests subsequently.

According to Weber, like Roman law, the *Rechtsstaat* was governed by a distinction between criminal and private law, which was "certainly unknown in the primitive administration of justice" (SL 647). Weber observes that "even in the late stages of complex developments" every action was relevant as a potential tort. All offenses were personal wrongs against a member of a kinship group, upon whom it was incumbent to seek revenge. Modern law seeks punishment primarily in criminal circumstances: the violation of a norm requires the public's or the state's sanctioning of the violator in the name of morality and/or expediency. On the other hand, private law seeks not punishment but "restoration of a situation which the law has guaranteed" (SL 647).

I cannot deal with Weber's fascinating account of the development of criminal law out of revenge, which clearly owes as much to Nietzsche as it does to Weber's empirical sources (SL 647–9).[27] Rather, I will emphasize Weber's provisional conclusions in this domain: (a) he is agnostic about the engine of legal development in the West – neither political nor economic factors are decisive (SL 650); (b) criminal law presupposes rules and application – the discretion of the household lord in meting out punishment does not qualify in this regard; and (c) public law emerges outside the household as offenses come to be perceived as threats to the greater community, especially in the areas of blasphemy or military disobedience. With respect to (a), Weber later remarks on the "indirect influence" of economic factors on the development of modern law. Three such indirect influences are the effects of "certain rationalizations of economic behavior"; freedom of contract associated with the market economy; and complex conflicts of interest that needed to be resolved legally (SL 655).

---

[27] Weber seems to read his historical evidence here and elsewhere through Nietzsche's account of the rise of morality and law from injury in *The Genealogy of Morals*. See Friedrich Nietzsche, *Basic Writings*, ed. and trans. Walter Kaufmann (New York: Random House, 1968).

But Weber insists that legal technique and political institutions were more decisive than economic factors. In any case, to reemphasize, contra the Habermas of TCA2, in SL Weber attributes no influence to the Protestant ethic in the development of law in the West.

The ramifications of (b) are more important for my purposes here; this seems to be the point of fixation for Weber's attempt to understand his contemporary legal predicament in terms of categories derived from the past. In a fashion important for Aristotle as well as the scholastic tradition, but in a way not really elevated to primacy until the Enlightenment, Weber understands law to be the opposite of discretion. Formal law is not the only way of constraining potentially arbitrary prudential power, but it may be the most efficient. Weber suspects or fears that the ability of law to perform such a function is deteriorating in his time as a result of the previously mentioned merging of administration with legislation, on the one hand, and with adjudication, on the other. Read alongside of his "Vocation" lectures and postwar essays on German politics, Weber's sections on imperium and the separation of powers sometimes seem to approximate a reading back of the phenomenon of *Führer* democracy or plebiscitary politics to premodern undeveloped legal forms.[28] Weber describes the former as a scenario where "the master remained more or less a law unto himself within his sphere and he was bound by legal rules only in very special cases" (SL 651). Modern law becomes the historical supercession of the punitive discretion of familial, religious, and military authorities by the "procedural formality or rule" (SL 651). Rules become the norm, and discretion becomes the exception rather than the reverse.

Weber stipulates that the patrimonial monarch is an advance on the household master because the former is subject to more formalized rules. But Weber is not concerned with the origins or trajectory of such a transition. In these passages, Weber's chief concern is the legal conditions of imperium – the power to punish disobedience through force or the threat thereof (SL 651). Imperium can be constrained through limitation or separation. The rights, whether legal or customary, of subjects of a particular imperium serve as *limits* on that power. The conflict of one imperium with another, whether equal or even somewhat subordinate to it, is the *separation* of power. Limitations and separation may coexist and, in fact, this coexistence for Weber "distinctively characterizes the modern state"

---

[28] See "The Profession and Vocation of Politics" and "Parliament and Government in Germany Under a New Political Order" in Weber, *Political Writings*, Peter Lassman and Ronald Speirs, eds. (Cambridge: Cambridge University Press, 1994), 309–69, 130–271.

(SL 652). He defines the state in this context as the consociation where bearers of legally defined imperia interact with each other and within their own spheres on the basis of preordained rules. The separation of powers was more hierarchical in ancient Rome and more fluid in feudal arrangements. But, following Montesquieu, Weber asserts that public law is not possible without the separation of powers. The more formal model of separation of powers – the one prevalent on the continent and in the United States, and the one in which jurisdictions are "dovetailed" rationally – makes possible a more "systematic theory of public law" (SL 653). On this basis, Weber concludes, only the West has checks and balances *and* the separation of powers.[29]

Weber observes that ancient Greece and Rome had quite systematic versions of the separation of powers, and then remarks that "everything else was essentially philosophy of state rather than constitutional law" (SL 653; RS 394). Presumably, the separation of powers is virtually synonymous with constitutional law – that is, the sorting out of institutional competences and the limiting of public power; all else is the matter of philosophical speculation. Along these lines, Weber asserts that feudalism did not have constitutional law because its separation of powers was merely the competition among privilege-holders and estates. An overarching structure and discrete delimitation of tasks are necessary conditions for what Weber calls *Staatsrecht*. However, it is not as if feudalism contributed nothing to the development of the modern separation of powers: Weber declares that the latter emerged out of the institutional characteristics of the personal authorities of separate estates, as well as Roman conceptions of the corporation, in addition to natural law doctrines and French legal theory (SL 653).

The issue of formally rational law emerges again in Weber's discussion of lawmaking and lawfinding (SL 653). Weber understands these two categories to comprise the legal activities of modern political institutions. Contemporary lawmaking is formally rational for Weber: it entails "the establishment of general norms which in the lawyers' thought assume the character of rational rules of law" (SL 653). Lawfinding is also formally rational, inasmuch as it is the application to concrete facts of, on the one hand, the norms created in lawmaking and, on the other, the

---

[29] On the conceptual distinction between, yet mutual deployment of, separation of powers and checks and balances, see Bernard Manin, "Checks, Balances and Boundaries: The Separation of Powers in the Constitutional Debate of 1787," in *The Invention of the Modern Republic*, Biancamaria Fontana, ed. (Cambridge: Cambridge University Press, 1994).

attendant logically deduced legal propositions of adjudication. Cases are subsumed under such rules in this process. There is further differentiation *within* lawfinding between substantive and procedural law, that is, the statutes to be applied and the rules guiding that application process. Weber emphasizes that this is not a timeless, transhistorical categorization of legal phenomena (SL 653). The development of and differentiation between lawmaking and lawfinding do not occur where adjudication *is* administration, that is, where decisions may vary from case to case due to the discretion of the arbiter, as in patrimonialism (SL 654). This implies that the distinction itself is endangered in the context of Weber's own analysis, given his own depiction of the relationship of adjudication and administration in the *Sozialstaat*.

According to Weber, neither legal norms, in the sense just described, nor a party's rights of appeal to them can exist in a scenario where adjudication and administration are blurred. Presumably, parties may have the "right" to appeal to precedent or custom or, as Weber mentions, their own status or privilege, but these are not formally rational principles. On the contrary, they are *concrete* standards, not what Weber defines as *general* norms: the right of a lord to X that is not also legally available to a serf is not a general norm. Moreover, the various and overlapping fora in which these disputes are adjudicated are not conducted according to criteria of strict application (SL 654). Thus, the absence of lawmaking and lawfinding entails the prevalence of "irrational adjudication," not only in primitive situations, but also in any context not directly influenced by Roman law (SL 654). This bold statement does not speak well for the *Sozialstaat*: by such standards, the latter might be interpreted as the reemergence of irrational adjudication, as Weber suggests more explicitly later on in SL.

When administration merges with adjudication, so-called corporatist arrangements supposedly reminiscent of feudalism encourage lawfinding on the basis of the *status* of collectively defined claimants rather than general *norms*. Even though Weber often qualifies this characterization, as noted previously, we might extrapolate from this analysis the conclusion that rights do *not* exist under the *Sozialstaat*: if the rationale of legal decisions is based on administrative measures, and if the substance of claims is based on the status of members of corporatist groups, then formal rights, general norms, and strict application are not in operation. At least this is the case when law as such is understood exclusively in light of Roman or bourgeois-liberal models.

But Weber's tortured equivocations over the broader ramifications of this logic continue throughout SL: he protests that he does *not* want to claim that all legal arrangements except Roman law and the *Rechtsstaat* are irrational – there are, after all, "different senses" of legal rationality (SL 655). Standards of rationality may be met whenever practices of "generalization" and "reduction" are performed: Weber describes these as the two-way, sometimes simultaneous, processes of, on the one hand, selecting the most appropriate general rule to apply to a particular case and, on the other, examining concrete facts to determine what kind of abstract rules may conform to it (SL 655). The arbiter engaged in such practices must reduce the many rationales related to a case to the most appropriate principles, and must identify from among the many facts involved in a case the most relevant (SL 655). And yet, Weber asserts that these practices cannot be found except in "late stages of legal modes of thought," where it serves as part of a "system" in the most rigorous sense:

According to present modes of thought it represents an integration of all analytically derived legal propositions in such a way that they constitute a logically clear, internally consistent, and, at least in theory, gapless system of rules, under which, it is implied, all conceivable fact situations must be capable of being logically subsumed lest their order lack an effective guaranty. (SL 656)

This description does not apply to English common law and, as Weber continually emphasizes, legal systems of "the past" (SL 656).[30] But even in contemporary regimes that aspire to such coherence, the system is a device for ordering legal data and does not really influence "the analytical derivation of legal propositions and the construction of legal relationships" (SL 656). A judge more confidently searches out a rule to apply to a particular case when certain that it indeed exists among all the statutes and propositions within the system. This fiction makes possible coherent adjudication and discourages judges from looking elsewhere – their imaginations or foreign regimes – for the standards to be applied. But it does not generate the logic of the principles themselves. Thus, a legal order may be rational without being systematic, even if the latter quality helps to increase the coherence of adjudication. Not satisfied with the irrational connotations of a legal system relying on "fictions" to provide coherence,

---

[30] Sally Ewing argues against interpretations that claim that Weber considered English common law as irrational jurisprudence. She shows that Weber recognized that English "empiricism" contributed greater calculability to the common law than, for instance, Kadi-like systems. See Ewing, "Formal Justice and the Spirit of Capitalism: Max Weber's Sociology of Law," *Law and Society Review* 21 (1987), 487–512.

we will observe how Habermas attempts to balance judicial discretion and preestablished rules and principles in my discussion of BFN in Chapter 4.

Weber proceeds to explain that lawmaking and lawfinding need not be rational as types, even though he has been using them as if they were in his analysis. They can be *formally irrational* when these processes resort to means that are beyond the grasp of the intellect – for instance, the procedures associated with oracles (SL 656). Such procedures – the way one approaches the oracle – may be formally quite rigid. But Weber declares that the outcomes are arbitrary and unpredictable, and hence irrational. Laws can be made and cases decided in such a manner. On the other hand, Weber attributes *substantive irrationality* to processes where the concrete factors of a particular case determine its outcome on extraneous ethical, emotional, or political grounds rather than general norms (SL 656). The facts of the case are not subsumed under rules but associated with less determinate norms resulting in ad hoc results. Not surprisingly, Weber uses this kind of language when discussing the adjudicative outcomes of *Sozialstaat* legal arrangements.

According to Weber, then, law may be rational either formally or substantively, but it is fully rational only if it is substantively and procedurally based on *general* characteristics. Formalism may be expressed in material or tangible ways, ways displaced through a concrete performance or action perceived as sense data: for instance, "the utterance of certain words, the execution of a signature, or the performance of a certain symbolic act with fixed meaning" (SL 657). In other words, the *act* of the official or the jurist contributes to the meaning of the law; the concrete activity – verbal or physical – of some ritual to some extent embodies a substantial meaning and imparts it to law. But the formalism that Weber seems to associate with modern legal formalism is more "logically" rational: "the legally relevant characteristics of the facts are disclosed through the logical analysis of meaning and where, accordingly, definitely fixed legal concepts in the form of highly abstract rules are formulated and applied" (SL 657). It is not the judge's banging of the gavel that adjudicates, but rather his or her application of general norms through logically verifiable procedures. Validity in the first type of formalism is enmeshed with substantive, doxic, religio-cultural norms that a judge is to actively uphold in legal practice, while validity corresponding to the second type of formalism is derived logically from abstract forms.

Does the acclamatory or plebiscitary aspect of the *Sozialstaat*, criticized by Habermas in STPS, constitute a new form of the more irrational kind of formalism, the kind employing concrete gestures and actions? Do gestures that ratify decisions already determined in advance – the parliamentary show of hands, the electoral confirmation, or the rank-and-file acclamation – signal a return of juridical substantive irrationality? Perhaps. Weber hints at this in the political writings mentioned earlier that are often criticized for promoting this model of politics.[31] But he distinguishes the performative type of substantive rationality from a different type that enlists "ethical imperatives, utilitarian and other expediential rules, and political maxims" (SL 657). Even though these are becoming more prevalent in the *Sozialstaat*, Weber distinguishes them from what is actually "modern" in an earlier sense, that is, what is logical, rational, and systematic (SL 657). He even invokes as a historical, and certainly crypto-normative, model the "gapless system of law," which he just recently in the text treated as merely an ideal type or heuristic device used by legal practitioners: "Only that abstract method which employs the logical interpretation of meaning allows the execution of the specifically systematic task, i.e., the collection and rationalization by logical means of all the several rules recognized as legally valid into an internally consistent complex of abstract legal propositions" (SL 657). In the previous chapter, we observed Habermas successfully expose the unexpressed normative expectations that Weber attaches to such methods and the vacant moral-practical substance actually residing in them in Weber's descriptions of them.

In this vein, Weber then proceeds to define the characteristics of systems marked by "the highest measure of methodological and logical rationality" (SL 657): (1) abstract legal propositions are applied to concrete fact situations in rendering decisions; (2) this application is performed logically; (3) these propositions must relate to each other in a gapless system, or one treated as such; (4) what cannot be construed rationally is judged to be irrelevant; and (5) all social action can be understood as reflecting or violating existing legal propositions, or else the system would not be "gapless" (SL 657–8). This model functions in SL as both an ideal type with which Weber evaluates legal arrangements and a concrete juridical configuration whose time has passed. Because he cannot distinguish between these two functions, his critique of the *Sozialstaat* proves to be as much an exercise in nostalgia as a robust historical, empirical, and (crypto-) normative analysis. Weber's view of history begins and ends with the *Rechtsstaat* model: how what precedes and succeeds it deviates from it,

---

[31] See Weber, "The Profession and Vocation of Politics" and "Parliament and Government," in Weber, *Political Writings*.

such that the logic of history is anachronistic and skewed to the characteristics of a specific period of history. Consequently, we can neither evaluate
patrimonial juridical reality with any accuracy nor formulate normative
possibilities for the *Sozialstaat* with any confidence. Perhaps these criticisms are inconsequential for Weber, who never claimed to be pursuing
these goals in SL; but they are potentially devastating for Habermas if
he, in fact, derived such presuppositions from Weber, because Habermas
claims to be able to, on the one hand, objectively analyze previous evolutionary epochs and, on the other, formulate emancipatory possibilities in
"late capitalism."

5. Organizations, Special Law, and the Law of the Land

If the *Rechtsstaat* is methodologically individualist, then organizations or
groups might be considered a potential threat to the determinacy, coherence, and rationality of the law. As Weber proceeds in SL, he examines the
extent to which this is borne out historically. "Groups," the very matter
of the feudal order and the social bases of the *Sozialstaat*, prove a difficult
topic for Weber to consider juridically. Tentative in outlining the legal
standing of feudal status groups and modern associational ones, Weber is
not sure whether or not the recent corporatist groups that he claims have
evolved from the associational ones are not, in fact, substantively akin to
feudal status groups.

In this context, Weber reiterates that, juridically, modern law consists
of legal propositions: "abstract norms the content of which asserts that a
certain factual situation is to have certain legal consequences" (SL 667).
Such propositions can be prescriptive, prohibitory, or permissive, the first
two constituting claims, the third privileges (SL 667). In the "present
economic order" privileges are of particular importance: freedoms such
as that of noninterference by third parties, especially state officials, or the
freedom to regulate one's own autonomy through contracts (SL 668). For
Weber, the significance of contacts is what separates modern substantive
law from "older law" (SL 669):

The farther we go back in legal history, the less significant becomes the contract
as a device of economic acquisition in fields other than the law of the family and
inheritance. The situation is vastly different today. The present-day significance of
contract is primarily the result of the high degree to which our economic system
is market-oriented and of the role played by money. The increased importance of
the private law contract in general is thus the legal reflex of the market orientation
of our society. (SL 671–2)

Modern contracts are completely different from the "status contracts" associated with earlier public and family law (SL 672). But what about twentieth-century corporatism?[32] According to Weber, what will eventually be called "corporatist" arrangements differ from feudal ones because they do not change the "total legal situation," as well as the wholesale social status of the persons involved, and they are not ordained by magical acts (SL 672). Certainly a marriage contract in a patrimonial setting that changed the social status and kinship associations of one or both of the parties *and* their families is not the same as a collective bargaining agreement that might alter the material existence of trade union members.

Nevertheless, contracts are potentially problematic for the rule of law because they may constitute "special law" outside of the system, and they may have ramifications for third parties who have not consented to the terms of the bargain (SL 694). In the modern setting, special law arises when two contracting parties "create law not only for themselves but also with operative effects as regards third parties . . . provided they comply with the substantive requirements" (SL 695). Weber remarks that this differs from forms of special law in the past (SL 695). But he seems to be speaking here about contracts formed under the *Rechtsstaat*. As the *Sozialstaat* emerges, do contracts take on more characteristics of premodern status contracts and create so much special law as to undermine the rule of law in general?

It is a truism that special or "particularist" law violates or "breaks" the law of the land. But Weber notes that this assessment is only correct with a significant qualification: "the state insisted almost everywhere, and usually with success, that the validity of these special laws, as well as the extent of their application, should be subject to its consent" (SL 695). Special law is not "lawless" when enacted at the pleasure of the centralized authority of the modern state, and signifies something else entirely when occurring in a system of variegated and overlapping legal authorities (SL 695). A particular "law community" (*Rechtsgemeinschaft*) in this context might be defined according to "birth, political, ethnic, or religious denomination, mode of life or occupation" (SL 695). The sorting out of the legal intricacies *within* these groups was conducted through

---

[32] On corporatism generally, see Howard J. Wiarda, *Corporatism and Comparative Politics: The Other Great Ism* (Armonk, NY: M. E. Sharpe, 1996); and with a more recent focus, Wolfgang Streeck and Philippe C. Schmitter, eds., *Private Interest Government: Beyond Market and State* (London: Sage, 1985); and Coen N. Teulings and Joop Hartog, *Corporatism or Competition?: Labour Contracts, Institutions and Wage Structures in International Comparison* (Cambridge: Cambridge University Press, 1998).

patriarchal arbitration, that is, authoritarianly, and *among* these groups through negotiation, that is, consensually (SL 695–6).

Weber again cautions against tracing out the logic of this account too far: it is not as if law was nonexistent in premodern arrangements. But in his estimation, it certainly was *underdeveloped*:

> The idea of generally applicable norms was not, it is true, completely lacking, but it inevitably remained in an undeveloped state; all law appeared as the privilege of particular individuals or objects or of a particular constellation of individuals or objects. Such a point of view had, of course, to be opposed by that in which the state appears as the all-embracing coercive institution. (SL 698)

Other forms of law, for instance, manorial law, coexisted with a general law of the land (SL 700). The "bourgeoisie," as Weber calls them, of both ancient Rome and the eighteenth century protested this state of affairs but never fully eradicated it. Weber remarks that modern law "has created anew a great mass of legal particularisms," but in a different manner than "the older corporate status groups" (SL 698). The bourgeoisie at first benefited from their use of special law in laissez-faire economic and *Rechtsstaat* political arrangements, but felt threatened as it became the instrument of organized labor and democratic parties by the end of the nineteenth century.

According to Weber, formal legal equality and the accompanying "integration of individuals and fact-situations into one compulsory institution," that is, the state, are the result of two great rationalizing forces: marketization and bureaucratization. The former renders associations voluntary, and law creation universally accessible, through freedom of contract. But Weber is no unequivocal advocate of "civil society."[33] Weber, the supposed theoretical counterweight to Marx, notes that the formal equality accompanying the process of autonomous association formation disproportionately benefits the propertied classes (SL 699). Thus, Weber does not attribute too much moral weight to the categories related to these developments and defines associational groups in terms of merely "metaphorical" autonomy (SL 699).

An association formed through such "metaphorical" autonomy is "a group of persons, which, though membership may fluctuate, is determinable, and whose members are all, by consent or enactment, under a *special law* depending on them for its modification" (SL 699, emphasis

---

[33] See Sung Ho Kim, "'In Affirming Them, He Affirms Himself': Max Weber's Politics of Civil Society," *Political Theory* 28, no. 2 (April 2000), 197–229.

added). Weber suggests that any group that forms itself, as it were, engages in the creation of special law to one degree or another. This definition applies to groups from various historical periods: clubs, businesses, municipalities, estates, guilds, labor unions, vassals, and so on. They are bound by norms other than those identifiable with a contract, and are constituted not so much by rules as by "reciprocal subjective claims" (SL 699). But under the guise of general examples, Weber still has in mind the more narrow comparison of feudal *ständische*, bourgeois associational and industrial corporatist groups and their respective relationships to law.

Immediately after the discussion of associations, Weber describes how modern law begins to differentiate between objective law and subjective right. The distinction between rights that pertain to individuals and those that pertain to groups has significance for the predicament of the *Sozialstaat*. According to Weber, "autonomy is exercised where the enacted rule has its normal source in a resolution; while we have a special case of regulation by virtue of freedom of contract where the rule is supplied by an agreement between concrete individuals" (SL 699). This distinction was always latent in legal arrangements but remained undeveloped before the emergence of modern law: even according to "the conceptions of earliest times, the distinction between enactment as the means of creating objective law and contract as the means of creating subjective rights was a familiar one, despite the great vagueness and fluidity of the transitions between them" (SL 706). The notion of rights is pivotal in the transitions from status to civil social groups and from overlapping legal jurisdictions to the bourgeois rule of law: "The general transformation and mediatization of the legally autonomous organizations of the age of personal law into the state's monopoly of law-creation found its expression in the change of the forms in which such organizations were legally treated as the bearers of rights" (SL 705). One should note the evolutionary overtones of this description in which the *Rechtsstaat* becomes the telos of legal history. As we saw in the previous chapter, in his mature works, Habermas would adopt the evolutionism of Weber, but depict instead the *Sozialstaat*, properly legitimated and theorized beyond further transformation, as the legal-rational telos of history. As we will see, this may account for the intensity of his response to the latter's possible supercession in his essays on globalization and European integration.

According to Weber, before the emergence of the *Rechtsstaat*, rights were protected through reprisal by the party whose "right" had been violated (SL 705). Eventually, corporate bodies were formed via endowment, that is, a juristic personality constituted by a plurality of persons recognized to represent the interest of those persons by rules and not on the basis of associational relations (SL 707). No longer kin but rather legal advocates represented parties. Advocates can take the form of a corporation, which is a fixed group, or the form of the state, an institution that is represented by its organs and based on obligation rather than interest (SL 707). In modern arrangements, one's rights may be protected by an association to which one belongs or a corporation in which one holds stock, or by the state, which monopolizes certain kinds of protection and pursues enforcement on that basis.

Weber then emphasizes an important difference between the authority–group relationship in modern and premodern arrangements. In particular, he points out, modern government is conducted through institutions rather than the corporate bodies that governed premodern politics:

It was the essentially technical needs of administration in the modern institutionalized state which led to the establishment as separate juristic persons of innumerable public enterprises such as schools, poorhouses, state banks, insurance funds, savings banks, etc.; having neither members nor membership rights but only heteronomous and heterocephalous organs, they could not be construed as corporations, and thus there was developed for them the legal concept of the "institutions." (SL 715)

Persons do not "belong" to the organizations that Weber mentions in this passage: they work for them or are the clients of them. The fact that there are associations to which members choose to belong is a result of the peculiar course of Western history. For Weber, the difference between the development of organizations in the West and those elsewhere was European patrimonialism's ultimately corporate rather than inherently patriarchal structure (SL 727). It was traditionally possible for Western groups to be autonomous, that is, capable of law creation, even before the emergence of modern law (SL 728).[34] With the exception of military

---

[34] Of course, Weber offers a more differentiated notion of the development of organizations *within* Europe as well: English organizations took the form of ecclesiastical bodies because the canon law never was counterbalanced there with Roman law (SL 721). Moreover, he argues that England experienced executive centralization under a powerful monarchy early, then civil-social independence, while the reverse was true in Germany (SL 721–2):

In consequence of the rigorous patrimonial central administration the integration of all associations in the state was at its maximum at the beginning of English legal history and had to undergo a gradual weakening from then. In Continental legal history, on

concerns, in most spheres the lord in Europe had to depend on the good will of a fairly independent administrative apparatus to achieve desired goals (SL 728).[35]

Subsequently, Weber suggests, modern law extends the possibility of contractual relations and the purposes for which they are formed, especially with respect to exchange of goods, personal work, and services (SL 729). But before succumbing to a Western chauvinism that celebrates the "freedom" that developed in Europe and not elsewhere, Weber warns that a study of "formal legal institutions" cannot explain whether there has been a real increase in the individual's ability to shape his or her own life or whether, in fact, the reverse is true: "The great variety of permitted contractual schemata and the formal empowerment to set the content of contracts in accordance with one's desires and independently of all official form patterns, in and of itself by no means makes sure that these formal possibilities will in fact be available to all and everyone" (SL 729). Weber insists that the legally secured distribution of property must also be taken into account (SL 729). A worker's right to contract work is not really a freedom, understood in terms of control of the conditions of one's life; a worker has virtually no say in the structure of the labor market itself and the conditions of his or her work. As we saw Habermas point out in

> the other hand, it was the bureaucratic princely state of modern times which broke the bonds of the traditional corporative autonomy; subjected to its own supervision the municipalities, guilds, village communities, churches, clubs, and other associations of all kinds; issued patents; regulated and controlled them; canceled all rights which were not officially granted in the patents; and thus for the first time introduced into actual practice the theory of "legists," who had maintained that no organizational structure could have juristic personality or any rights of its own except by virtue of a grant by princeps. (SL 724)

> But the French Revolution destroyed corporations and voluntary associations, as, Weber avers, every radical democracy is wont to do (SL 724). Such a sharp break with the past never occurred in English corporation law (SL 724).

[35] Berman and Reid discuss the legal and sociological factors to which Weber attributed the ability of Europe's "traditionalism," as opposed to other types around the globe, to produce modernity out of itself: see "Max Weber as Legal Historian" in Turner, ed., *The Cambridge Companion to Weber*, 231. After all, Weber claims in SL that the canon law of the Middle Ages was "much more rational and more highly developed" formally than other types of sacred law (SL 828). The Christian Middle Ages more or less preserved, for Weber, the rationality of classical antiquity, especially in the case of the bureaucratic organization of the church (SL 828–9). The canon law served as a guide for secular law on the road to rationality (SL 829). The individual churches were the first juridical institutions, and as such made possible the legal conception of public organizations as corporations (SL 829).

the previous chapter, this is especially true under Weber's paradigm and paragon of law – the *Rechtsstaat*. As we will see, despite these admissions here, later in SL Weber describes the attempt of workers to exert more control through the *Sozialstaat* over these circumstances as a threat to law.

But in these passages Weber is adamant: formal legal freedoms are more appropriately understood as the freedom of property owners to exercise "power over others" (SL 730). A freedom that is fully accessible to some but not others is not really universal, and thus the "generality" of the *Rechtsstaat* must be called into question. These are some of the most emphatic passages in SL: Weber observes how a decrease in *formal* coercion may engender an expansion in *concrete* coercion: "The exact extent to which the total amount of 'freedom' within a given legal community is actually increased depends entirely upon the concrete economic order and especially upon the property distribution. In no case can it simply be deduced from the content of law" (SL 730; cf. 731). Domination in contemporary labor markets is not just *hidden* by the law, as some critics suggest, but is also actually enabled by the latter's guarantee of inequitable property relations (SL 731).

It is almost as if Weber needs to convince himself of the conditions that make the rise of the *Sozialstaat* necessary in these exceptional passages of SL. Just when the reader might think that Weber has indeed become the forerunner of neo-conservative apologists for the market and its most accommodating type of law, he suddenly goes "red," or at least a dark shade of pink. Most of SL seems concerned with privileging modern formal law as the paragon of justice and rationality and with denouncing any deformalization of it as an irrational and arbitrary threat – a return of the long repressed past. Here Weber is more judicious: he discusses democratic socialism's opposition to both market coercion *and* purely personal claims to authority. Social democracy would like to recognize only objectively abstract laws, not falsely abstract ones like those of the market. Therefore, Weber points out, social democrats share with market apologists repugnance to personal or concrete authority, even as it operates through a "special kind" of impersonal coercion that does not overtly discriminate against workers, consumers, producers, and so on (SL 731). The consequences of such abstract domination, after all, can be quite concrete, Weber asserts, extending to the complete loss of an individual's economic existence. Furthermore, while the concrete domination associated with capitalism may in fact be impersonal – that is, "drained of all normal sentimental content" – it also may be allowed to expand further than has any kind of domination in history:

The more comprehensive the realm of structures whose existence depends in a specific way on "discipline" – that of capitalist commercial establishments – the more relentlessly can authoritarian constraint be exercised within them, and the smaller will the circle of those in whose hands the power to use this type of constraint is concentrated and who also hold the power to have such authority guaranteed to them by the legal order. (SL 731)

In the final sections of SL, Weber implies that despite their preference for no domination – abstract or concrete – advocates of social democracy and economic justice will facilitate the kind of unprecedented concrete domination mentioned in this passage. They will have to resort to the kind of internal discipline necessary to challenge the abstract imperatives and concrete practices of private property and the market, not to mention the external mechanism of the state to achieve their ends. But before confronting legal change in his concrete historical moment, Weber treats it as a theoretical problem in the abstract.

6. Weber, Law, and Social Change

The law is the guideline of a *normal* order. Why does it change? In particular, if modern, formally rational law is so rational, why might it need to be amended? Weber addresses this question, which subterreaneously concerns the issue of law and social change. Weber starts in his contemporary context: he remarks that "at the present time," new legal rules emerge through conscious choice, that is, through lawmaking conducted according to constitutional requirements (SL 753). This presupposes two levels of will: a preestablished one in the constitution and the immediate one motivating the statutory process.

This form of lawmaking is generally supposed to stand in opposition to a customary law associated with the past. Customary law, like English common law, "emerges" rather than being actively "made." But as Weber points out, customary law itself is fairly modern (SL 753). The modern definitions of customary law are but "theoretical constructs" (SL 753). Customary law serves a conceptual purpose by providing a gray area around the opposition of statutory law and judge-made law. More specifically, Weber insinuates that the notion of customary law gives a more rational air to statutory law (SL 754). But Weber does not pursue this issue further, even as it bears a resemblance to his *Rechtsstaat*–patrimonialism contrast, concluding with a swipe at legal sociologists who attack customary law as a straw man (SL 753). The more interesting question is: why at the time that law is perceived in terms of will – the will of the demos or the will of the judge – does a notion of an organic or spontaneous, long-developing law come into play, especially at this point in SL?

According to Weber, legal norms have their origin in habit that subsequently becomes binding (SL 754). Consensus over expectations regarding others' behavior then acquires the guaranty of coercive enforcement. Again, this is an appropriate theorization of the initial juridical circumstances, but why should expectations change? Weber responds: "Even in this purely hypothetical construction there arises the question of how anything could ever change in this inert mass of canonized custom which, just because it is considered binding, could never give birth to anything new" (SL 754). One reason Weber offers is "unperceived changes in meaning"; that is, a new situation is addressed with old law (SL 755). Or new law is applied without being recognized as such to an old or even a new factual situation (SL 755). And, of course, the law and the situation may change. But Weber gives no explanation for the cognitive dissonance in these cases. What would prevent such recognition of novelty or anachronism? On the one hand, Weber concedes that "the external conditions of social life" change unbeknown to the participants, but also that actors interested in a concrete end are the sources of a "new line of conduct" (SL 755). This is particularly troublesome in the case of capitalism, which changes on the basis of anonymous developments and action based on interests. But Weber does not attempt to resolve this problem here.

Change can also come through judicial initiative since judges do not merely restore a status quo ante or establish norms that would have been binding by consensus understanding or agreement (SL 758). Weber suggests that a judge's "decision of individual cases always produces consequences which, acting beyond the scope of the case, influence the selection of those rules which are to survive as law" (SL 758). A judge is involved in the simple application of norms to a case only when dealing with formal procedural issues. Concrete cases require some concrete reasons, such that a judge is to some degree creating "the empirical validity of a general norm" as law, because the decision carries over into the future, presumably in precedent and even legislation.

Weber suggests that the utter malleability of law generally is demonstrated by the fact that even Mohammed and Yahweh change their mind on law. But judges generally have an incentive to be consistent: continuity increases legitimacy and so is self-perpetuating. Therefore, judges try to adhere to the purported "persistently correct decision" (SL 759). Thus,

Weber concludes that new legal norms arise from (1) the standardization of certain consensual understandings" and (2) judicial precedent, as in English common law (SL 759). Weber deems the initiative for new law from above as very different from the modes of "our present society" (SL 760). Weber seems to think of both social democratic and capital-interested legislation as bottom-up phenomena. Bureaucratic change via regulation as opposed to lawmaking does not seem to count for Weber. Because the former, unlike the latter, cannot be legitimated, it seems to be a reversion to a pre-imperium situation of nonlegality: "Wherever there arose an imperium (i.e., an authority whose functions are specifically par-ticularized as distinguished from the unlimited domestic authority), we find the beginnings of the distinction between 'legitimate' command and the norms by which it is 'legitimated'" (SL 764).

In less *Rechtsstaat*-centric moments, Weber interprets similar differen-tiations as forms of the separation of powers: the "Germanic" distinction between lawfinding and law enforcement, the Roman practice of interces-sion by magistrates with concurrent powers against each other, as well as the necessity of their agreement in cases of administrative justice. These constitute "formal" arrangements of law and its administration (SL 773). But formal arrangements require concrete persons: Weber asserts that trained specialists have always facilitated the development of law (SL 775). Private counselors and attorneys and, eventually, professional lawyers sat-isfied and increased the need for specialized knowledge, which, Weber hints, almost always results from the increased significance of commerce (SL 775). Legal experts are either trained *empirically*, as if learning a craft, like apprentices learning from practitioners, or *theoretically* and scientif-ically in special schools (SL 784–5). In a sense, they can emphasize either *Faktizität* (empirical facticity) or *Geltung* (abstract validity).

In the former case, which conforms to the guildlike English approach, notwithstanding statements to the contrary in other parts of SL, Weber baldly states, "no rational system of law could emerge, nor even a ratio-nalization of the law as such" (SL 787). The concepts deployed by such an approach are too intimately connected with the concrete events of everyday life, which are themselves determined by external criteria. As such, the concepts deployed are not "general concepts" that abstract away from concrete instances and are not determined by "logical interpretation of meaning," neither generalization nor subsumption (SL 787). Weber argues that such an approach jumps too freely from fact to fact, case to case: "In the purely empirical conduct of legal practice and legal training one always moves from the particular to the particular but never tries to move from the particular to general propositions in order to be able subsequently to deduce from them the norms for new particular cases" (SL 787). Interestingly, Weber associates the empirical approach with "the word"; legal words are stretched to cover concrete instances rather than composed in propositions under which concrete instances are subsumed. A circumstance obtains where *material* governs the law through abuse of words rather than the converse circumstance, where reason governs the world through logical propositions.

Weber suggests that the situation of the craft-apprentice training of lawyers is completely the opposite of that where lawyers are "school-trained":

The legal concepts produced by academic law-teaching bear the character of abstract norms, which, at least in principle, are formed and distinguished from one another by a rigorously formal and rational logical interpretation of meaning. Their rational, systematic character, as well as their relatively small degree of concreteness of content, easily result in a far-reaching emancipation of legal thinking from the everyday needs of the public. The force of the purely logical legal doctrines let loose, and a legal practice dominated by it, can considerably reduce the role played by considerations of practical needs in the formation of the law. (SL 789)

Even legal training conducted by priests in seminaries is highly rational, according to Weber's account, if not juristically formal. It aims at certain morally defined material goods, on the one hand, but, on the other, is indulgent of highly abstract theorizing characteristic of the "uninhibited intellectualism of scholars" (SL 789). But he notes that its rationality is bound by the constraints of tradition (SL 790).

7. Formal and Substantive Rationalization of Law

Weber emphasizes time and again the preeminence of political authority in determining the particular form a certain legal arrangement will take. In the subsection of SL dealing with the general conditions of legal formalism (SL V, 1), Weber recapitulates his understanding of the history of the relationship between political authority and formally rational law. He remarks that "older forms of popular justice," that is, not yet rationally formal legality, originated in the corporatist negotiation between kinship groups (SL 809). The centralization of authority in the European monarchies, on the other hand, set in motion the administrative rationalization through which bureaucratic officials subsequently would rationalize legal procedure "in form and substance" (SL 809). Weber suggests that these officials did not set out to rationalize law as a goal in itself but merely as a means to more effective governance (SL 809). But he cautions against interpreting these motivations as purely technocratic rather than oriented toward general ethical goals (SL 810).

Moreover, militating against a monolithic portrait of this development, Weber acknowledges that just because a specific authority may have desired control in certain domains does not mean that the result was formally rational law. In particular, Weber shows that authority based on personal loyalty or democratic foundations may issue "nonformal" results (SL 811). Enlightened despots and democratic demagogues, for instance, "may refuse to be bound by formal rules, even by those they have made themselves" (SL 811). Here Weber begins to pose an irreconcilable conflict between the abstract formalism of legal determinism and the desire of authority to attain substantive goals that will continue throughout the balance of SL (SL 811).

Weber then accentuates the kind of "freedom" that regularity engenders: juridical formalism enables the legal system to operate like "a technically rational machine" that ensures the maximum freedom for individuals and groups based on the accurate prediction of legal consequences (SL 811). For this kind of freedom to be realized, Weber claims that "rational proof and the logical derivation of decisions" had to triumph over methods centered on oracular pronouncement and physical contest (SL 812). Weber celebrates the fact that formal procedure "pacifies contest" through "fixed and inviolable 'rules of the game'" (SL 811) rather than the physical contests that were once the only accepted way of revealing the truth. Weber emphasizes that what may seem obvious to contemporary readers was not always the case: it took ages before formally rational procedure became accepted as a fact-finding method (SL 811). Weber never goes so far as to associate the contemporary controversy over legal determinacy – over the legal status of "facts" – with the revival of informal adjudicative procedures, though it is no great leap to venture such an association.

But, along the lines of his Marxoid sentiments discussed earlier, Weber reminds the reader that formal freedom is not freedom per se. He notes how conservative forces at first oppose formal justice because it decreases dependence on authority, but then democratic partisans oppose the latter for undermining majority rule and for serving as an obstacle to redistributive impulses:

> Formal justice guarantees the maximum freedom for the interested parties to represent their formal legal interests. . . . To democracy, however, it has been repugnant because it decreases the dependency of the legal practice, and therewith the individuals, upon the decisions of their fellow citizens. Furthermore, the development

of the trial into a peaceful contest of conflicting interests can contribute to the further concentration of economic and social power. In all these cases formal justice, due to its necessarily abstract character, infringes upon the ideals of substantive justice. (SL 812–13)

Those who "wield economic power" depend on the "abstract character" of formal justice to further their interests, but also to further the ideology of opening up opportunities for individuals against "authoritarian control" or "irrational mass emotions" (SL 813).

Weber does not dispel this image of democratic justice: again, he interprets the use of juries in ancient democracy as "khadi-justice" – ad hoc, inconsistent, unprincipled, susceptible to prevailing passions (SL 813).[36] In fact, Weber, at least in these passages, cannot conceive of a democracy that might be bound by the formal rule of law:

Quite generally, in all forms of popular justice decisions are reached on the basis of concrete, ethical, or political considerations or of feelings oriented toward social justice. Political justice prevailed particularly in Athens, but it can be found even today. In this respect, there are similar tendencies displayed by popular democracy on the one hand and the authoritarian power of theocracy or of patriarchal monarchs on the other. (SL 813)

Weber returns to the purported incompatibility between political justice and formal justice in democracies in the sections explicitly devoted to the *Sozialstaat* toward the end of SL.

Returning to the origins of rationally formal law in the West, Weber focuses on the political power of princes, magistrates, and officials (SL 839). This power certainly effected the development of special law, particularly as it concerns the relationships of patron and client, master and servant, and lord and vassal (SL 839). But Weber emphasizes how, in the attempt to overcome estate privileges and the vestiges of estate law, the patrimonial monarchs contributed to the development of rational-formal law (SL 846). In particular, ministers and lawyers were able to ally their professional interests with that of the prince to further accelerate the process (SL 846): "The needs of those interested in increased rationality, [that is,] the growing predominance of formal legal equality and objective formal norms, coincide with the power interests of the prince as against the holders of privilege.... The alliance of monarchical and bourgeois interests was, therefore, one of the major factors which led towards formal legal rationalization" (SL 846–7).

---

[36] A more serious treatment of the Khadis, or the religious courts of Islam, can be found in Noel J. Coulson, *Conflicts and Tensions in Islamic Jurisprudence* (Chicago: University of Chicago Press, 1969).

Obviously, the contribution of the patrimonial monarchs to the development of modern law has limits. Weber mentions how these monarchs, when attempting to escape the binding formal laws that they made for themselves, veered toward the dissolution of law into administration (SL 843–4). Through the struggle to keep the monarchs true to such bindings, the bourgeoisie displaced their former allies in the revolutions of the eighteenth century. Weber notes that even when following its own rules, patrimonial authority is not fully rational because it tends to pursue substantive goals that undermine a formal legal system:

> Although the patriarchal system of justice can well be rational in the sense of adherence to fixed principles, it is not so in the sense of a logical rationality of its modes of thought but rather in the sense of the pursuit of substantive principles of social justice of political, welfare utilitarian, or ethical content. Again law and administration are identical, but not in the sense that all administration would assume the form of adjudication but rather in the reverse sense that all adjudication takes the character of administration. The prince's administrative officials are at the same time judges, and the prince himself, intervening at will into the administration of justice in the form of "cabinet justice," decides according to his free discretion in the light of considerations of equity, expediency or politics. (SL 844–5)

Weber ranks the Napoleonic Civil Code as a paragon of rational law alongside the practical law model, Anglo-Saxon law, theoretical-literary law, and Roman law (SL 865). Weber admires the formal elegance of the Napoleonic system, its lucidity, clarity, and simplicity, and the "precise intelligibility in its provisions" (SL 865). But it is not free of drawbacks; its rule-based simplicity has rendered it lacking in substantive principles: "as a result of the abstract total structure of the legal system and the axiomatic nature of many provisions, legal thinking has not been stimulated to a truly constructive elaboration of legal institutions" (SL 865). Its rules must be adapted to on a case-by-case basis since the former do not represent articulations of "broader principles" (SL 865). According to Weber, the Napoleonic Civil Code approximates Bentham's ideal of purely rational law because it is free from historical prejudice, and its substantive content derives almost exclusively from "sublimated common sense" (SL 866). But the Code has a tendency to sacrifice "juristic sublimation to vivid form" (SL 866). Thus, perhaps providing evidence that Habermas himself did not use in his reconstruction of the morally substantive assumptions of Weber's SL, he reveals himself to be no admirer of legal form for the sake of mere form in the discussion of the Napoleonic Civil Code.

Speaking of Habermas's critique of Weber, at this point in SL, the latter reinvokes the sociological perspective on legal validity to discuss natural law: legal rectitude or correctness is sociologically relevant to the extent that it conditions the behavior of legal actors, whether lawmakers, legal practitioners, or social groups (SL 866). These actors have the *conviction* that law is legitimate, that is, they *believe* that legal maxims are binding on grounds of reigning principles rather than naked power (SL 866). These principles undergirding most rational-positive systems, especially in postrevolutionary France and the United States, constitute modern natural law. Unlike earlier natural law, which traces its legitimacy to divine or personally charismatic origin, on the one hand, and majoritarian-positivist law, which traces its legitimacy to parliamentary enactment, modern natural law legitimates legal maxims by tracing them to "immanent and teleological qualities" located in nature or reason (SL 867, 869). Weber declares that natural law is the "only consistent type of legitimacy" appropriate to a postreligious age (SL 867). But since Weber is skeptical of the efficacy of natural law, it is disappointing that he does not elaborate on what he means by "consistent." Throughout SL, one gets the overwhelming impression that Weber believes a formally rational *Rechtsstaat*, defined *apart* from natural law, is the most consistent form of modern legitimacy.

This problem becomes more pressing as Weber asserts that natural law is inherently "substantive" and that there can be no inherently "formal" type of natural law. Even the apparently formally based contract version of natural law presupposes some substantive notions of peaceful agreement, reciprocity, free and rational subjects, and so on. This obtains whether the contracts are legitimated upon actual agreements or reasonable standards derived from hypothetical agreements (SL 868–9). The most important implications of this type of natural law are the civil liberties and especially the freedom of contract enshrined in modern constitutions (SL 869). In fact, Weber admits that from the perspective of natural law, it is appropriate to interpret administrative or redistributive policies as a violation of the latter freedom: "for example, every act of social welfare legislation prohibiting certain contents of the free labor contract, is on that account an infringement of freedom of contract" (SL 869).

Again prefiguring the right-wing version of the dialectic of enlightenment made popular by European neo-conservatives – that is, the enlightenment devours itself – Weber notes how natural law formally strengthened the development of logically abstract law and juridical procedure, but also substantively expanded the domain of rights that were to be protected and then advanced by the law (SL 873). The latter substantive development undermines the former, which makes it possible to begin with. Once "discredited" by, among other things, "anti-metaphysical radicalism," Weber suggests that natural law legitimations decline but never fully disappear: again invoking antinomial oppositions, Weber asserts that "the conflict between the axioms of substantive and formal natural law is insoluble" (SL 874). The formalism of the modern *Rechtsstaat* battles with the substantive demands of an emerging *Sozialstaat*, while the natural law origins of both dissipate. Beneath this battle, however, the legitimate underpinnings of a healthy contest of principles are no longer very firm:

In consequence of both juridical rationalism and modern intellectual skepticism in general, the axioms of natural law have lost all capacity to provide the fundamental basis of a legal system.... Even the most convincing norms arrived at by abstraction seem to be too subtle to serve as the bases of a legal system. Consequently, legal positivism has, at least for the time being, advanced irresistibly. The disappearance of the old natural law conceptions has destroyed all possibility of providing the law with a metaphysical dignity by virtue of its immanent qualities. In the great majority of its most important provisions, it has been unmasked all too visibly, indeed, as the product or the technical means of a compromise between conflicting interests.... [T]his extinction of the metajuristic implications of the law...also effectively promoted the actual obedience to the power, now viewed solely from an instrumentalist standpoint, of the authorities who claim legitimacy at any moment. Among the practitioners of the law this attitude has been particularly pronounced. (SL 874–5)

These are fateful words indeed, as before too long, German lawyers and judges would prostitute themselves to the most unlawful "legitimate" powers.[37] Perhaps due to the fact that Weber would be deprived of the benefit of witnessing this for himself, and notwithstanding his previous condemnation of the legal profession – of which he was a member – he manages some fairly objective observations here: Weber insists that lawyers are conservative in general, resisting innovation generated from below, such as social ideals, and from above, such as expansion of power (SL 875). But in specific cases, he points out that lawyers have been the champions of the underprivileged and the legally disadvantaged, as well as the main agents of various bourgeois revolutions (SL 875). But in the contemporary context, Weber notes, lawyers "are inclined to stand on the

---

[37] See Ingo Müller, *Hitler's Justice: The Courts of the Third Reich*, trans. Deborah Lucas Schneider (Cambridge, MA: Harvard University Press, 1991). Weber's prophecy would be both reissued and fulfilled by Schmitt, *Legality and Legitimacy*.

side of 'order,' which in practice means that they will take the side of the 'legitimate' authoritarian political power that happens to predominate at the given moment" (SL 876). These insights suggest that Weber does not attribute altruism to lawyers who are attempting to put legal means at the disposal of "the demand for substantive justice by certain social class interests and ideologies" (SL 894). Here he resumes his diatribe against "the ideologically rooted power aspirations" of lawyers who encourage the "anti-formal tendencies" of modern law (SL 894).

8. Formal versus Substantive Law and the *Sozialstaat*

In the concluding sections of SL, Weber tries to define standards of legal validity that are generally relevant and yet can still accommodate the transformation that is taking place, as it were, under his feet. He finds that he cannot satisfactorily define such standards, even though he has done so in previous pages, and instead confronts head on the novelty of law's predicament in the *Sozialstaat*. These sections are filled with language that evokes visions of historical obsolescence and sweeping social change.

Weber begins by recapitulating the rational and systematic character of modern legislation, qualities that distinguish it from other types of law throughout history (SL 880). Yet, Weber declares that it is difficult to define rationally legal formalism because its qualities are somewhat ambiguous, and adds, "indeed, this ambiguity is a direct result of more recent developments" (SL 880). Most treatments of SL focus on Weber's seemingly confident distinction between sociological and juridical analyses of modern law in the section "Economy and Social Norms" (SL 311–38). However, here Weber explicitly concedes that his own historical context impinges on his ability to formulate abstract analytic categories. The rising "substantivism" associated with the *Sozialstaat* interferes with the formulation of a definition of rationally formal law, at least one that is presently operational.

Weber then adopts a standpoint characteristic of the formally rational paradigm that he has just balked at defining: he remarks that the efficacy of "ancient principles" (*alten Prinzipien*) interlocking right and law, particularly those associated with membership in status groups or tribes, as well as the attendant special courts and procedures that adjudicated them, have been relegated "to the past" (SL 880). This statement is certainly true from the vantage point of the nineteenth-century *Rechtsstaat*, which, presumably, had eliminated these premodern concretist juridical entities forever. But Weber stops and reverses this line of argument: "neither all special and personal law, nor all special jurisdictions have disappeared completely. On the contrary, very recent legal developments have brought an increasing particularism within the legal system" (SL 880). Weber now adopts the standpoint of the emerging *Sozialstaat* that is rapidly superseding the *Rechtsstaat* and recognizes that substantive elements akin – perhaps superficially, perhaps not – to premodern ones are reappearing, particularly in the sphere of commercial law (SL 880).

Increasingly, Weber suggests, the regulation of contracts and the definition of enterprises constitute special law, that is, law "determined either by substantive qualities of an individual transaction, especially its intended meaning, or by the objective association of a transaction with the rational organization of an enterprise" (SL 881). This means that bargains and agreements are no longer governed by rules that apply to all transactions, but rather are determined by the concrete aspects of the bargain itself. The parties to transactions effectively make law for themselves rather than seeing to it that the transaction conform to standing laws. While these special laws are not determined by the participants' membership in a status group, as was the case in premodern legal arrangements, the groups involved, such as labor or capital, to some extent establish the terms and the outcomes of the proceedings (SL 881).

But rather than collapse contemporary labor or administrative law mechanically into premodern forms of law, Weber insists on distinguishing what he calls "class law" from "status group law" (SL 881). Unlike many pluralists in his day, Weber does not interpret corporatism or pluralism as the quasi-revival of medieval guild arrangements.[38] Yet, on the other hand, he does not completely rule out such an interpretation, remarking that his own proposed "contrast with the past is but a relative one" (SL 881). The distinction between class and status law might be interpreted merely in terms of degrees because they have been, in fact, "essentially the same" throughout history (SL 881). Weber concedes that the difference is largely relative: the procedures for becoming a member of a particular group, such as a merchant, under the jurisdiction of modern special law require only the application for a license or privilege (SL 881). It is a kind of soft *ständische* delimitation, unlike medieval ones, which were much more difficult to attain.

But Weber emphasizes that these new types of association are, in fact, adjudicated in ways quite reminiscent of earlier modes of status

[38] See Paul Q. Hirst, ed., *The Pluralist Theory of the State: Selected Writings of G. D. Cole, J. N. Figgis, and H. J. Laski* (London: Routledge, 1994).

law: "Many of these modern special laws are also combined with special courts and procedures of their own" (SL 882). According to Weber, the emergence of modern particularist law can be traced to the increased occupational differentiation and greater leverage of industrial and commercial pressure groups (SL 882). In addition, concerned parties presently desire more expeditious and concretely appropriate resolution of disputes than might be achieved through formally rational procedures (SL 882). But Weber cautions against attributing the modern deformalization of law to these causes alone, as they are only a few "among a whole series of similar contemporary phenomena" (SL 882).

Perhaps surprisingly, Weber does not here, as he does elsewhere in the SL, almost exclusively blame organized labor and/or popular appeals to social justice for causing the proliferation of special law. The "propertied classes" who initially most benefited from the formalism of modern law are rather active participants in its decline according to Weber's account here. In terms that anticipate Habermas's attribution to representatives of capital a role commensurate with that of labor in the emergence of the *Sozialstaat*, Weber describes how the impatience of economic power with the formal aspects of the *Rechtsstaat* exacerbates the so-called indeterminacy of law associated with state regulation and redistribution:

The expectations of parties will often be disappointed by the results of a strictly professional legal logic. Such disappointments are inevitable indeed where the facts of life are juridically "construed" in order to make them fit the abstract propositions of law and in accordance with the maxim that nothing can exist in the realm of law unless it can be "conceived" by the jurist in conformity with those "principles" which are revealed to him by juristic science.... To a large extent such conflicts are the inevitable consequence of the incompatibility that exists between the intrinsic necessities of logically consistent formal legal thinking and the fact that the legally relevant agreements and activities of private parties are aimed at economic results and oriented towards economically determined expectations. (SL 885)

While property interests contribute to the deformalization of laws in *Sozialstaat* arrangements, Weber, perhaps now adopting the standpoint of legal rationality, most severely scorns the threat to formal law launched from the other direction: namely, the "new demands for a 'social law' based on such emotionally colored ethical postulates as 'justice' or 'human' dignity" (SL 886). True, Weber recognizes that these demands are a response to business dominance in legal spheres specifically and "the modern class problem" generally (SL 886). But Weber seems determined to characterize these demands for social justice in terms of dangerous irrationality or contemptible emotionality. Not only labor, but also special interest groups and ideologically motivated lawyers, challenge legal formalism by factoring in issues such as "economic duress" on, or asymmetries in, the capabilities of legal parties involved in contracts (SL 886). From a legal standpoint, these are "entirely amorphous" *ethical*, and not rigorously *juridical*, standards whose legitimation lies with substantive notions of justice and not formal aspects of legality (SL 886). The two are fundamentally incompatible for Weber. He blames progressive lawyers for pursuing this agenda because it better rewards them than the formally rational model in a number of respects: they can satisfy their desire for self-aggrandizement, express their ethical-emotional inclinations, and alleviate their boredom with formal adjudication (SL 886).

While Weber does not come to the following conclusion, his presentation of the evidence, and its location in his work, suggest that the attitude and behavior of contemporary lawyers are the result of a particular crisis of adjudication, and not merely an indication of the lawyerly disposition of jurists generally or even within a thriving *Rechtsstaat* particularly. The lawyers' disposition and Weber's account of it here bear the traces of, to use an unfashionable term, "ideology." Weber's description of it does not match the care with which he intuits the subjective disposition of legal actors throughout the rest of the work, even in the passages devoted to subjects' "belief" in legitimacy that we observed Habermas criticize as deficient in the previous chapter. Weber's account of the motivations of lawyers in the emerging *Sozialstaat* raises, but does not explain, the following questions: until very recently in Weber's context, why did some jurists completely ignore the idea that even the most formally rational law entails some law creation by judges?[39] Why does this issue of judge-made law become more intense in the contemporary controversies between the Free Law and the Historical schools, mentioned by Weber, than it had been only fifty years earlier?[40] Weber exposes the disastrous results of judges acting as they believe legislators would in cases where statutes do not provide clear rules: the ensuing "value-compromises" lead to the

[39] See Korioth, "The Shattering of Methods in Late Wilhelmine Germany," 41–50. He introduces essays by Weber, Jellinek, Kelsen, and Schmitt from the first decade of the twentieth century that grapple with the limits of formally positivist conceptions of judicial application.
[40] See Caldwell, *Popular Sovereignty and the Crisis of German Constitutional Law*, 41–4, 52–4.

disabling of abstract norms, the rise of concrete evaluations, and therefore "not only nonformal but irrational lawfinding" (SL 887). But it sounds as if this is only a recent state of affairs.

It is quite possible that these controversies do not reflect timeless questions that plague the formal law of the *Rechtsstaat* – after all, they were seldom raised during its mid-nineteenth-century pinnacle. These issues that would later be grouped under the "indeterminacy of law" thesis made famous by the Legal Realist movement and especially the CLS movement are rather indications of the specific circumstances of the emerging *Sozialstaat*, even if Weber does not explicitly link them to them. Weber criticizes the jurists of his time who celebrate as normative opportunities the inevitability of judge-made law and the indeterminacy that accompanies it. But Weber does not link these developments to the phenomena that he described just a few pages earlier: the fact that social groups, most notably labor and capital, are negotiating law whose content is dictated by the concrete specifics of the disputes and the agreements, the interests of the parties themselves, and the decisions of the arbitrators presiding over these cases.

This situation, as much as the selfish or emotional disposition of lawyers, more directly accounts for the prevalence of "gaps" in the law and of "concrete decisions" in adjudication, as well as the growing difficulty of applying general norms to concrete cases (SL 887).[41] Weber criticizes the lawyers who promote this situation – perhaps appropriately – of fleeing "into the irrational" and away from "the increasing rationalization of legal technique" (SL 889). But it is not clear that their autonomous behavior and desire "to heighten their feeling of self-importance and sense of power" is the sole or even most important cause of the situation at hand (SL 889).[42]

---

[41] See Michael Stolleis, "Die Entstehung des Interventionsstaates und das öffentliche Rechtsstaat," *Zeitschrift für neuere Rechtsgeschichte* 11 (1989), 129–47.

[42] In these passages, Weber notes the differences in the continental and common law approaches to legal interpretation and attributes these to the idiosyncrasies of the respective legal professions (SL 889): namely, the fact that the former applies legal propositions logically derived from statutory texts, while the latter is practiced "essentially as an empirical art" (SL 890–1). He associates these differences with political development only secondarily and with economic factors even more remotely (SL 889–90). But it is not clear what exact causal weight should be attributed to legal training, and why political factors are somewhat determinate and economic ones only tangential. Either self-evidently relying on his other analyses of the rise of capitalism or shutting these out completely in the legal context, Weber declares: "Once everything is said and done

This voluntarist account of the crisis of formally rational law continues as Weber assesses the contemporary role of expanding democracy. As
discussed in the previous chapter, Weber understands popular demands
for justice to undermine formal legal rationality (SL 892). In particular, the
institution of juries, which he associates with "irrational khadi justice,"
has only affective or emotional justifications for Weber. The jury trial
"appeals to the sentiments of the layman, who feels annoyed whenever
he meets with formalism in a concrete case, and it satisfies the emotional
demands of those underprivileged classes which clamor for substantive
justice" (SL 892).[43] As in ancient Rome, Weber avers, jury selection in contemporary liberal democracies is the site of severe class conflict (SL 892).
Rather than choosing to test empirically the republican intuition that collective bodies of citizens will reach the most rational or at least most
fair outcome, Weber selects an example that irrefutably demonstrates
their bias: in Germany, predominantly male juries will rarely convict
another man of rape unless they are assured of the "virtue" of the female
accuser (SL 893). Weber takes a further slap at German manhood by
noting, "in Germany female virtue is not held in great respect anyway"
(SL 893). Notwithstanding the accuracy of this anecdote – and however
heartening is Weber's sensitivity to the issue of gender inequality – one
still must ask: is this the most representative example by which we should
evaluate the efficacy of juries?

Previously in the text, Weber opened the possibility that the collapse
of formal law is due to socioeconomic and historical developments such
as structural changes in bargaining and conflict resolution within *Sozialstaat* arrangements. However, we just observed that Weber ultimately
chooses to emphasize voluntarist factors like the motivations of lawyers
and class partisans. At the close of SL, this voluntarism translates into
a largely ideational account of the crisis of formal law. Weber expressly
minimizes causes associated with "technical and economic developments"
and, in a rather hyper-Kantian fashion, holds up categorical antinomies
as the source of the contemporary crisis and controversies. He attributes
the latter to "the insoluble conflict between the formal and the substantive

---

about these differences in historical developments, modern capitalism prospers equally
and manifests essentially identical economic traits under legal systems containing rules
and institutions which considerably differ from each other at least from the juridical
point of view" (SL 890).

[43] For a refutation of the thesis that coherent justice is incompatible with extensive democratization, see Ian Shapiro, *Democratic Justice* (New Haven, CT: Yale University Press,
1999), which, in fact evaluates the example of juries, 35, 50–1.

principles of justice, which may clash with one another even where their respective protagonists belong to one and the same social class" (SL 893).[44] At this crucial point in SL, two competing ways of *conceiving* the institutionalization of justice through law, formally or substantively, are the source of the contemporary crisis, not the structural deficiencies of the *Rechtsstaat* associated with economic chaos and inequality that necessitated redress through *Sozialstaat* strategies. Weber seems to flee from further interrogation of the way the current theoretical controversy is embedded within a structural transformation and elevates the former to a timeless irresolvable status.

In any case, Weber predicts that the "informal administration of justice" may not ultimately benefit the working class in the way that legal ideologues and labor organizers promise (SL 893). Shifting the grounds of his critique yet again, Weber turns to the standpoint of social class: the hoped-for "bureaucratized judiciary" will still be composed of elite recruits who can turn only so far away from the interests of the ruling class (SL 893). In one of his more categorical statements, Weber asserts that the law is, after all, a conservative institution that inhibits "creativity" in almost all contexts (SL 894). Even before the development of formally rational law, which imposes certain restrictions on juridical behavior, earlier procedural formalism and precedence reliance hindered innovation. This is a curious claim to make given that the context in which it is uttered is precisely characterized by the prevalence of judge- and lawyer-initiated "innovation." Weber has been complaining about this covertly or expressly throughout the work. In this rather spiteful instance of *Schadenfreude*, Weber seems to be warning the adherents of social democracy that, despite apparent advances in recent years, the legal system is not the appropriate vehicle for achieving their ends. But does he fear that they will fail or rather succeed? Weber may be guilty of whistling in the dark.

On the heels of these outbursts, Weber suggests that with the exception of legal prophets (e.g., Moses), most legal actors in any context will be reluctant to admit that they actively *create* law. They prefer to understand and present themselves as mouthpieces of extant norms and as appliers of law rather than its originators (SL 894). But Weber's contemporary circumstances may encourage more frequent fresh creation and innovation

---

[44] A recent example of the long tradition focusing on Weber's fixation on antinomial or incommensurable principles is John Patrick Diggins, *Max Weber: Politics and the Spirit of Tragedy* (New York: Basic Books, 1996). See Richard Wolin's review of the book, which takes up these issues in *The New Republic* (26 September 1996).

of the law – with deleterious implications: "the juristic precision of judicial opinions will be seriously impaired if sociological, economic, or ethical argument were to take the place of legal concepts" (SL 894). Again, Weber understands the prevalence of these approaches as almost personal "reactions" to the dominance of specialization and rationalization in modern law that create the conditions of a new structural scenario (SL 894). Not to engage in chicken-and-egg quagmires, but if judges are responding to and taking advantage of a new complexity in the law, the *Rechtsstaat* must no longer be as formally elegant and its workings no longer so discretely transparent. Or is the behavior of lawyers and judges not the agent of a transformation, as Weber seems to assert so desperately in these passages, but rather a symptom of an already-changed scenario, one whose structural characteristics Weber had associated earlier in SL with the recent adjudication of organizational relations?

Weber chooses to conclude on the more "subjective" or "voluntarist" note: since the law is becoming more technical and specialized, jurors and lay judges will be deployed more often in an attempt to compensate for this development politically, that is, by democratic access to the legal apparatus. But, again, Weber is caught in a tautology: does the formal rationality of the *Rechtsstaat* cause or allow inequalities and pathologies to which the demand for regulations and the redistributions that characterize the *Sozialstaat* is the subjective response and concrete measure of redress? Or is it *Rechtsstaat* rationality itself, linearly conceived, that has become so sheerly rational and specialized that the social democratic outcry is a natural response to it? Put bluntly: what is the source of contemporary legal irrationality, the *Rechtsstaat* or the *Sozialstaat*? Weber does not answer explicitly. In either case, he insists, no normative content, whatever the aspirations of legal subjects and actors, can succeed in filling contemporary law:

Inevitably the notion must expand that the law is a rational technical apparatus, which is continually transformable in the light of expediential considerations and devoid of all sacredness of content. This fate may be obscured by the tendency of acquiescence in the existing law, which is growing in many ways for several reasons, but it cannot really be stayed. All of the modern sociological and philosophical analyses, many of which are of a high scholarly value, can only contribute to strengthen this impression, regardless of the content of their theories concerning the nature of law and the judicial process. (SL 895)

Contemporary law may appear to be increasingly moral, Weber warns, but the forces advancing this moralization will bring about only a new formalism that, detached from the specific formally rational characteristics of the *Rechtsstaat*, is actually irrational. In the previous chapter, we observed Habermas's uncovering the practical morality that lay beneath Weber's description of *Rechtsstaat* rationality. And in the next chapter, we will see how Habermas attempts to rectify the irrational pathologies that Weber insisted were inherent in *Sozialstaat* law. Here I will continue to emphasize the historical logic accompanying Weber's analysis and begin to draw out its implications.

Throughout the bulk of SL, Weber has been operating with a rather abstract narrative of the history of legal rationalization. Patriarchal households and then patrimonial monarchies, characterized by a fusion of legislation, execution, and adjudication and the preponderance of groups, are succeeded by the *Rechtsstaat*, characterized by its specific institutional and sociopolitical separations and a focus on individual freedom *to* contract and *from* state interference. The relationship between the two models is not one attributable to causality but one characterized by *idealtypische* contrasts. I have argued in this chapter that this particular narrative of legal rationalization is motivated by Weber's inability to analyze the emerging *Sozialstaat* in positively empirical and appropriately historical terms and his need to subsume it under the categories of patrimonialism and, sometimes, the reverse. Consequently, the *Rechtsstaat* becomes the paragon of rational law now in dire jeopardy or actually having become obsolete. But in the dominant account of SL there is no motor of causality between patrimonialism and the *Rechtsstaat,* and only inconsistent ones posited between the latter and the *Sozialstaat.*

But in the passage cited at length earlier, Weber attempts to fit this narrative into his more causally concerned rationalization thesis. In this account, the process of rationalization and specialization that culminated in the formalism of the *Rechtsstaat* continues to drive on, eventually undermining it in the *Sozialstaat.* Rationalization leveled and rendered uniform the hierarchical and overlapping jurisdictions of the *ständische* Middle Ages, only to facilitate new irregular legal arrangements among different occupations and between labor and capital at the turn of the twentieth century. In his account here, there *is* historical continuity throughout Western history, one familiar to students of Weber's rationalization thesis but that is, by and large, surprisingly absent from the bulk of SL. It also bears similarity with the social evolutionism that Habermas adopts in his mature writings; an evolutionism in which social actors adapt through learning processes to new structural constraints. In this case, social agents pursuing egalitarian measures – specifically, economic actors seeking equilibrating policies and lawyers and jurists seeking their own aggrandizement – adapt to law as a "rational technical apparatus...continually transformable in the light of expediential considerations," with results that are deformingly irrational.

Weber's historical logic becomes a little clearer in the short history of global legal development he subsequently provides in the final pages of SL. Weber confesses that his account is purely theoretical, but he assures the reader of the general accuracy of his unabashedly evolutionary account. Weber suggests that law develops in a series of successive stages: the charismatic revelation of prophets, the precedent-based practice of legal honoratiores, law imposition by secular or theocratic powers, and, finally, the systematization of law and its administration by formally trained experts (SL 882). This process suggests to Weber that formalism initially emerges from the strict procedures of primitive magical/legal practice, proceeding then to increasingly rational forms of lawmaking and lawfinding, sometimes taking a detour through theocratic or patrimonial substantive agendas (SL 882). Eventually law achieves "logical sublimation," "deductive rigor," and "rational technique," that is, the formally rational characteristics of the *Rechtsstaat* (SL 882).

Weber concedes that this line of development is not followed everywhere in either process or result, and that deviations are usually attributable to political intervention and reigning power competitions, such as those between secular and theocratic authorities (SL 882–3). But this account does confirm a particularly important aspect of Weber's understanding of legal-historical development: any departures from this general schema are to be understood as pathological reversions to irrationality and dangerous regressions to arbitrariness. From this standpoint, it would be difficult to understand any departure from the *Rechtsstaat* – even ones that would correct the deficiencies of the socioeconomic arrangement concomitant with it – as anything other than a signal of crisis and collapse. Throughout SL, Weber attempts to struggle out of this corner into which he boxes himself. But because the departure from formalism is not law, which had reached a privileged conceptual pinnacle in the *Rechtsstaat* and Weber's account of it, Weber (1) cannot entertain the new legitimately juridical aspects of *Sozialstaat* law and (2) cannot ascertain those aspects of the new historical configuration that are not regressive and threats to freedom. As Weber mentions earlier, the real injustices of the *Rechtsstaat* cannot be successfully criticized from the juridical standpoint alone. But Weber's SL, read in tandem with his more expressly political writings of the period, show that he cannot appreciate the progressive possibilities of law in the *Sozialstaat*.[45]

One might be tempted to attribute to Weber's class position the drawbacks of his analysis of law and the decline of the *Rechtsstaat*. Obviously, Weber harbors many of the prejudices of the nineteenth-century bourgeois society that formed him and that he knows is collapsing before him.[46] For instance, his discussion of the domains that once did or should pertain to private and public law overtly brackets the authoritarian aspects of the private that were *not* dissolved by the *Rechtsstaat*. The authority of the landlord and the head of the family resembles that of the manorial lord and remains protected with the rise of private law. In other words, laissez-faire bourgeois society held within it the patrimonial concrete domination that Weber later would attribute to the *Sozialstaat*. It did not take the rise of the *Sozialstaat* to raise the specter of authoritarianism in the nineteenth and twentieth centuries – it was quite compatible with the *Rechtsstaat*. As noted earlier, Weber acknowledges this but never integrates it into his analysis, instead choosing to consign his observations along these lines to a Marxoid subsection of the work.

Weber could have elaborated on how the widespread lack of access to courts, as well as the reluctance of courts to engage in certain jurisdictions, facilitated a greater level of lawlessness in the nineteenth century than is generally acknowledged. The lawlessness of an absent state, or a state restrained by the power of certain groups of socioeconomic elites, could be even *guiltier* of an unjust relationship with society than one that tries

---

[45] On the specific ways that Weber misses the compatibility of *Sozialstaat* practices and legal standards, see Kettler and Meja, "Legal Formalism and Disillusioned Realism in Max Weber," 329–31. On this issue in general: in the European context, see Günther Teubner, ed., *Dilemmas of Law and the Welfare State* (New York: de Gruyter, 1988), and Neil MacCormick, *Legal Right and Social Democracy: Essays in Legal and Political Philosophy* (Oxford: Clarendon Press, 1984); and in the U.S. context, Cass R. Sunstein, *After the Rights Revolution: Reconceiving the Regulatory State* (Cambridge, MA: Harvard University Press, 1990); Sunstein, *Free Markets and Social Justice* (Oxford: Oxford University Press, 1997); and Bruce Ackerman, *Social Justice and the Liberal State* (New Haven, CT: Yale University Press, 1981).

[46] For explorations along these lines, see the following contributions to Asher Horowitz and Terry Maley, eds., *The Barbarism of Reason: Max Weber and the Twilight of Enlightenment* (Toronto: University of Toronto Press, 1994): David Beetham, "Max Weber and the Liberal Political Tradition," 99–112; and Tracy Strong, "Max Weber and the Bourgeoisie," 113–26.

to ameliorate injustice, however imperfectly.[47] Weber never raises this issue to question the validity and force of what would become the neo-conservative critique of the *Sozialstaat*.

Conclusion

Perhaps more than any other segment of Weber's *Economy and Society*, SL bears the traces of the context in which it was written. Weber does not formulate ideal types for legal phenomena that are as abstract as, for instance, those illustrating the legitimate types of authority: in certain respects, "formally rational law" is too closely identified with the *Rechtsstaat*, a highly specific historical configuration, to function like the category of "traditional authority." Moreover, when Weber delves into law's historical past, he seldom writes in a way that approaches the more "pure" kind of history to be found in, say, his sociology of religions: he constantly resorts to comparison and contrast – sometimes implicit, more often explicit – with the emerging realities of the *Sozialstaat*. We may conclude that the present imposes itself on both the timeless and the determinably past aspects of Weber's analysis of law, that is, on the formulation of analytical concepts and the pursuit of historical fact.

More alarmingly, these abstract categories and historical examples, already to some extent "contaminated" by the present context, are then deployed in Weber's description and evaluation of the present. The historical categories that Weber revives largely consign the emerging future to some kind of replay of the past, and hence, given his normative privileging of *Rechtsstaat*, a regression into civilizational decline. Can social change be tracked properly and normative implications prescribed convincingly through such a methodology? Even without offering a more viable alternative at this juncture – a justifiable demand – the answer is clearly, no. Yet, the question itself is especially pressing for research in our own time, especially for attempts to grapple with large-scale changes perhaps as dramatic as that which confronted Weber. In Chapter 6, I will consider the literature on European integration as a subcontext of the transformation represented by globalization. Law, again, will be at the center of

---

[47] See Michael Mann, *The Sources of Social Power: The Rise of Classes and Nation-States, 1760–1914*, Vol. 2 (Cambridge: Cambridge University Press, 1993); and Louis Adamic, *Dynamite: A Century of Class Violence in America, 1830–1930* (New York: Left Bank Distribution, 1990).

attempts to apprehend the nature of the transformation and secure the means of preserving or advancing progressive political agendas within it. These fields of research have lacked the guidance, however flawed, of a figure of Weber's stature and brilliance, and, ironically, they often retrace theoretical steps reminiscent of the master without the suggestive benefits of his efforts. In Chapter 5, I will evaluate Habermas's impressive attempt to assert himself as *the* theorist of European integration in a more successful way than Weber was *the* theorist of the *Sozialstaat*. But first, in the next chapter, we have to examine the legally enabled, deliberatively rational model of the *Sozialstaat* that Habermas formulates to address the social pathologies and legal dead ends exposed by Weber, ones that Habermas wishes to transpose to the supranational level in his writings on the EU.

4

Habermas's Deliberatively Legal *Sozialstaat*

Democracy, Adjudication, and Reflexive Law

Between Facts and Norms,[1] Jürgen Habermas's magnum opus of legal and state theory, clarifies the model of a communicatively grounded and legally facilitated social democracy, a model anticipated in *Public Sphere* and more generally elaborated in TCA.[2] In this chapter, I focus on Habermas's attempt to address problems that have their roots in Weimar debates over law and democracy, and that can be traced back even further to Weber's legal sociology. In particular, I address Habermas's efforts to (1) translate his system/lifeworld theory of modernity into juridical terms; (2) formulate a theory of constitutional democracy that corrects the inadequacies and avoids the excesses of narrowly proceduralist or excessively substantive alternatives; (3) develop a theory of legal adjudication that is neither rationally incoherent nor inherently elitist; and (4) explicate a strategy by which the advantages of the *Rechtsstaat* and *Sozialstaat* models of law might be made efficacious in contemporary circumstances.[3] In

---

[1] Jürgen Habermas, *Between Facts and Norms: Contributions to a Discourse Theory of Law and Democracy* (1992), trans. William Rehg (Cambridge, MA: MIT Press, 1996), hereafter BFN. Amended translations conform to Habermas, *Faktizität und Geltung: Beiträge zur Diskurstheorie des Rechts und des demokratischen Rechtsstaats* (Frankfurt a.M.: Suhrkamp, 1992), hereafter FG.

[2] Habermas, *The Structural Transformation of the Public Sphere: An Inquiry into a Category of Bourgeois Society* (1962), trans. Thomas Burger with Frederick Lawrence (Cambridge, MA: MIT Press, 1989), hereafter STPS; *The Theory of Communicative Action, Vol. 1: Reason and the Rationalization of Society* (1981), trans. Thomas McCarthy (Boston: Beacon Press, 1984), hereafter TCA1; *The Theory of Communicative Action, Vol. 2: Lifeworld and System: A Critique of Functionalist Reason* (1981), trans. Thomas McCarthy (Boston: Beacon Press, 1987), hereafter TCA2.

[3] For previous treatments of some of these issues, see Klaus Eder, "Critique of Habermas' Contribution to the Sociology of Law," *Law and Society Review* 22 (1988), 931–44;

addition, I lay the groundwork for a critique of Habermas's attempt to transpose this model to a supranational level, a critique to which I will devote the next chapter in its entirety.

By now, we should not be surprised to find in the title of BFN categories familiar from Weber's "Sociology of Law" and from the latter's essay on "Legal Theory and Sociology."[4] Habermas's tome, almost as mammoth as Weber's, purports to mediate the opposition between the empirical facticity (*Faktizität*) and abstract validity (*Geltung*) expressed in its title, and he discusses contemporary scholarly approaches that prioritize each. Yet, behind the norm dismissing the factually fixated systems theory of Niklas Luhmann,[5] a theory frequently criticized in the work, looms the specter of Carl Schmitt; and behind the empirically blind normativity of John Rawls[6] stands the figure of Hans Kelsen. According to Habermas, Luhmannian "sociological theories of law" convey a "false realism that underestimates the empirical impact of the normative presuppositions of existing legal practice" (BFN xl), while the Rawlsian "philosophical theories of justice" are problematically formulated "in vacuo" socially – that is, to a great extent oblivious to social reality and the politically marginalizing effects of purely abstract categories (BFN 57). I explore Habermas's negation of these mutually insufficient positions presently. In Chapter 5, I will ask whether his mediation of them is appropriate for a contemporary crisis of the state, one in which the *Sozialstaat* is being superseded, or, on the contrary, is an unwittingly anachronistic effort that replays the earlier Weberianly cast crisis of an emerging *Sozialstaat*.

Walter T. Murphy, "The Habermas Effect: Critical Theory and Academic Law," *Current Legal Problems* 42 (1989), 135–65; Karlo Tuori, "Discourse Ethics and the Legitimacy of the Law," *Ratio Juris* 2 (1989), 125–43; Wibren Van der Burg, "Jürgen Habermas on Law and Morality: Some Critical Comments," *Theory, Culture & Society* 7 (1990), 105–11; William E. Scheuerman, "Neumann v. Habermas: The Frankfurt School and the Rule of Law," *Praxis International* 13 (1993), 50–67; and Mathieu Deflem, "Law in Habermas' *Theory of Communicative Action*," *Philosophy & Social Criticism* 20 (1994), 33–42.

[4] Weber, "Economy and Social Norms" and "Sociology of Law" in *Economy and Society: An Outline of Interpretive Sociology*, Guenther Roth and Claus Wittich, eds., 2 vols. (Berkeley: University of California Press, 1978), 311–38, 641–899, hereafter SL; and Weber, "On Legal Theory and Sociology" (commentary on Hermann Kantorowicz, 1911), trans. Belinda Cooper, in Bernhard Schlink and Arthur Jacobson, eds., *Weimar: A Jurisprudence of Crisis* (Berkeley: University of California Press, 2000), 50–4.

[5] See Niklas Luhmann, *Legitimation durch Verfahren* (Darmstadt: Luchterhand, 1969) and *A Sociological Theory of Law*, trans. Elizabeth King and Martin Albrow (Boston: Routledge & Kegan Paul, 1985).

[6] See John Rawls, *A Theory of Justice* (Cambridge, MA: Harvard University Press, 1971) and *Political Liberalism* (New York: Columbia University Press, 1993).

1. Habermas on Language and Law, Lifeworld and System

In BFN, Habermas continues to engage Weber's undertheorized account of legality and legitimacy in terms of his system–lifeworld distinction (BFN 169ff., 295–302, 319–21). As elaborated in Chapter 2, this distinction was originally set out most fully in his two-volume social-theoretical epic TCA.[7] Habermas's TCA-based account of modernity provides the basis for his efforts to fill the normative deficit left by Weber's approach to law, wherein law is *not* regarded as an institution that reflects deliberatively derived moral consensus, but rather as an expression of concrete force. The BFN attempt to draw out the normative dimension from Weberian legal sociology is tied to Habermas's reconfiguring the model of state and society presupposed by traditional social theory. In this effort, Habermas detaches the economy from "the society" component of the nineteenth-century binary state/society model and attaches it to "the state," thereby forming what he calls the "system," that is, that part of modern social structures concerned with the material reproduction and administrative regulation of society. Habermas argues that the system functions primarily through the language of strategic rationality.

What remains of society in the nineteenth-century model Habermas re-constructs as the lifeworld, that is, that part of modern social structures

---

[7] On the relationship between TCA and BFN, see Kenneth Baynes, "Democracy and the *Rechtsstaat*: Habermas' *Faktizität und Geltung*," in Stephen K. White, ed., *The Cambridge Companion to Habermas* (Cambridge: Cambridge University Press, 1995); Dews, "Agreeing What's Right," *London Review of Books* 1, no. 9, (May 13, 1993), 26–70; and Deflem, "Law in Habermas' *Theory of Communicative Action*." The ensuing discussion in this section is a necessarily brief, but hopefully not excessively crude, summary of the combined arguments of the two works, as well as those of two important works written by Habermas in the years between the publication of TCA and BFN: see Habermas, *Moral Consciousness and Communicative Action*, trans. Christian Lenhardt and Shierry Weber Nicholson (Cambridge, MA: MIT Press, 1990) and *Justification and Application: Remarks on Discourse Ethics*, trans. Ciaran Cronin (Cambridge, MA: MIT Press, 1993). For excellent discussions of Habermas's communicative ethics, see the essays by Stephen K. White, Georgia Warnke, J. Donald Moon, Mark Warren, and Simone Chambers in White, ed., *The Cambridge Companion to Habermas*; David Ingram, "The Limits and Possibilities of Communicative Ethics for Democratic Theory," *Political Theory* 21 (1993); *The Communicative Ethics Controversy*, ed. Seyla Benhabib and Fred Dallmayr (Cambridge: MIT Press, 1990); James Bohman, "Communication, Ideology and Democratic Theory," *American Political Science Review* 84 (1990); 94–109; Jean Cohen, "Discourse Ethics and Civil Society," *Philosophy and Social Criticism* 14 (1988), 315–29; Seyla Benhabib, "The Utopian Dimension in Communitarian Ethics," *New German Critique* 85 (1985), 83–96; and Agnes Heller, "The Discourse Ethics of Habermas: Critique and Appraisal," *Thesis Eleven: Rethinking Social and Political Theory* 10–11 (1984–5), 5–17.

comprising the family, free associations, religion, and so on. The life-world reproduces culture symbolically through a communicative ratio-nality characterized by an implicit intention to reach understanding in virtually every utterance of communication. Habermas emphasizes the heterogeneous character of the lifeworld when he describes the commu-nicative activity that people practice in the institutions of civil society, such as public spheres and weak and strong publics. These informal insti-tutions are the loci that generate what he terms "communicative power" (BFN 151–7). The lifeworld is economically dependent on the system to provide the material requisites of life, and is politically dependent on it to enforce the communicatively derived decisions generated through civil society, public spheres, and discursive publics. However, the lifeworld is potentially threatened by the social inequalities generated by the econ-omy and the potentially arbitrary administrative activities performed by the bureaucratic state apparatus, pathologies of modern life identified by Habermas as the "colonization of the lifeworld."

Habermas characterizes law as the mediator between the lifeworld and the system, the "transformer" that converts the communicative language of the lifeworld into the strategic language of the administrative state and the economy (BFN 56, 169). He purports to overcome the Webe-rian dilemma of formal procedures of lawmaking and factual instances of compliance that have no inherent normative content by rethinking polit-ical will formation in terms of a discourse theory of society. In so doing, Habermas claims to evade the problems of both "liberal" and "repub-lican" models of will formation. The former engenders a legitimation deficit by assuming preformed and somewhat rigidly held interests that either prevail, fail, or are compromised in the lawmaking process, thereby necessarily creating political losers. The latter constrains the possibilities of democracy by placing limits on what is open for discussion in polit-ical deliberation, for instance, the status of the republican polity itself.[8] Habermas outflanks both models by seeking to include all persons and possibly to gain the assent of *most* communicative actors affected by a particular law or policy.

Habermas thereby conceptualizes law in a way that renders its func-tioning both normatively rich and substantively rational. He avoids the coercive shadow of a law enforced upon those who have not consented

---

[8] On the liberal versus republican debate in constitutional law, see Cass R. Sunstein, "Prefer-ences and Politics," *Philosophy & Public Affairs* 20 (1991), 3–34; and Sunstein, "Beyond the Republican Revival," *Yale Law Journal* 97 (1988), 1539–54.

to it by guaranteeing that the collective and potentially unanimous will of a populace (or a particular part thereof) affected by a law is reflected in the making and enforcement of that law through the establishment of a communicative process free of coercion and capable of facilitating the transformation of interests and positions. Furthermore, Habermas ensures that law will not be accepted by its authors/subjects as mere convention by building into the process of lawmaking institutional opportunities for understanding, and therefore for the emergence of the best justifications for policy decisions, and by fostering compromises that are not necessarily the result of strategic bargains (BFN 180).

In the next section, I discuss just how Habermas understands law to simultaneously protect the lifeworld from the pathological excesses of an economically/bureaucratically functioning system and, conversely, to ensure that the system performs *only* as the rational instrument of the lifeworld. Moreover, Habermas purports to undertake this task without lapsing into, on the one hand, holistic and thereby potentially authoritarian notions of a quasi-homogeneous, democratic people or, on the other, excessively formalistic accounts of the relationships of legal actors and subjects that result in weak and vulnerable models of constitutional democracy. However, to conclude this section, I offer a brief clarification and defense of Habermas's discourse theory of law.

In assessing the merits of BFN, many critics appear to misapprehend the linguistic underpinnings of discourse theory when they suggest that Habermas arbitrarily insists on potentially unanimous consensus building in lawmaking and constitution making. One articulate, though in this instance misguided, commentator states that "the insistence on rational argumentation seems to be dictated more by the preferences of the discourse theorists than by any presupposed rules of language."[9] This common objection ignores Habermas's central arguments concerning the mutual understanding necessarily taken for granted in every act of speech. Even the most hostile or aggressive verbal directive assumes certain abilities of reception on the part of the addressee. When confronted with such assumptions, the aggressive addresser can either rationally accept the egalitarian notions presupposed in his speech act or concede that he is committing an irrational act, in which case he removes himself from the realm of rationally productive discourse and denies himself the privileges that, at least in the legal and political realms, coincide with consistent

---

[9] James Herget, *Contemporary German Legal Philosophy* (Philadelphia: University of Pennsylvania Press, 1996), 55.

argumentation.[10] The exposure of inconsistency invites a moment in which authority is challenged. The obvious historical examples of naked oppression to which critics often gesture as proof of the inefficacy of emancipatory discourse are rife with precisely the kinds of restrictions on free speech that Habermas suggests are performative self-negations on the part of those who wield power. Indeed, the example of Thrasymachus from Plato's *Republic* and the blush that Socrates induces in him reveal that power, no matter how cynically asserted, to be effective, must be communicatively legitimated by those over whom it is exercised.[11] This can, but need not necessarily, initiate a cycle of less legally restricted communication, which leads to further progressive political practice, which itself leads to more substantive forms of communication, and so on.[12] In this historical possibility lies the source of discourse theory's subversive and emancipatory potential.

Critics often resort to the charge that Habermas is "playing games" when he supposes the possibility of less coercive or even noncoercive communication, particularly when they attack the "ideal speech situation," which actually holds a relatively limited place in Habermas's generally more sociologically concrete theory.[13] Establishing rules for an imaginary

---

[10] See Stephen K. White, *The Recent Work of Jürgen Habermas: Reason, Justice and Modernity* (Cambridge: Cambridge University Press, 1990), 50, 56.

[11] Plato, *The Republic*, trans. G. M. A. Grube (Indianapolis: Hackett, 1997).

[12] David Dyzenhaus argues that in even the most "wicked" regimes, such as apartheid South Africa, it was the duty and sometimes the practice of officials, especially legal officials, to expose the inconsistent and hypocritical rationales of public officials making and enforcing unjust policies, and that this had, and could have had, an even more corrosive effect on the regime. See Dyzenhaus, *Judging the Judges, Judging Ourselves: Truth, Reconciliation and the Apartheid Legal Order* (Oxford: Oxford University Press, 1997). In my review of the book (*New York University Review of Law and Social Change* XXV, no. 1 [1999]), I suggest that such a practice should be generalized into a kind of judicial civil disobedience that might be deployed even in supposedly more just liberal democracies.

[13] See Ota Weinberger, "Habermas on Democracy and Justice: Limits of a Sound Conception," *Ratio Juris* 7 (July 1994), 239–53; Michael K. Power, "Habermas and the Counterfactual Imagination," *Cardozo Law Review* 17 (1996), 1163–89; and Herget, *Contemporary German Legal Philosophy*, especially, 59. For a much more measured consideration and critique of Habermas on these grounds, see White, *The Recent Work of Jürgen Habermas*, 55–6. Gutmann and Thompson offer an alternative deliberative theory of democracy unencumbered by the more elaborate philosophical/sociological justifications, and often more controversial expectations, of Habermas's approach. See Amy Gutmann and Dennis Thompson, *Democracy and Disagreement* (Cambridge, MA: Harvard University Press, 1996). Whether it is any less open to criticism because of these differences, see Stephen Macedo, ed., *Deliberative Politics: Essays on Democracy and Disagreement* (Oxford: Oxford University Press, 1999).

game that no one else plays purportedly exhibits the trivially tautological character of discourse theory. But the point of discourse theory is not, as many suggest, that advocating its adoption in law and politics is equivalent to "telling someone that if he or she wants to play tennis, the rules of tennis must be followed."[14] Rather, it means that if two or more persons want to play tennis correctly and fairly, certain strictures apply. To play without a net is, according to communicatively established understanding, not to play tennis properly. Moreover, to play with the hand of one of the participants tied behind her back is to play inequitably. Most importantly, according to Habermas, the rules of law and politics are (factually) and should be (normatively) open-ended and subject to the constant and perpetual discussion, evaluation, and transformation of the rules of social life. This can never be conducted unilaterally or "monologically," in the style of Rawls's original position: this would entail, without consultation with socially or historically real others, arbitrary decisionism.[15] Therefore, the making and enforcement of laws and measures necessarily involves the input of all those affected by a particular policy. Habermas's writings, perhaps BFN most of all, show that the offhand dismissal of the jurisprudential usefulness of discourse theory by many critics can be justified only if the question of legitimacy is to be banished from the legal and political spheres.

2. Beyond Formalist and Vitalist Notions of Constitutional Democracy

The legitimacy problems of formal law can only be solved if the concrete aspects of legal systems can be linked with the abstract ones, most pressingly legal coercion and legal norm formation. Therefore, to establish more firmly accountability within the discourse theory of law, Habermas reconstructs the mutual relationship of facticity and validity (BFN 416), which is generally treated as separate and even competing entities in the self-understanding of German legal sociology and philosophy. In Chapter 1, we witnessed perhaps the most succinct version of this opposition in Weber's early social and legal theory essay, as well as the way these categories played out in Weimar debates over law in the *Sozialstaat*. The significance of these respective categories of "formalist" or "concretist"

---

[14] Herget, *Contemporary German Legal Philosophy*, 59.

[15] On the importance of fully considering concrete others in critical discourse theory, see Seyla Benhabib, *Situating the Self: Gender, Community, and Postmodernism in Contemporary Ethics* (London: Routledge, 1992), 1–22, 68–88, 148–241.

constitutional democracy and their relationship to each other reached a rather precarious point in the legal and political debates surrounding Germany's first attempt at democracy in the Weimar Republic, and arguably foreshadowed the Republic's eventual collapse and the subsequent triumph of National Socialism. The efforts of Hans Kelsen can be understood as an attempt to maintain a formal conception of legal normativity that allows for the expansion of democracy under welfare state conditions while, on the other hand, the work of Carl Schmitt represents a jurisprudential attempt to coerce the conformity of society with supposedly irresistible factually structural imperatives of concrete state intervention, a move that entails authoritarian consequences. The collapse of Weimar is often viewed as the victory of the latter hyperfactual over the former overly normative position, a victory all too easily facilitated by the inherent weakness of the former and the ruthlessness of the latter, that is, validity subdued by facticity. While the Weimar ghost of Carl Schmitt is treated in a mostly subtextual manner in BFN, Habermas more directly addresses Kelsen, Schmitt's primary Weimar interlocutor and critic. Kelsen's legal positivism was a progressive legal theory that sought to render state activity accountable to popular sovereignty through procedural means.[16] Habermas finds the Kelsenian tradition of procedural jurisprudence overly susceptible to "realist" dismissal by present-day hyperempirical interpreters such as Luhmann, who may share none of Schmitt's political predilections but whose skepticism regarding sheer normativity may corrode, in an equally devastating manner, the substantive efficacy of communicative power in procedural legality. In short, Habermas takes up the mission of mediating legal facticity and validity left unresolved by Weber, hypostatized by Schmitt and Kelsen, and valiantly if imperfectly attempted by jurists Richard Thoma and Hermann Heller.

Recall how in his previous work, Habermas subjected Weber's sociology of law, with its thin notion of legal validity, to an immanent critique that revealed the ways that procedural legality could, despite Weber's

---

[16] In a compelling interpretation, Dhananjai Shivakumar emphasizes Kelsen's affinities with Weber's neo-Kantianism over his more generally discussed relationship to Kantianism writ large in an effort to preserve the viability of Kelsen's jurisprudential methodology. See Dhananjai Shivakumar, "The Pure Theory as Ideal Type: Defending Kelsen on the Basis of Weberian Methodology," *Yale Law Journal* 105, no. 5 (1996), 1383–414. As I will discuss, Habermas attempts to address the deficiencies of both Weberian and Kelsenian methodologies, though himself employing something of a neo-Kantian approach in that effort.

assertions, entail substantive legitimacy.[17] Weber's work left open the question of whether the simple fact of the law – its recognition or its formal validity – was sufficient to render it substantively rational or legitimate. Whereas Schmitt cynically answered the riddle in the negative in *Legality and Legitimacy*,[18] and Luhmann, on the basis of sociological assumptions similar to those held by Weber and Schmitt, answered it with only a weak affirmative in *Legitimation Through Procedures*,[19] Kelsen's constitutional theory is the most elaborate effort to solve definitively this dilemma in favor of *formal proceduralism* or legal positivism.[20] Therefore, in BFN Habermas fully engages Kelsen's theory.

Again, Habermas has come to accept Weber's diagnosis of modernity, understood in terms of the destruction of socially legitimating natural law by the polytheism of a pluralizing enlightenment (BFN 145). In terms recalling the secularization thesis that I suggested crept into Habermas's theory in TCA, Habermas asserts that modern rationalization entails a "linguistification of the sacred," a sacred that once made the conventional background of the lifeworld more rigid (BFN 24). In TCA, Habermas suggested that the sacred "shrinks" under the expansion of communicatively generated rational criticism (TCA2 88). Hence, in BFN, he suggests that law and authority become legitimate in this post-secularization world only through broader democratization where more and more persons participate in the creation of lifeworld understandings (BFN 443). Habermas, however, acknowledges that the overtly formalist solutions of the early modern period do not hold sufficient legitimating potential on either normative or empirical grounds (BFN 146), and so he lays out two alternative versions of modern validity, both of which were previously analyzed by Weber: the factually based, empirically ascertained notion that registers

---

[17] See also Johannes Winckelmann, *Legitimität und Legalität im Max Webers Herrschaftssoziologie* (Tübingen: J. C. B. Mohr [Paul Siebeck], 1952).

[18] See Carl Schmitt, *Legality and Legitimacy* (1932), trans. Jeffrey Seitzer; intro. John P. McCormick (Durham, NC: Duke University Press, 2004).

[19] Luhmann, *Legitimation durch Verfahren*. On Luhmann and Schmitt, see Jean L. Cohen and Andrew Arato, *Civil Society and Political Theory* (Cambridge, MA: MIT Press, 1992), 323–5.

[20] For a more general overview of legal positivism, see the classics H. L. A. Hart, *Essays in Jurisprudence and Philosophy* (Oxford: Oxford University Press, 1983); Lon L. Fuller, *The Morality of Law* (New Haven, CT: Yale University Press, 1969); and Joseph Raz, *The Morality of Freedom* (Oxford: Clarendon Press, 1986). See also more recent considerations by Anthony J. Sebok, "Misunderstanding Positivism," *Michigan Law Review* 93 (1995), 2054–132; and Michael Stokes, "Formalism, Realism and the Concept of Law," *Law and Philosophy* 13 (1994), 115–59.

average compliance with the law and the normatively inclined notion of subjective recognition of the law's legitimacy (BFN 54).

As noted before, both are fundamentally unstable conceptions; in the former, the subjective aspect of the participant's attitude toward the law is rendered unimportant in comparison to her possibly coerced factual compliance with it, while in the latter, this subjective disposition is rendered inaccessible to social scientific observation, hence is potentially indeterminate, and further is formulated in terms of a "belief" that need not have a rational basis. In the first conception, the subject is conceived as a strategic actor for whom the law is merely a fact that structures behavior. In the second, the subject "believes in" the law with no assuredly rational account as to why, or whether, she will continue to do so, and with no observable or necessary link with the structure of the law itself (BFN 31). Thus, in Habermas's estimation, neither instrumentalism nor conventionalism is a sufficiently substantive legal orientation for ameliorating the risk of coercion and promoting the primacy of communicative over administrative power (BFN 33).

Kelsen's legal positivism remains a sophisticated attempt to combine these two notions of validity by transposing the requisite but inaccessible normativity of the subjective participant into the procedures of the law itself, thus cushioning the potential coerciveness of the law's positive facticity in state enforcement. However, Habermas perceptively illustrates how the attempt to embed normativity *within* institutional procedures of lawmaking actually forsakes any connection with real subjective personalities and hence defers *too much* to factual necessity. For Kelsen, the positive quality of a law itself renders that law legitimate; the fact that it was made by a set of procedures that ultimately can be traced back through other prearranged procedures to a previously established popular sanction renders it correct. Hence, for Habermas, Kelsen's famous "ought" in his "normativist" scheme of jurisprudence is ultimately "empirical" and not really "deontological" because it is constituted by state sanction and divorced from continuous interaction with subjectively normative practices. In Kelsen's elaborate architectonic construction of multiple, hierarchically arranged levels of norms, the persons who initially author these norms are either fictive or eclipsed soon after the act of authorship (BFN 86). Kelsen thus encourages those approaches to law that devote attention only to the already established formal procedures, and that themselves quickly expose the law's lack of normative resonance: "Once the moral and natural person has been uncoupled from the legal system, there is nothing to stop jurisprudence from conceiving rights along purely functional lines. This doctrine of rights hands on the baton to a systems theory that rids itself by methodological fiats of all normative considerations" (BFN 87).

Drawing upon arguments he expounded as early as in his classic essay "Dogmatism, Reason, and Decision,"[21] Habermas unmasks the fluidity that actually obtains between one-sided approaches emphasizing either facticity or validity when he demonstrates how a Kelsenian normativity is ultimately reliant upon a decisionist moment, a moment reminiscent of the Schmittian "decisionism" against which it is opposed in Kelsen's own self-understanding (BFN 38). Kelsen's tracing of all statutory validity to a basic will at the constitution's founding that serves as the "ground-norm" from which all others derive ultimately amounts to a might-makes-right proposition and leaves administrative policies beyond the reach of communicative regulation. Hence, Habermas charges, normativism "exhausts itself in the legalism of a political domination construed in positivist terms" (BFN 89). The democratic potential of this sovereign will is rendered static and normatively unaccountable. According to Habermas, in a theory like Kelsen's,

> The source from whence positive law may derive its legitimacy is not successfully explained. To be sure, the source of all legitimacy lays in the democratic lawmaking process, and this in turn calls on the principle of popular sovereignty. But the legal positivism, or *Gesetzespositivismus*, propounded in the Weimar period by professors of public law does not introduce this principle in such a way that the intrinsic moral content of the classical liberties...is preserved. In one way or another, the intersubjective meaning of legally defined liberties is overlooked.... (BFN 89)

Kelsen's type of legal formalism is not interactively dynamic because it cannot ensure that the imperatives of administrative power remain accountable to the democratic will. Once this will is all but metaphysically constituted in a founding act, or less dramatically in a parliamentary election, it has insufficient means to influence systemic forces continually. Through his discourse theory, however, Habermas purports to infuse Kelsen's merely formal characteristics of the law with a normative substance that would better ensure its legitimacy: "The law receives its full normative sense neither through its legal form per se [e.g., Kelsenian positivism], nor through an a priori moral content [e.g., natural law or

---

[21] Habermas, "Dogmatism, Reason and Decision: On Theory and Practice in Our Scientific Society" (1963), in *Jürgen Habermas on Society and Politics*, Steven Seideman, ed. (Boston: Beacon Press, 1989).

Rawlsian liberalism], but through a procedure of lawmaking that begets legitimacy" (BFN 135). To be more specific, if at every level of opinion and will formation, and law- and policymaking, there are structures in place that facilitate the full communicative interactions that lead to general assent, then the formality of legality can be rendered substantively legitimate: "If discourses...are the site where a rational will can take shape, then the legitimacy of law ultimately depends on a communicative arrangement: As participants in rational discourses, consociates under law must be able to examine whether a contested norm meets with, or could meet with, the agreement of all those affected" (BFN 103–4).

In contrast to Kelsen and Schmitt, who both presuppose something like a static will at the original moment of a constitution's founding (BFN 202), Habermas theorizes a process of will formation – a "concept of the political" standing as an alternative to both liberal and authoritarian models (BFN 150–1) – that is open to constant change but nevertheless remains stable through adherence to the procedures themselves: "The preferences entering into the political process are viewed not as something merely given but as inputs that, open to the exchange of arguments, can be discursively changed" (BFN 162–8, 181). The universality of "general assent" or "reasonable consensus" engendered by such proceedings ensures legitimacy that may be defined in terms of lifeworld control of the system (BFN 147, 155).[22] According to Habermas, a discourse theory of popular sovereignty poses no danger to liberty because it necessitates the inclusion and possibly the assent of everyone affected (BFN 89). Moreover, this theory requires deference to more rational arguments in general discussion, including those regarding the very definition of rights previously conceived of as prepolitical and potentially untouchable (BFN 89).

---

[22] Habermas's emphasis on the potential for "general assent" or "reasonable consensus" in societal and parliamentary will and opinion formation has already sparked vigorous commentary. In addition to Herget, *Contemporary German Legal Philosophy*, see William Rehg and James Bohman, "Discourse and Democracy: The Formal and Informal Bases of Legitimacy in Habermas's *Faktizität und Geltung*," *Journal of Political Philosophy* 4 (1996); William E. Scheuerman, "Between Radicalism and Resignation: Democratic Theory in Habermas's *Between Facts and Norms*" paper presented at the American Political Science Association annual meeting, San Francisco, August 29–September 1, 1996; Kenneth Baynes, "Democracy and the *Rechtsstaat*," and Simone Chambers, "Discourse and Democratic Practices," in White, ed., *The Cambridge Companion to Habermas*; Charles Larmore, "The Foundations of Modern Democracy: Reflections on Jürgen Habermas," *European Journal of Philosophy* 3 (1994), 55–68; Bernhard Peters, "On Reconstructive Legal and Political Theory," *Philosophy & Social Criticism* 20 (1994), 101–39; and Robert Alexy, "Basic Rights and Democracy in Habermas' Procedural Paradigm of the Law," *Ratio Juris* 7 (1994), 131–50.

For Habermas, subsequent liberal attempts to shore up the deficiencies of a Kelsenian normative framework perform scarcely better in addressing the Weberian normative void ultimately perpetuated by Kelsen himself. Rawls, for instance, ignores the factual side altogether, thus providing a reverse image of Kelsen, who, for his part, pays too much attention to legal form and not enough to its potentially normative content (BFN 60–1). However, Habermas's desire to build legitimacy into the legal order entails abandonment neither of Rawlsian moral-political normativity nor of Kelsenian formal-legal normativity. In fact, the latter still holds a par-ticular attraction for Habermas. Because of the Kantian inclinations of the work, which will be discussed later, Habermas deems "economical and elegant" certain characteristics of the liberal, statute-positivism tradition, of which Kelsen is the greatest representative, and he remarks that they "still have a certain suggestive power even today" (BFN 190). Habermas has in mind the fact that statutes are produced through parliamentary procedure, formulated in general terms, and subsumptive in character; that is, these statutes presuppose the hierarchy of the constitution over the legislature and the latter over the executive (BFN 191). In terms of Chapter 2, this hierarchy reflects the extent to which the different insti-tutions embody mutual understanding.

Thus, Habermas reconstructs the Kelsenian theory of formal law, essen-tially produces a substantive theory of legal procedure, and highlights the relationship of Kelsen's theory of popular sovereignty to the more author-itarian ones against which it is opposed in its self-understanding. Yet, having done so, Habermas is careful to distance his own conception of popular sovereignty from Rousseauian-cum-Schmittian interpretations, in which the political will of an empirically and physically existing col-lective group or community is prioritized over formal legal and constitu-tional procedures (BFN 102–3). In fact, Habermas appears to be *so* deeply concerned by the implications of this "concretist" notion of democracy that it often appears to cloud his thinking in other areas. For instance, the shadow of Schmitt prevents Habermas from seriously considering the creative and productive use of the executive branch exhibited in the separation of powers and checks and balances in various constitutional contexts – for example, that the executive might hold some leverage over the other branches through agenda-setting or popular appeals not neces-sarily dangerously "plebiscitary" in character. On the contrary, Habermas asserts rather curtly that such functions "are excluded" from his theory, and he raises in retort the ominous specter of *Führerdemokratie*: "Anyone who would want to replace a constitutional court by appointing the head of the executive branch as the 'Guardian of the Constitution' – as Carl Schmitt wanted to do in his day with the German president – thwarts the meaning of the separation of powers in the constitutional state into its very opposite" (BFN 241–2).

Habermas's somewhat extreme stance in this particular instance carries over to his criticisms of constitutional theorists like Bruce Ackerman, Frank Michelman, and Werner Becker, all of whom, he claims, unwittingly revive quasi-Schmittian notions of democracy. Habermas expresses grave reservations regarding Ackerman's "vitalist" constitutional approach to "constitutional moments," which he associates with the Schmittian notion of *Ausnahmezustand*, or the "exception" (BFN 277–8). He softens this charge somewhat in reference to Michelman (BFN 279), as well as to Becker, in whose empiricist (that is, overly "*faktische*") account of democracy Habermas finds shades of decisionism (BFN 295). In fact, at times it seems as though Habermas's own discourse-theoretic *Sozialstaat*, in its adamant insistence on multivocal (in contradistinction to monolithic) expressions of popular will, is expressly formulated in opposition to a Schmittian notion of democracy (BFN 136, 563, n. 75). But surely any political theory that calls itself democratic – that is, that understands itself as being grounded in a will of the people, however intersubjectively or procedurally conditioned – runs the risk of being considered Schmittian. More fine-grained differentiations among different means of ascertaining a "popular will" than Habermas offers at this point in BFN seem necessary.[23]

In any case, on the basis of the analysis conducted in Chapter 2, as well as my remarks here, Habermas can be understood to have solved at a certain high level of abstraction the dilemma left by Weber's legal sociology. The normative vacuum exposed in Weber's account is filled by Habermas's discourse theory of law, which postulates that law can be formulated in such a way as to garner and reflect the assent of those over whom it applies. This rules out the potential coercion entailed in arbitrary enforcement of the law over particular subjects and the potential irrationality of a formalist conception that allows for any outcome to be deemed valid provided it has complied with established procedure. Because the procedures themselves, as conceived by Habermas, are infused

---

[23] For instance, I distinguish the "attenuated plebiscitarianism" of any robust democratic theory from "vitalist plebiscitarianism" characteristic of Schmittian fascism in my "From Constitutional Technique to Caesarist Ploy: Carl Schmitt on Dictatorship" in *From Bonapartism to Fascism: Studies in the History and Theory of Dictatorship*, Peter Baehr and Melvin Richter, eds. (Cambridge: Cambridge University Press, 2005).

with the possibility of coercion-free communication and are amenable to change on the bases of such communication, the formalism of the law is neither empty nor irrational. Moreover, because the will to which lawmaking and law enforcement are accountable is *not* theorized as a singular homogeneous will, as conceived by competing Schmittian and Kelsenian constitutional notions, but is instead understood as anonymous and manifold, Habermas avoids the irrational excesses of nationalist or homogeneity-enforcing expressions of democracy.

Throughout this work, and as will become even more pronounced in Chapter 5 and the Conclusion, I criticize Habermas's privileging of a transhistorical, Kantian approach to law over a more Hegelian, historically specific one. However, here Habermas's "flight from Hegel" serves him well in at least one regard: he refrains from elaborating the particular qualities of the institutions that constitute the lawmaking transition from lifeworld to law itself, or of those institutions by which law fastens the interests of the lifeworld to the system. While many consider this omission a flaw,[24] Habermas is consistent in leaving the determination of these institutions to the decisions of deliberating democratic publics and not to the ruminations of German philosophers.

3. Rational and Democratically Accessible Adjudication

BFN offers a comprehensive account of how modern law facilitates the potential for democratic communicative power such that systemic threats posed by state power and economic inequality are checked or redirected at every institutional level.[25] The constitutional means of achieving this, articulated in anti-Weberian or reconstructed-Weberian terms, were already foreshadowed in *Communicative Action*, as we observed in Chapter 2. In BFN, Habermas tackles another aspect of modern law that Weber's legal sociology posed as problematic, rationally democratic politics: adjudication. Habermas attempts to demonstrate how communicative procedures can be built into the postparliamentary – and traditionally only quasi-democratically legitimate – judicial practices of constitutional government. As we observed in Chapters 1 and 3, adjudicative rationality and legitimacy were called into question by the rise of the *Sozialstaat*: can

---

[24] See, for instance, Chambers, "Discourse and Democratic Practices."
[25] On the important differences between the preparliamentary and parliamentary modes of communication in Habermas's "two-track" approach, see Baynes, "Democracy and the *Rechtsstaat*," 216.

legal interpretation be coherent under regulative and redistributive conditions, and are judges sufficiently connected to the democratic process? In BFN, Habermas specifically addresses the question of how law is to be interpreted "with both internal consistency and rational external justification so as to guarantee simultaneously the certainty of law and its rightness" (BFN 199). Habermas carefully considers three post–natural law approaches to contemporary adjudication – hermeneutics, realism, and positivism – as well as the sophisticated proposals of Ronald Dworkin and Klaus Günther, but he is most intensely interested in the wholesale assault on adjudication launched by scholars associated with the Critical Legal Studies (CLS) movement.²⁶

As with most of the legal issues that Habermas sets out to clarify, Weber initially frames the dilemma entailed by adjudication. In a famous passage from SL, Weber compares conceptions of the judge, on the one hand, as a vending machine into whose head the appropriate statutes and case materials are poured and from whose mouth pops forth the eternally correct decision, and, on the other, an unbounded creator of law who negotiates the fundamentally unbridgeable gap between rule and case with his or her own ultimately arbitrary decision (SL 979, 756; cf. 656, 811, 895, 1395). These two paradigms confront each other in the judge-as-automaton versus judge-as-lawgiver models (SL 758, 894; cf. 979, 1395). In SL and elsewhere, Weber is ambivalent as to which model corresponds most closely to reality. Habermas seeks to move beyond these alternatives by evaluating contemporary attempts to resolve the dilemma of adjudication.

According to Habermas, the alternative of *legal hermeneutics* is too compromised democratically for it to serve as a viable, present-day interpretive model for the law (BFN 244). By prioritizing historical precedent in the negotiation of law and case, legal hermeneutics simply depends too heavily on "received," and hence potentially dogmatic, judicial tradition, however loosely one conceives of tradition. Habermas is

---

²⁶ See Ronald Dworkin, *Taking Rights Seriously* (Cambridge, MA: Harvard University Press, 1977); *A Matter of Principle* (Cambridge, MA: Harvard University Press, 1985); and *Law's Empire* (Cambridge, MA: Harvard University Press, 1986); Klaus Günther, *The Sense of Appropriateness: Application Discourses in Morality and Law* (Albany: State University of New York Press, 1993); Roberto M. Unger, *Law in Modern Society* (New York: Free Press, 1976); Mark Kelman, *A Guide to Critical Legal Studies* (Cambridge, MA: Harvard University Press, 1987); Alan Hunt and Peter Fitzpatrick, *Critical Legal Studies* (Oxford: Blackwell, 1987); and Andrew Altman, *Critical Legal Studies: A Liberal Critique* (Princeton, NJ: Princeton University Press, 1990).

nevertheless careful to acknowledge the sophistication of legal hermeneutics in addressing the complex relationship between a rule and its application: the context or situation of application is, to some extent, *defined* by being brought into proximity with a law, while the law is only made concrete in its application to a specific case (BFN 244). Rule and case are not hypostatized opposites that must be reconciled but rather entities whose own meaning emerges only in proximity to each other.

In much the same way that he theoretically undresses poststructuralism elsewhere,[27] Habermas reveals *legal realism's* inability to justify its own normative goals once it has exposed as ideology the normative claims of the judicial system (BFN 244). It completely reduces law to politics and overemphasizes the naked value preferences of judges (BFN 244). On the other hand, according to Habermas, *legal positivism* ignores social context and is insensitive to the threat of vested interests, rendering the approach unresponsive to the needs of substantive democracy. Moreover, Habermas reiterates his distrust of the latent decisionism in the positivist theory of adjudication: given the strict formalism of positivism, when the rule is unclear because of the inevitable indeterminacy of language, the judge is given unnecessarily wide discretion in rendering a decision (BFN 200).

Habermas finds the adjudicative philosophy of Dworkin much more successful in linking a theory of legal coherency with legal legitimacy.

---

[27] For instance, in only the most recent of such criticisms, Habermas charges that advocates of postmodernism have a naive "linguistic idealism," thinking that merely uttering something or formulating alternatives in words makes them somehow "real" in practice, and that, moreover, they grossly underestimate the universal achievements of modernity. See Habermas, *The Postnational Constellation: Political Essays*, Max Pensky, ed. (Cambridge, MA: MIT Press, 2001), 146, hereafter PC. Furthermore, Habermas observes that "from the correct premise that there is no such thing as a context-transcendent reason, postmodernism draws the false conclusion that the criteria of reason themselves change with every new context" (PC 148). Habermas counters that enlightenment depends not only on general exclusion – which was already aspired after in the world's religions – but also on the development of discourses directed by principles criticizable on precisely the grounds that they were not sufficiently inclusive (PC 148). He also detects a certain symbiosis of postmodernism and neoliberalism: "For different reasons, postmodernism and neoliberalism thus ultimately share the vision of the lifeworlds of individuals and small groups scattering, like discrete monads, across global, functionally coordinated networks, rather than overlapping in the course of social integration, in larger, multidimensional political entities" (PC 88). Habermas may speak too broadly when criticizing postmodernism: see my "Derrida on Law; Or, Poststructuralism Gets Serious," *Political Theory* 29, no. 3 (June 2001), 395–423. See also Stephen K. White, *Political Theory and Postmodernism* (Cambridge: Cambridge University Press, 1991).

Dworkin's distinction of principles and rules avoids both positivist and antipositivist responses to the apparent indeterminacy of the law: only the conflict of either/or rules makes for "decisionistic" resolution in adjudication. Principles, on the other hand, do not have this zero-sum quality (BFN 208–9). Habermas is inclined to accept Dworkin's call for a work-in-progress approach to legal principles wherein coherency follows from – rather than is presupposed by – the principles themselves (as in the more often criticized Rawlsian approach). For Dworkin, according to Habermas, "the task does not consist in the philosophical construction of a well-ordered society whose basic institutions would embody principles of justice [but rather] in the discovery of valid principles and policies in the light of which a given, concrete legal order can be justified in its essential elements such that all the individual decisions fit into it as parts of a coherent whole" (BFN 212).

Habermas also locates in Dworkin the grounds to refute the radical CLS critique of adjudication – the contemporary manifestation of the legal realist assault on formal law that also happens, wittingly or unwittingly, to reproduce some of the arguments used by Schmitt in his Weimar assault on liberal law.[28] Habermas's initial improvement on CLS can be found in his more sophisticated understanding of the source and role of the different and often opposing values that are invoked in twentieth-century legal adjudication (BFN 388–409). For Habermas the competing market and welfare state, individualistic and communitarian values of, respectively, autonomy/self-interest and solidarity/altruism are not reified as warring aspects of the human psyche, as they often are by CLS.[29] That CLS ultimately attributes such impulses to the potentially ahistorical realm of human psychology would not be so problematic had CLS not detected them, to begin with, in the midst of a very concrete historical situation. It is through the study of the consequences of postwar materialized administrative and contract law that CLS detects the interplay of

---

[28] On this comparison, see William E. Scheuerman, *Between the Norm and the Exception: The Frankfurt School and the Rule of Law* (Cambridge, MA: MIT Press, 1994), and John P. McCormick, "Three Ways of Thinking 'Critically' about the Law," *American Political Science Review* 93, no. 2 (June 1999), 413–28.

[29] See Jay Feinman, "Critical Approaches to Contract Law," *University of California Law Review* 30 (April 1983), 829–60; Gary Peller, "Debates about Theory Within CLS," *Lizard* 1 (1984), 21–39; and James Boyle, "The Politics of Reason: Critical Legal Theory and Local Social Thought," *University of Pennsylvania Law Review* 133 (April 1985), 685–780.

the different competing and contradictory values that render the law supposedly indeterminate.[30] While these values certainly have psychological
attributes,[31] Habermas chastises "hastily generalized historical studies"
of the law (BFN 216) and proceeds to discuss the decisive historical quality
of these values.

For Habermas, the emphasis on *freedom* that accompanies market
arrangements of state and society in the nineteenth-century *Rechtsstaat*
was expressed in formal strategies of law. The greater need for socioeconomic regulation in the twentieth century required social democratic
arrangements that institutionalized *equality* through the materialized law
of the *Sozialstaat* (BFN 216, 221). Since both right and left recognize
that liberty and equality, as well as individualism and altruism, are requisite components of a robust social order, Habermas is not surprised
or alarmed that they should compete in contemporary legal debates. His
negotiation of the two principles, however, hinges to a great extent on
his response to the indeterminacy critique. Drawing on Dworkin again,
Habermas claims that the supposed indeterminacy of law does not result
from the structure of the law itself understood in terms of linguistic limitations, political pressure, or judicial preference. Rather, it quite often
simply reflects judges' failure to put forth the best arguments in particular
cases (BFN 214). Judges, as human beings, are not perfect interpreters
of the law. Moreover, the institutional history to which they regularly
have recourse often resists fully rational reconstruction in adjudication.
As legal hermeneutics points out, but perhaps celebrates too uncritically,
judges do not stand outside of history and must deal with the baggage
that they inherit from the tradition in which they are embedded – even
when applying formal standards (BFN 214). Neither of these facts implies
a structural indeterminacy in the law. In fact, there is much evidence that

---

[30] Along these lines, Christian Joerges demonstrates quite convincingly how German representatives of critical legal theory have explored the historical and sociological relationship of law and society more rigorously than their North American counterparts
like realism and CLS. See Joerges, "*Politische Rechtstheorie* and CLS: Points of Contact
and Divergence," in C. Joerges and David M. Trubek, eds., *Critical Legal Thought: An
American–German Debate* (Baden-Baden: Nomos, 1989), 597–643. For an historical-
institutionalist alternative to CLS in the U.S. context, see Rogers Smith, "After Criticism:
An Analysis of the Critical Legal Studies Movement," in Michael McCann and Gerald
Houseman, eds., *Judging the Constitution* (New York: Little, Brown, 1989), 92–124.

[31] Mark Warren, in particular, draws upon Habermas in a discussion of the psychological
dimensions of contemporary democratic theory. See Warren, "Can Participatory Democracy Produce Better Selves?: Psychological Dimensions of Habermas's Discursive Model
of Democracy," *Political Psychology* 14, no. 2 (1993), 209–34.

the deliberate infiltration of personal preference or political pressure in adjudication is *far* less pervasive than CLS would have it.[32]

For Habermas, the de facto strategy of reducing all cases to "exceptions" leads CLS to the conclusion that since there is no coherence to liberal-democratic law, there is no justice. Because each law is capable of contradicting another, a fact exacerbated by subjective judging, the whole legal order is suspect. But Habermas argues that at base CLS confuses legal *rules* with legal *principles* (BFN 216–17). Rules are norms specified for application in particular cases: for instance, stipulations for drawing up wills or traffic laws. As discussed before, rules are often preceded by an "if" clause, which clearly identifies the application situation: if circumstance X obtains, then procedure Y is in order (BFN 208). Principles, on the other hand, are general legal standards with far fewer prespecified application guidelines. The meanings of procedural rights, human rights, or equal protection are ultimately made specific in interpretation and application (BFN 172, 208). Rules may collide in irreconcilable ways, but they do not constitute the broader workings of justice as such, as do principles.

In fact, rules are *supposed* to conflict because they are so finely specified for particular situations that the legal system depends on their conflict. This kind of conflict can be interpreted as *facilitating* the determinacy of the system rather than as thrusting it into indeterminacy jeopardy (BFN 217). Rules are highly determinate because they set the conditions of their own application. They are what Habermas calls "self-executing" laws, whereas principles like equality or mutual recognition are "implemented along administrative paths" where their meaning is fully fleshed out (BFN 172). Principles are necessarily indeterminate, to some extent, because they do not apply themselves but rather require "additional specification"

---

[32] Michel Rosenfeld and Ernest Weinrib show how judges cannot shift interpretive strategies without extensive, substantive, and therefore prohibitive justification. See Rosenfeld, "Deconstruction and Legal Interpretation: Conflict, Indeterminacy and the Temptations of the New Legal Formalism," in Drucilla Cornell, Michel Rosenfeld, and David Corlson, eds., *Deconstruction and the Possibility of Justice* (New York: Routledge, 1992), 152–210; and Weinrib, "Legal Formalism: On the Immanent Rationality of the Law," *Yale Law Journal* 97 (May 1988), 949–1016. David Shapiro enumerates the various costs that judges incur from deciding subjectively in "Courts, Legislatures, and Paternalism," *Virginia Law Review* 74 (April 1988), 519–75. And Charles Yablon argues that despite the many pertinent factors that CLS brings to light, it is remarkable just how *predictable* judicial decisions really are. See Yablon, "The Indeterminacy of the Law: Critical Legal Studies and the Problem of Legal Explanation," *Cardozo Law Review* 6 (Summer 1985), 917–45.

(BFN 217). All principles are necessarily indeterminate because they do not apply themselves. They must be examined to see if another principle better conforms to a particular case (BFN 216–17). In application, all suitable normative reasons must be collected and then the situation itself interpreted:

If the "collision" between norms being weighed in the interpretive process led one to infer a "contradiction" within the system of norms itself, then one would be confusing the norm's "validity," which it enjoys in general insofar as it is justified, with its "appropriateness" for application in particular cases. If instead one explains the indeterminacy of valid norms in terms of argumentation theory, then a contest of norms competing as prima facie candidates for application in a given case makes good methodological sense. (BFN 218)

There is an intimate relationship between rules and principles, for Habermas, but they ought not to be conflated in the way that CLS collapses them.[33] Because CLS, like Schmitt, perceives *all* law as rules and, more importantly, caricatures liberalism as ultimately doing the same, they set up a false either/or dilemma for liberal adjudication. Thus viewed, all legal materials are potentially in chaotic disagreement with one another. The conflating of rules and principles is at the root of Schmitt's and CLS's exaggerated characterization of formalism: since they group all liberal law under the blanket term "formal," and do not acknowledge that formal and substantive modes of law can coexist in the liberal rule of law, they encourage the appearance of arbitrary and conflicting practices that may not actually exist upon more differentiated analysis. In fact, it is precisely because CLS, like the positivism it criticizes, views the whole liberal legal system as merely a set of rules, that it can move effortlessly from statutes to constitutions, gaps to exceptions, even if without the malicious political intent of Schmitt. Habermas remarks that one of the traditional ways of avoiding rule conflict in the law, in cases where it might be confusing rather

---

[33] Neil MacCormick explains the rule–standard (read: principle) relationship a bit more concretely than Habermas, but in a way that corresponds quite closely with Habermas's understanding: for instance, "the rule is that prosecutors must prove their cases beyond a reasonable doubt. It is by incorporation in a rule that the relevant standard is made the law's standard. But for the rule incorporating it, it would not be true that the criminal standard of proof is proof beyond a reasonable doubt. . . . Hence there is no polar opposition between rules and standards. It takes a rule to make a standard legal; it may take a standard to make a rule satisfactorily workable. That there can be rules which do not incorporate standards does not show that standards can operate legally without incorporation in rules." See MacCormick, "Reconstruction After Deconstruction: A Response to CLS," *Oxford Journal of Legal Studies* 10 (Winter 1990), 539–58, here 545. See also the original formulation: Dworkin, *Taking Rights Seriously*, 22–8.

than instructive, is the recourse to exception clauses (BFN 208). Schmitt infamously exploited this by reading a built-in exception clause into the entire statutory legal system (understood as a collection of exceptionable rules), with disastrous results. CLS does not consider the ramifications that follow from this logic: if all laws have exception conditions, so too does the legal order itself, which is therefore suspendable in the name of a sovereign popular will.

In its own caricature of legal formalism, CLS very often assails a straw man: even the most stringent legal formalists acknowledge a necessary but not devastating lack of total determinacy in the liberal rule of law.[34] For Habermas, the formalism of the law has a very precise meaning. Formalism pertains primarily to the law's construction: that is, it is logically correct and established through prearranged procedures. The decisive aspect of the adjudication of principles, however, is not necessarily an airtight formalism, but rather the determination of appropriateness for a particular case (BFN 218). According to Habermas, in the application of principles all suitable normative reasons must be collected and then the situation itself interpreted. From a high level of abstraction, the formal modes of law, associated, for instance, with principles of criminal justice like retribution, appear irreconcilable with the more concrete, or material, modes of law that actualize the principle of substantive equality through social welfare provisions. But each is appropriate to a vastly different set of cases. To illustrate this point: Michel Rosenfeld and Ernest Weinrib each have used the distinction between corrective and distributive justice to clear up misunderstandings stemming from conflations of the two. The primarily backward-looking quality of corrective justice – redressing a wrong already perpetrated by means of procedures previously established – makes its workings appear relatively transparent. The future-directed quality of distributive justice deals with quantities not always known in advance – how much of what, to whom, and by what means? This seems terribly vague by contrast with criminal justice codes.[35] CLS lumps the two modes together in an attack on "the law."

Just because the conditions of principle adjudication cannot, nor should not, be fully laid out in advance, this does not render them hemorrhaging wounds in the body legal. It is largely their open-endedness that

---

[34] See Weinrib, "Legal Formalism"; Frederick Schauer, "Formalism," *Yale Law Journal* 97 (March 1988), 509–48; and a special "Symposium on Legal Formalism" in the *Harvard Journal of Law and Public Policy* 16 (Autumn 1993), 579–860.

[35] See Rosenfeld, "Deconstruction and Legal Interpretation," and Weinrib, "Legal Formalism."

gives the process a public and democratic quality. According to Habermas, in legal discourses of application, competing parties and state authorities present arguments over which norms are most relevant to the facts of a case (BFN 172). There are two interpretive steps for judges, the outcomes of which are not foreordained: the description of facts and the description of norms (BFN 218). As Habermas writes, "once the situational features of the case have been described as exhaustively as possible from all normatively relevant points of view," the appropriate principle can be selected (BFN 260). When one norm is selected over another for application, it does not invalidate, nullify, or render irrational those not chosen. "Recessive principles," those that are decided to be less relevant, according to Habermas, do not lose validity for a case like rules, but only their "contextual relevance" (BFN 209). CLS does not distinguish between principles contradicting one another per se and those that collide in a particular case (BFN 216). Because a particular principle was not applied does not render it at war with other principles or with the system as a whole. "A plausible connection [is maintained] between the pertinent norm and the norms that.... do not prevail such that the coherence of the rule system as a whole remains unaffected" (BFN 260). This is not an ideological weighing or privileging of one over the other, but rather a process of logical selection.

Schmitt and CLS, for their part, basically pose an ultimatum between nineteenth-century-style formal law and twentieth-century-style material law, each of which, if practiced alone in an "advanced" industrial legal order, would compromise the coherence and legitimacy of adjudication. If one observes and evaluates the operation of *Sozialstaat* materialized law with the standard of nineteenth-century formal law, the former is likely to appear incoherent or indeterminate. If one approaches them with historical and analytical honesty, however, as Schmitt intentionally and CLS inadvertently do not, each type of law can be equally coherent or determinate in its appropriate sphere of jurisdiction. How might this be accomplished?

As I will explain more elaborately in the next section, Habermas proposes a "reflexive" approach that draws upon one or the other type of law, formal or material, depending on its appropriateness for particular circumstances (BFN 393). The explicit judicial choice of either formal or material paradigms, those associated previously with private market participants and entitlement-receiving clients, helps in the selection of principles, such as freedom of contract or substantive equal opportunity

(BFN 216, 221). Understanding law in terms of formal and material paradigms relieves the judge of "the hypercomplex task of surveying an unordered set of prima facie valid principles and norms" and applying them to cases (BFN 221). It is democratic to the extent that laypersons participate and determinate to the extent that the process, if not the results, is coherent and predictable (BFN 221). This is no doubt the kind of differentiated analysis of adjudication that Roberto Unger dismisses as "hocus pocus."[36] But the flexible interpretation of principles that Habermas describes does escape the major thrust of Unger's critique because it does not operate exclusively in the "subjective" domain of the jurist. The responsibility of deploying principles means that judges, except on obvious occasions of gross misconduct, are not, as in one side of the Weberian model of adjudication, unencumbered creators of law. Habermas draws on Dworkin again to demonstrate how judges appeal to the principles that were invoked and deployed by lawmakers, who in turn are responsive to those invoked by deliberative publics. This ties individual cases and decisions to the normative substance of the whole legal order. Under Habermas's model, courts need only be more specific in invoking principles associated with liberty or equality. Whether or not a court "gets it right," the fact that it has signaled which set of principles it deems appropriate makes its decision more decipherable on appeal, should there be one. Determinacy has not been lost in the process but rather affirmed.

Drawing upon the discourse theory of constitution making and lawmaking analyzed in previous sections, Habermas understands adjudication as a rational moment within a normatively rich constitutional order. Again, Habermas conceives constitutional orders such that at every level of opinion and will formation, and law- and policymaking, there obtain the structures to facilitate full communicative interaction leading to general assent. As a result, the *formality* of legality can be rendered *substantively* legitimate: "if discourses . . . are the site where a rational will can take shape, then the legitimacy of law ultimately depends on a communicative arrangement: as participants in rational discourses, consociates under law must be able to examine whether a contested norm meets with, or could meet with, the agreement of all those affected" (BFN 103–4). The universality of, and continual intervention by, "general assent" or "reasonable consensus" proffered by such proceedings ensures legitimacy

---

[36] Roberto M. Unger, *The Critical Legal Studies Movement* (Cambridge, MA: Harvard University Press, 1986), 578.

defined in terms of social control of the state and the economy (BFN 147, 155).[37]

In Habermas's "reflexive strategy," the requirement of finding the appropriate principle for a specific case means that the judicial process cannot, and should not, be preordained before judging. Therefore, contra the other antinomic pole of Weber's analysis, this theory of adjudication is no more comparable to the objectively predictable workings of a machine than it is equivalent to the arbitrary whim of judges. Supposedly "critical" opponents of the liberal rule of law, like CLS or Schmitt, hence deploy determinacy in the wrong sense. Habermas suggests that those so fixated on indeterminacy must themselves expect a predetermined outcome in the judicial process. Seen in this light, the contingency celebration of CLS is revealed to be something of a latent craving for "necessity," something vigorously argued against in their work.[38] For Habermas, the appropriate expectation from procedural rights in the legal system is neither certainty of outcome nor arbitrary pronouncements from lawgiver judges, but rather clarification of the pertinent facts and legal questions (BFN 220).

According to Habermas's democratic proceduralism wherein adjudication is tied into communicative practices, affected parties should be confident that the procedures leading to judicial decisions regarding rules and principles entail relevant reasons, and not arbitrary ones (BFN 220). Formal law promises no stronger guarantee of determinacy than that. As Lawrence Solum succinctly puts it, legal formalisms "can significantly constrain outcomes even if they do not mechanically determine them."[39] CLS and Schmitt claim that liberal-democratic adjudication violates a

---

[37] The relationships of law, communicative rationality, and constitutional democracy are extensively explored in the Anglo-American reviews of BFN: see Seyla Benhabib, "Review of *Between Facts and Norms*," *American Political Science Review* 91 (September 1997), 712–14; Peter Dews, "Agreeing What's Right," *London Review of Books* (13 May 1993); David Dyzenhaus, "The Legitimacy of Legality," *University of Toronto Law Journal* 46 (1996), 129–80; David Rasmussen, "How Is Valid Law Possible?" *Philosophy and Social Criticism* 20, no. (1994), 21–46; Michel Rosenfeld, "Law as Discourse: Between Democracy and Rights," *Harvard Law Review* 108 (March 1995), 1163–89; Cass R. Sunstein, "Democracy Isn't What You Think," *New York Times Book Review* (18 August 1996), 29; Stephen K. White, "Review of *Faktizität und Geltung*," *Political Theory* 24 (February 1996), 128–30; as well as a special double issue of the *Cardozo Law Review* 17, "Habermas on Law and Democracy: Critical Exchanges" (March 1996), 767–1684.

[38] Most dramatically by Roberto M. Unger, *Politics, a Work in Constructive Social Theory* (Cambridge, MA: Harvard University Press, 1987).

[39] Lawrence Solum, "On the Indeterminacy Crisis: Critiquing Critical Dogma," *University of Chicago Law Review* 54 (March 1987), 462–503, here 475.

promise for determined outcomes that it never made to start. To this extent, they play what might be called "determinacy blackmail" with the rule of law. Thus, with the aid of Dworkin, and Günther as well, Habermas undermines the once reactionary, now supposedly progressive, strategy of reducing all cases to "exceptions" and utilizing the ensuing exposé of the indeterminacy of the liberal rule of law as the point of departure for a wholesale overhaul of it. After all, according to Habermas, CLS claims that there is no coherency to liberal-democratic law, hence no justice.

But Habermas subsequently parts company with Dworkin and Günther. By placing far too much emphasis on the individual judge – likening her to "Hercules," in fact – Dworkin is too "monologic" for Habermas. And Günther, by setting out too strong a distinction between rules and principles, as well as justification and application, endangers the very legal determinacy he seeks to uphold. By contrast, for Habermas, the way in which something is rationally justified cannot be wholly divorced from the manner in which (and the means with which) it is applied. As a solution to these deficiencies, Habermas introduces his "dialogic approach" to adjudication, an approach that takes into account multiple perspectives in the process:

Whether norms and values could find the rationally motivated assent of all those affected can be judged only from the intersubjectively enlarged perspective of the first person plural. This perspective integrates the perspectives of each participant's worldview and self-understanding in a manner that is neither coercive nor distorting. The practice of argumentation recommends itself for such a universalized ideal role taking practiced in common. As the reflective form of communicative action, argumentation distinguishes itself socio-ontologically, one might say, by a complete reversibility of participant perspectives that unleashes the higher-level intersubjectivity of the deliberating collective. In this way Hegel's concrete universal is sublimated into a communicative structure purified of all substantial elements. (BFN 228)

There is much more that could be said here with respect to the substantive qualities of Habermas's own legal hermeneutics.[40] However, in line with Habermas's invocation of Hegel at this juncture, I would like to raise questions about the way in which Habermas decontextualizes legal theory in BFN, the ramifications of which threaten the contemporary pertinence of his theses. To be sure, as I have reiterated again and again in previous chapters, Habermas never engaged in a simple-minded reduction of

---

[40] See Stephen M. Feldman, "The Persistence of Power and the Struggle for Dialogic Standards in Postmodern Constitutional Jurisprudence: Michelman, Habermas and Civic Republicanism," *Georgetown Law Journal* 81 (1993), 2243–90.

ideas to a socioeconomic or materialist base. STPS, for instance, demonstrated a sophisticated understanding of the way that theoretical positions, philosophical ideas, and cultural understandings interacted with particular sociohistorical moments. Indeed, recall that Habermas made it clear that the "bourgeois public sphere," although located within the complex of nineteenth-century, liberal, laissez-faire capitalist societies, could not be reduced to the mere ideological expression of them (STPS 160, 257).

In BFN, however, Habermas seems to have ceased to inquire about the sociohistorical status of theoretical utterances and has instead come to take them almost exclusively at intellectual face value – that is, purely at the level of theory. Throughout the work, particularly when treating competing interpretive strategies of jurisprudence, the question for Habermas is almost exclusively one of principles and how they are interpreted, and not one of the moment that informs and to some extent motivates a particular emergence of principles (e.g., BFN 252). As I will elaborate further in the next chapter, just as Habermas does not sufficiently contextualize within a transformation of state and society in the early twentieth century, the neo-Kantian categories of Weber's sociology of law (facticity and validity), he does not locate the contemporary legal-theoretical controversies of constitutional adjudication addressed earlier in their own changing historical context. In other words, many of the legal-theoretical positions analyzed by Habermas and explicated earlier might have been more comprehensively treated had they been examined on sociohistorical grounds along with ratio-normative ones. Habermas fails to entertain the issue of whether the competition between the variously reconstructed formalism of Dworkin, Raz, and Rawls, and the chauvinistic antiformalism of CLS are themselves characteristic of a crisis of the state in the post-Fordist Western European and North American countries, just as such a competition was indicative earlier this century of crisis and change in legal debates in Germany and elsewhere. It is remarkable that the "indeterminacy" thesis, one of the subtexts of Weimar debates during the transition to the *Sozialstaat*, should again emerge with such vitality in a post-1970s transition away from this model.[41] As we will see in the next

---

[41] See Gosta Esping-Andersen, ed., *Welfare States in Transition: National Adaptations in Global Economies* (London: Sage Publications, 1996). Fortunately, there is some dialogue between the Kantian formalist and Nietzschean antiformalist approaches to law in this context, as reflected by the debate between Charles Larmore and Drucilla Cornell. See Drucilla Cornell, "Time, Deconstruction and the Challenge to Legal Positivism: The Call for Judicial Responsibility," *Yale Journal of Law and the Humanities* 2 (1990), 267–97; and Larmore's response: Charles Larmore, "Law, Morality, and Autopoiesis in

section, these arguments about the purported prevalence of legal indeterminacy remained largely the possession of neo-conservatives and were not taken completely seriously during the period of *Sozialstaat* stability in the decades immediately following World War II.[42] At one time, this historical repetition would have struck Habermas in a significant way, and he would have pursued it in terms of its relationship to dramatic social and historical change, or at least the issue of ideology. One might wonder, considerations of tragedy and farce aside, why the arguments employed by legal realism during the emergence of the *Sozialstaat* to justify quite plausible, if not fully effective, state intervention in the name of social justice are replicated by CLS at the present time in the name of nearly uninstitutionalizable goals. In Habermas's earlier work, this likely would have been understood as an ideological symptom of the historical transformation and perhaps the normative exhaustion of the previous model.

But to sum up this section on the intricacies of Habermas's analysis of contemporary legal adjudication, which includes his critique of legal hermeneutics, legal realism, and legal positivism, his critical appropriation of Dworkin and Günther, and his rather devastating assault on CLS (BFN 194–204), I say this: rather than inquire into the sociopolitical context of the legal theories in question, Habermas tends to take them at intellectual face value, that is, exclusively at the level of their logical principles and normative justifications. One of the implications of the arguments developed earlier, however, is that an adequate engagement of contemporary legal theories necessarily entails examination not only of their ratio-normative defensibility but also of their relation to contemporary societal dynamics such as the status of the state, as well as statutory and constitutional law, under conditions of a transforming postwar *Sozialstaat* and emerging scenarios of globalization and supranational developments, such as the EU associated with it.

The fact that the "indeterminacy of law" emerges as a theme of legal debate during both the Weimar Republic and the present sociohistorical juncture raises the question of whether there are any structural similarities between these respective contexts. Such similarities may indeed

Niklas Luhmann," *Cardozo Law Review* 13 (1992), 505–9. Perhaps the most chauvinistic antiformalist is Stanley Fish: see Fish, *There's No Such Thing as Free Speech and It's a Good Thing Too* (New York: Oxford University Press, 1994).

[42] The champion of this position was, of course, Friedrich A. Hayek. See Hayek, *Law, Liberty, and Legislation: A New Statement of the Liberal Principles of Justice and Political Economy*, 3 vols. (Chicago: University of Chicago Press, 1976).

be found in dramatic, if qualitatively different, crises of the state. Had Habermas positioned himself in BFN vis-à-vis his interlocutors in such a manner – certainly without ignoring the normative-rational weight of their positions – he would perhaps have thought about the relationship between validity and facticity, determinacy and indeterminacy in different, more historically sensitive, ways. Habermas's failure to historicize adequately normative prescriptions is central in the next section as I examine his attempt to merge the respective advantages of the nineteenth- and twentieth-century "paradigms" of law as a response to the historical dilemma handed down to him by Weber. I postpone until the next chapter my critique of Habermas's contemporary writings on Europe. I will fault him for failing to consider whether EU governance portends a twenty-first-century paradigm of law generated by a new structural transformation, not one that can be captured by the combination of juridical responses to the two previous transformations that we see him theorize in the next section.

4. Selecting Nineteenth- or Twentieth-Century Paradigms of Law

In works as early as *Public Sphere*, we observed Habermas struggle with the pathological consequences of the transition of law from the relatively laissez-faire arrangements of the nineteenth century to the more state-interventionist scenario of the twentieth – pathologies already presciently perceived by Weber in his sociology of law and exploited by neo-conservative critics in the Federal Republic of Germany (BRD). At the conclusion of STPS, Habermas proposed novel, legally instituted, publicity- and discussion-promoting reforms to ameliorate the deleterious aspects of *Sozialstaat* social and political arrangements. In BFN Habermas revisits the BRD *Rechtsstaat/Sozialstaat* legal controversy, but proposes a different way of resolving it.

The ostensible "zero-hour" founding of the BRD after World War II compelled its legal theorists and practitioners to confront in a rather abrupt manner the predicament of law in an industrial democracy. While other Fordist-democratic regimes were able to adapt somewhat gradually to the consequences of an increasingly interventionist state in the twentieth century (or even, in the U.S. context, manage to conceal such consequences), the BRD confronted head-on these realities and their legal ramifications for the rule of law. Specifically, they had to resume the theoretical-practical experiment of a constitutionally democratic *Sozialstaat* that had been broken off with the collapse of Weimar and the rise of the pathological Nazi "*Sozialstaat.*" As discussed in earlier chapters, two aspects of the historical transformation from the *Rechtsstaat* to the *Sozialstaat* are a novel relationship of state and society, on the one hand, and of governmental branches, on the other. As Weber explained quite well, the traditional nineteenth-century conception of the rule of law posited the law as a set of clearly defined rules that kept apart from each other, on the one hand, state and society, and, on the other, legislative, administrative, and judicial branches of government in a way that preserved individual freedom. Law that is subsequently put into the service of the twentieth-century *Sozialstaat*, so the argument goes, suffers a crisis of indeterminacy as state activity blurs the distinction between state and society, and among governmental institutions as well. Put briefly, as sociopolitical relations become muddled, so too do the rules designed to coordinate them. State encroachment upon society and against the individual is difficult to discern and counteract.

The debates over this historical transformation raged in the immediate postwar period but reached particular intensity in the 1970s.[43] Habermas revisits these debates in the elaboration of his discursively social democratic theory of law and constitutionalism in BFN. He specifically takes up the task of reconciling the competing claims to justice of respective sides of the debate over the *Sozialstaat* so as to formulate a theory of law that preserves liberty, as in the *Rechtsstaat* model, and pursues equality, as in the *Sozialstaat* one. How can the vast inequalities generated by capitalist

---

[43] Some of the main figures of these debates were Ernst Forsthoff, "Begriff und Wesen des sozialen Rechtsstaats" (1954), in Forsthoff, ed., *Rechtsstaatlichkeit und Sozialstaatlichkeit* (Darmstadt: Wissenschaftliche Buchgesellschaft, 1968), and Forsthoff, *Verfassungsprobleme des Sozialstaats* (Münster: Aschendorff); Wolfgang Abendroth, "Zur Funktion der Gewerkschaften in der westdeutschen Verfassungsdemokratie," *Arbeiterklasse, Staat und Verfassung* 43 (1952), 127–48; and Abendroth, "Zum Begriff des demokratischen und sozialen Rechtsstaates im Grundgesetz der Bundesrepublik Deutschland" (1954), in *Antagonistische Gesellschaft und politische Demokratie: Aufsätze zur politischen Soziologie* (Neuwied: Luchterhand, 1967); Peter Häberle, "Grundrechte im Leistungsstaat," *Veröffentlichungen der Vereinigung der Deutschen Staatsrechtslehrer* 30 (1972), 43–131; Erhard Denninger, *Der gebändigte Leviathan* (Baden-Baden: Nomos, 1990); Dieter Grimm, *Die Zukunft der Verfassung* (Frankfurt a.M.: Fischer, 1991); and, perhaps most importantly, Ernst-Wolfgang Böckenförde, *Staat und Gesellschaft* (Darmstadt: Wissenschaftliche Buchgesellschaft, 1976); and Böckenförde, *Staat, Verfassung, Demokratie.* (Frankfurt a.M.: Fischer, 1991). Peter Caldwell provides an excellent account of the early BRD debates, moreover, one that demonstrates that these debates did *not* emerge from a "zero hour": see Caldwell, "Is a 'Social *Rechtsstaat*' Possible?: The Weimar Roots of a Bonn Controversy," in *From Liberal Democracy to Fascism: Political and Legal Thought in the Weimar Republic*, eds. P. C. Caldwell and W. E. Scheuerman (Atlantic Highlands, NJ: Humanities Press, 2000).

political economy be minimized in ways that do not infringe upon the individual liberties necessary for a thriving civil society? As mentioned in the section on Habermas's theory of adjudication, he develops a "reflexive theory of law" that allows political public spheres and legal institutions – embedded institutionally within a deliberatively democratic framework – to avail themselves of either *Rechtsstaat* formal law or *Sozialstaat* material law, depending on its appropriateness for the case at hand. This enterprise can be understood as Habermas's attempt to theorize a *Sozialstaat* adequate to the challenges of the twenty-first century.

In Habermas's account, which follows closely Weber's analysis as explicated in Chapter 3, the traditional *Rechtsstaat* presupposes the two great "separations" mentioned earlier: first and foremost, a sociological separation of state and society. State activity is confined to the guarantee of internal and external security of citizens, with the assumption that a self-regulating market economy will provide the substantive means by which all or at least the vast majority of citizens can achieve a good life (BFN 174–5). The *Rechtsstaat* separation of state and society ensures the rule of procedurally legitimated law rather than the rule of executive-enacted force. The executive arms of government merely concretize in specific circumstances the general contents of statutes; they serve to make real the semantic formulas of abstract and general norms (BFN 188–9). Thus, the grammar of legal rules itself has a distinctive character under the *Rechtsstaat*: abstract, general, formal, and *conditional*. As described earlier, the latter characteristic is best illustrated by the "if x, then y" formulation of law under the *Rechtsstaat*. The structure of law itself limits state activity: the state may take appropriate action y only if certain circumstances x arise in social reality (BFN 208).

Along with the sociological separation of state and society, the *Rechtsstaat* depends on the political requirement of the separation of powers, in which courts function as semiautonomous institutions. In Habermas's account, courts function as neither the puppets of legislatures that make laws nor the ignored-as-irrelevant weaker institutional siblings of executive authorities. Rather, courts are granted powers of oversight over and against both of these ostensibly more powerful arms of government. While to some extent bound by the terms of statutes produced by parliamentary majorities in adjudication, constitutional courts in many contexts have had the authority to strike down such legislation on the basis of constitutional principles. Moreover, while possessing no specific enforcement powers of their own, courts have been served with more or less good faith by the effective enforcement of their judicial decisions by executive actors.

Thus, a functioning separation of powers is an institutional sine qua non of the traditional *Rechtsstaat* (BFN 245–6, 431).

In other words, in this admittedly highly abstract model, proper court activity under the rule of law entails a certain balance between autonomy from, and dependence on, other institutional actors. The result of this limited autonomy or enabled constraint, depending on how one looks at it, is an institutional safeguard against the more political branches of government. The latter might encroach upon the basic constitutional principles of the regime itself, such as protection of minorities, equality before the law, state nonintervention into spheres of economic freedom, the prohibition against ex post facto judgment, the relatively consistent reliance on precedent, and so on.[44]

Thus, the delicate institutional position of the judiciary in the *Rechtsstaat* is preserved by the form of the kinds of laws legislated and adjudicated in this stylized nineteenth-century model. Confined to the adjudication of cases testing statutes dealing with criminal law and a narrow conception of property, courts were seldomly perceived as illegitimately encroaching on the responsibilities of the other branches. Therefore, they were rarely treated in a hostile manner by the other branches that would threaten their autonomy. When courts did challenge the activity of other state institutions, they did so on the basis of explicit and often written constitutional provisions that were not open to varied or controversial interpretation.

As parliaments begin enacting, and courts gave up resistance to, the legislation or management of an increasingly industrial economy in the late nineteenth and early twentieth centuries, we perceive the emergence of the welfare state, or *Sozialstaat*. Again, following Habermas, courts now adjudicate more substantively defined principles of liberty and equality transcending those narrowly associated with property rights. State activity in all branches of government becomes concerned with issues of redistributive taxation, the collective organization of labor, worker safety, social insurance, discouragement of monopoly, public control of fiscal markets, and so on. As the state intervenes in the market for purposes of regulation and redistribution, "the classical scheme for separating branches of government becomes less tenable the more laws lose the form of conditional programs and assume instead the shape of substantive goal-oriented programs" (BFN 190). Consequently, the judicial and

---

[44] On general elements of the rule of law, see George P. Fletcher, *The Basic Concepts of Legal Thought* (Oxford: Oxford University Press, 1996).

executive branches exercise considerable discretion in the interpretation and application of laws that are no longer formally specific (BFN 190): "As a rule these 'materialized' laws...are formulated without proper nouns and directed to an indeterminate number of addressees.... " (BFN 190). The normative intent of broad policies is lost in the vagaries of application, or, conversely, democratically unaccountable, bureaucratic, or judicial officials arbitrarily enforce policies with dubious normative content.[45]

So-called *classical* administration under the *Rechtsstaat* was reactive to actual and specific social events, functionally divided among branches, restrained in its approach to intervention. This gives way to *service* administration under the *Sozialstaat*, which provides public goods, infrastructure, planning, and risk prevention to society. Service administration, unlike classical administration, is necessarily future-oriented to often-hypothetical situations and is expansive in approach (BFN 431). Law no longer looks like conditional propositions with universal claims but rather takes the form of special legislation, experimental temporary laws, broad regulative imperatives with uncertain prognoses, and blanket clauses, all couched in indefinite statutory language (BFN 431).[46]

The conservative critics of the *Sozialstaat*, some of whom, as pointed out in Chapter 2, were former Nazis, conceived the traditional *Rechtsstaat* in such a way that the rule of law encompassed only rights against the state, legal guarantees of public order, and prohibitions on the abuse of "economic liberty" – all maintained through general and abstract law. On the basis of this strict conception of the traditional *Rechtsstaat*, the *Sozialstaat* appears to be a "corruption" of or "upheaval" against law itself (BFN 245–6, 431). The very nature of law might be compromised by recourse to less than clearly defined conditional phrases and declarative imperatives that enable broad policies, fundamentally infused with appeals to substantive principles – a "remoralization," a "deformalization" of law, if you will (BFN 246), or what I have referred to as "materialized" law throughout this work. An unhinging of executive and judicial activity from the express will of the legislature likewise jeopardizes separation of powers, resulting in the illegitimate expansion of executive

---

[45] On the issue of legal indeterminacy, see the literature on CLS in the previous sections. On this theme understood more generally in contemporary theory, see Benjamin Gregg, "Possibility of Social Critique in an Indeterminate World," *Theory and Society* 23 (1994), 327–66; and James Bohman, *New Philosophy of Social Science: Problems of Indeterminacy* (Oxford: Polity, 1991).

[46] See Scheuerman, *Between the Norm and the Exception*.

and judicial power vis-à-vis the legislature (BFN 246, 431). In short, for critics, the *Sozialstaat* obscures the clarity and mechanical application of *Rechtsstaat* law due to the vagueness of social law and the discretion it affords its enforcers and adjudicators (BFN 188–9). This sacrifices the freedom of individual actors vis-à-vis the state in the name of social projects meant to coercively enforce egalitarianism. Legal indeterminacy means that executive and judicial arms usurp the position of legislatures. Society, it would seem, now suffers the intrusion of executive and judicial decrees.

So, much of the discourse distinguishing the two paradigms of the rule of law serves to validate either the neo-conservative or the social democratic visions of law. In his resolution of the dispute, Habermas does not choose between these two positions that sometimes seem to deliberately misread each other. Habermas asserts that there is compatibility and a mutually enforcing relationship between the traditional *Rechtsstaat* and the *Sozialstaat* – a mutuality institutionalizing the indispensability of freedom and equality for each other.[47] Habermas identifies this as the internal relation of private and public autonomy (BFN 135). As I will demonstrate, Habermas's *Aufhebung* of what he calls "bourgeois-formal law" and "welfare state-material law" privileges neither the formal character of law construction and adjudication, on the one hand, nor the substantive content of economic equality, on the other; rather, it is a discourse-centered process that renders contemporary law constituent of and by both (BFN 134).

Habermas's discourse theory of law has as its goal not just the protection of equal private rights or the realization of the principles of social justice, but the retention of both in the achievement of "an exclusive opinion- and will-formation in which free and equal citizens reach an understanding on which goals and norms lie in the equal intent of all" (BFN 270). The essence of law is not just the pursuit of economic gain or the attainment of economic equality, but the realization of an active – or

---

[47] For other considerations on the compatibility of the rule of law and the welfare state, see, in the European context, Günther Teubner, ed., *Dilemmas of Law and the Welfare State* (New York: de Gruyter, 1988), and Neil MacCormick, *Legal Right and Social Democracy: Essays in Legal and Political Philosophy* (Oxford: Clarendon Press, 1984); and in the U.S. context, Cass R. Sunstein, *After the Rights Revolution: Reconceiving the Regulatory State* (Cambridge, MA: Harvard University Press, 1990), and Sunstein, *Free Markets and Social Justice* (Oxford: Oxford University Press, 1997); Bruce Ackerman, *Reconstructing American Law* (Cambridge, MA: Harvard University Press, 1983), and Ackerman, *Social Justice and the Liberal State* (New Haven, CT: Yale University Press, 1981).

rather interactive – pursuit of the conditions by which these may be expanded in nonpathological (i.e., capitalist exploitative or state-socialist repressive) means. Habermas proposes a "reflexive" approach to law whereby lawmakers and law adjudicators explicitly invoke the principles and methods characteristic of either the *Rechtsstaat*'s bourgeois formal law or the *Sozialstaat*'s material law (depending on whether a particular case suggests liberty-allowing or equality-encouraging priorities) (BFN 393, 410).

The reflexive approach – that is, explicitly invoked popular, legislative, *and* judicial *choice* of either formal or material paradigms, those associated previously with private market participants and entitlement-receiving clients – helps in the selection of principles for adjudication, such as freedom of contract or substantive equal opportunity (BFN 216, 221). Claimants, legislators, and judges should explicitly invoke either formal or material paradigms. Habermas proposes that the option of choosing between them should become part of citizens' discourse, legislative language, and judicial practice. In other words, appeals to formal or material law should be as commonplace in policy debates as are appeals to the First Amendment or the Equal Protection Clause in the United States. The invocation of principles associated with *Rechtsstaat* freedom or *Sozialstaat* equality provides clearer guidelines to governmental actors for the appropriate means of implementation. Rather than an undifferentiated demand for "regulation," the reflexive theory of law provides an intermediary step that clarifies the goals of particular social policy by its advocates, critics, formulators, and implementers.

To that extent, Habermas argues, "the outcome of a procedure then becomes predictable for the parties...insofar as the pertinent paradigm determines a background understanding that legal experts share with all citizens" (BFN 221). The explicit invocation of specific principles during a law's formulation, in claimants' activity, and in judges' decisions counteracts the charge of "vagueness" against *Sozialstaat* material law. In its policymaking function, as in its adjudicative aspect mentioned in the previous section, the reflexive approach is democratic because laypersons participate in the process and determinate to the extent that the procedures, if not their outcomes, are coherent and predictable. Habermas hopes that critics of *Sozialstaat* law will be satisfied that a place is made for formal-*Rechtsstaat*-type law within his reflexive model. Basically, *Rechtsstaat* formal law is not overwhelmed by *Sozialstaat* decree in the model. Additionally, the more substantively material law characteristic of welfare state regulation is explicitly guided by specific principles that prevent it from facilitating unbounded administrative domination. For

Habermas, determinacy will not be lost but rather can be better assured in contemporary legal practices. Habermas's reflexive approach, however, begs the question of whether the neo-conservatives engaged in the *Sozialstaat* law debate would want to deploy material law in even a partial or limited capacity. It still is quite controversial whether critics would be willing to concede that equal protection–like principles could ever be invoked to justify wide-scale state intervention that they never considered legitimate in the first place. But Habermas never addresses this point.

However, in a vein potentially even more troubling for Habermas's theory: Habermas's understanding of the *cause* of the shift from formal to materialized law, as much as his understanding of its effects, may limit the success of his endeavor to transcend both kinds of law in BFN. Again, his reflexive strategy moves from one paradigm to the other, depending on the particular needs of deliberative lawmaking publics in various legislative, executive, and adjudicative contexts: "Today the political legislator must choose from among formal, material and procedural law according to the matter that requires regulation" (BFN 438). Habermas develops a method that allows for voluntary *selection* of either type of law, depending upon the discursively derived choice of the persons affected by the proposed policy. He refers to bourgeois formal law and welfare state deformalized law as "the two most successful paradigms..., which are still competing today" but does not clarify the status of this competition – specifically, to what extent it is played out on ideological or sociological terrain, or indeed some synthesis of the two (BFN 117).

Whereas *Public Sphere* concluded with legal-deliberative recommendations whose possibilities and constraints were made fairly specific, in BFN *Rechtsstaat* and *Sozialstaat* approaches, which Habermas showed to have been embedded within specific socioeconomic complexes in the past, have no such concrete referents in the present. Habermas makes no explicit attempt to ground his "higher third" in the possibilities afforded by contemporary socioeconomic conditions. On this basis, it might be suggested that Habermas's definitions of bourgeois rule of law and welfare-state law are potentially voluntaristic, emphasizing the idealistic characteristics of epochs in a way that may obfuscate their sociostructural status in the present crisis of the state. For instance, Habermas attributes the motor of each respective model to "claims of rights by market participants," on the one hand, and "claims of entitlements by welfare clients," on the other (BFN 221; FG 271). In other words, these epochs were generated to a large extent by the demands of social agents, with no reference to the conditions that inspired or shaped those demands.

Habermas claims that "the social-welfare model emerged from the reformist critique of bourgeois formal law" (BFN 401; FG 484), thus underemphasizing the structural conditions that facilitated, if not forged, such a model – conditions that were in fact of central importance in *Public Sphere*. The constraints on communicative action delineated in that book are given little attention in BFN and seem to indicate that Habermas's efforts already presuppose the more substantive communicative-participatory state of affairs that he is encouraging with the discourse theory of constitutional democracy. Such constraints are absent from Habermas's explanation of how many of the so-called deficits of the *Sozialstaat* model turn out to be largely matters of perspective on the part of the particular subjects:

> It is only a particular paradigmatic understanding of law in general that causes the objective legal content apparently to drop out of some basic rights [in the *Sozialstaat*]. This understanding stems in turn from how a particular historical situation was perceived through the lens of social theory, that is, a situation in which the liberal middle class had to grasp, on the basis of its interest position, how the principles of the constitutional state could be realized. (BFN 251)

The potentially ideational/voluntarist assumptions of Habermas's account are perhaps best reflected by the very notion of "paradigm shifts," referred to in the previous passage, made famous by Thomas Kuhn.[48] In BFN, Habermas repeatedly refers to the transition from *Rechtsstaat* to *Sozialstaat* law in terms of such paradigm shifts (BFN 252, 397). The Kuhnian concept, however, suggests that the way in which objective conditions are perceived by a particular community of observers is almost exclusively determinate of its reality: Habermas argues that paradigm shifts are to be explained in terms of the perception that a particular paradigm has become "dysfunctional." It is this subjectivist understanding of legal history that affords Habermas the opportunity – through the prospective choices of deliberating subjects within overlapping public spheres – to preserve and reject selectively particular elements from previous paradigms as ingredients of a new one at any moment of law- or policymaking.[49]

In setting out such an approach, Habermas departs from critical theory to the extent that he does not reflect upon the status of his model

---

[48] See Thomas Kuhn, *The Structure of Scientific Revolutions* (Chicago: University of Chicago Press, 1962).

[49] Robert Pippin derides as "paradigm relativism" the way that the mature Habermas seems to account for nonstructural social change. See Pippin, *Idealism as Modernism: Hegelian Variations* (Cambridge: Cambridge University Press, 1997), 168.

in relation to the historical moment in which it emerges. As I suggest subsequently and in later chapters, this historical context may not be amenable to *either* formal *or* materialized strategies of law (or some combination thereof), but rather may entail wholly new options for wholly new circumstances. But even before grounding my own critique in contemporary structural possibilities and constraints, I can suggest on formal-methodological grounds that Habermas's reflexive strategy runs the risk of approximating a social democratic philosophy of will: a subjectivist philosophy that wavers between the ideal constructions of the theorist and the demands, perceptions, and expressions of particular social groups. As mentioned previously, Habermas has simultaneously sought to distance his theories from potentially authoritarian "philosophies of consciousness," as well as, in BFN, homogenizing notions of popular sovereignty. Through this paradigm-dependent model, Habermas, on the one hand – quite appropriately – leaves the discussion and decision over the mode of law appropriate to a specific situation to the practices of the community directly affected by it. However, on the other hand, because of transepochal, evolutionary, and ideational sociohistorical presuppositions, as we observed in Chapter 2, he has set out in advance the emancipatory options – options confined to one of either two or, if somehow combined, three juridical possibilities. Yet, since the relationship between the discursive publics and the observations of the theorist, on one side, and sociological reality, on the other, is not mediated in a more explicit manner, both remain unreconstructed Kantian antinomies in BFN and hence ideological assertions.

For Habermas, because the conditions that obtained under the two respective previous paradigms came to be seen as dysfunctional, this fact – as much as or more than the empirical reality of actual dysfunctionality – becomes sufficient grounds for an ideally created supercession of one or both paradigms. Habermas is surely correct to insist that "a social theory claiming to be 'critical' cannot confine itself to describing the relationship of norm and reality solely from the perspective of an observer" (BFN 109). However, he seems to move to the opposite extreme in BFN and appears to privilege inordinately participants' perspectives or consciousness: "The tacit assumption that these two [legal] paradigms exhausted the alternatives was questioned only after the dysfunctional side effects of the successfully implemented welfare state became pressing political issues" (BFN 390). For Habermas, it is therefore the ensuing politicization that directly results in "the search for a new paradigm beyond the familiar alternatives" (BFN 390). But the structural conditions that inspired such dissatisfactions and politicizations would also provide important hints regarding the concrete constraints on and the historical status of emancipation in an emerging historical circumstance.

To be sure, Habermas claims that the newly theorized reflexive paradigm must preserve the liberty-upholding and solidarity-instilling aspirations of the two previous ones (the respective *Rechtsstaat* and *Sozialstaat* paradigms) without, like them, undermining the possibility of their historical realization through the pathological consequences emerging from them (socioeconomic injustice and state paternalism, respectively). Moreover, Habermas insists that given present societal realities, his discourse-theoretic paradigm must not anachronistically hope to preserve irretrievable aspects from the previous paradigms (BFN 249). On this basis, in a telling passage he criticizes Ernst-Wolfgang Böckenförde's nostalgia for certain irretrievable aspects of the nineteenth-century *Rechtsstaat*:

The liberal paradigm of law is certainly not a simplifying description of a historical starting point that we could take at face value. It tells us, rather, how the principles of the constitutional state could be realized under the hypothetically assumed conditions of a liberal economic society. This model stands and falls with the social-theoretic assumptions of classical political economy, which were already shaken by Marx's critique and no longer hold for developed postindustrial societies in the West. In other words the principles of the democratic constitutional state must not be confused with one of its context-bound historical modes of interpretation. (BFN 250)

In other words, Böckenförde ought not to confuse liberal democracy, as such, with an idealization of the *Rechtsstaat*. However, Habermas's supposed overcoming of the two paradigms of law also "stands or falls" on "context-bound" assumptions about the historical status of the *Sozialstaat* that may "no longer hold for developed postindustrial societies" (BFN 250). In the next chapter, I will ask whether Habermas himself attempts to revive aspects of the *Sozialstaat* within the supranational institutions of the EU in just as nostalgic a fashion as Böckenförde attempts to revive the *Rechtsstaat* under irreversible *Sozialstaat* conditions. But the normative-empirical limits of Habermas's explicitly state-centric model are already discernible in BFN.[50]

Why does Habermas think he can escape the ideological anachronism he attributes to Böckenförde, which, as we know from Chapters 2 and 3,

---

[50] Neil Brenner convincingly demonstrates that BFN presumes a relatively unchanging welfare state model: see Brenner, "The Limits of Civil Society in the Age of Global Capital: A Critique of Jürgen Habermas's Mature Social Theory" (M.A. thesis, Department of Political Science, University of Chicago, 1993).

could just as easily be associated with Weber? The answer may lie in Habermas's succinct summation of his historical-paradigmatic approach:

The desired paradigm should satisfy the best description of *complex* societies; it should illuminate once again the original idea of the self-constitution of a community of free and equal legal citizens [bourgeois rule of law]; and it should overcome the rampant particularism of a legal order that, having lost its center in adapting to the uncomprehended complexity of the social environment, is unraveling bit by bit [in *Sozialstaat* materialized law]. (BFN 393, first emphasis added).

In BFN, Habermas seeks to infuse the new reflexive paradigm with a normativity that has been drained from social-scientific accounts of the *Sozialstaat* by "a functionalistically prejudiced understanding of law fixated on government action" that "conflates legitimacy and efficiency" (BFN 434, 444; FG 524, 525). But his failure to give a more full account of the sociostructural bases of the new paradigm, except through repeated references to systemic "complexity," undermines the potential efficacy of the proposed paradigm. As we observed in Chapter 2, works such as LC and TCA themselves showed the intimate link between inefficiency and crises of legitimacy, especially when the former facilitates inequitable capital accumulation, the stultification of effective political participation, and the clientalization of citizens. It thus would seem that Habermas's "third way" in democratic constitutional theory, elaborated in BFN, is grounded upon a Weberian secularization-cum-complexity view of empirical reality, presented in systems-theoretic language upon which is superimposed a philosophically idealistic conception of paradigm shifts. If so, this would render Habermas's conception of present socioeconomic reality merely a further "differentiating" *Sozialstaat* paradigm that already obtains in essence, one whose worst pathology is a "rampant particularism." It obscures other pathologies of the *Sozialstaat*, such as continued material inequality, citizen clientalization, and participatory stultification.

To this charge, perhaps surprisingly, given the primacy of these other pathologies in his past work, Habermas explicitly pleads guilty: "The social-welfare project must neither be simply continued along the same lines nor be broken off, but must be pursued at a higher level of reflection" (BFN 410). This injunction, however, presupposes a socioeconomic structure already in place and may not entertain the notion of its *fundamental* change. In STPS, Habermas had criticized the tendency to "derive the essence" of capitalism per se from the "unique historical constellation" of laissez-faire capitalism in Great Britain at the transition from the eighteenth to the nineteenth century (STPS 78–9). However, Habermas's own tendency in BFN to derive the essence of contemporary state–economy–society relations from the equally historically unique model of the post–World War II *Sozialstaat* seriously hampers his attempt to ground sociologically his contemporary normative project.[51] That we will observe Habermas waver on this issue of continuity and change in contemporary political economy in his essays on the EU indicates his awareness of a tension here, even if it is less than fully clear that he is equipped or determined to resolve it.[52]

Habermas's discussion of the feminist critique of formal and welfare state law, the place in BFN where he intends to make his reflexive approach most concrete, exemplifies these problems (BFN 409–27). Habermas draws upon literature that demonstrates the various ways in which women were marginalized and exploited under a formal law paradigm blinded to women's needs by andro-centric notions of neutrality – a paradigm that tacitly condoned the subjection of women in the name of state nonintervention. He also acknowledges the feminist indictment of the welfare-state legal paradigm that manipulated and enforced female dependency through the promulgation of policies over which women had little control. Habermas suggests that a new legal paradigm might emerge from feminist "demands" for alternative types of legal practice; that is, legislation and policies could be crafted that draw upon the former traditions that prevent both state intrusion and clientalization of welfare recipients, yet continue to provide the substantive service and support of welfare-state policies.[53] However, once again, Habermas's focus on the "demands" of the legal subjects in question entails a neglect of the sociostructural context within which these persons are situated. In this

[51] David Held criticizes Habermas along similar lines in Held, "Crisis Tendencies, Legitimation and the State," in *Habermas: Critical Debates*, eds. John Thompson and David Held (Cambridge, MA: MIT Press, 1982), 193–4.

[52] Not that there is a self-evident answer to the question: see the essays contained in Herbert Kitschelt, Peter Lange, and Gary Marks, eds., *Continuity and Change in Contemporary Capitalism* (Cambridge: Cambridge University Press, 1999).

[53] Habermas directly engages the work of Seyla Benhabib, Nancy Fraser, and Iris Marion Young in these sections of BFN and throughout the book (BFN 419–20, 563, 550). See Benhabib, *Situating the Self*; Fraser, *Unruly Practices: Power, Discourse, and Gender in Contemporary Social Theory* (Minneapolis: University of Minnesota Press, 1989); and Iris Marion Young, *Justice and the Politics of Difference* (Princeton, NJ: Princeton University Press, 1990). However, Nancy Love argues that Habermas does not go far enough so as to truly *incorporate* the concerns of feminist theorists: see Love, "Language and Gender in Habermas's Legal Turn," in John P. McCormick, ed., *Confronting Mass Democracy and Mass Technology: Essays on German Social and Political Thought from Nietzsche to Habermas* (Durham, NC: Duke University Press, 2002).

case, Habermas's discussion of feminist legal theory fails to consider the ways in which the increasing number of women entering the work force over the last twenty-five years in Organization for Economic Coop- eration and Development (OECD) countries may have contributed to the changing political and legal agendas of feminists, and it occludes the necessity of taking into account present structural possibilities and constraints.

It should be pointed out that in the last chapter of BFN, Habermas claims to begin "historically situating" his project (BFN 395) and expresses a renewed sensitivity to the "structural transformation of soci- ety" (BFN 516), to the "qualitative transformation of state tasks" (BFN 427), and, further, to "the unavoidable results of structural changes in state and society" (BFN 430). Yet, his conception of historical change throughout BFN is ultimately grounded upon a notion of an "outmoded paradigmatic understanding" (BFN 423). Habermas's attempt to tran- scend both *Rechtsstaat* formal and *Sozialstaat* materialized legal models, as originally set forth as a historical dilemma by Weber, amounts to an abstract negation of each option against the other – an attempt to over- come two historical pasts that is nevertheless itself theoretically blind to the historical present (BFN 445). Even though he eventually grapples with the feminist literature on *Sozialstaat* law, in his treatment of paradigm shifts Habermas reveals himself actually to be addressing those controver- sies between left-liberals and neo-conservatives over welfare-state policy that were prefigured in Weber's writings – debates within which the status of the welfare state itself is taken for granted.[54] While within the bound- aries of BFN Habermas may concede that *Sozialstaat* reality is growing ever more complex, he does not entertain the notion that it is changing qualitatively. This sets up the paradox that, on the one hand, an extant scenario can be reformed, but, on the other, its growing complexity sug- gests a situation moving beyond the grasp of conscious choice and control. Georg Lukács perceived this same tension in Weber and offered a vision of how to seize what was to him the immediately apparent dynamic of dramatic change to promote progress: a notion of history that was pre- cisely under the control of those human actors who needed to be made

---

[54] For attempts to confront the transformation of the welfare state and the role of women within it under post-Fordism or globalization, see Anna Yeatman, "Women's Citizenship Claims, Labour Market Policy and Globalization," *Australian Journal of Political Science* 27 (1991), 449–61; and L. McDowell, "Life without Father and Ford: The New Gender Order of Post-Fordism," *Transactions of the Institute of British Geographers* 16 (1992), 400–19.

aware of it, instead of a notion that portrayed these actors as beguiled into passivity and resignation by linear and deterministic notions of ever-increasing societal rationalization and specialization.[55] These are themes whose ramifications for law and socioeconomic change will be addressed in the book's Conclusion.

5. Conceptual Paradigms and Historical Configurations of Law

Whether one would find it simply another affirmation of the power of Minerva's owl, Habermas's attempt in BFN to resolve the law and *Sozialstaat* debate, and to solve the predicament of the rule of law in Fordist nation-states more generally, may be too little, too late. BFN certainly offers an articulate reconception of the relationship of *Rechtsstaat* and *Sozialstaat* types of law, a convincing refutation of the indeterminacy critique of the latter type of law, and keen prescriptions for the appropriate deployment of one or the other paradigm. Yet, it is somewhat disconcerting that such a work should have come at a time when its geopolitical and sociological conditions of possibility are so questionable. As we will see in the next chapter, in works subsequent to BFN, Habermas argues for the transmissibility of his model to supranational levels, specifically that

---

[55] Georg Lukács, one of Weber's closest and perhaps most singularly brilliant students, chose not to privilege one theoretical pole of validity or facticity over the other. Instead, in an unfortunately understudied legal section of his *History and Class Consciousness* collection of 1923, Lukács calls for a Hegelian mediation and overcoming of such false – that is, independently empty and ineffectual – oppositions as Kelsenian abstract validity and Schmittian concrete factuality, categories he calls "antinomies of bourgeois thought." See Lukács, *History and Class Consciousness*, trans. Rodney Livingstone (Cambridge, MA: MIT Press, 1988), 95–8, 256–71. Lukács uses this phrase to demonstrate the link between the supposedly mutually indissoluble "ideal" versus "reality" poles of Kantian philosophy and the methodology practiced by neo-Kantians such as Lukács's mentor, Weber. This methodology is perhaps best exemplified by Weber's sociological approach, which applies subjectively constructed "ideal types" to concrete empirical reality. Lukács, for his part, attempted to ground these poles of validity and facticity in the respective abstract and concrete moments of both Marx's analysis of commodity form, exchange value, and use value, and the historical dynamics of capitalism. In joining the Communist Party, he sought the practical overcoming of these oppositions and the socioeconomic reality with which they corresponded, first in the present moment of revolution and eventually in apologies for Lenin and Stalin. Despite the particularly misguided activity that resulted from Lukács's attempted transcendence of Weber's neo-Kantian categories, the spirit of this Hegelian–Marxist theoretical-practical project was passed down to his progeny in the so-called Frankfurt School of Critical Social Theory. It is to this legacy that Jürgen Habermas is today the preeminent heir. I discuss this response in my "Transcending Weber's Categories of Modernity?: Left and Right 'Weberians' on the Rationalization Thesis in Interwar Central Europe," *New German Critique* 75 (Fall 1998), 133–77.

of the EU.[56] He seems to recognize in the development of supranational organizations a symptom of, or reaction to, a new phase in the history of capitalism. But the adequacy of the reflexive theory of law for such a new phase remains to be demonstrated rather than assumed.

It would, after all, seem somewhat naive for Habermas to expect that the demands of justice on the law can be satisfied in a *new* transformation of capitalism by combining the outcomes of two *previous* transformations of capitalism. The formal-legal arrangements of the *Rechtsstaat* and the material ones of the *Sozialstaat* were embedded in specific socioeconomic arrangements: moments crudely understood as nineteenth-century laissez-faire and twentieth-century Fordist political economies. While still an open question, should we expect legal strategies adequate to a new socio-economic moment to amount to a combination of the last two? Unless we understand the emergence of *Sozialstaat* law as some combination of the *Rechtsstaat* with common law, Roman law, or canon law – which is the logic of Habermas's legal-historical narrative read backward – the prospects for predicting the future on the basis of a *fusion* of discrete juridical pasts are not very hopeful. Therefore, the limits of the reflexive theory of law in the present historical constellation may be set by Habermas's failure to elucidate the *new* legal strategies for pursuing justice that cannot be derived by the selection of one or the other previous strategies.

Recent scholarship suggests that standards of both the traditional and the social democratic rule of law are being challenged and, to some extent, compromised by supranational developments associated with globalization and regionalization.[57] Some argue that international legal fora are threatened by a *greater* encroachment on their functioning by state and

---

[56] See Habermas, *The Postnational Constellation: Political Essays*; *The Inclusion of the Other: Studies in Political Theory*, Ciaran Cronin and Pablo de Grieff, eds. (Cambridge, MA: MIT Press, 1998), hereafter IO; "The European Nation-State and the Pressures of Globalization," *New Left Review* 235 (1999), 46–59, hereafter NLR; "Beyond the Nation-State?: On Some Consequences of Economic Globalization," in E. O. Eriksen, and J. E. Fossum, eds., *Democracy in the European Union: Integration Through Deliberation?* (London: Routledge, 2000), 29–41, hereafter DEU; and "Warum braucht Europa eine Verfassung?" in Habermas, *Zeit der Übergänge* (Frankfurt a.M.: Suhrkamp, 2001), 104–29. I cite the English translation by Michelle Everson, sponsored by the European University Institute: "So, Why Does Europe Need a Constitution?" (http://www.iue.it/RSC/EU/Reform02.pdf), hereafter RSC.

[57] The following volumes lay out quite well the constraints on an expansion of the rule of law in the global arena while nevertheless advocating the pursuit of this very possibility: Hans Kochler, *Democracy and the International Rule of Law: Propositions for an Alternative World Order* (Berlin: Springer Verlag, 1995); David Held, *Democracy and the Global Order: From the Modern State to Cosmopolitan Governance* (Stanford, CA: Stanford University Press, 1995); and Günther Teubner, ed., *Global Law without a State* (London: Dartmouth Publishing, 1996).

multinational actors than national courts have been by their domestic institutional counterparts. For instance, one body of literature argues that the enforcement of ECJ decisions are at the mercy of the potentially arbitrary whims of authorities, such as the Council of Ministers and national judiciaries, not directly linked to them institutionally through territorially bound constitutions.[58] The work of these more skeptical students of EU law and the ECJ suggest that a rule of law other than one confined exclusively to economic integration is not likely to emerge in the near future of the EU. Moreover, given the lack of autonomy attributed to the Court in this literature, serious questions are raised about the ECJ's ability to conduct even such a narrowly defined task as strict common-market-making by standards of the formal paradigm described in Habermas's reflexive theory. One of the ramifications of this perspective is that European law will function exclusively in a manner akin to nineteenth-century national law in the United States, that is, adjudicating only the contemporary equivalent of narrow property rights and free trade. The Euroskeptic literature suggests that it would be merely speculative to ask whether the purview of supranational court jurisdiction will be expanded to include substantive social and political concerns any time soon.

As one might expect, we will see Habermas argue for an expansion of European law culminating in a full-fledged continental constitution that generates the circuit of communication conducted by "a European-wide, integrated public sphere . . . , a civil society encompassing interest associations, nongovernmental organizations, citizens' movements, etc., and naturally a party system appropriate to a European arena" (IO 160). In support of Habermas's prescriptions, the boldest claim of scholars optimistic about the supranational normative potential of EU law is that the economic sphere of adjudication explicitly granted to the ECJ is presently, and will increasingly, "spill over" into social and political ones.[59] In line

---

[58] See Geoffrey Garrett, "International Cooperation and Institutional Choice: The European Community's Internal Market," *International Organizations* 46 (Spring 1992), 533–60; Geoffrey Garrett and Barry Weingast, "Ideas, Interests and Institutions: Constructing the European Community's Internal Market," in Judith Goldstein and Robert Keohane, eds., *Ideas and Foreign Policy* (Ithaca, NY: Cornell University Press, 1993), 173–206; and Geoffrey Garrett, R. Daniel Keleman, and Heiner Schulz, "The European Court of Justice, National Governments, and Legal Integration in the European Union," *International Organizations* 52 (Winter 1998), 149–76.

[59] The following argue that the EU as it exists now is already a constitutional order: Anne-Marie Burley and Walter Mattli, "Europe Before the Court: A Political Theory of Legal Integration," *International Organization* 47 (Winter 1993), 41–75; Anne-Marie Slaughter-Burley, "New Directions in Legal Research on the European Community,"

with Habermas's expectation that the EU will repeat the process of legally steered marketization-cum-democratization experienced by nation-states, these scholars claim that the ECJ will continue to subtly argue that economic integration cannot be achieved without the integration of social spheres as well. A fully common market cannot function properly without universal levels of private and social insurance, environmental protection, medical benefits, worker compensation, and so on. Thus will the EU become a supranational social democracy through law. Along the lines of the formal law in the bourgeois *Rechtsstaat*, independence from other EU institutional actors and consistency of adjudication are maintained throughout the system. The optimistic account of social spheres integrating through economic ones also suggests that a European *Sozialstaat*, adjudicated by something like welfare-state material law, is possible and likely. Habermas's reflexive theory of law would hence appear to be potentially operational on a supranational level.[60]

Before turning to Habermas's more elaborate account of EU law and democracy in the next chapter, here I will briefly test Habermas's reflexive theory of law, as expressed in BFN, against the charges of the more skeptical literature on democracy in the EU. Habermas's account presupposes courts that are entrenched in national-constitutional orders. Given the extent to which Habermas links judicial activity to democratic practices in his discourse theory of law, his model may not suffer from the legitimacy deficit generally directed against court-centric accounts of constitutional democracy. However, Habermas's model may make assumptions about courts that may not be generalizable from the Fordist nation-state to the supranational level where law is now functioning. In this sense,

---

Journal of Common Market Studies 31 (September 1993), 391–400; Joseph H. H. Weiler, "The Transformation of Europe," *Yale Law Review* 100 (1991), 2403–83; Weiler, "A Quiet Revolution: The European Court of Justice and Its Interlocutors," *Comparative Political Studies* 26 (January 1994), 510–34, and Weiler, "The Reformation of European Constitutionalism," *Journal of Common Market Studies* 35 (March 1997), 97–131; Alec Stone, "What Is a Supranational Constitution?: An Essay in International Relations Theory," *Review of Politics* 56 (Summer 1994), 441–74, and Stone, "Governing with Judges: The New Constitutionalism," in Jack Hayward and Edward C. Page, eds., *Governing the New Europe* (Durham, NC: Duke University Press, 1995), 286–314; Karen J. Alter, "The European Court's Political Power," *West European Politics* 19 (July 1996), 458–87; and Alec Stone Sweet and Thomas L. Brunell, "Constructing a Supranational Constitution: Dispute Resolution and Governance in the European Community," *American Political Science Review* 92 (March 1998), 63–82.

60　I discuss these competing literatures in John P. McCormick, "Supranational Challenges to the Rule of Law: The Case of the European Union," in David Dyzenhaus, ed., *Recrafting the Rule of Law* (Oxford: Hart Publishing, 1999).

by so carefully resolving a previous debate regarding law and democracy, Habermas may have left himself at something of a disadvantage in addressing the present one. Despite criticisms like those launched by neoconservatives against the *Sozialstaat*, the territorial cohesion of national constitutional orders like the Federal Republic of Germany shielded courts from excessive backlash and spared them unfaithful enforcement of their decisions within the Fordist nation-states of the postwar era. Habermas takes this for granted as a situation that obtains now and will do so for the immediate future in the EU. Almost two centuries of entrenched arrangements of the separation of powers in the liberal democracies of Europe and North America insulated courts from shocks caused by the transition to the *Sozialstaat* from the *Rechtsstaat* that might otherwise have thrown courts from the historical vehicle of constitutional politics.

On the most superficial level, the depiction of constrained ECJ adjudication in the skeptical literature does not seem the fertile ground in which Habermas's liberty- and equality-guaranteeing reflexive model of law may develop. Perhaps the role of national courts in successfully carrying out the social welfare projects of the twentieth century could not have been predicted in the nineteenth century. Admittedly, much of the evidence would have argued against it. But there are further problems for Habermas's prognostications. In the previous section, I sympathetically presented Habermas's distinction between rules and principles in adjudication, particularly how they relate to earlier historical paradigms of law in a liberal-democratic framework. However, it is precisely this distinction that at this juncture is especially problematic at the supranational level. It is presently either too easy or too difficult to delineate juridical *principles* in supranational configurations, even one as relatively homogeneous as the EU. If the governing principles of a juridical unit like the EU pertain merely to the regulation of an economic free-trade zone, for instance, then those principles will clearly be too thin to preserve the gains of liberal or social democracy associated with two or three centuries of expanding civil and social rights. According to Court-skeptical scholars, appeals by European citizens or associations to the ECJ on the grounds of more *substantive* principles of justice, and attempts by the ECJ to address them, will be resisted by nation-states. While the autonomy of the ECJ is a hotly contested issue in European studies, its activities are no doubt constrained to a significant degree by the preemptive and reactive pressure of EU member states.[61]

---

[61] A paper argues that member states ignore or repudiate the principles justifying ECJ decisions even while enforcing them: see Lisa J. Conant, "Containing Justice: Institutional

In his EU writings, Habermas will assert supranational legal protection as the necessary response to the expanding transnational power of economic, and hence political, actors. But evidence suggests that this supranational juridical development is presently stymied by the still quasi-sovereign nation-states. The EU member states may have suffered some loss of sovereignty to the extent that they participate in the process of integration as compensation for economic losses that some attribute to international developments. These states are, however, still sufficiently strong, and jealous of what sovereignty they still hold, to be capable of blocking the extension of civil and social principles of justice to the adjudication processes of the ECJ.[62] Habermas takes note of this retrenchist behavior on the part of the member states (IO 124), but does not construe it as a particularly significant obstacle to the development of his prospective communicatively and constitutionally democratic European continental regime (IO 127). On the contrary, he urges state actors to undertake the "heroic effort" to promote actively the development of supranational institutions that could replace the actors themselves, or at least replicate themselves on a continental level (IO 124).

But, on Habermas's own terms, within the gap between the nation-states' declining ability to secure and advance principles of social justice themselves (as a result of evaporating tax bases, increased environmental threats, anti-immigrant and minority-unfriendly policies, etc.) and their reluctance to fully accede these responsibilities to fora like the ECJ lies the abyss of the supranational democratic possibilities of Habermas's

---

Constraints on European Law," paper presented at the annual meeting of the American Political Science Association, Boston, 3–6 September 1998. This does not speak well of the ECJ's ability to incrementally establish, for instance, judicial independence, precedence, stability, and, of course, determinacy over time. Add to this the general obscurity of the ECJ in the public consciousness of European citizens: see Gregory A. Caldeira and James L. Gibson, "The Legitimacy of the Court of Justice in the European Union: Models of Institutional Support," *American Political Science Review* 89 (June 1995), 356–76, and we have, at this point in time, a less politically independent and popularly legitimate agent of transnational social change than many progressives would like. I introduce these examples not to hold the future of a supranational legal-democratic order hostage to present political constraints. In this historically open-ended and politically fluid situation, such a strategy would be as theoretically insufficient as idle speculation. I invoke these facts merely to make the point that these present constraints must be more fully integrated into prognostications, such as Habermas's, concerning future possibilities of law and democracy in the EU. An account of the development of the EU that makes plain the limits on the possibility of supranational development autonomously of the member states is Andrew Moravcsik, *The Choice for Europe: Social Purpose and State Power from Messina to Maastricht* (Ithaca, NY: Cornell University Press, 1998).

[62] See Garrett, Keleman, and Schulz, "The European Court of Justice, National Governments."

theoretical framework as laid out in BFN.[63] If the ECJ is to adjudicate exclusively on the basis of market-related *rules*, and merely hortatory appeals to *principles* associated with civil, social, and human rights, then the subtle distinction and interplay of rules and principles upon which Habermas bases his rationally democratic theory of adjudication would appear virtually ineffectual in the EU context. There is obviously significant debate on the extent to which pessimism is warranted concerning social welfare in contemporary Europe.[64] But it is precisely the existence and importance of such debates that render problematic their absence from Habermas's discourse theory of law in BFN. In short, law in the EU is precisely the kind of supranational law that is developing in ways that may not necessarily be understood in the traditional terms of international, constitutional, and statutory law. Habermas cautions that the adequacy of his theoretical framework may not be relevant until some time in the future (BFN 501–3, 506–7), but it is worth while to test its substance against the findings of contemporary research since he provided no guidelines for its possibilities and constraints in BFN. His analyses of democracy in the EU may provide more of this necessary historical-structural aspect of contemporary critical social and political theory.

Conclusion

At one point in the discussion of the reflexive theory of law in BFN, Habermas highlights the historical limitations of understanding law in terms of

[63] In any case, there is disagreement in empirical studies between those who argue that globalization undermines national welfare states (cf. Jean-Marie Guéhenno, *The End of the Nation-State*, trans. V. P. Elliott [Minneapolis: University of Minnesota Press, 1995]) and those who suggest that the evidence is far from clear and may, in fact, suggest that globalization encourages domestic public spending on the redistribution of resources and risk (Elmar Rieger and Stephan Leibfried, "Welfare State Limits to Globalization," *Politics and Society* 26 [September 1998], 361–88).

[64] The serious question of expanding social welfare to the European level is extensively explored in the individual or collaborative work of Stephan Leibfried and Paul Pierson: see Stephan Leibfried and Paul Pierson, "Prospects for Social Europe," *Politics and Society* 20 (September 1992), 333–66; and "Semi-Sovereign Welfare States: Social Policy in a Multitiered Europe," in Leibfried and Pierson, eds., *European Social Policy: Between Fragmentation and Integration* (Washington, DC: Brookings Institution, 1993), 43–77, and Pierson, "The New Politics of the Welfare State," *World Politics* 48 (January 1996), 143–70. The authors, while relatively sure of the stability of European member-state welfare regimes, in any event, unlike Habermas, suggest that whatever the future shape taken by a European social regime, its trajectory will certainly be vastly different from those of individual European social states. They label expectations like Habermas's concerning the nation-state-replicating path of development of a European welfare regime the "Stockholm fallacy."

paradigms. But he has in mind the traditional resistance of bourgeois formal law adherents to the development of materialized *Sozialstaat* law,
not the resistance of Habermas's own understanding of the two earlier
paradigms to new, perhaps supranational, paradigms:

> Paradigms harden into ideologies insofar as they systematically *close themselves
> off* from the perception of *radically new situations* and *resist different interpre-
> tations* of rights and principles, interpretations that press for acknowledgment
> in the light *of radically new historical experiences*.... [They] stabilize themselves
> through professionally and judicially institutionalized monopolies on interpreta-
> tion and *permit only internal revision* according to their own standards. (BFN
> 221, emphases added)

This is an excellent description of Weber's response to *Sozialstaat* law
and could, ironically, be said of Habermas's *Sozialstaat* framework itself.
In BFN, Habermas's discourse theory of law has to some extent closed
off, resisted, and insulated itself against reflections on the law's radically
new historical situation. To that extent, the book falls somewhat short
of the standards set in his early work and his own adoption of the strictures of critical theory. Obviously, the simple assertion of "history" or
the injunction toward the more fine-grained analysis of "context" will
not automatically or satisfactorily address the deficiencies of either liberal normative theory or its concrete-fixated assailants.[65] But, as I hope
to show in the next chapter, the combination of the concretely historical
and categorically universal methods practiced in Habermas's early efforts,
and still alluded to in his later ones, offers a viable provisional guide for
thinking critically about the law in the new century.

---

[65] See Ian Shapiro, *Political Criticism* (Berkeley: University of California Press, 1990),
207–13.

5

Habermas on the EU

Normative Aspirations, Empirical Questions, and Historical Assumptions

In 2005 a proposed constitution was rejected by several member states of the EU, largely because its proponents failed to articulate a grand vision of a legally, socially, and politically integrated Europe.[1] Jürgen Habermas, arguably Europe's greatest living philosopher, is virtually the only scholar or public intellectual to set out the requisite comprehensive vision of constitutional democracy in the EU. This chapter evaluates the strengths and deficiencies of Habermas's vision of supranational democracy in Europe. Habermas argues that the EU will solve socioeconomic problems posed by globalization, as well as capitalize on legal and cultural possibilities opened by it: on the one hand, the EU will address the threat that increased capital mobility poses to the European welfare state; and, on the other, a constitutionally integrated Europe will generate a postnational citizenship that accommodates the multicultural dimensions of contemporary member states.

I demonstrate that the plausibility of Habermas's normative vision of the EU hinges on two contradictory accounts of globalization: the dominant theme of his essays, the historical continuity of globalization within the history of capitalism, supports Habermas's vision of supranational constitutional-social democracy but does not portend the overcoming of exclusionist identity politics that is central to Habermas's theory of postnational citizenship. Conversely, alternate strains of Habermas's account of globalization – those that depict it as an example of historical disrupture

---

[1] Nevertheless, pronouncements on the death of EU constitutionalism are certainly premature: see the symposium "The EU Constitution: RIP?" *Political Science and Politics* 39, no. 2 (April 2006), 237–72.

or what he once called a "structural transformation" – raise doubts about the possibility of a supranational constitutional-welfare regime even as they render conceivable a transcendence of the elite-manipulated politics of ethnic and cultural exclusion. In the next chapter, I will suggest that empirical evidence suggests that the emerging European polity will look very different than the supranational constitutional state (*Rechtsstaat*) or welfare state (*Sozialstaat*) that Habermas describes and will resemble a *Sektoralstaat*: a polity in which different policy spheres are governed by those most closely affected by or most interested in them, a development with dire implications for democratic rule, legal authority, and material equality in Europe's future – ramifications not properly addressed by Habermas.

The problem that globalization poses for political progressives is often framed in terms of the following two questions. (A) Does increased capital mobility undercut the power of states to advance social justice on a domestic level? There is growing concern that tax bases and regulatory capacities in postindustrial democracies have been undermined by the ability of capital to move sites of production and corporate headquarters abroad or by the credible threat to do so.[2] (B) Can international institutions, movements, and associations advance cosmopolitan and universal schemes of rights against states that do not observe such rights with respect to minorities, women, workers, immigrants, the environment, and as on? Such postnational human rights strategies capitalize on recent developments such as increased migration flows, changes in workforce demographics, and greater awareness of the policy implications of multiculturalism and environmentalism.[3] However, the two questions to some extent

[2] See Paul Hirst and G. Thompson, *Globalisation in Question: The International Economy and the Possibilities of Governance* (Cambridge: Polity Press, 1996); Susan Strange, *The Retreat of the State: The Diffusion of Power in the World Economy* (Cambridge: Cambridge University Press, 1996); Saskia Sassen, *Globalization and Its Discontents* (New York: New Press, 1996); Sassen, *Losing Control?: Sovereignty in an Age of Globalization* (New York: Columbia University Press, 1998); and Christian Barry and Thomas Pogge, eds., *Global Institutions and Responsibilities: Achieving Global Justice* (Cambridge: Blackwell, 2006).

[3] See Seyla Benhabib, *The Rights of Others: Aliens, Residents and Citizens* (Cambridge: Cambridge University Press, 2004); Thomas W. Pogge, ed., *Global Justice* (Cambridge: Blackwell, 2001); David Held, *Democracy and the Global Order: From the Modern State to Cosmopolitan Governance* (Stanford, CA: Stanford University Press, 1995); Yasemin Nuhoglu Soysal, *Limits of Citizenship: Migrants and Postnational Membership in Europe* (Chicago: University of Chicago Press, 1994); Arjun Appadurai, *Modernity at Large: Cultural Dimensions of Globalization* (Minneapolis: University of Minnesota Press, 1996); and D. Archibugi, D. Held, and M. Koehler, eds., *Transnational Democracy* (Cambridge: Polity Press, 1998).

stand in tension with or work against each other: the first is motivated by trepidation over diminished state capacity in the sphere of political economy, while the second seeks to accelerate the diminution of the state's autonomy to carry out repressive political and social policies. Nevertheless, both questions assume a new status for the state in the contemporary world.

Habermas attempts to theorize both of these concerns in the context of the EU, which, despite recent setbacks, still serves as the best test case for an analysis of postnational politics. In essays composed since the publication of BFN, some of which have been collected in the volumes *The Inclusion of the Other* and *The Postnational Constellation*,[4] Habermas operationalizes the normative blueprint of the former work in contemporary historical-empirical circumstances often identified with globalization. One might justly expect that among contemporary social and political theorists, Habermas is best equipped to confront the kinds of questions just raised, given his previous efforts at combining moral-philosophical, social-scientific, and historically grounded modes of analysis. While Habermas may have rivals in each of these separate scholarly spheres, he has been a peerless practitioner of the kind of interdisciplinary research necessary to even begin confronting a problem as multifaceted and potentially overwhelming as globalization. For instance, in contrast to Rawls's justifications for economic redistribution and, more recently, global justice,[5] Habermas's efforts have seldom been entirely confined to the realm of "the ought," but have incorporated state-of-the-art knowledge

---

[4] See Habermas, *Between Facts and Norms: Contributions to a Discourse Theory of Law and Democracy*, trans. William Rehg (Cambridge, MA: MIT Press, 1996), hereafter BFN; *The Inclusion of the Other: Studies in Political Theory*, Ciaran Cronin and Pablo de Grieff, eds. (Cambridge, MA: MIT Press, 1998), hereafter IO; "The European Nation-State and the Pressures of Globalization," *New Left Review* 235 (1999), 46–59, hereafter NLR; "Beyond the Nation-State?: On Some Consequences of Economic Globalization," in E. O. Eriksen and J. E. Fossum, eds., *Democracy in the European Union: Integration through Deliberation?* (London: Routledge, 2000), 29–41, hereafter DEU; *The Postnational Constellation: Political Essays*, Max Pensky, ed. (Cambridge, MA: MIT Press, 2001), hereafter PC; and "Warum braucht Europa eine Verfassung?" in Habermas, *Zeit der bergänge* (Frankfurt a.M.: Suhrkamp, 2001), 104–29. I cite the English translation by Michelle Everson, sponsored by the European University Institute: "So, Why Does Europe Need a Constitution?" (http://www.iue.it/RSC/EU/Reform02.pdf), hereafter RSC.

[5] See John Rawls, *A Theory of Justice* (Cambridge, MA: Harvard University Press, 1971); and *The Law of Peoples: With the Idea of Public Reason Revisited* (Cambridge, MA: Harvard University Press, 1999). See the review of the latter by Charles Beitz, "Rawls's Law of Peoples," *Ethics* 110 (July 2000), 670–75.

of "the is" as well.[6] As I have shown in Chapters 1 and 2, Habermas's "critical theory" at its most incisive has been characterized by concern with an ought inhering immanent to the is – particularly a constantly and often rapidly changing is.[7]

Habermas conceives of the EU as a postnational vehicle to preserve and advance the liberal and social democratic achievements of the European nation-state – significantly, one that will abstain from the domestically and externally directed xenophobia and ethnocentrism to which the nation-state has been susceptible in the past. In his estimation, the EU might facilitate the self-government and economic equality necessary for human autonomy without the war, genocide, and discrimination that render the former impossible. Yet, Habermas's analysis of the problems raised by globalization and potentially solved by the EU relies on an account of the historical development and the political economy of the modern European nation-state that exhibits serious tensions with – indeed, directly repudiates – his own earlier but still relevant writings. This chapter demonstrates how Habermas wavers between historically continuous and discontinuous accounts of globalization, each of which makes more or less plausible particular aspects of his normative vision of the EU.

The tension between these two views exemplifies the extent to which Habermas's understanding of historical transformation within modernity has changed from earlier work, as well as his recent tendency to paper over the pathologies of the *Sozialstaat*. Each of these mature "turns" in his work renders problematic the coherence and persuasiveness of Habermas's analysis of EU supranational democracy: Habermas often describes the implications of globalization in ways that are reminiscent of the transformation from *Rechtsstaat* to *Sozialstaat* arrangements that was the central focus of *Public Sphere*. Moreover, the legitimation and clientalization problems that Habermas previously identified and criticized in the Fordist state would conceivably persist and perhaps proliferate in the conduct of

---

[6] See Thomas McCarthy, *The Critical Theory of Jürgen Habermas* (Cambridge, MA: MIT Press, 1978); Seyla Benhabib, *Critique, Norm and Utopia: A Study of the Foundations of Critical Theory* (New York: Columbia University Press, 1986); Stephen K. White, *The Recent Work of Jürgen Habermas: Reason, Justice and Modernity* (Cambridge: Cambridge University Press, 1990); and Kenneth Baynes, *The Normative Grounds of Social Criticism: Kant, Rawls, and Habermas* (Albany: State University of New York Press, 1991).

[7] Most explicitly and impressively in Habermas, *The Structural Transformation of the Public Sphere: An Inquiry into a Category of Bourgeois Society*, trans. T. Burger with F. Lawrence (Cambridge, MA: MIT Press, [1962] 1989), hereafter STPS.

supranational governance. Habermas renders these issues subordinate to, respectively, themes of historical continuity and welfare-state efficiency in the essays under consideration. Habermas's aspirations for supranational democracy in Europe are compelling in many important respects. But because Habermas's analysis of the EU abandons the sensitivity to both historical change and the constraints posed by political economy that set him apart from normative theorists in the past, I argue that the methodological approach of these essays undermines the efficacy of his normative vision today. In short, like Weber, when confronted with a daunting structural transformation, Habermas resorts to an unsubstantiated historical narrative and an unreflective ideational construction of the past in comparison with/in contrast to the present so that the present might be grasped more facilely. That Habermas engages in such moves to highlight optimistic rather than Weberianly pessimistic possibilities does not mitigate the undertheorized quality of the moves themselves.

The first section (1) elaborates Habermas's account of the problems posed by globalization that, to his mind, necessitate the continued development of the EU; subsequent sections explicate (2) Habermas's contradictory account of the history of the nation-state and (3) outline his legal discourse model of EU democracy. In conclusion, I (4) develop an immanent critique that uses Habermas's previous historical and empirical work, and the presuppositions of his present work against the dominant historical-empirical logic he enlists in recent essays to ground his normative vision of supranational democracy in Europe. Having criticized the internal contradictions within Habermas's analysis of the EU in this chapter, in Chapter 6, I will explore the limits of Habermas's vision of the European *Sozialstaat* by juxtaposing it with the *Sektoralstaat* model of supranational governance that I suggest is emerging in the EU. This political configuration is composed of both the transnational "comitological" or "infranational" policymaking that presently operates under the auspices of the European Commission and the eventuality of "multiple policy Europes" within the EU, a scenario in which different combinations of member states will constitute separate energy, defense, trade, communications, welfare, and environmental regulatory regimes.

1. Global Problems to Be Solved by EU Democracy

In the essays under consideration, Habermas flirts with the identification of globalization as a structural transformation, demurs from such a step, but then proceeds as if it is in fact such a transformation in his description of phenomena associated with globalization. Consistent with the two facets of globalization (A and B) laid out earlier, Habermas acknowledges that globalization entails various developments that are not strictly "economic," for instance "the intercontinental dissemination of telecommunications, mass tourism, or mass culture [as well as] the border crossing risks of high technology and arms trafficking, the global side-effects of overburdened ecosystems, or the supranational collective network of governmental or non-governmental organizations" (PC 66). But he insists that the "most significant dimension" of globalization is, in fact, the economic one (PC 66). Habermas defines economic globalization in both quantitative and qualitative terms: on the one hand, as a quantitative increase in the interdependence of national economies on industrial goods produced elsewhere and, on the other, in terms of a qualitative change in the kinds of goods exchanged. Unlike products manufactured in Fordist-industrial arrangements, those produced and transported via new communication technologies can be "stored and then consumed at different locations far removed from one another" (DEU 31).

Consequently, the world economy is now "transnational" and no longer "international" since national boundaries have become blurred, and the political scope of states is no longer determined by "the strategic decisions of other nation-states, but by *systemic* interdependencies" among them (DEU 32). The conduct reflective of these arrangements, and the risks entailed by them, can no longer be predicted or calculated by projecting the behavior of strategic actors, as might have been possible in the state system (DEU 32). Habermas is adamant that the Fordist, industrial, international state system has been displaced and, concomitantly, so has its greatest normative achievement: "the globalization of the economy, no matter how we look at it, destroys a historical constellation in which, for a certain period and a favored region, the welfare-state compromise was possible" (DEU 33). The endangered status of the postwar nation-state's social welfare functions, in what seems to be a structural transformation of the state–economy relationship, is Habermas's first concern in these essays.

As I show, Habermas equivocates on the nature and extent of this transformation from the Fordist nation-state constellation to the new transnational one associated with globalization in a way that will have serious ramifications for his contemporary normative prescriptions. Certainly, Habermas's language often conjures images of structural transformation, as when he speaks of the changing "locus of control" from "space to time" and the replacement of "rulers of territory" by "masters of speed" (PC 67). But Habermas ultimately punts on the "transformation" question: "Whether we understand economic globalization as the accelerated continuance of long-established trends or as a transformation to a new transnational form of capitalism, it nonetheless shares the disturbing traits common to all accelerated processes of modernization" (RSC 8). Thus, having raised the possibility that globalization represents a new structural transformation, Habermas then identifies it as a mere "structural adjustment" like others that have asymmetrically distributed social costs (RSC 8). Nevertheless, as we will see, this new asymmetrical redistribution of social costs and burdens seems so drastic as to signal a new historical configuration. While these essays waver over continuity and innovation, *Public Sphere* suggested that new historical configurations require new institutional means to secure normative ideals, new or old. Put simply, Habermas wavers over continuity and innovation throughout the essays.

The issue of structural transformation does not subside as Habermas invokes Karl Polanyi's *Great Transformation* to assess the substance and magnitude of globalization.[8] According to Habermas, Polanyi wrote *Transformation* to explain fascism's pathological response to unregulated capitalism and wound up predicting the emergence of the Bretton Woods arrangements of the postwar world. However, Habermas admits that globalization may portend a historical change comparable in magnitude to the rise of capitalism itself and not just the mini-eras within it, such as the interwar and postwar periods:

Since [the book's publication], the balancing act of a successful political closure with the political deregulation of global markets has come to an end. A new opening, this time via financial markets, has once again transformed the international division of labor. The dynamics of the new global economy explain the renewed interest in the dynamic of the international economy that Polanyi explored. That is, if a "double movement" – the deregulation of world trade in the nineteenth century, and its re-regulation in the twentieth – can serve as a model, then we may once again be standing on the brink of a "great transformation." Polanyi's perspective, in any case, poses the question of how the political closure of a globally networked, highly interdependent world society would be possible without regressions – without the same sorts of world-historical tremors and catastrophes that we know from the first half of the twentieth century, and that spurred Polanyi's investigation. (PC 85)

---

[8] See Polanyi, *The Great Transformation: The Political and Economic Origins of Our Time* (1944), fore. Joseph E. Stiglitz, intro. Fred L. Block (Boston: Beacon Press, 2001).

Even if Habermas stops short of explicitly declaring as structural transformations the transitions between these mini-eras within the late twentieth century – between what he calls the "organized modernity" of the immediate postwar epoch and the "liberally expanded" modernity dated roughly since the 1970s – he too is concerned with directing these developments in a "non-regressive" manner (PC 86).

Therefore, Habermas clearly accepts as fact the globalization scenario raised by question (A): state capacity for economic regulation and redistribution is diminishing as a result of the internationalization of financial markets and industrial production. Without qualification, Habermas speaks of

the ever-widening gap between the limited room for nation-states to maneuver and global economic imperatives that are less and less susceptible to political influence. . . . [W]ith the recent trend toward the denationalization of the economy, national politics is gradually losing its influence over the conditions of production under which taxable income and profits are generated. Governments have less and less influence over enterprises that orient their investment decisions within a global horizon. They are caught in the dilemma of having to avoid two equally unreasonable reactions. A policy of protectionistic isolationism and the formation of defensive cartels is hopeless; but balancing the budget through cutbacks in the domain of social policy is no less dangerous in view of its likely social consequences. (IO 122–3)

States *could* exert more control over the economy through regulation and redistribution, in this account, but doing so would undercut their own competitiveness in the global market. However intimidating it may be, globalization is not an "evolutionary given," according to Habermas; it is amenable to political control, understood not as a reversal of recent trends, but rather as a *corrective*: for instance, short-term unemployment can be corrected by education, training, and modest transfers, while long-term unemployment can be addressed through negative taxation (RSC 8–9). Though globalization need not entail a structural transformation of the state and an inevitable diminishing of its power, states seem to be moving in this direction nonetheless:

There is neither a linear relationship between the globalization of markets and reduced state autonomy, nor is there a necessarily inverse relationship between employment levels and social welfare: quite independently from intensified external global pressure, governments have also had to learn to take a less dominant position within national arenas, laying an increasingly mediation-oriented role in their interaction with influential social actors. Social science literature has highlighted the co-operative characteristics of a modern state that has been captured within bargaining processes and must deal with more or less self-assertive parties. Although the state retains its exclusive recourse to the legitimate mechanisms of coercion, it must seemingly and ever more regularly refashion its operations to convince and to convert rather than to command. (RSC 10)

Even if governments "retain adequate options" over employment and social welfare, Habermas notes that global competition has reduced levels of corporate taxation (RSC 11).

Habermas also worries that, beyond the parameters of political economy, the state's reluctance to use its monopoly on coercion means that it no longer manages security and environmental threats unilaterally, or even through conventional treaties: "The spread of technology and weapons, and above all of ecological and military risks, pose problems that can no longer be solved within the framework of nation states or by the traditional method of agreements between sovereign states" (IO 106).

Certainly, there is no consensus over the extent to which aspects of this scenario over which Habermas equivocates actually obtains in reality. Well-established arguments demonstrating a correlation between extensive exposure to international markets and increased domestic expenditure have been revived and recast in debates over globalization.[9] Moreover, there is evidence to suggest that nation states can cooperate to solve ecological and military problems without sacrificing sovereignty; in other words, the necessities of the international realm can be met by nationstates acting collectively through treaties.[10] Habermas is willing to admit as much with respect to the containment and regulation of war, but he is less optimistic on environmental issues (IO 126), accidents, and ecological changes such as Chernobyl, the ozone hole, and acid rain (PC 68).

---

[9] See David R. Cameron, "The Expansion of the Public Economy: A Comparative Analysis," *American Political Science Review* 72, no. 4 (1978), 1243–61; Geoffrey Garrett, "Global Markets and National Politics: Collision Course or Virtuous Circle?" *International Organization* 52, no. 4 (Fall 1998), 787–824; Garrett, *Partisan Politics in the Global Economy* (Cambridge: Cambridge University Press, 1998); Dani Rodrik, "Why Do Open Economies Have Bigger Governments?" *Journal of Political Economy* 106, no. 5 (1998), 997–1032; Carles Boix, "Partisan Governments, the International Economy, and Macroeconomic Policies in Advanced Nations, 1960–93," *World Politics* 53 (October 2000), 38–73; and Brian Burgoon, "Globalization and Welfare Compensation: Disentangling the Ties That Bind," *International Organization* 55, no. 3 (Summer 2001), 509–51.

[10] See John Gerard Ruggie, ed., *Multilateralism Matters: The Theory and Praxis of an Institutional Form* (New York: Columbia University Press, 1993); and Andrew Moravcsik, *The Choice for Europe: Social Purpose and State Power from Messina to Maastricht* (Ithaca, NY: Cornell University Press, 1998).

However, he ultimately concedes that "global environmental consortia" work effectively, if not optimally (PC 69).

These are important debates in the contemporary literature on globalization. But I do not intend to criticize Habermas for being insufficiently attentive to all facets of contemporary empirical research. That is always too convenient a way of dismissing the arguments of a normative theorist, even one as empirically curious and well grounded as Habermas. Moreover, Habermas recognizes that growing social inequalities, despite the decline of Keynesianism and the increase in global competition, cannot be causally attributed to globalization at this point in time (PC 91). But he worries that exact measurements of the relationship between social democracy and international exposure are difficult because workforces have changed and grown as a result of women, immigrants, and economic refugees entering the ranks in the last generation (PC 91).[11] Habermas notes that right now, nation-states continue to benefit from economic productivity even under the postindustrial conditions he describes; certainly, doomsday prognoses regarding "technological unemployment" have not been borne out (PC 90). But he is adamant that since the 1970s, economic growth and unemployment rates have been uncoupled, with growth seeming to result in increased unemployment, for which the United States and the United Kingdom have compensated with the creation of low-wage sectors. The latter development, rather than solving economic problems, only serves to perpetuate impoverishment and marginalization, and requires increasing state repression and decreasing social solidarity (PC 91). Thus, if Habermas's account of globalization does not incorporate all aspects of the contemporary political economy literature, it certainly engages most of the prevailing arguments within it.

So, how does Habermas more specifically accentuate the diminishing state capacity to regulate economic forces? He declares that nation-states are increasingly inadequate because they make decisions on a territorial basis, while "in an interdependent world society there is less and less congruence between the group of participants in a collective decision and the total of all those affected by their decision" (PC 70). In particular, he continually invokes the prospect of "footloose capital" that might exercise its "exit option" whenever a government attempts "to protect social standards, maintain job security, or preserve its own ability to manage

---

[11] On these and other dimensions of changing labor-market dynamics, see Bruce Western, *Between Class and Markets: Postwar Unionization in the Capitalist Democracies* (Princeton, NJ: Princeton University Press, 1997).

demand" by constraining the conditions for domestic investment (NLR 50). As he remarks:

Capitalism's new, apparently irrevocable globalizing dynamic drastically reduces the G7 states' freedom of action, which had enabled them, unlike the economically dependent states of the Third World, to hang on to a relative degree of independence. Economic globalization forms the central challenge for the political and social orders that grew out of postwar Europe. (PC 49)

In addition, he emphasizes the greater influence exerted over domestic affairs by economic actors lying outside individual states: for instance, "international stock exchanges have now taken over the function of assessing national economic policies" (NLR 50).

In this vein, Habermas claims that governments are at the mercy of an independent "symbolic economy" in which these swiftly reacting international exchanges "evaluate," and of course influence, domestic interest rate policies and budgetary measures according to investment-friendly criteria (DEU 31). In addition, the state now has rival policymakers in the International Monetary Fund (IMF), the General Agreement on Tariffs and Trade (GATT)–created World Trade Organization (WTO), the World Health Organization, the International Nuclear Regulatory Agency, and various agencies of the United Nations (PC 70). The result of all these developments is not, as their spokespersons would assert, increased efficiency and abundance within national economies but rather much more ominous social developments: the supplanting of politics by markets results in the vicious cycle of soaring unemployment, strained social security systems, and shrinking national insurance contributions (NLR 50).

States risk exacerbating these problems by attempting to address them through business-unfriendly deficit spending and likewise have little leverage to forge long-term partnerships with capital that might be socially beneficial: "The global networking of financial markets encourages short-term investments and accelerates capital flows," such that mobile capital "can more readily slip through the fingers of national fiscal authorities" (DEU 31). In particular, low-skilled blue-collar workers in low-technology industries suffer from the independence of multinational corporations that move direct investment around to their best advantage (DEU 31). Workers, not the wealthy, are affected by the fact that taxes on high incomes, corporations, and capital gains have fallen since the 1980s, while excise and middle-income taxes have risen (PC 69). Habermas suggests that transnational economic actors attempting to dodge taxes, and the political imperatives of "direct investments," are motivated by the neo-liberal/

internationalist fantasy of achieving "harmoniously equilibrated production sites and … a symmetrical division of labor," which, like older Marxian delusions, underestimates and miscalculates the severity of the inevitable and perhaps perpetual "transitional" period requisite to realize such a result, that is, the "valley of tears" it will be necessary to traverse (NLR 51). Thus, according to Habermas, the postwar era is reaching its end due to both structural and ideological threats to the "welfarist domestication of capitalism": respectively, economic globalization *and* neo-conservatism/neo-liberalism (PC 48).[12] After all, as stated earlier the *Sozialstaat* has practical remedies at its disposal – radical redistribution to the lowest quintile, widespread sharing of capital assets, or raising the minimum wage – but ones that are not acceptable from reigning interest, property, and value perspectives that largely regard the *Sozialstaat* as a "misdevelopment" (PC 92). Therefore, it is not only for structural but also for ideological reasons that Habermas declares that supranational coordination of labor policy is necessary (PC 92).[13]

Habermas muses over the potentially dreadful ramifications of continued and extended state capitulation to mobile economic power, particularly through recourse to supply-side policies that attempt to control demand but exact heavy social costs in the effort (PC 77):

The social consequences of an abdication of politics, which tacitly accepts a chronically high level of unemployment and the dismantling of the welfare state as the price to be paid for international competitiveness, are already discernible in the OECD countries. The sources of social solidarity are drying up, with the result that the social conditions of the former Third World are becoming commonplace in the urban centers of the First World. These trends are crystallizing in the phenomenon of a new "underclass." (IO 122–3)

---

[12] As a cautionary note, Fritz Scharpf suggests that the globalization issue is not so simple as blaming the "usual suspects" for the economic problems of European countries since the 1970s: the ubiquitous laments over "institutional rigidities, union power and the burdens of the welfare state." Scharpf, *Governing in Europe: Effective and Democratic?* (Oxford: Oxford University Press, 1999), 124. These neo-liberal explanations do not confront "critical structural factors," particularly those related to gender demographics, such as the fact that unemployment figures neglect the impact of women in the workforce, or the separate taxation of spouses' incomes, or the impact of day-care availability on the labor market, as well as the fact that unemployment figures are open to political manipulation in general. See Scharpf, *Governing in Europe*, 125. This is not to mention the impact of increased incarceration rates on political economy; see Bruce Western and Katherine Beckett, "How Unregulated Is the U.S. Labor Market?: The Penal System as a Labor Market Institution," *American Journal of Sociology* 104 (1999), 1030–60.

[13] It should be noted that, as we observed him do so in Chapter 2, Habermas again finds it necessary to savage the neo-conservative/neo-liberal ideology of the bourgeois formal law revived anachronistically and cynically in these contemporary circumstances (PC 93–4).

What distinguishes the emerging underclass from earlier incarnations of
the poor is the nearly permanent and quasi-unalterable nature of their condition: specifically, their complete exclusion from the systems of employment, education, housing, and family benefits (DEU 30). Habermas avers
that the ensuing "de-solidarization will inevitably destroy a liberal political culture" (DEU 30). In almost apocalyptic terms, he speaks of the
resulting "autonomization of globalized networks and markets," a "fragmentation of public consciousness," and a "crippling fatalism" reminiscent of the "Old Empires" (IO 158). Even worse than the material poverty
engendered by a world economy beyond political control is the despair
that results from the absolute inability to *improve* what Habermas refers
to as "the postindustrial misery of the 'surplus' population produced by
the surplus society" (IO 158). Such poverty and despair occasion more
frequent crimes against life and property, to which the only state response
still legitimate, according to neo-liberal logic, is the imposition of *order*: in
such a world, "prisons and the organization of internal security" will be
the only government-sponsored "growth industry" (IO 123). Habermas
insists that this is not a strictly North–South hemispheric problem, since
a loss of solidarity *within* Europe is indicated by antiredistributive movements in Italy against the south of the country and in Germany among
the *Länder* and against the former East (PC 72).

One might ask if this scenario is really new at all. Perhaps what is most
chilling about Habermas's account of this impending future is how reminiscent it is of the present and the recent past. Indeed, are the causes of
such conditions to be found in globalization or do they predate the eclipse
of Fordist political-economic arrangements? Certainly, massive poverty
existed in the industrial democracies before the more recent transnational-
ization of production and exchange, as Habermas's own work conveys.[14]
I discuss this in the next section. For now, we would have to concede
that the globalization scenario (A) described earlier, as recapitulated by
Habermas, one that would lead to increasing inequalities of wealth within
the nations of the North Atlantic rim, and particularly between the North-
ern and Southern Hemispheres, is a qualitatively new epoch in the history
of capitalism (IO 126). Again, Habermas demurs from designating it as
such even if his account clearly raises the issue.

Besides the demise of distributive justice, Habermas points out how
this postnational scenario portends a collapse of public policy in general.
On the one hand, globalization potentially facilitates universal interaction

---

[14] See Habermas, *Legitimation Crisis*, trans. Thomas McCarthy (Boston: Beacon Press,
1975), hereafter LC.

by spreading natural languages through the electronic media; but, on the other, it more extensively proliferates the insular and encoded languages that pertain to money and the law (IO 120–1). The esoteric codes and rules that govern semiautonomous social and economic spheres inhibit open communication and prevent such spheres from being evaluated by persons most affected and perhaps legitimated by standards common to all. If state-facilitated political integration and standardization were obsolete then we would find ourselves living in what Habermas calls a "postpolitical world" where "the multinational corporation becomes the model for all conduct" (IO 125). He ascribes a "Hobbesian" character to this world, yet "Luhmannian" seems the more appropriate adjective: Habermas conjures a neo-liberal nightmare where a decentered array of "self-reproducing and self-steering functional systems" incessantly run according to their own logics. General authority is replaced with rule by quango, nothing collective transcends differentiated subfields, and nothing public prevails; rules are "legitimate" simply because they are imposed and followed, and not because they are rationally formulated or generally applied through consent (IO 125).

Habermas suggests that while national politics, to some extent, is deliberatively inclined, contemporary global politics is not, and thus cannot sustain solidarity-preserving regulation and redistribution:

In a politically constituted community organized via a state, [sociopolitical] compromise formation is more closely meshed with procedures of deliberative politics, so that agreements are not simply produced by an equalization of interests in terms of power politics.... [O]n the international level this "thick" communicative embeddedness is missing. And a "naked" compromise formation that simply reflects back the essential features of classical power politics is an inadequate beginning for a world domestic policy. (PC 109)

Habermas does concede that the contemporary negotiations of intergovernmental accords are not structured by power politics alone, but also by a "normative framing" (PC 109), and, indeed, might be developed further in such a direction by greater inclusion of nongovernment organizations (NGOs) and recourse to global referenda (PC 111).

Despite his pessimism regarding global politics and his worries over increasing economic injustice, Habermas notes that the fatalism that accompanies most descriptions of globalization must be combated and can be done so by transcending a national-state perspective:

It is a paradoxical situation. We perceive the trends toward a postnational constellation as a list of political challenges only because we still describe them from the familiar perspective of the nation-state. But the more aware of this situation we become, the more our democratic self-confidence is shaken; a confidence that is necessary if conflicts are to be perceived as challenges, as problems awaiting a political solution. (PC 60–1)

Habermas warns against "alarmist feelings of enlightened helplessness" that encourage policy inclinations toward mere "intelligent management" of "forced adaptation to the pressure to shore up purely local positional advantages" (PC 61). Habermas understands such local-instrumental behavior as leading to a trivialization and desubstantialization of political controversy. This is a perfect milieu for the "forced cheerfulness" of neo-liberal politics, a milieu in which money and "political charisma" favor the recent wave of right-wing "outsider" personalities (PC 80). Habermas must have in mind Perot, Buchanan, Berlusconi, Haider, and LePen.

Habermas insists that neither local instrumentalism nor national protectionism is an appropriate solution to the emerging problematic; instead, he proposes a general policy of "anticipative, intelligent and sustainable adaptation of national conditions to global competition" (DEU 32). Habermas offers two possible and not necessarily mutually exclusive ways of realizing this adaptive policy: on the one hand, the attempt to "cushion" its impact at the national level; or, on the other, the effort to "catch up" with it through supranational politics (NLR 52–3). Such cushioning at the national level would entail a reversal of the reigning antipublic, neo-liberal value orientation of general publics and perhaps, more concretely, the enactment of a state-guaranteed citizen income (DEU 32–3). But if the budgets of national governments are, in fact, severely constrained as a result of global competition, then Habermas indicates that something more radical may be in order (DEU 33): namely, the transfer of redistributive and regulatory functions from "the nation-state to larger political units" so as to more assuredly "catch up" with a "transnationalized economy" (DEU 33). This would signify the requisite "political response" to the contemporary dilemma: the search for "appropriate forms for the democratic process . . . beyond the nation-state" (PC 61).

Along these lines, then, in order to forestall the dawning of the global "involuntary risk society" and the shortsightedness of "locational competition" just described (IO 150; PC 62), Habermas envisions and endorses the development of "continental regimes" in North America, Asia, and Europe (IO 150, 107), regimes that would evolve out of the present institutional frameworks of, respectively, the North American Free Trade Association (NAFTA), Asia-Pacific Economic Cooperation (APEC), and the EU (DEU 33). Since a world state is "unlikely" (DEU 37), these continental regimes might eventually provide the "requisite infrastructure" at an intermediary level between the United Nations and the nation-states (IO 107) to facilitate the conduct of "a global domestic politics" and prevent the chaos of ungoverned economic and policy actors (NLR 48). The emergence and conduct of NAFTA and Association of Southeast Asian Nations (ASEAN), for instance, already suggest that the distinction between foreign and domestic policy is growing increasingly "blurry" (PC 71). What are the incentives or constraints that will encourage the appropriate policy actors to drift in this "continental" direction? Habermas suggests that globalization will eventually set concrete limits to the continued externalization of unpleasant consequences by actors unconcerned with the consequences – in other words, the shifting of costs and burdens to other sectors, regions, cultures, and generations without immediate reprisals and costs (DEU 36). Somewhat mitigating the hopelessness of the nightmare scenario he outlined previously, Habermas suggests that the world is becoming too small for some areas of it to persist in passing on, rather than dealing with, social, economic, and environmental problems. Perhaps the globe itself presents limits to the perpetual sloughing off of market capitalism's pathological outcomes and presents the opportunity for the continental regimes to emerge as rational coordinators of appropriate solutions.

But, in advocating regional or continental regimes, Habermas demonstrates that he is not an unequivocal advocate of *universal* citizenship, for he insists that citizenship can be grounded in *universalist* principles but must be realized in *particular* forms of life (PC 107): "even a worldwide consensus on human rights could not serve as the basis for a strong equivalent to the *civic* solidarity that emerged in the framework of the nation-state. Civic solidarity is rooted in particular collective identities; cosmopolitan solidarity has to support itself on the moral universalism of human rights alone" (PC 108). The particularity of regions might provide a concrete specificity to create a solidarity that "the world," as such, would not: "I see no structural obstacles to expanding national civic solidarity and welfare-state policies to the scale of a postnational federation. But the political culture of a world society lacks the common ethical-political dimension that would be necessary for a corresponding global community – and its identity formation" (PC 109).

To Habermas's mind, the highest priorities of such continental regimes would be the amelioration of the postindustrial misery of an increasingly inegalitarian world: "If the welfare state is to be preserved at least in its essentials and if the creation of a separate underclass is to be avoided, then institutions capable of acting supranationally must be formed. Only regionally comprehensive regimes like the [EU] can still affect the global system along the lines of a coordinated world domestic policy" (IO 157–8). In terms of social solidarity, redistribution requires proactive citizenship, human rights only a reactive one (PC 108): concrete solidarity forms the infrastructure upon which integrative institutions may be built, while abstract rights can be observed by punishing their violation after the fact. Habermas admits, however, that "the idea of supranational politics catching up with globalized markets" has not yet even attained the status of a "project" (DEU 35). But, according to Habermas, supranational social democracy must be pursued at the continental level or nowhere at all, because its feasibility is diminishing on the national level and, again, is improbable at the global one: "a *global welfare regime* seems a quite rapturous, if not bizarre idea" (DEU 35). He insists that a "world domestic policy" conducted by continental regimes is not the same thing as a single "world government"; he is in favor of the first but not the second (PC 104). And the fears of right-wing, antiglobalists notwithstanding, he suggests that "despotic world rule" is not only undesirable but also not likely (PC 106). The continental regimes will interact *not* in the manner of administrative components of a single state but rather in a manner that requires a "less demanding basis of legitimacy in the organizational forms of an international negotiation system" (PC 109).

But Habermas does not think that simply identifying the problems associated with globalization suggests the institutional and cultural specifics of the solution to them in the EU, the most developed of the nascent continental regimes that he mentions. Habermas is still sufficiently sensitive to history to look to the *development* of the problems for insight into the particulars of their solution. Habermas claims that the history of the nation-state suggests how the latter may be overcome in a salutary rather than a regressive manner at the supranational level. He states that "the institutionalized capacity for democratic self-determination, the political integration of citizens into a large scale society counts among the undisputed historical achievements of the nation-state" (PC 71), and that these functions are what must be preserved in supranational institutions. I will examine whether Habermas's account of that history can support his conclusions concerning the overcoming of the nation-state.

2. The History of the State as a Guide to the Present

Habermas claims that the "unprecedented increase in abstraction" engendered by globalization is "merely the continuation of a process" that began with the initial development of the nation-state (IO 107). Just as authority accrued to a higher institutional level and extended over a wider territorial expanse in the state-building process, globalization presently abstracts away from and beyond the local and national to the regional and universal. Potentially important differences between the two moments of this "continuous" dynamic are an increased integration in the first and the danger of heightened disintegration in the second. State building was directed by the centralized administrative authority of newly empowered bureaucracies in tandem with market forces, while globalization is driven by a diverse array of international actors and a global market significantly free from state direction. While the nation-state initiated "a more abstract form of social integration beyond the borders of ancestry and dialect," for social integration to continue today, this process must move to "a further abstractive step" (PC 18). As we will see, because Habermas understands the abstraction process of state formation to be one of transhistorical continuity, whatever minor variations occur within it, he claims that we can evaluate the emergence of "postnational societies from the very historical model we are on the point of superseding" (IO 107).

In other words, since the same process that gave rise to state dominance is contributing to its demise, gains and losses of this outcome might be inherent in the process itself: "Though the national state is today running up against its limits, we can still learn from its example" (IO 117). Habermas's main question and purpose are whether the integration of democratic citizenship previously achieved within the nation-state can be carried out on a supranational level without recourse to the ethnic identity enlisted by the former in this effort (IO 117). Habermas avers that attention to an ongoing historical process does not compel us, as if by fate, to reexperience the same pathologies that plagued the nation-state: "there are no laws of history in the strict sense, and human beings, even whole societies, are capable of learning" (IO 123; cf. NLR 47). Recall from Chapter 2 that Habermas understands social evolutionism in cognitive-adaptive, not deterministically teleological, terms, and he does not resort to historical determinism, but he does think that historical trends provide road maps to paths that may or may not be taken in the present and the future.

Contrary to the stereotypes of both early-modern state building and contemporary globalization, Habermas insists that the crucial issue is not the "openness or closedness" of the state's boundaries – its purported integrity in the former case and its porousness in the latter (PC 82). Much more important to the history of the state is the interaction between two social processes, one pertaining to networks and one to lifeworlds: the functional integration of individuals through market exchange and their cultural integration through mutual understanding, intersubjectively shared norms, and collective values (PC 82). Building on his uncoupling of system and lifeworld theory of modernity, and invoking the "pluralism of worldviews" account to which it has been increasingly wedded, Habermas declares that "European history since the Middle Ages" has been marked by the interaction of networks and lifeworlds (PC 82). Lifeworlds have been the intuitive background for the development of networks that then force the former to adapt continually to their imperatives. Not surprisingly, Habermas describes this in secularization terms: "growing pluralism loosens ascriptive ties to family, locality, social background, and tradition. . . ." (PC 83). To be sure, Habermas's secularization account lacks the tragic air of Weber's: Habermas asserts that the "overlapping projects for a common political culture" required by contemporary supranational demands could be derived from "the common historical horizon that the citizens of Europe already find themselves in" (PC 103). More specifically, he asserts that European history has been characterized since the Middle Ages by a series of tensions unlike those that have beset any other culture: secular–ecclesiastical, regional, town–country, Protestant–Catholic, faith–knowledge, colony–metropole, and so on (PC 103). In this very ideas-based, very transhistorical narrative, Habermas resorts to many "since the Middle Ages" references. He suggests that these tensions across the history, modern and premodern, of Europe contribute to the decentered perspectives, critical reflection, distance on prejudices, overcoming of particularisms, engendering of tolerance, and institutionalization of disputes that characterize the best of Western development (PC 103).

Habermas also observes that the tenuous relationship between state power and market dynamics is another issue that is not novel or peculiar to the situation of globalization – indeed, he recognizes it as an additional constant in the history of the modern West. The European state always maintained a rather precarious relationship with markets: Traditionally,

the financial needs of the state are met by a privately generated tax income. The price the administrative system pays for the benefits of [its] functional specialization is its dependence on the performance of an economy regulated by markets. Although markets can be established and regulated by political means, they obey a logic of their own that escapes state control. (IO 109)

The state flourished by resorting to the partial, but never total, regulation of these markets. States were dependent on the capitalist economy to the extent that revenues were derived from taxes, until finally the *Sozialstaat* succeeded in "regulating national economies without, however, destroying the self-regulating mechanism of the market" (DEU 33). But Habermas reiterates that the globalized economy increasingly "evades the grip" of even such partial state regulation.

However, in his account of the rise of the European state, while Habermas acknowledges state dependence on a market economy, he does not attribute the former's genesis to socioeconomic factors; markets only further the development of the state once it is already established. In fact, in these essays, Habermas's notion of the origins of the modern state is largely ideational. As indicated earlier, much like the later Rawls,[15] Habermas absorbs a secularization account of modernity, one that posits an emergent pluralism of worldviews in the early modern period that necessitated the development of centralized secular authority to control it (IO 111). In such accounts, whether Habermas's or Rawls's, these ideological developments themselves do not seem to be socioeconomically conditioned at all. Moreover, Habermas somewhat erroneously associates confessional conflicts with the demise of "divine right" rather than identifying it as one of the sources of the latter's emergence (IO 111). The divine right of the absolutist period was in many respects a provisional *solution* to the disorder of unruly religious pluralism.[16]

This ideational account of historical change has ramifications for Habermas's prognosis concerning supranational democracy, as we will see. At this juncture, I would merely point out that these observations differ rather drastically from those presented in Habermas's *Public Sphere*, a work that (a) integrated ideas and empirical facts in the subtle transitions of history and (b) emphasized the decidedly abrupt character of change between epochs *within* modernity as opposed to a generalized continuity *of* modernity. As discussed in Chapter 2, the ideals of the bourgeois public sphere were conditioned by the expanded exchange of commodities in the market and the emergence of social labor. Moreover, the periodization central to his analysis in that work was not "feudal–modern," as it is in the essays under consideration, but rather the more fine-grained distinction among feudal, absolutist, mercantilist, laissez-faire, and Fordist phases of modern history.

In these essays on the EU, Habermas attributes the development of the modern state to the interaction of and tension between formal citizenship

---

[15] See John Rawls, *Political Liberalism* (New York: Columbia University Press, 1993).

[16] See Charles Tilly, ed., *The Formation of National States in Western Europe* (Princeton, NJ: Princeton University Press, 1975).

and ethnic nationality (IO 113). Citizenship, based on popular sovereignty and universal rights, justifies political participation, then socioeconomic entitlement, and develops in "the communicative context of the press, and from the discursive struggle for power of political parties" (PC 102). But Habermas suggests that this was insufficient to "mobilize" people for the domestic or international tasks of state building, and appeals to "nationhood" served to fill the motivational vacuum (IO 115): "National consciousness owes its existence to the mobilization of enfranchised voters in the political public sphere, no less than to the mobilization of draftees in defense of the Fatherland" (PC 102). In other words, "democratic citizenship" was not a self-motivating phenomenon and proved necessary but not sufficient for the task of social integration without the accompaniment of an unattractive politics of ethnic and cultural homogeneity. Habermas invokes his now famous notion of "constitutional patriotism" (IO 114) as a progressive alternative that was never satisfactorily practiced outside of the "immigration nations."[17] According to this ideal, national substance was understood in terms of the interpretation of one's own constitution over time rather than by appeals to a prepolitical identity located in either common ethnicity or even language. In this alternative account of nationalism, while admitting that political mobilization "depends on a prior cultural integration" (PC 64), Habermas insists that political identity is not fundamentally primordial: "peoples come into being only with their state constitutions" (NLR 57).

Nevertheless, the substantively formal sociopolitical integration associated with citizenship and constitutional patriotism will not be easy to carry over in a supranational age. Habermas notes that contemporary cultural circumstances entail, on the one hand, a hardening of ethnic identities such as national majorities and minorities, but also, on the other, a fragmenting and fracturing of them to an individual level via the materialism of global capitalist culture. He suggests that "both tendencies strengthen centrifugal forces within the nation-state, and will sap the resources of civil solidarity unless the historical symbiosis of republicanism and nationalism can be broken, and the republican sensibilities of populations can be shifted onto the foundations of constitutional patriotism" (PC 76). Habermas asks "whether here, in Europe and in the Federal Republic of Germany,

---

[17] Habermas's "constitutional patriotism" is often invoked as a slogan but seldom interrogated as a concept. A notable exception is Patchen Markell, "Making Affect Safe for Democracy?: On 'Constitutional Patriotism,'" *Political Theory* 28, no. 1 (February 2000), 38–53.

a cosmopolitan consciousness – the consciousness of a compulsory cosmopolitan solidarity, so to speak – will arise" (PC 112). This requires a tight intra-European solidarity and a weaker but still substantive solidarity with peoples of other continental regimes throughout the world.

Habermas may seriously overestimate the extent to which constitutional patriotism was ever realized *anywhere* outside of the writings of Kant, even – or especially – in "immigration nations" like the United States.[18] There certainly are more than glimpses of the nonexclusionary proceduralist and deliberative aspects of nationhood in Habermas's own account of early-nineteenth-century European civil society in *Public Sphere*. But that work is notorious for overlooking virulent nationalism, ethnic prejudice, the subjection of women, and class oppression in the bourgeois public sphere.[19] To be sure, Habermas managed to show in that work how democratic citizenship did in fact serve as a powerful ideal immanent within historical practice, as well as the only possible rival to nationalism for putting flesh on the bones of formal constitutional liberties, universal rights and popular sovereignty. Citizenship at its best in the past and, Habermas will hope, in the future is characterized by the substantive social, public, and political *exercise* of formal rights rather than the mere *enumeration* or even *observance* of them: "The true functional requirements for democratic will-formation [are] the communicative circuits of a political public sphere that developed out of bourgeois associations and through the medium of the mass press.... This process gives rise to public opinions that aggregate themes and attitudes to the point where they exercise political influence" (IO 153). Formal citizenship entails a substantive practice and result: Habermas argues that it must have a "use-value," a concrete payoff in social, ecological, and cultural terms, to be meaningful (PC 77).

However, Habermas insists that nationalism too often trumped such substantive democratic practice, often resulting in "the expulsion of enemies of the state" and even "the annihilation of the Jews" (PC 18). The sheer artificiality of nationalism, in particular, makes it susceptible to manipulation by elites. Consequently, the progress of democratic citizenship could be derailed by appeals to homogeneous identity on the part of

---

[18] See Rogers Smith, *Civic Ideals: Conflicting Visions of Citizenship in U.S. History* (New Haven, CT: Yale University Press, 1997).

[19] See Oskar Negt and Alexander Kluge, *Public Sphere and Experience: Toward an Analysis of the Bourgeois and Proletarian Public Sphere*, trans. P. Labanyi, J. O. Daniel, and A. Oksiloff (Minneapolis: Minnesota University Press, 1993); and Craig Calhoun, ed., *Habermas and the Public Sphere* (Cambridge, MA: MIT Press, 1992).

officials who could not or would not facilitate social and political justice: for instance, the fact that "domestic conflicts can be neutralized by foreign military successes rests on a socio-psychological mechanism that governments have repeatedly exploited" (IO 114). Nationalism could always be whipped up in military engagements to distract from the deficiencies of domestic policies and politicians.[20]

During the Cold War, however, such options were not available to policy elites in European nation-states. Despite gesturing to a learning process through which policy elites voluntarily sought to avoid economic mistakes of the interwar period that Polanyi pointed out led to fascism, war, and genocide (PC 48), Habermas admits that these elites were actually *forced*, under novel geopolitical circumstances, to facilitate democratic citizenship through a more responsible domestic politics:

> Under the umbrella of a nuclear balance between the superpowers, the European countries – and not just the divided Germany – could not conduct a foreign policy of their own. Territorial disputes ceased to be an issue. Internal social conflicts could not be diverted outward but had to be dealt with in accordance with the primacy of domestic politics. Under these conditions it became possible to uncouple the universalistic understanding of the democratic constitutional state to a large extent from the imperatives of a power politics guided by national interests.... (IO 119)

Postwar social democracy carries out this "welfare-state pacification of class antagonism" through expanded social security, reforms in education, family policy, criminal law, the penal system, data protection, and so on, as well as tentative provisions for gender equality (IO 119). Habermas asserts that "within a single generation the status of citizens, however imperfect, was markedly improved in its legal and material substance" (IO 119).

But Habermas's account of the welfare state here contravenes his own analyses in important earlier works such as *Public Sphere*, LC, and TCA[21]: he now describes Fordist policies as if they "benefited the population as a whole," when he had previously emphasized their discriminatory and

---

[20] In this sense, Habermas equivocates on the thesis associated with David Miller's *On Nationality* (Oxford: Oxford University Press, 1997), which posits that welfare state consolidation required the undergirding of nationalism: here Habermas suggests that nationalism *distracted* from substantive welfare issues, while later he will admit that nationalism *provided* some of the infrastructure for social democracy. His ultimate point is that political culture and redistributive politics can be sustained through an intersubjectively not ethnically based solidarity (PC 99).

[21] Habermas, *Theory of Communicative Action*, vols. 1 and 2, trans. T. McCarthy (Boston: Beacon Press, 1984/1987), hereafter TCA.

marginalizing affects. Whereas Habermas previously charged the mass party/corporatist state with infantilizing what were once deliberating publics, in these essays he remarks that it "improved the general level of education" (IO 121). Moreover, the following descriptions are simply not consonant with the pathologies of the welfare state diagnosed by Habermas in these earlier works: "citizens intuitively realized that they could succeed in regulating their private autonomy, and that an intact private sphere is in turn a necessary precondition of such political participation" (IO 120). All discussion of the self-defeating and intrusive public policy of LC and TCA, as well as the stultification of the populace by the plebiscitary politics of the welfare state in STPS, seem to have vanished. As Habermas moves up to a supranational level, he becomes much less stringent on standards for democratic practice at the national and subnational levels. For instance, is the following statement a watering down of his previous nationally based standards for deliberative democracy and a capitulation to localized acclamatory democracy?:

Within democratic constitutional states, the public communicative infrastructure plays the ideal-typical function of crystallizing problems of common social concerns within discourses, such that citizens are given the opportunity to orient themselves in line with equally weighted arguments and take a positive or negative stance on controversial contributions. The largely implicit and fragmented yes/no reactions to better or less well-founded alternatives are the tiny particles, which, on the one shorter-term hand, accrue to immediately influential opinions and, on the other longer-term hand, make themselves felt in underlying political attitudes and democratic electoral results. (RSC 19)[22]

Continuing along these lines, Habermas concludes, "national economies provided a range of opportunities for redistribution that could be exploited, through wage policies and – on the side of the state – welfare and social policies, to satisfy the aspirations of a *demanding* and *intelligent* population" (IO 121, emphasis added).[23] These great achievements of

---

[22] At one point, Habermas concedes the inadequacy of postwar national politics but resorts to referenda, place markers for deliberation translating into action, for supranational accountability: "Political decisions in polarized consensus-based democracies are notoriously intransparent. Europe must therefore consider the use of Europe-wide referenda in order to give citizens a better opportunity to influence the character of policies" (RSC 27).

[23] Rather than complicit in the political apathy of *Sozialstaat* politics, in these essays Habermas presents mass communication as progressively integrating in an almost unqualified way: "National consciousness has derived as much from the mass communication of newspaper readers as from the mass mobilization of conscripts and voters. It has been no less shaped by public discourse on the influence and governing power of competing

the now glorified *Sozialstaat* include substantive living conditions, educational opportunities, and leisure time to foster creativity – in other words, the "preconditions for effective democratic participation" (RSC 4). He characterizes these as the successful *materialization* of "formal state guarantees and the rule of law," a process "identified by Max Weber" (RSC 4). Presumably, Habermas feels that his reconstruction of Weber has been so complete that he may now invoke him as an advocate for, or at least neutral witness to, the *Sozialstaat* realization of the claims of the *Rechtsstaat*, and not as a paranoid critic of the transformation. But has Habermas provided us with sufficient resources to follow him in such a move?

In these writings on globalization and the EU, Habermas will repeatedly invoke the example of "a broad democracy that works reasonably well," or at least does so within the nation-states of the postwar North Atlantic rim (NLR 47). Habermas identifies the welfare state, the social project achieved during the Hobsbawnian "Golden Age" of the postwar years, as "a specific culture and way of life that is today under threat" (RSC 7). On that basis he poses the question: "Can this form of the democratic self-transformation of modern societies be extended beyond national borders?" (NLR 47). But before this question can be answered, it must be pointed out that Habermas did not previously believe, nor does he now demonstrate, that the *Sozialstaat* operated in such a manner *within* national borders. Habermas may gesture to the clientalization critique of Western welfare states by noting how they hardly encouraged "their clients to take charge of their own lives" in an unambiguous way (NLR 47). He even invokes his former intellectual opponent, Michel Foucault,[24] to accentuate the problems of bureaucratization and normalization in the *Sozialstaat*, but winds up emphasizing the successes of liberalism, constitutionalism, and democracy within the latter configuration (DEU 33). In the most effusive language, he asserts, "In the third quarter of [the twentieth] century, the welfare state did succeed in substantially offsetting the socially undesirable consequences of a highly productive economic system in Europe and the OECD states. For the first time in its history, capitalism did not thwart fulfillment of the republican promise to include all citizens as equals before the law; it made it possible" (NLR 47).

political parties than by the construction of proud national histories" (RSC 17). Recall that *Public Sphere* showed mass communication to be as, or more, stultifying than it was edifying or progressively integrating.

[24] For critical cross-comparisons of Habermas and Foucault, see Michael Kelly, ed., *Critique and Power: Recasting the Foucault/Habermas Debate* (Cambridge, MA: MIT Press, 1994), and White, *The Recent Work of Jürgen Habermas*, chap. 6.

Again, in terms that almost directly repudiate the arguments of the earlier works mentioned previously, Habermas speaks of how "successful government steering mechanisms in domestic economies stimulate growth and so secure vital bases for their legitimation" that are being undermined by globalization (NLR 50). In this respect, the history of the national welfare state, once a concrete object of critique, now seems to function as an "as if" proposition in Habermas's theory: supranational possibilities apparently must be measured against an idealized older model of the state. In TCA and BFN, Habermas balanced progressive possibilities of the Fordist welfare state against the structural impediments to those possibilities. In these essays, the analysis has tipped decidedly in favor of ideal possibilities, while attention to constraints remains largely gestural.

This move in Habermas's present analytical method raises the larger question of how one can reliably evaluate the present social scientifically: it points to the possibility that the only way an emerging social reality can be grasped is through an unlearning or exaggeration of what was a rather sophisticated understanding of a previous one. Of course, Habermas has been accused of just such an idealization of, for instance, the bourgeois public sphere in his attempt to delineate the normative possibilities of the *Sozialstaat* that superseded it.[25] But if such moves were in fact unavoidable, then the enterprise of critical theory as espoused by Habermas, particularly in his early work, would be severely jeopardized. The latter demands that normative standards be derived from present reality understood beyond mere ideological distortions of it. In other words, critical democratic theory is not supposed to adopt as its standpoint of critique a construction from an idealized past, but rather the immanent possibilities of present socioeconomic circumstances. Habermas follows in Weber's footsteps here, since Weber evaluated the *Sozialstaat* with categories, albeit dripping with pejorative connotations, derived from medieval patrimonialism and contrasted with a sanitized depiction of the *Rechtsstaat*.

Besides exaggerating the efficacy and normative accomplishments of the *Sozialstaat*, Habermas overextends state capacity to integrate local particularity in the course of nation building. The state *and* capital both integrated acutely diverse and multifarious local, cultural, and religious particularities over quite an extended period of time. Habermas suggests, "in the West, this process of nation-state formation, which interconnects and mixes tribes and regions, took more than a century" (IO 153). But

---

[25] See Calhoun, ed. *Habermas and the Public Sphere*.

this is a gross understatement: it took as many as three centuries, if not more, to accomplish this – a fact to which *Public Sphere*, in particular, was more sensitive. Indeed, elsewhere, Habermas equivocates on the difficulty of the national integration project in these essays: "The universalistic reformulation of inherited loyalties to village and clan, landscape and dynasty was a difficult and protracted process, and it did not permeate the entire population until well into the twentieth century, even in the classical nation-states of the West" (PC 18). In any case, by fixating exclusively on the ideological dimension of nationalism, rather than the social bases and consequences of state building, Habermas presents a distorted picture of how easily the state was consolidated. One might say that Habermas relies disproportionately and inappropriately on one Anderson over the other – that is, Benedict over Perry.[26] In so doing, Habermas places himself in a rather peculiar position: he argues that the nation-state was easily consolidated – easily precisely because it relied on this pathological element of substantive identity. But it is this undesirable accelerator that Habermas hopes to jettison at the supranational level. By emphasizing the purported ease with which the state constructed itself through ideological means, and by grossly neglecting the economic ones by which it did so, Habermas, at least in this instance, makes his subsequently presented case for consolidating a continental or global order more plausible than may be appropriate. How can the EU integrate democratically in as facile a manner as the nation-state if Habermas wishes to jettison the catalyst of the earlier integration process, exclusionist/xenophobic identity construction? In general, ideational accounts like the one Habermas has adopted in these essays tend to overestimate continuity and encourage notions of inevitability, whether these are ultimately evaluated positively or negatively. This would seem to be confirmed by the contrast between *Public Sphere* and Habermas's later works that I presented in Chapter 2, as well as the analyses of his mature works by McCarthy, Benhabib, and Honneth that I drew upon there.

Habermas may qualify his overall account by asserting that "national consciousness and social solidarity" were only "gradually produced with the help of national historiography, mass communications, and universal conscription" and that this was a "learning process" (NLR 58). But he does not distinguish how civil society–centered modes of integration

---

[26] See Benedict Anderson, *Imagined Communities: Reflections on the Origin and Spread of Nationalism* (London: Verso, 1991); and Perry Anderson, *Lineages of the Absolutist State* (London: Routledge, 1996).

associated with mass communication differed from those, such as mass conscription, associated with nationalism.[27] At his most differentiated, he concedes that state building required both "projections of shared descent" and practices of formal citizenship: "the nation oscillates between the imaginary organicity of a *Volksnation* and the legal construct of a nation of citizens" (PC 101–2). If the EU is to integrate along the lines of the nation-state, how will it do so without such a crucial-cum-unsavory component of the integration process? At other moments, when relying most heavily on the historical continuity of the nation-state, Habermas cheats somewhat by implying that procedural democracy temporally followed nationalism and therefore need not persist: "if [the state] form of collective identity was due to a highly abstractive leap from the local and dynastic to national and then to democratic consciousness, why shouldn't this learning process be able to continue?" (PC 102).

Also, in the absence of nationalism, what already had been an extended process at the national level would presumably become an even longer one supranationally. Habermas guards against such criticisms by asserting that a "federal European state will, in any case, be of a different caliber than national federal states; it cannot simply copy their legitimation processes" (NLR 58). But, as we have seen already and as I will confirm later, by emphasizing historical continuity, much of his account assumes that it will. Habermas asserts that European "experiences of successful forms of social integration have shaped the normative self-understanding of European modernity into an egalitarian universalism that can ease the transition to postnational democracy's demanding contexts of mutual recognition for all of us – we, the sons, daughters, and grand-children of a barbaric nationalism" (PC 103). But his own account suggests that it might not be so easy.

In fact, from a standpoint that takes into account the vagaries and intricacies of state formation in the West, it is not clear whether the following description really portends the demise of the state at all: "Today we live in pluralistic societies that are moving further and further away from the model of a nation state based on a culturally homogeneous population. The diversity of cultural forms of life, ethnic groups, religions and world-views is constantly growing" (IO 117). This scenario need not entail anything more unruly and variegated than the kind of multiplicity that was eventually accommodated or homogenized *by* the nation-state – at least

---

[27] See Theda Skocpol, *Protecting Soldiers and Mothers: The Political Origins of Social Policy in the United States* (Cambridge, MA: Harvard University Press, 1995); and Margaret Levi, *Consent, Dissent and Patriotism* (Cambridge: Cambridge University Press, 1997).

Habermas provides no evidence for why we should think so. However "multicultural" contemporary societies may be, are they really more variegated than were European localities and provinces prior to the state-building projects of the national monarchs? The role of Christianity, always exaggerated as an integrative force in feudal Europe by modernization accounts, was probably not nearly so homogenizing at this time as corporate capitalism or the bureaucratic state became in later centuries. In short, it is not clear what the relative ease or difficulty of the rise of the modern state portends for an emerging international order beyond the state in Habermas's account.

In any case, in accord with globalization scenario (B) mentioned at the outset, Habermas believes that the contemporary multicultural diversity that has been accelerated by increased migration is a progressive development to the extent that it contributes to the dissolution of the social foundations of nationalism – provided that multiculturalism does not entail the internal repression of members of particular identity groups. Habermas suggests that multiculturalism should be conducted *beyond* formal national politics, but conducted in pursuit of agendas that combine liberal and civil rights strategies, on the one hand, *with* social and cultural ones, on the other (IO 117–18).[28] Habermas advises that this agenda ought to be pursued at the supranational as well at the micro-local level, as should strategies targeted at socioeconomic equity. Despite notable instances of state recalcitrance at this very moment when the state is "most overwhelmed,"[29] Habermas avers that the European nation-state

should make the heroic effort to overcome its own limitations and construct political institutions capable of acting at the supranational level. Moreover, the latter would have to be connected to processes of democratic will-formation if the normative heritage of the democratic constitutional state is to function as a break on the at-present unfettered dynamic of globalized capitalist production. (IO 124)

Habermas repeats that the "exemplary case" of the EU "naturally comes to mind" as the direction to be followed for "democracy functioning beyond the limits of the nation-state" (PC 88; NLR 53). How does he

---

[28] See Will Kymlicka, *Multicultural Citizenship: A Liberal Theory of Minority Rights* (Oxford: Oxford University Press, 1995); Joseph Carens, *Culture, Citizenship and Community: A Conceptual Exploration of Justice as Evenhandedness* (Oxford: Oxford University Press, 2000); Seyla Benhabib, *Transformations of Citizenship: Dilemmas of the Nation State in the Era of Globalization* (Assen: Van Gorcum, 2001); and Iris Marion Young, *Democracy and Inclusion* (Oxford: Oxford University Press, 2001).

[29] See Paul Pierson, "The New Politics of the Welfare State," *World Politics* 48 (January 1996), 143–70.

evaluate this potential, normatively and realistically, and handicap the European "gamble on a postnational democracy" (PC 88)? Habermas insists that the nation-state cannot "regain its old strength by retreating into its shell" (PC 81). Rather, it can only regain such strength by no longer operating as a state in the traditional sense, but instead by more firmly embedding itself in a continental and supranational order. But, as I suggest subsequently, Habermas may conceive of the EU as a state writ large rather than as a truly novel amalgamation of states.

3. The Form and Content of EU Democracy

Habermas admits that "more than one lesson" can be drawn from the evolution of the EU so far (IO 123). For instance, one might interpret the EU as a development that actually exacerbates the problems of globalization, particularly the lack of accountability or "autonomization" of bureaucracies (IO 123). As he surveys the political situation of the EU, Habermas observes that a "thick horizontal net stretched over markets by relatively weak political regulations is being expanded by even more weakly legitimated authorities" (PC 98). In this light, he acknowledges the "dangerous legitimation deficiencies" of the Brussels bureaucracy, which is perhaps too far removed from a political base in the localities of the member states (IO 151). From this standpoint, the EU could be deemed one of the "self-programming administrations and systemic networks" at odds with "democratic processes" (IO 151) that we observed Habermas criticizing in Section 1. Weak legitimation procedures might have been appropriate to market integration but not political integration:

To date, the decisions of the Commission and Council of Ministers were largely legitimated through Members' state channels. This legitimation gauge, however, belongs to a model of international treaty-based intergovernmental government that was appropriate only to the extent that market-creating policies were the sole object pursued. The absence of *European* citizenship-based solidarity now becomes apparent to the same degree that the Council of Ministers and the Commission can no longer restrict themselves to the negative coordination of operational constraints (freedoms) and must stray across the border into the positive coordination of distributive intervention. In some estimates, the implementation of decisions taken in Brussels already makes up 70% of all national legislation; subject matter that is never exposed to political debate in national arenas and to which only paid-up European card carriers have access. (RSC 15)

Habermas predicted that EU enlargement would complicate things further: "the expansion of the Union to include a further twelve economically and socially heterogeneous countries has intensified the complexity of a demand for rule- and decision-making capacity that cannot be satisfied without further integration or a 'deepening' of the integration process" (RSC 13). Thus, Habermas does not depict EU policy as presently conducted in an unequivocally sanguine light: in particular, he complains that the harsh immigration regulations creating a "fortress Europe" violate the asylum rights enshrined in Germany's constitution (PC 73). But Habermas decides to explore more optimistic possibilities, given the indeterminacy of Europe's situation as he writes and the alarming ramifications of the more pessimistic scenario that he outlined earlier (IO 123). He is not willing to dismiss the possibility that the EU can compensate for the functional losses of the nation-state in ways that do not "snap the chain of democratic legitimation" (NLR 53): Habermas understands "the European project" as a common effort by European national governments "to win for themselves in Brussels a degree of the interventionist capacity that they have lost at home" (RSC 14).

But a potential problem with a continental- or specifically EU-centered solution to the problem of capital mobility becomes immediately apparent: *bigger* institutional structures do not automatically entail *better* adeptness at controlling global capital. Habermas concedes that "the creation of larger political entities does not by itself alter the process of competition between local production sites, that is, it does not challenge the primacy of market-led integration per se" (NLR 54). Some might contend that anything short of the "world regime" that Habermas claims is unlikely would fail in this endeavor. But such objectives rest upon a somewhat mechanical spatial logic whereby territorial authority readily translates into economic control. Drawing upon the "global limits" logic that I recounted earlier, Habermas argues that the development of multiple continental regimes means that fewer actors might better coordinate common policies: "With each new supranational regime, the number of political actors decreases, while the club of those few actors fills who are at all capable to act on a global scale, and are able to co-operate for reaching arrangements as to the project and the implementation of an economic world order" (DEU 34).

But even if he does not go about it in a crude manner, Habermas does seem to adhere to the notion that institutional size corresponds with some capacity for economic control: for instance, he claims that the size of the nation-state – smaller than the ancient empires but larger than city-states – was ideal for administrative control in the early modern period (DEU 33). To be sure, he does not define the nation-state solely in terms of its size; the unprecedented functional specialization of its administrative capacities remains a more distinctive characteristic for Habermas (DEU 33). Nevertheless, whether a world state or, more likely for Habermas, a "club" of continental regimes can direct or control markets, he recognizes that they will fall short, just as did nation-states, in one important regard: "markets, unlike polities, cannot be *democratized*" (NLR 54, emphasis added). But even if continental regimes fail at the task of fully democratizing markets, Habermas presumes that their larger territorial authority and coordination with other supranational units will enable them to carry out the kind of regulation previously exercised by the national *Sozialstaat* (PC 77): Habermas is confident that the EU, like nation-states, can take up the task of "correcting markets and establishing redistributive regulatory mechanisms," and not leave such correction and redistribution to "markets themselves" (NLR 56).

Habermas identifies Europe's single monetary system as a potentially powerful vehicle of economic regulation and eventual sociopolitical integration. The EMU would lead to common financial, economic, and social policies, notwithstanding continued resistance against attempts to assign essential statelike competences to the EU in ways that supposedly "relativize" sovereignty (IO 124). Along these lines, Habermas proceeds to catalog the features that still qualify the EU as an international organization and not yet as something approximating a sovereign state: It was established by treaty, *not* a constitution. It holds no monopoly on violence and bears no sovereignty recognized according to domestic or international standards (IO 155).[30] The European Parliament (EP), a plausible vehicle of more directly popular supranational legitimation, is equipped with only weak competences for the time being (IO 155). Habermas thinks that the EP needs to draw more public attention to itself but need not necessarily assume budgetary sovereignty at this point in time (RSC 19). In contrast to Lionel Jospin's proposal for a new "European Congress" composed of national parliamentarians, Habermas suggests that "parliamentary legitimation of the EU would be increased were a portion of European parliamentarians *concurrently* to be members of national representative bodies or were the, to date somewhat neglected, 'Conference of Committee for European Affairs' to breathe renewed life into the horizontal *exchange* between national parliaments" (RSC 27–8, emphasis added).

---

[30] In terms of structural reforms in these spheres, Habermas suggests that the EU, backed by a European army, should "speak with one voice in matters of foreign and security policy in order better to present its own perceptions within NATO and the UN Security Council" (RSC 6).

Despite these deficient aspects of the EU, Habermas understands European *law* (technically EC law) to exercise a supreme authority over nation-states unlike that generated by any other international organization in the world, including the United Nations. He recognizes that the discrepancy between the non-state quality of EU institutions and the authority of European law is one of the sources of the "oft-bemoaned democratic deficit" in Europe (IO 155). Yet despite this situation, Habermas urges his readers not to view European institutions as *illegitimate* or even only *distantly legitimate* in the way that, for instance, the WTO is justifiably viewed. EU institutions are merely *indirectly* legitimate: the legitimacy of the EU flows from citizens *through* the member states, and law, as I will discuss, is crucial to this process (IO 155–6).[31]

Despite its non-state status, therefore, Habermas notes that the institutions of the EU could be quite easily transformed into legitimizable statelike organs: the EP could function as a conventional legislature; the EC could be converted into a cabinet; the Council of Ministers into an Upper House; and the ECJ might continue to be empowered along the lines of a U.S. or German-style constitutional court (IO 156). The 2000 Nice conference, for instance, gave the EU Charter of Human Rights "a proclamatory rather than binding status," but the ECJ references it, infusing supranational adjudication with a greater moral-political resonance (RSC 23). Indeed, the treaties that established the EC and EU certainly left these institutional possibilities open: Habermas notes that the first generation of EU founders, such as Robert Schuman, Conrad Adenauer, and Alcide de Gaspari, had no problem speaking in terms of an eventual "United States of Europe" (RSC 3). Yet, he acknowledges that many of today's European elite, whether due to a "healthy realism," "counterproductive timidity," or "outright defeatism," consider even the word "federalism" to be "offensive" (RSC 3).[32]

But Habermas's ultimate priority in exploring the legitimacy question is not formally institutional, but rather substantively political. He exclaims

---

[31] Habermas cites European social legislation that promotes gender equality and the approximately 300 ECJ decisions that promote social law and the compatibility of national welfare standards with the European market functioning (PC 96). But he notes that these policies and decisions do not affect the crucial spheres of taxation and distribution that require substantive political pressure (PC 97).

[32] Nevertheless, even supranational skeptics acknowledge the possibility that the EU might be reformed along federal or quasi-statist lines: see Geoffrey Garrett and George Tsebelis, "The Institutional Determinants of Supranationalism in the European Union," *International Organization* 55, no. 2 (2001), 357–90. Moreover, in 2001, German Chancellor Gerhard Schroeder proposed reforms in just such a spirit, and the Laeken Conference called for a constitutional convention that just might adopt them.

that the EU organs just mentioned must be "filled with life," not just formally empowered, if they are to do more than merely "accelerate the autonomization of bureaucratized politics" (IO 156). The risk that formal legitimacy may mask or engender substantive alienation is magnified at the supranational level given the greater distance between EU institutions and national/local populaces (IO 157). Therefore, in addition to being "repositioned" from a treaty organization toward a basic lawlike Charter, the EU must foster a sociological basis that includes a "common practice of opinion- and will-formation" (PC 100). But Habermas does not consider whether a debate over a formal constitution may yet engender substantively social results. A European constitution would provide a "catalyzing impetus" intensifying and directing a European civil society, public sphere, and political culture toward "convergence":

Europe must reflexively re-apply to itself the logic of the circular process that witnessed the mutual reinforcement of the democratic state and the nation. The starting-point would be a constitutional referendum precipitating a Europe-wide debate. The constitutive process is itself a unique instrument of cross-border communication. It is a potential *self-fulfilling prophecy*." (RSC 18)

But Habermas here straddles notions of novelty and continuity, sometimes implying that a European people in fact *already* exists: he asserts at other moments that Europe need not attempt what the French and American revolutionaries accomplished (with various levels of bloodshed) since "the constitutive question is no longer integral to the problems we are seeking to solve" (RSC 4). In other words, we already know what we wish to achieve and what the polity is that will achieve it. Europe needs only "a new format to safeguard the great achievements of the nation state beyond national borders" (RSC 4).

Habermas asserts that what is *most* needed to promote democracy at a supranational level is the development of "a European-networked civil society, a European-wide political public sphere, and a common political culture" (IO 156). He insists that social movements and NGOs, *not* governments, are the best agents of a European or global integration project (DEU 37). While Habermas welcomes "the world-wide development of an informed political opinion- and will-formation [capacity]," he acknowledges that the over 350 international NGOs devoted to economic order, peace, and ecology are in no position to secure it (DEU 35). If they focus their energies on states, the latter may be unable to address their concerns for the reasons sketched in Section 1; if they target international institutions such as the WTO or the UN, these associations may bring insufficient leverage to bear on these international institutions to be effective. Thus, according to Habermas's account, by developing within and focusing upon continental institutions such as the EU, these associations can begin the process of accomplishing the goals of global justice associated with proposition (B) raised at the outset of this book. In short, transnational associations operating outside the context of continental regimes are too weak, and the bureaucratic structures of the continental associations as they presently exist are too formal. Together, they might comprise what is for Habermas the appropriate form–content relationship for the conduct of supranational politics:

Interests currently segregated along economic, professional, confessional, ideological, class, regional and gender lines will, once beyond the borders of the nation state, begin to overlap. Such a transnational fusion of parallel interests and value-orientations would encourage the creation of a European party system and transnational networks. Territorial forms of organization would in this manner be transformed in line with functional principles to create the associational relationships that could form the core of a European civil society. (RSC 19)

Thus, Habermas does not mechanically invoke "civil society" to breathe life into the dormant body of integrated Europe. He does, however, wish to refine the way that a European civil society might address the problems of a postnational situation. At this point in his analysis, Habermas attempts to sort out empirical and normative concerns: "Any assessment of the chances for a European-wide democracy depends in the first place upon empirically grounded arguments. But we first have to determine the functional requirements; and for that, the normative perspective in which these requirements are justified is crucial" (IO 158). In other words, a normative ideal, generally informed by historical and empirical factors, must be elucidated *first*. *Then* the functional mechanisms necessary to bring this about must be delineated. And *then* the resulting architecture must be reexamined empirically for its feasibility. But I will argue that because Habermas has sufficiently repudiated or ignored his own practice of historical and empirical methodology a priori, he seriously hinders his ability to conduct this third stage of analysis. This is particularly acute regarding his treatment of welfare-state pathologies; elite-manufactured or -exploited identity politics; and the trajectory of social change within modernity. Indeed, in his own recent work, Habermas occasionally asserts the necessity of sorting out historical continuity and discontinuity so as to make normative prescriptions, even if he does so himself when carrying out his analysis of supranational democracy: "The continuities of social modernization extending through the century can only inadequately teach us what is characteristic of the 20th century as such. Thus, historians tend to punctuate the historical flow of their narratives with events, rather than trends and structural transformations. And indeed the physiognomy of a century is molded by the caesurae of great events" (PC 43). These are methodological standards that hearken back to Habermas's earlier work, and ones by which I will measure his enterprise throughout the balance of this chapter.

In this effort to sort out normative priorities, Habermas identifies four perspectives on integration: cosmopolitan, market European, Eurofederalist, and Euroskeptic (NLR 56). Cosmopolitans view the EU as a step toward world government: a world without political demarcations. We have seen that Habermas is wary of undifferentiated formulations of such a goal. Market Europeans understand the EU to be nothing more than a free-trade zone, an environment for commercial exchange and little else. Habermas affiliates this view with the example of a Deutsche Bank spokesman, who "can only regard as 'academic' the debate over the alternative 'state alliance' or 'federal state'" (NLR 56). Market Europeans are content with arrangements established by international treaties aimed at promoting "negative" integrative functions such as dismantling trade barriers and constructing market institutions (PC 79). But Habermas points out that no positively integrative functions can result from treaties, except limited ecological ones; and that to successfully address the economic, social, and political unintended consequences of a "Market Europe" or a "Businessman's Europe," a constitution is required (PC 79).[33] In this vein, Habermas avers that the EU "requires a form of abstract solidarity" that cannot be generated by "the cool calculation of individual advantage" but rather by "a consciousness of collective belonging" (PC 18). The EU requires "a common value orientation" rather than mere "economic expectations" (RSC 7). In his proposal for a continental federal system that serves a European-wide civil society, Habermas will reveal himself to be something of a Eurofederalist. Eurofederalists must "design a future Europe in contrast to the status quo that the market Europeans would like

---

[33] The market Europeans demonstrate for Habermas that neo-liberals need not necessarily be antisupranational: on economic grounds they favor a continental market, while many social democrats oppose such a market on Euroskeptic grounds (PC 95). However, he notes that social democratic, as opposed to more conservative, Euroskeptics assume that the nation-state encouraged "non-economic practices, institutions, and mentalities" that institutionally embedded *national* systems of production, systems that would not necessarily be re-embedded anywhere else in the global system under contemporary circumstances (PC 95).

to see maintained; one that can stir the imagination and help to initiate a broad public debate over the common issues for different national arenas" (PC 98). Therefore, despite having stated at times that a "constitutive moment" is not necessary, he asserts, "the Maastricht intergovernmental agreement lacks that symbolic depth which political constitutive moments alone possess" (RSC 4). But his rejoinders to market Europeans notwithstanding, Habermas devotes most of his energy engaging the last of these approaches to integration, the Euroskeptic perspective.

Habermas sharply criticizes Euroskeptics – even moderate ones like Dieter Grimm[34] – who claim that European law is a significant threat to the sovereignty of individual European states. Habermas retorts that European law is obviously far less erosive of state sovereignty than are, for instance, the dynamics of contemporary capitalism. Replicating arguments for state regulation of markets in the mid-twentieth century, Habermas argues that the EU will save the state from itself much as the *Sozialstaat* saved capitalism from itself (IO 158). A remedy, now EU policy, that seems to undermine an entity, here the state, is presented by Habermas as actually furthering the latter's interests by other means. The semiofficial manifesto of Euroskepticism, the "Maastricht Decision" of the German Federal Constitutional Court,[35] states that the EU need not functionally and should not normatively take on statelike characteristics. Functionally, the decision shares the view of "intergovernmentalist" interpreters of the EU: states lease out, or pool together, competences for specific tasks without sacrificing sovereignty (IO 151).[36]

Normatively, as Habermas points out, the decision replicates the logic of nationalist, prepolitical identity notions of democracy in the following way: it claims that there must be a concrete and homogeneous European demos for there to be a European state or statelike entity. He argues that the "no-demos-thesis" put forth by Euroskeptics undermines "the voluntaristic character of a contractual nation" (RSC 17). To be sure, the Maastricht Decision – which, as Habermas notes, actually contradicted earlier decisions of the German court that accepted prevailing relations between Germany and the EU (IO 152) – has proved to be more bark than bite in practice. Yet, Habermas worries that the Euroskeptic perspective

---

[34] See Dieter Grimm, "Does Europe Need a Constitution?" *European Law Journal* 1 (November 1995), 282–302. See also Ernst-Wolfgang Böckenförde, *Welche Weg geht Europa?* (Munich: Siemens Stiftung, 1997).

[35] See the "Maastricht Decision" of the German Federal Constitutional Court. 2 BvR 2134/92, 2BvR 2159/92. *Europäische Grundrechte Zeitschrift* (1993), 429–47.

[36] See Moravcsik, *The Choice for Europe*.

contributes to an emerging alliance in European member states between economic protectionism and cultural chauvinism characterized by

ethnocentric rejection of diversity, xenophobic rejection of the other, and antimodernist rejection of complex social conditions. Such sentiment is directed against anyone or anything that crosses national borders – the arms-smugglers and drug-dealers or mafiosi who threaten domestic security, the American movies and flood of information that threaten national cultures, or the immigrant workers and refugees who, like foreign capital, threaten living standards. (NLR 52)

Indeed, Euroskeptics are learning that they can make "common cause" with the qualified supranationalism of the market Europeans "to freeze the status quo of an economically integrated but still politically fragmented Europe. But the price for this status quo is paid in the coin of growing social inequalities" (PC xviii).

Habermas charges that Euroskepticism carries the dangerous logic of nationalism – a logic with an unfortunate past in Europe – into debates over integration. The fact that it has any traction at all in contemporary debates over the EU raises questions about Habermas's aspirations for postnationalist forms of political integration. The empirical facts of increased migration flows and a more extensive multicultural composition of contemporary societies do not necessarily rule out ideological reactions to them.[37] Moreover, in responding to both the Euroskeptics and market Europeans, Habermas manages to show that in the academic literature, neither neo-realists nor neo-functionalists are correct: the state is not the *only* institution to carry out formative politics, and market integration in and of itself will not lead to political integration (PC 98). Contra the Euroskeptics more specifically, Habermas reiterates liberal and social democratic criteria of what makes a "people": neither a prepolitical substance or will nor a common enemy, but rather a set of practices and procedures actively engaged in by citizens through which social bonds are forged. In fact, he asserts that this substance-through-procedure mode of social integration should and can obtain more readily on the supranational level than it did on the national level:

The forms and procedures of the constitutional state, together with the democratic mode of legitimation, simultaneously forge a new level of social integration. Democratic citizenship establishes an abstract, legally mediated solidarity between strangers. This form of social integration, which first emerges with the nation state, is realized in the form of a politically socializing communicative context ... [and] not simply by administrative means. (IO 159)

[37] See Jacob Levy, *The Multiculturalism of Fear* (Oxford: Oxford University Press, 2000).

In other words, supranational democracy does not pertain to the organs of the EU alone, which by themselves might perpetuate the globalization pathology of autonomous bureaucracies. And it is certainly not entailed by an exclusionary definition of what it means to be "European," which would, on the other hand, replicate the worst forms of nationalism, past and present, extending them to a continental level. According to Habermas, European democracy entails interaction by associations like those mentioned earlier, associations targeting political institutions beyond the state but below the highest global level:

The initial impetus to integration in the direction of a postnational society is . . . the communicative network of a European-wide political public sphere embedded in a shared political culture. The latter is founded on a civil society composed of interest groups, nongovernmental organizations, and citizen initiatives and movements, and will be occupied by arenas in which political parties can directly address the decisions of European institutions and go beyond mere tactical alliance to form a European party system. (IO 153)

Habermas admits that contemporary nation-states themselves may not fully live up to the standards that he establishes for supranational popular government (IO 160). While I will address this later, for Habermas this fact is, in and of itself, no reason not to pursue such standards at the EU level (IO 160).

Thus, not only the pathologies of the political-economic dimension of globalization – that is, question (A) – concerns Habermas, but also a failure to address the political-cultural possibilities opened by it – those associated with issue (B). At stake, he insists, is

more than just the question as to whether the EU can, by harmonizing divergent national fiscal, social, and economic policies, win back the leeway that nation-states have lost; after all, the European economic zone is still relatively insulated from global competition, thanks to a tightly-woven regional network of trade relations and direct investments. The debate between Euroskeptics and Eurofederalists hinges above all on whether the EU, despite the diversity of its member-states, with their many different peoples, languages and cultures, can ever acquire the character of an authentic state, or must rather remain the prisoner of neo-corporatist systems of negotiation. (NLR 57)

The EU must simultaneously tame economic globalization and facilitate transnational cultural interaction; in fact, the latter may be as difficult as the former. The "neo-corporatist" tag raises the issue of whether national identities will merely horse-trade, as did labor, management, and interest groups during the Fordist era, as opposed to fully deliberating and consensually agreeing upon policies collectively. While social and citizen solidarity (NLR 57) have been historically limited to national boundaries, they must now extend to "the citizens of the Union in such a way that, for example, Swedes and Portuguese, Germans and Greeks are willing to stand up for one another" (DEU 34) – they must develop what Habermas calls "transnational trust" (PC 102). Veering toward the nationalism–welfare-state thesis that he earlier resisted, here Habermas argues that citizen solidarity is necessary for twenty-first-century social democracy: "clearly, redistributive programs are difficult to execute politically, not least since modernization's losers no longer belong to an identifiable industrial class with a strong veto vote" (RSC 9). He concedes that the majority needs to have a conscience for social justice and a belief that the disadvantaged are still members of the "dominant political culture" (RSC 9). European citizens need to be identified beyond a common passport to entail a mutually recognized common political existence that might undergird a robust common social policy (PC 99). To this end, a European civil society may require "a common grounding in foreign languages" (NLR 58), but *not* the imposition of one or some languages over others. Habermas mentions the television network Arte as a forum that promotes bilingualism, and he might have added MTV Europe (RSC 20). Furthermore, Habermas considers whether English assuming the role of "a working tool" or even a "second mother tongue," as it does in the Netherlands and the Scandinavian countries, could meet the problems posed by thirteen different officially recognized languages in Europe (RSC 21). But Habermas warns that European *integration* must not repeat coercive national *homogenization*; or, in his terms, integration should be characterized by "harmonization not *Gleichschaltung* . . . the gradual elimination of the social divisions and stratification of world society without prejudice to cultural specificity" (NLR 59). While nationalist collective belonging was "the product of national elites" in the nineteenth century, today it must be produced from a "communicative context stretching over national public spheres" (PC 18).

Habermas attempts to guard against the impression that he is simply combining and transposing up to the continental level the individual national civil societies of Europe; he attempts to show that he has something more differentiated and perhaps historically novel in mind when he proposes the further "opening" of the "still integral communication cycles of national arenas *to one another*":

The stratification of the different – regional, national and federal – instances of political opinion formation assigned to individual levels of the multi-level political system leaves us with the false picture of a "super" public sphere superimposing itself upon its national counterparts. Instead, distinctly national, but mutually translated, communicative cycles must embrace one another such that relevant contributions are osmotically extracted from each national arena. (RSC 20)

In short, he proposes a historically unprecedented reshaping of the space of communication.

The kind of communication that Habermas understands as sustaining a simultaneous nontechnocratic and nonxenophobic democracy will be encouraged and materially instantiated through EU law. As mentioned at the outset, Habermas recognizes that law can function as a popularly inaccessible administrative code. But as he reconstructs it according to the arguments of BFN that I explicated in the previous chapter: when law is formulated within a civil society of free associations, through deliberating political publics and open parliamentary statute making, and then ultimately enforced by an accountable executive, it is the best way of translating popular will into public policy.[38] In fact, it is the encoded character of law that makes administrations and markets understand the otherwise spontaneous and unruly expressions of society. For Habermas, law is therefore both institutionally administrative and socially participatory because it translates popular will into government action. It is generated by public communication but also reaches back into society to foster the conditions of further communication.

If a European civil society is not yet fully developed, European law almost certainly is. Thus, according to Habermas's theory, law is not only the connecting tissue between an emerging European civil society and the organs of the EU, but also a potential generator of further democratic activity in the former and enhanced responsiveness by the latter. This emphasis on law is what enables Habermas to transpose the architecture of BFN, largely constructed with a nation-state in mind,[39] up to a supranational level:

The ethical-political self-understanding of citizens in a democratic community must not be taken as a historical-cultural a priori that makes democratic will-formation possible, but rather as the fluid content of a circulatory process that is generated through the *legal institutionalization of citizen's communication*. This

---

[38] See John McCormick, "Three Ways of Thinking 'Critically' about the Law," *American Political Science Review* 93, no. 2 (June 1997), 413–28; and McCormick, "The Sociology and Philosophy of Law during Crises of the State: Max Weber and Jürgen Habermas," *Yale Journal of Law and the Humanities* 9, no. 2 (June 1995), 297–344.

[39] See Neil Brenner, "The Limits of Civil Society in the Age of Global Capital" (M.A. thesis, Department of Political Science, University of Chicago, 1993).

is precisely how national identities were formed in modern Europe. Therefore it is to be expected that the political institutions that would be created by a European constitution would have a catalytic effect. (IO 161, emphasis added)

Law, including the "higher" law of a constitution, is the conductor for an "identity" that is constantly formed and re-formed through interaction and policymaking. But what about the strong claim that national identities were formed "precisely" along these legal-procedural lines? Is this consistent with Habermas's alternately elite-centered or administratively centered account of nationalism presented earlier – an account that acknowledged the power of exclusionary identities in the mobilization of popular participation?

Here it might be appropriate to question the adequacy of this conception of procedural substance in Habermas's proposal for a European civil society. How can law and the associative life of civil society really integrate the EU now in a way that Habermas admits that nationalism did, and proceduralism alone did not, on the state level in previous centuries? The latter, after all, had precisely these procedural means at its disposal in the form of market-related associative life and the institutions affiliated with the *Rechtsstaat* but made recourse to the sinisterly "positive" or "substantive" attributes of nationalism. Or at the very least, the state combined proceduralism with heavy doses of nationalism. Again, the Euroskeptic perspective that Habermas engages in these essays reminds us that there are other problematic or unsavory sentiments and movements already available in contemporary Europe that cynical elites might exploit.[40] There certainly are cynically unifying imaginaries available to potential European nationalists or culturalists or continentalists that could stymie integration – or, conversely, *promote* a kind of pathologically coercive integration that Habermas would find most disagreeable. In this light, the problem of social integration may amount to something more than "a bottleneck in the process of European unification" or a lack of "cosmopolitan solidarity" (DEU 36–7); there may be active efforts to halt or undo the development of such noncoercive unity and solidarity.

Habermas largely overlooks this problem in these essays. There certainly are allusions to a progressively positive vision of Europe: for

---

[40] See Mark Hayes, *The New Right in Britain: An Introduction to Theory and Practice* (New York: Pluto Press, 1995); Martin Schain, "The National Front and the Legislative Elections of 1997," in Michael Lewis-Beck, ed., *The Legislative Elections of 1997 in France* (New York: Chatham House, 2001); and Meredith W. Watts, *Xenophobia in United Germany: Generations, Modernization, and Ideology* (New York: St. Martin's Press, 1997).

instance, the "European value order" characterized by labor movements, ecclesiastical social doctrines, and social liberalism (RSC 9), a value order that positions Europe as the social democratic conscience and model for the rest of the world (RSC 12). Habermas again makes reference to the "fundamental structural conflicts and tensions" to which "Europeans have reacted productively" throughout their history such that they learned "to live with permanent conflict and to engage reflexively with their own traditions," even if this has occurred during "the knotty course of painful and fateful developments" (RSC 22). He points to Europe's ban on the death penalty and overwhelming support for an International Crimes Tribunal, which demonstrate that Europe is the home of human rights (RSC 23). But for Habermas, it is precisely the "historical experiences" and the *lessons* of nationalism that serve as the unifying principle of something *alternative* to nationalism on the European level. Europe must unite because it must *avoid* what precisely it once was: Habermas conceives of this mixture of "negative" and "positive" European identity in the following terms:

The catastrophes of two world wars have taught Europeans that they must abandon the mind-sets on which nationalistic, exclusionary mechanisms feed. Why should a sense of belonging together culturally and politically not grow out of these experiences – especially against the rich background of shared traditions which have long since achieved world-historical significance, as well as on the basis of the overlapping interests and dense networks of communication which have more recently developed in the decades of economic success of the European Community? (IO 152)

The "painful learning process" typified by "National Socialist excess" shows that Europe must integrate in a more substantive manner: Habermas asserts that "neither 'assimilation,' nor simple 'co-existence' (in the sense of a shaky *modus vivendi*) are models that are suited to this history; a history that has taught us that we can create ever more abstract forms of 'solidarity with strangers'" (RSC 23). In fact, according to Habermas, nationalism can be replaced as a binding substance by Europe's "shared historical experience of having happily *overcome* nationalism" (IO 161, emphasis added). Appealing to the concrete historical example of national integration in Germany (PC 18), Habermas surmises "perhaps German federalism, as it developed after Prussia was shattered and the confessional division overcome, might not be the worst model" (IO 161). Nor might it be the best. If one dwells on this example at any length, one must confront the fact that this "success story" was interrupted by the failure of supranationalism after World War I and the rise of Nazism in the midst of a crisis of global capitalism, and ultimately brought to fulfillment through the impetus of a victorious enemy and in the presence of an occupying army.[41]

I should make it clear that Habermas ought not to be criticized for making "unlikely" prescriptions about the future. Habermas is not a predictive theorist. Social scientists, even – or perhaps especially – German social philosophers cannot predict the future: having demonstrated the "empirical pre-conditions" for European democracy, Habermas states that the EU must confront the "voluntaristic gap," a gap that can only be overcome if integration moves beyond "the mere abstractions of administrative measures and scientific discourse" (RSC 24). In other words, European democracy will only come to be if Europeans *want* it and *act* to bring it about. He himself admits the difficulty of assessing the evidence and making recommendations regarding globalization: as much as an empirically verifiable reality, Habermas is examining a "discourse whose outcome cannot be predicted" but for which he would like to lay out the "burdens of proof" (PC 90). In this spirit, I evaluate Habermas's account according to the standards, logic, conclusions, and "burdens of proof" of his own earlier and recent research. Since, as we will see, Habermas's arguments about a prospective postnational future rest so firmly on interpretations of a nation-state-dominated past, his own work in the area of state theory is obviously fair game.

4. Critical-Historical Limits of Habermas's Theory of EU Democracy

My immanent critique of Habermas's analysis of democracy in the EU emphasizes the following three points, all of which were alluded to in previous sections: (a) the relationship of state integration of multiplicity and locality in the past and the tasks of supranational integration today; (b) Habermas's retrospective romanticizing of the national *Sozialstaat*; and (c) the contradictions in and the ramifications of his "continuity" account of the history of the state. As the previous chapter should make plain, I do not take issue with much of the content of Habermas's normative aspirations for the EU. If European civil society is indeed capable of overcoming the excesses of ethnic, religious, and/or national identity, then by Habermas's logic, we might hope that EU membership will be

---

[41] Habermas remarks that the allied victory "sparked" democracy in the Federal Republic, but he does not consider the extent to which it *imposed* democracy (PC 47). See Max Pensky, "Editor's Introduction" (PC xv–xvi).

expanded eastward in time to include not only postcommunist states, but also Turkey and Israel. This eventuality would go a long way to diminish apprehension over the possibility that the EU might resort to unifying conceptions reminiscent of "Christendom" in its traditional and even more unsavory secular forms.[42] Such an outcome certainly would require a more differentiated reconstruction of European citizenship than Habermas undertakes here.[43] The more pressing question here is whether Habermas adequately specifies the historical-empirical conditions necessary to justify this overcoming of nationalism and the other pillar of his theory, the supranational extension of European social democracy.

As we have seen, Habermas expounds an historical narrative of the nation-state according to which its gradual emergence and impending eclipse can be conceived as a progressive increase in abstraction. He presents this course as a linear development, even if he avoids designating a particular telos. Habermas suggests the following with the sometimes "painful" process of abstraction entailed by state building in mind: "there is no reason to presume that such a form of civic solidarity will find its limits at the borders of the nation state" (RSC 17–18). The question is whether this will occur without the aforementioned pain, or whether we can foresee what kind of pain more precisely this will entail. However, there is a tension in these essays that sets out and then relies on this account of the modern state: as we observed in Section 1, Habermas also describes a postpolitical horror show portended by globalization, a neoliberal nightmare characterized by no public provision for common goods of any kind. When raising this very real alternative scenario, Habermas resorts to a language and logic that suggest qualitative historical change – structural transformation, if you will – that is not consistent with historical continuity in any obvious way. It is the presupposition of continuity, the dominant theme of Habermas's account in these essays, that makes

---

[42] I explore these issues in the thought of one notorious "Europeanist"; see my "Carl Schmitt's Europe: Cultural, Imperial and Spatial Proposals for European Integration, 1923–1955," in *The Darker Legacy of European Law: Legal Perspectives on a "European Order" in the Fascist Era and Beyond*, C. Joerges and N. S. Ghaleigh, eds. (Oxford: Hart Publishing, 2005). Habermas dismisses Christendomesque aspirations – what he calls the "Carolingian objective" of a "Christian European homeland" – that some of the EC's founders harbored (RSC 6).

[43] See the essays included in Klaus Eder and Bernhard Giesen, eds., *European Citizenship: National Legacies and Transnational Projects* (Oxford: Oxford University Press, 2001); and Seyla Benhabib, "Who Are 'We'? : Dilemmas of Citizenship in Contemporary Europe," in *The Claims of Culture: Equality and Diversity in the Global Era* (Princeton, NJ: Princeton University Press, 2002).

plausible the robust supranational social democracy that will purportedly regulate the elusive dynamics of capitalism without the inconvenient obstacles of national borders. Yet, Habermas does not reconcile these two alternative views of historical change, nor does he justify his ultimate adoption of and reliance on the latter, more optimistic account. He seems motivated by a professed anxiety over the intolerable nature of the former possibility, and perhaps too readily accepts the implications of the "global limits" argument, but does not incorporate them systematically into the historical narrative of continuity, as I will explain.

By leaving unreconciled the two contradictory accounts of globalization in these essays – drastic qualitative change that results in apocalyptic social, political, and economic outcomes versus continued increasing abstraction that facilitates a plausible supranational extension of the welfare state – and by not justifying the theoretical apparatus he employs in selecting one over the other, Habermas finds himself in a somewhat awkward position. His account aspires to a radical break with nationalism that on the face of things may not be compatible with a relatively easy extension of the *Sozialstaat*. Habermas's historical account of the dynamics of globalization does not conclusively show why both outcomes should or could be expected to emerge in tandem. If globalization can be characterized as a qualitative break, then the first desideratum of overcoming nationalism could, as a novel phenomenon, be plausible, but the second one of supranational social democracy certainly not – at least not without further elaboration. On the other hand, if globalization is in fact part of a larger historical continuity, then the second goal of welfare-state transposition seems much more likely than the first, since nationalism seems still inherent in the process itself.

To be more specific, if modern history proceeds as a continuous dynamic, then capital might indeed prove controllable on a global level. Since the nation-state managed significant if never complete regulation and redistribution vis-à-vis markets, continental regimes could be expected to do so as well. But two aspects of Habermas's own work, subsidiary here and central elsewhere, raise doubts about this eventuality. Habermas's depiction of globalization in these essays hearkens back to his STPS description of the transition from laissez-faire/liberal to administrative/welfare state capitalism, an account in which the preservation of the normative advantages of the previous model remained decidedly precarious in the second, or at least required a thinking through of alternative means to preserve them in a new historical configuration. Doubts about Habermas's model of supranational social democracy are compounded by his previous work such as LC and TCA that analyzed the crisis-ridden, redistributively insufficient, and pathology-inducing qualities of the national *Sozialstaat* even as he reconstructed the model in more emancipatory ways. In the essays on the EU, the national *Sozialstaat* is supposed to serve as an unqualified, viable model for just and efficient social integration in the future. Furthermore, historical continuity in the development of the nation-state would suggest that an integrating supranational polity would also make use of exclusionary and homogenizing notions of identity rather than forsake them, as Habermas hopes – at least he does not explain why social democratic advantages should carry over through the transition to supranational arrangements while cultural disadvantages reminiscent of nationalism will not.

Put in terms of Habermas's critique of Weber's SL, discussed previously: the relatively separate state–society relationship that conditioned the emergence of the bourgeois public sphere in the nineteenth-century *Rechtsstaat* was not sustained or extended with the emergence of the *Sozialstaat*, but rather was largely overcome and perhaps even extinguished by the latter. Habermas suggests that normative aspirations remained constant throughout the transformation but that the institutions that might realize them had to change. If the phenomena associated with globalization constitute a similar structural transformation, as his account suggests when he speaks in terms consistent with scenario (A), then this might portend the demise of the Fordist institutional arrangements of the twentieth century rather than their extension to supranational levels. If social change within modernity entails dramatic rupture and discontinuity, as *Public Sphere* suggests (STPS 9, 17–18, 78, 224), then a supranational extension of the *Sozialstaat* would not be expected, and the institutions that could realize its normative goals would need more careful and specific demonstration to be rendered plausible in Habermas's present reflections.

If, on the other hand, social changes within modernity are not nearly so drastic as the one between feudalism and modernity, as suggested by Habermas's later writings such as TCA (TCA1 199, 221, 260; TCA2 119, 174, 178), then the more continuous and linear understanding would lend feasibility to an extension of the welfare state at a continental level. Habermas claims to "use the concept of globalization . . . to describe a process, not an end-state" (PC 65). But how does this viewpoint coincide with his assertion of an end of the nation-state epoch in other moments of the essays? In the latter case, globalization would then succeed the nation-state as a new, if not final, epoch. The distinction between a "process" and an "end state" is potentially meaningless since the stateifi-cation/societalization process led to a new epoch, that of the *Sozialstaat*, in STPS, even if Habermas never fully worked out continuity/discontinuity issues and hence periodizations in that work. But the nation-state *is* an end state if Habermas conceives of supranational institutions replicating its form.

Put differently, in *Public Sphere*, Habermas could only show with great difficulty how the normative goals of the *Rechtsstaat* could be attained in the *Sozialstaat* (e.g., STPS 208–9), but he proposed socioinstitutional reforms through which they might be realized at the book's conclusion. Habermas ascended to the more abstract level of social and political the-ory in TCA and BFN, respectively, to delineate more optimistically the emancipatory possibilities of twentieth-century nation-states, but only by directly identifying the complex structures of the *Sozialstaat* with "moder-nity" itself and by neglecting moments of qualitative change within the latter historical configuration. Yet, in redescending from these theoreti-cal heights to engage what, in certain moments of his account, is a *new* transformation of state and economy under conditions of globalization, Habermas has not resumed historical-empirical analysis according to the same standards of *Public Sphere* – that is, not in a way that finely details the material gains and losses of the historical transformation. On the con-trary, Habermas's view of the possibilities of the new scenario is purely stereoscopic: either an optimistic or a pessimistic extension of some facet of the previous form of the nation-state constellation. Habermas chooses to emphasize, perhaps arbitrarily, the general conditions that might bring about the more optimistic scenario. But this move results in a promo-tion of the *Sozialstaat* model at the supranational level in terms rendered highly questionable by other aspects of Habermas's own efforts here, as well as his more historical and social scientific work of the past.

Rather than a failure to consult empirical research in contemporary social science literatures, I first wish to attribute these deficiencies to the unreconciled contradictions in Habermas's own account of the processes leading to contemporary circumstances and his refusal to reconsider the methodology of his earlier work that may in fact be more appropriate to the present moment. In other words, in this chapter, I consider this to be a conceptual or categorical problem rather than a factual or informa-tional one. In the next chapter, I consider the extent to which Habermas's *Sozialstaat* model of EU democracy conforms to the reality of *Sektoral-staat* governance that seems to be prevailing at the supranational level. By the standards set here, Habermas should have provided better theoretical justification for abandoning his earlier views of the nature of historical change *to* the *Sozialstaat* and the limitations of political economy *within* Fordist postwar nation-states. Habermas may well have changed his mind on the worth of the kinds of normative insights provided by these earlier methods, but his famous reservations about and lamentations over "philosophies of history" are not sufficient to this end. Indeed, the earlier approach reflected in STPS should be acknowledged in, if not integrated into, his present analysis, precisely because it was directed at a phenomenon – qualitative social change *within* rather than *to* modernity – that seems to have more in common with present circumstances than do his later writings, like TCA and BFN. It may be that Habermas casts modern history as continuity in the main thrust of these recent essays for the same reason he did so in his mature social and political works: as *a direct response* to the uneasy normative conclusions of his earlier historical works, such as *Public Sphere*, that emphasized structural change. In a way potentially consistent with STPS, Habermas states that economic globalization does not pose a threat to "functional and legitimate democratic processes as such," but rather to the nation-state as the "institutional form" in which these processes operate (PC 67); it only constitutes a "disempowerment" of the nation-state (PC 69). But, with little qualification, he upholds the EU as a communicatively sustained supranational social democracy precisely on the institutional model of the nation-state, as well as in line with the developmental logic of it.[44]

Whatever Habermas's motives in emphasizing such a temporal trajectory, historical continuity does not necessarily guarantee the sanguine results for which he hopes: if continuity governs the history of the state, then might not history be more likely to repeat itself than take abrupt and unexpected changes in course, such as that entailed by the discarding of nationalism? If so, apropos of criticisms raised at the end of the previous section, it is especially alarming that Habermas provides no firmer evidence in support of the possibility of overcoming xenophobia in Europe.

---

[44] Habermas attempts to preempt criticisms that might imply that he is transposing a nation-state model up to the EU level: he states that the EU cannot simply copy extant national constitutions such as Germany's, or level out European nationalities, or melt them down into a "Nation of Europe" (PC 99). But even the specifics of his recommendation replicate institutional attributes of national constitutional democracies: for instance, Habermas favors an "upper house," derived from federal nation-states, in EU constitutional arrangements to preserve individual state power (PC 99). But I believe I have shown that the continuity in the history of the state implies a historical logic that is resistant to historical novelty entailed by structural transformations.

Why will elites confronted with the integration deficiencies of supranational politics in Europe not be tempted to appeal to substantive and exclusionary identities, as did their counterparts in the earlier history of the nation-state? The infamous Huntington scenario[45] whereby continental cultural difference leads to violent conflict may have little foundation in empirical reality.[46] But it is not ruled out by Habermas's account of the history of the state on either factual or historical grounds.

Returning to the plausibility of European social democracy in Habermas's essays – the creation of "a social Europe that can throw its weight onto the cosmopolitan scale" (PC 112) – the status of transformations to and from the *Sozialstaat* is not the only issue at stake. Precisely *how* the *Sozialstaat* functions is also a problematic issue in Habermas's prescriptions for the EU. State regulation of society and the economy that he once showed to be a self-contradictory and crisis-ridden operation is presented in these essays on globalization and the EU as the paragon of redistributive and solidarity-inducing efficiency. He admits at certain points that the welfare-state compromise was by "no means the ideal solution" to the political-economic dilemma of capitalism, but he insists that it did succeed in keeping the social costs of capitalism down to a minimum (DEU 33). But such statements stand in marked contrast with those found in Habermas's previous work such as LC (LC 41–5, 50–61) and *The New Conservatism*.[47] Whereas the latter works grappled with the problematic relationship of capital and the state in the postwar era – a relationship rife with pathological unintended consequences in both material and ideological domains – this recent work does not demonstrate how the EU would adequately address these problems or, for that matter, the one of capital flight that he emphasizes so dramatically.

If globalized capital is as slippery as Habermas's depiction in these essays suggests, then it presumably could elude regional or continental regimes as easily as it has the state. The ramifications of this are exacerbated by Habermas's retrospective romanticizing of the national

---

45 See Samuel P. Huntington, *The Clash of Civilizations and the Remaking of World Order* (New York: Touchstone Books, 1998).

46 Consult Bruce Russett and John R. Oneal, "The Kantian Peace: The Pacific Benefits of Democracy, Interdependence, and International Organizations, 1885–1992," *World Politics* 52, no. 1 (October 1999), 1–37; and Russett, *Triangulating Peace: Democracy, Interdependence, and International Organizations* (New York: Norton, 2000).

47 See Habermas, *The New Conservatism: Cultural Criticism and the Historians' Debate*, trans. Shierry Weber Nicholsen, intro. Richard Wolin (Cambridge, MA: MIT Press, 1989).

Sozialstaat: if, according to Habermas's earlier work, the national welfare state did not sufficiently control and regulate markets and compensate for their deleterious effects, despite its territorial authority, why should we expect continental regimes to do so with any efficiency? Here Habermas remarks that the EU can "affect" or put a "brake" on the dynamic of global capital, but he also intimates that the latter is a *qualitatively different* and not just *quantitatively extended* kind of capitalism – one that may not be controlled, albeit imperfectly, in the manner of classic social democracy at whatever territorial expanse.[48] At some moments in these essays, Habermas attributes global capital's elusiveness to what is qualitatively new in its emerging forms of production, transportation, and consumption, but generally he understands it in terms of the expansion of a relatively similar and constant phenomenon beyond national borders.

The former understanding makes the case for a supranational welfare state exceedingly difficult but the latter not all that easier: the one would require an unprecedented regime of regulation and redistribution for which no previous configuration might serve as a reliable model, while the latter would be beset by the same or exacerbated inefficiencies and pathologies as the national *Sozialstaat*, perhaps to such an extent as to risk its sustainability altogether. The "global limits" logic that Habermas invokes (DEU 36) buttresses his case regarding the geographic constraints that would compel an unprecedented engagement with regulatory and redistributive issues among continental regimes. But this presupposes that globalization signals the quantitative extension of previous forms of capitalism, and not a qualitative break from them, such that territorial scope and proximity still translate into significant regulative capacity. In any case, Habermas does not fully explore the ramifications of both the quantitative and qualitative aspects of globalization and the tensions between them that his account raises. The global limits argument is further undermined by the fact that Habermas never previously attributed *Sozialstaat* misfunctioning to its tendency to slough off costs and burdens abroad. Here and elsewhere, Habermas describes the welfare state's regulative successes and failures exclusively in terms of its own internal capabilities, so that any diminishing capacity to export costs should not render it any more effective at a national or supranational level.

---

[48] On the difficulties of regulating Fordist capitalism, an account that influenced Habermas, see Claus Offe, *Contradictions of the Welfare State*, ed. J. Keane (Cambridge, MA: MIT Press, 1984).

All of these criticisms may be beside the point. In these essays, Habermas simply may formulate an *ideal* of social democracy on the basis of a stylized version of the nation-state of the past that might serve as a normative yardstick for the institutional future of the EU. In this sense, perhaps he has moved definitively into the realm of Kantian ideal theory and permanently away from more specific neo-Hegelian historical-institutional analyses.[49] But Habermas's injunction, mentioned earlier, to sort out functional, empirical, and normative aspects of the present situation (IO 158) suggests that he still wishes to practice something more than ideal theory that is applied to empirical circumstances. Such an approach falls into subjective–objective and ideal–real Kantian dichotomies that critical theory sought to overcome. It is one thing for self-understood "normative" theorists such as Rawls to confine their speculation about the ethical possibilities of a cosmopolitan world to a rather high level of abstraction. It is quite another matter in the case of a theorist like Habermas, who has prided himself on being the practitioner of a "critical," interdisciplinary, social science agenda for some time.

From the standpoint of this analysis, it is ironic that in these writings Habermas accuses Hegel and Marx of retrospectively romanticizing aspects of late medieval and early modern guild-style corporatism and warns against attempts at idealizing the postwar *Sozialstaat* (PC 86). He tries to set an evaluative balance in the latter instance that he himself cannot maintain:

> Although we should take care not to assume an uncritical view of the achievements of the social welfare state, we must also not blind ourselves to the costs of its "transformation" or collapse. One can remain sensitive to the normalizing force of social bureaucracies without closing one's eyes to the shocking price that a reckless monetarization of the lifeworld would demand. (PC 87)

But he never reconciles these statements that hearken back to *Public Sphere* and even LC with his continuity account of nation-state development and his idealization of the *Sozialstaat*, which undergirds these essays on Europe.

There have always been some questions about the adequacy of Habermas's analyses of the *Sozialstaat*, both in general and for a post-Fordist

---

[49] For compelling quasi-Kantian endorsements of strategies for global justice, see Charles R. Beitz, *Political Theory and International Relations* (Princeton, NJ: Princeton University Press, 1999), 125–220; and Thomas W. Pogge, *World Poverty and Human Rights: Cosmopolitan Responsibilities and Reforms* (Oxford: Polity, 2002), 27–51.

scenario.[50] But this is less of a concern here than the fact that Habermas seems to completely abandon or leave unacknowledged his earlier *Sozialstaat* analysis, whatever its shortcomings. For Habermas's prescriptions to carry more weight in the context of these essays, he needs to integrate such work more actively and extensively in his present engagement with the dilemmas posed by globalization, especially the EU – or at least justify why he has dispensed with the earlier approach. When a theorist such as Habermas abandons, even reverses, the analysis of one sociopolitical configuration at the moment when he is confronted by a new one, it raises the – admittedly unfashionable – issue of ideology.[51]

The question is whether this dilemma is the result of, on the one hand, a permanent change in Habermas's thought toward the ideal and away from the historical – one inspired by personal predilections or career trajectory – or, on the other, is generated by the nature of the reality confronting Habermas the social scientist. In other words, does historical change cause researchers to reevaluate previous epochs, especially the one immediately preceding the present, in a way that allows the emerging one to conform more easily to one's normative preferences? In this sense, Weber and Habermas both turn to the past to confirm a present that reflects their respective theoretical dispositions, pessimistic or optimistic. Habermas's stated methodological goals in these essays seem to imply that he aspires to something more than a loose application of ideal theory to contemporary circumstances. Thus, we need to look past personal predilections and career trajectory and fully consider the effect of these novel circumstances on Habermas's present categories and mode of analysis. The interrogation of Weber's SL in Chapter 3 set the groundwork for such an examination, and my engagement with the literature on democracy in the EU from which I draw a *Sektoralstaat* model in the next chapter attempts to carry it forward and situate it in contemporary circumstances.

The issue of historical methodology, as well as the specter of ideology raised earlier, pose the following generalizable question regarding

---

[50] See Moishe Postone, "History and Critical Social Theory," *Contemporary Sociology* 19 (March 1990), 170–6; and Postone, "Political Theory and Historical Analysis," in *Habermas and the Public Sphere*, ed. Craig Calhoun (Cambridge, MA: MIT Press, 1992), 164–80.

[51] Michael Rosen provides sound and refreshingly unideological, philosophical grounds for approaching *Ideologiekritik* with skepticism in *On Voluntary Servitude: False Consciousness and the Theory of Ideology* (Cambridge, MA: Harvard University Press, 1996).

Habermas's analysis in the essays under consideration here: can any social science adequately apprehend the present by glossing over or jettisoning knowledge of the past? Many scholars of European integration, like Habermas, will project a vibrant supranational social-constitutional democracy as Europe's future. On the other hand, many other researchers who have devoted years to tracing both the deficiencies of the welfare state *and* the imperfections of democratic accountability in liberal democratic states now lament the demise of regulatory policy and the growing democratic deficits in supranational organizations like the EU.[52] This too is a phenomenon worth considering in greater depth if we are to take seriously changes as vast as those affiliated with globalization and the EU, and the way we should go about analyzing them.

Conclusion

In this chapter, I have suggested that by minimizing the traumatic nature of previous transformations of the nation-state and overestimating the accomplishments of the *Sozialstaat*, Habermas may too readily accentuate the feasibility of a kind of perfected state at the European level; he may render too plausible the development of a "continental regime" to *aufheben*, as it were, the best of the nation-state, while shedding its excessive tendencies. Habermas's account of the history of the state exhibits a tension between continuity and discontinuity that provides no clear reason why one should expect that the transition to supranational citizenship and economic regulation will be as, or any more, continuous than was the transition from the nineteenth-century *Rechtsstaat* to the twentieth-century *Sozialstaat* configuration. This problem is particularly acute because the more pessimistic possibility outlined by Habermas conforms with a conception of historical change reminiscent of Habermas's earlier and more empirically grounded work such as *Public Sphere*, work that analyzed the previous transformation in terms of large-scale historical discontinuity. Yet, without substantive justification, Habermas chooses to carry out the bulk of his analysis in these essays on the EU with the conceptual apparatus that he developed in later work, such as TCA, which biases his account in favor of less wholesale, less drastic, and potentially less intimidating historical change within modernity.

---

[52] A rather sophisticated representative of this shift, which I treat in the next chapter, is Fritz Scharpf, *Governing in Europe: Effective and Democratic?* (Oxford: Oxford University Press, 1999).

By setting out something less than an empirically and historically informed normative framework for a postnational future, as we will see, Habermas's work on the EU shares widespread assumptions with many theoretical engagements with the prospect of democracy in Europe. Most speculation about supranational institutions – optimistic and skeptical – tends to reify some aspect of the nation-state that used to be problematic or contested, and deploy it as evidence for the development of a certain vision of sociopolitical arrangements under supranational developments. As we will see, supranationalists posit something approximating a constitutional-social democracy at the continental level, while intergovernmentalists predict a persistence of state treaty negotiations as the core of future European politics. I will venture to guess that European politics will look very different than what is presupposed by either of these models and, on the contrary, will resemble what I call a *Sektoralstaat*: a polity in which different policy spheres are governed by those most closely affected by or most interested in it, and that this will have serious ramifications for democratic rule, legal scope, and material equality in Europe's future – ramifications not necessarily well met by the Habermasian paradigm.

6

The Structural Transformation to the Supranational *Sektoralstaat* and Prospects for Democracy in the EU

Clearly, European integration is central to the project of advancing democratic principles and practices in a dawning supranational age.[1] In the 1990s, as the primarily economic entity, the European Community, became the quasi-political EU, observers began to ponder integration's relationship to wider-scale phenomena associated with internationalization, multilateralism, or globalization.[2] Since the emergence and maintenance of the modern state was integral to the achievements of liberal

---

[1] See Andrew Moravcsik, The Choice for Europe: *Social Purpose and State Power from Messina to Maastricht* (Ithaca, NY: Cornell University Press, 1998); Neil MacCormick, *Questioning Sovereignty: Law, State, and Nation in the European Commonwealth* (Oxford: Oxford University Press, 1999); G. F. Mancini, *Democracy and Constitutionalism in the European Union* (Oxford: Hart, 2000); Philippe C. Schmitter, *How to Democratize the European Union . . . and Why Bother?* (Lanham, MD: Rowman & Littlefield, 2000); Larry Siedentop, *Democracy in Europe* (New York: Columbia University Press, 2001); and Klaus Eder and Bernhard Giesen, eds., *European Citizenship: National Legacies and Transnational Projects* (Oxford: Oxford University Press, 2001).

[2] Consult Robert Keohane and Stanley Hoffmann, eds., *The New European Community: Decisionmaking and Institutional Change* (Boulder, CO: Westview Press, 1991); William James Adams, ed., *Singular Europe: The Economy and Polity of the European Community after 1992* (Ann Arbor: University of Michigan Press, 1992); Alberta Sbragia, ed., *Euro-Politics: Institutions and Policymaking in the "New" European Community* (Washington, DC: Brookings Institution, 1992); Gary Marks, Fritz Scharpf, Philippe Schmitter, and Wolfgang Streeck, eds., *Governance in the European Union* (London: Sage, 1996); John Gerard Ruggie, ed., *Multilateralism Matters: The Theory and Praxis of an Institutional Form* (New York: Columbia University Press, 1993); John Dunn, ed., *Contemporary Crisis of the Nation State?* (Oxford: Blackwell, 1994); and David Held, *Democracy and the Global Order: From the Modern State to Cosmopolitan Governance* (Stanford, CA: Stanford University Press, 1995). On the last work, see John P. McCormick, "Review of David Held's *Democracy and the Global Order,*" *Constellations: An International Journal of Critical Democratic Theory* 4, no. 3 (January 1998), 44–53.

and social democracy in the last three centuries, the state's precarious position in globalization debates, as discussed in the previous chapter, has become cause for serious consternation among progressives of many stripes. Integration raises momentous questions concerning the institutional and legal means by which democratic principles and practices may be preserved and perhaps even advanced at a potentially novel supranational historical moment.[3] In this context, and notwithstanding recent setbacks in the ratification process of a European constitution,[4] the EU remains *the* crucial test case for exploring the possibility of democracy beyond the state.

Among the now seemingly innumerable attempts to make sense of these developments, both European and global, Jürgen Habermas's foray into EU analysis stands out for its high level of normative sophistication and empirical sensitivity. As discussed in the previous chapter, Habermas attempted to transpose his discursive legal theory of democracy, developed in BFN, from a state to a European level.[5] The previous chapter employed immanent critique to evaluate Habermas's EU model "internally," that is, on the basis of its own conceptual logic and the critical historical and social scientific strictures of his own earlier works. This chapter operates more "externally" to his framework: it situates Habermas's prognosis for EU democracy (1) within debates over integration in the contemporary empirical literature and (2) against a model of the emerging European polity that I derive from the latter. First, I compare and contrast

---

[3] For the EU's own understanding of its relationship to democratic traditions and principles, see the Commission of the EC, "A White Paper on European Governance – 'Enhancing Democracy in the European Union,' Work programme," SEC (2000) 1547/7 final, 11 October 2000 (http://europa.eu.int/comm/governance/work/en.pdf); see also the speech of the German foreign minister, Joschka Fisher, concerning an emerging "European Federation" in Berlin, 12 May 2000.

[4] Developments can be followed at the EU website, http://europa.eu.int/.

[5] See Habermas, *Between Facts and Norms: Contributions to a Discourse Theory of Law and Democracy*, trans. William Rehg (Cambridge, MA: MIT Press, 1996), hereafter BFN; *The Inclusion of the Other: Studies in Political Theory*, Ciaran Cronin and Pablo de Grieff, eds. (Cambridge, MA: MIT Press, 1998), hereafter IO; "The European Nation-State and the Pressures of Globalization," *New Left Review* 235 (1999), 46–59, hereafter NLR; "Beyond the Nation-State?: On Some Consequences of Economic Globalization," in Erik O. Eriksen and John E. Fossum, eds., *Democracy in the European Union: Integration Through Deliberation?* (London: Routledge, 2000), 29–41, hereafter DEU; *The Postnational Constellation: Political Essays*, Max Pensky, ed. (Cambridge, MA: MIT Press, 2001), hereafter PC; and "Warum braucht Europa eine Verfassung?" in Habermas, *Zeit der Übergänge* (Frankfurt a.M: Suhrkamp, 2001), 104–29. I cite the English translation by Michelle Everson, sponsored by the European University Institute: "So, Why Does Europe Need a Constitution?" (http://www.iue.it/RSC/EU/Reform02.pdf), hereafter RSC.

Habermas's approach to that of supranationalist and intergovernmental-ist EU scholars; and then I examine whether his theoretical framework can accommodate the reality of the *Sektoralstaat* model of governance that I claim is emerging at the European level.

Given the more intensely legal focus of Habermas's recent work, perhaps it should be no surprise that his model of a continental, constitutional-social democracy places him more or less on the side of academic lawyers who have advanced the supranationalist vision of the EU.[6] The supranationalist scholars, who for a long time had champi-oned integration spearheaded by the ECJ, have amassed evidence that makes it plausible to ask whether a constitutional order, as rich as any national liberal or social democratic regime, is emerging in Europe and now makes possible the transposition of the *Rechtsstaat*, and eventually even the *Sozialstaat*, to a supranational level.[7] These jurists have quite successfully demonstrated the substance and significance of formal-legal integration within the EU, but may have overestimated the likelihood that the latter would spill over into more substantive policy spheres requir-ing the expansion of a supranational European polity to address them.[8] However, political scientists who depict the EU as an intergovernmental organization that serves state interests by means of novel treaty arrange-ments fiercely criticize the supranationalists.[9] In the estimation of such

---

[6] While I will associate Habermas's vision of Europe most closely with that of recent legal supranationalists, there are elements in his model, particularly his aspirations for a com-mon European political culture, that go back to Ernst B. Haas, *The Uniting of Europe* (Stanford, CA: Stanford University Press, 1958).

[7] I will rely both generally and specifically on the following landmark articles from the early 1990s: those collected in J. H. H. Weiler, *The Constitution of Europe: "Do the New Clothes Have an Emperor?" and Other Essays* (Cambridge: Cambridge University Press, 1999); and Anne-Marie Burley [Slaughter] and Walter Mattli, "Europe Before the Court: A Political Theory of Legal Integration," *International Organization* 47 (Winter 1993), 41–75. Weiler's book, in particular, has a curious feel: parts written before or during the mid-1990s, and left relatively unrevised, quite convincingly demonstrate the substance and significance of formal-legal integration within the EC, and hence the germs of a suprana-tional constitutional order. But Weiler's later essays and the layers of revisions added to earlier ones concede that the supranationalist vision may overestimate the likelihood that Court-accelerated integration in narrow economic areas can spill over so as to foster the expansion of a genuinely progressive continental regime in Europe.

[8] Although Weiler, for instance, is more worried than is Habermas about the problem of an exclusionary "European nationalism" rising at the EU level within such a supranational polity. See Weiler, *The Constitution of Europe*, 94–5.

[9] See Geoffrey Garrett, R. Daniel Keleman, and Heiner Schulz, "The European Court of Justice, National Governments, and Legal Integration in the European Union," *Interna-tional Organizations* 52, no. 1 (Winter 1998), 150; Garrett and Barry Weingast, "Ideas, Interests and Institutions: Constructing the European Community's Internal Market," in

scholars, the EU cannot develop beyond the parameters of state interests because the member states have quick and effective recourse to curtail or roll back any maverick behavior on the part of European institutional actors such as the ECJ.

But it is more than possible that both poles of this controversy operate within historically anachronistic frameworks: specifically, the more supranationally sanguine lawyers with whom Habermas is aligned impose a twentieth-century *Sozialstaat* model upon the EU, while the Euroskeptic social scientists read the situation in eighteenth- or nineteenth-century terms according to which states, acting as independent, rational actors, can opt in and out of treaties at will and determine the inner workings of EU policy through their still considerable sovereign powers.[10] However, the contemporary European situation calls for the analysis of a qualitatively new kind of polity that cannot be captured by conceptions of either a constitutional-federal state "writ large" or the power politics of individual treaty signatories.[11] With this in mind, the *Sektoralstaat* model I formulate here combines insights from, on the one hand, studies of the transnational comitological or infranational policymaking that presently operates under the auspices of the European Commission; and, on the other, growing consensus over the eventuality of "multiple policy Europes" within the EU. In this scenario, different combinations of member states will constitute separate energy, defense, trade, communications, welfare, environmental, and other regulatory regimes.[12] Building on the historical-normative analysis of transformations of law and democracy developed throughout

Judith Goldstein and Robert Keohane, eds., *Ideas and Foreign Policy* (Ithaca, NY: Cornell University Press, 1993), 193; and Garrett, "International Cooperation and Institutional Choice: The European Community's Internal Market," *International Organizations* 46 (Spring 1992), 171.

[10] Or, alternately, in more sophisticated versions of this model, states strategically avoid having to take blame for certain difficult policy courses themselves by attributing responsibility to European institutions: see Moravcsik, *The Choice for Europe*.

[11] Weiler, in particular, attempts to be more differentiated theoretically in this regard: he distinguishes two forms of supranationalism – on the one hand, a more conventional "United States of Europe" and, on the other, a historically new, "more attenuated Community vision." See Weiler, *The Constitution of Europe*, 246; cf. also 250, 270. He affiliates himself with the latter model but consistently evokes images recalling the former, even conceding that the supranational model ultimately assumes a statelike form (283). Generally, supranationalists speak as if they think of the emerging EU polity as a sui generis development, but because they provide few institutional specifics about what that new form might be, they fall back on a federal *Sozialstaat* model.

[12] This eventuality is most explicitly predicted by and advocated in Fritz Scharpf, *Governing in Europe: Effective and Democratic?* (Oxford: Oxford University Press, 1999); and Schmitter, *How to Democratize the European Union*.

this book, I seek to evaluate this emerging configuration to ascertain how much the Habermasian model can be adapted to it.

Thus, this chapter will depart from the usual method of evaluating European integration in two ways: it sets out a concrete *Sektoralstaat* model of what the EU is and increasingly will be (both micro- and macro-sectorally) rather than engage in abstract speculations on "democracy in Europe." In a Habermasian spirit, I will show how the *Sektoralstaat* model of governance in the EU does in fact accentuate deliberation among interested parties in microspheres of transnational policymaking – but in a rather un-Habermasian fashion: that is, it *also* insulates those spheres from public and governmental oversight and regulation through which, for example, the *Sozialstaat* attempted to guarantee the equity and transparency of participation, redistribution, negotiation, and bargaining for citizens in different aspects of their public lives.

As we observed in Chapter 4, Habermas argued that those *Sozialstaat* guarantees were sanctioned by universal principles institutionalized in constitutional orders and protected, albeit imperfectly, by practices of judicial review. The delegative characteristic of the materialization of law proved to be compatible with constitutional equal protection at the national level but may not be so at a more institutionally fragmented supranational level. Notwithstanding lingering assumptions concerning the power of the ECJ and recent attempts to ratify a European constitution,[13] these institutions are/will be markedly less powerful at the Union level than they were in the *Sozialstaat* and are likely to remain so for structural reasons I will address. But Habermas is completely silent and hence relatively unhelpful on the question of federalism, particularly as

---

[13] The new attention to normative issues and conventional constitutionalization in EU practices was reflected in the proclamation of the EU Charter of Fundamental Rights (Nice, 7 December 2000) (O.J. 2000, C 346/1 of 18 December 2000) and the European Council's Laeken Declaration (14–15 December 2001) on a constitutional convention, which convened in March 2002 (http://europeanconvention.eu.int/plensess.asp?lang=EN). Far ahead of the recent official and scholarly wave on formal constitutionalism in Europe has been the work of Richard Bellamy and Dario Castiglione: see Bellamy and Castiglione, "Between Cosmopolis and Community: Three Models of Rights and Democracy within the European Union," in *Reimagining Political Community: Studies in Cosmopolitan Democracy*, D. Archibugi, D. Held, and M. Köhler, eds. (Oxford: Polity Press, 1998); "The Normative Challenge of a European Polity: Cosmopolitan and Communitarian Models Compared, Criticized and Combined," in *Democracy and the EU*, Andreas Follesdal and Peter Koslowski, eds. (Berlin: Springer, 1998); and "'A Republic, If You Can Keep It': The Democratic Deficit and the Constitution of Europe," in *The European Union and Its Order*, Zenon Bankowski and Andrew Scott, eds. (Oxford: Blackwell, 2000).

federal arrangements impact equal protection in the sphere of social welfare. If, as I suggest, the EU *Sektoralstaat* will permit individual member
states to opt in or out of different energy, defense, trade, communications,
welfare, environmental, and other subpolities, does this mean that the EU
will be a "Union" that tolerates – in de jure and not just de facto manner
– greater disparities of material welfare, economic liberty, and social protection among its component parts than any federal state permitted in the
Sozialstaat era? We will have to look beyond Habermas in an attempt to
answer this question.

1. Legal Integration and the Supranationalist Model

Weber observed that lawyers marched at the head of every modern revolution.[14] To whatever extent European integration can be viewed as a revolution,[15] law is unequivocally central to the EU's development. While the
law's influence on integration had perhaps been overstated in the past,[16]
today even the most realist commentators marvel at the transnational
force of European law.[17] As I discuss in this section, the supranationalist
literature successfully establishes the general autonomy and efficacy of
the ECJ and EU law to such an extent that the EU may be said to satisfy
certain fundamental criteria of the *Rechtsstaat* elaborated in Chapters 1
and 2. However, whether the rule of law at a European level can fully take
the place of law in liberal democratic nation-states or, more hopefully, further advance principles associated with both *Rechtsstaat* and *Sozialstaat*
models of the state remains an open question.

   If we think of modern democracy institutionally, that is, in terms of
the governmental branches or departments through which popular will
has been expressed and progressive policy has been made in most liberal

---

[14] Max Weber, "The Profession and Vocation of Politics," in *Political Writings* (Cambridge:
Cambridge University Press, 1992), 328.

[15] See Joseph H. H. Weiler, "The Quiet Revolution: The European Court of Justice and Its
Interlocutors," *Comparative Political Studies* 26, no. 4 (January 1994), 510–34.

[16] For example, A. W. Green, *Political Integration by Jurisprudence* (Leyden: Sijthoff, 1961);
Mauro Cappelletti, ed., *Integration Through Law* (Berlin: de Gruyter, 1986). An indispensable contemporary guide to the role of law in European integration is Neil Mac-
Cormick, ed., *Constructing Legal Systems: "European Union" in Legal Theory* (Amsterdam: Kluwer, 1997).

[17] See Robert Keohane and Stanley Hoffmann, "Conclusions: Community Politics and Institutional Change," in William Wallace, ed., *The Dynamics of European Integration* (London: Pinter, 1990), 261–82; and Keohane and Hoffmann, *The New European Community*. While most law that I discuss in this chapter is technically "European Community
law," I will simplify matters by using the terms "European law" or "EU law."

democracies, legislative and judicial organs have enjoyed noteworthy successes. According to Habermas's normative reconstruction of historical reality in BFN, legislatures have successfully reflected and channeled popular will (BFN 181–3, 277–8, 383). More controversially, Habermas's model suggests that twentieth-century courts have proven to be faithful allies of progressive politics, despite the ostensibly antidemocratic nature of judiciaries and their historical role in resisting the advance of substantive democracy in many contexts (BFN 167–8, 240–2, 262–6). Not merely the passive or rhetorical upholders of static conceptions of rights, at times judiciaries also have been active in the advancement of evolving and expanding conceptions of civil and social rights in postwar North America and Europe.[18] On the basis of these traditions, or simply in the search for novel paths of further democratization, many have expressed high expectations for judicially driven, ECJ-centered progressive political strategies beyond the state in Europe.[19]

As the supranationalists point out, the ECJ has become the EU institution perhaps most autonomous of member state influence, even if it is hardly free of it. The court is also the European institution with which individuals within member states have the most substantively direct relationship. This relationship is reminiscent of citizen–government relations within conventional nation-states and not, like other forms of EU–citizen interactions in the most powerful EU organs, relationships largely mediated through the offices of the heads of state, ranking ministers, or appointments to the European Commission (EC).[20] Unlike the EC, the Council of Ministers, and the European Council,[21] the ECJ's policy

---

[18] For support of Habermas's view of courts, consult Morton Horwitz, *The Warren Court and the Pursuit of Justice* (New York: Hill and Wang, 1998) in the U.S. context; and in the German one, Donald P. Kommers, *The Constitutional Jurisprudence of the Federal Republic of Germany* (Durham, NC: Duke University Press, 1997), 241–97.

[19] This is not to say that there is no consciousness of the limits on the extent to which legal integration can serve European-democratic ends: see, for instance, Weiler, *The Constitution of Europe*, 62.

[20] The Commission is a seventeen-member body composed of a president and one or two nominees from each member state, approved by the European Parliament, for a five-year renewable term. The Commission functions as the administration of the EU. See Neill Nugent, *The Politics and Government of the European Union* (Durham, NC: Duke University Press, 1996), 150–78.

[21] The Council of Ministers is composed of the ranking member state ministers of whatever policy sphere is being dealt with at a given meeting of the Council: the foreign ministers, the energy ministers, and so on. The European Council is the meeting of the respective heads of governments of the member states. See Nugent, *The Politics and Government of the European Union*, 178–96.

adjudication is least beholden to *direct* member state input and/or sanction. (The exact extent of the ECJ's susceptibility to influence by the member states, more generally, is one of the central questions at issue in the next section.) As I discuss later, European citizens interact with the ECJ through more intimate channels – appeals through local courts – rather than other, more distant member state organs.

The ECJ's policy purview may be less wide-ranging than that of the other EU institutions and certainly less than that of the high courts of most nation-states (e.g., it lacks explicit criminal, family, educational, health, and, effectively so far, social and human rights jurisdictions). Nevertheless, supranationalist scholars insist that the expanding spheres of economic integration (single market, environmental and consumer protection) at some point began to overlap with many, if not all, social policy concerns. Most importantly, they emphasize the extent to which national courts refer cases to the ECJ, and how often and faithfully the former abide by the Court's rulings upon return. The Court successfully established the doctrinal supremacy of European law over member state law through the following jurisprudential principles: *direct applicability* establishes the immediate validity of EU law within member states without the necessity of subsequent member state measures (i.e., enabling or specifying acts); *direct effect* enjoins member state courts to recognize European law's conferring of rights, or imposing of obligations, on particular individuals; the principle of *primacy*, while not mentioned in the treaties of the Community or, more recently, the Union, is assumed in ECJ and member state court decisions and establishes the supremacy of EU law over member state law on treaty-related matters, even those already dealt with in member state constitutions.

Over the life of the Community, the ECJ expanded not only its own jurisdiction, but also, some would say, the power of Europe: it invoked Article 235 to adjudicate international agreements, emergency food relief to developing countries, Community constitutional innovation, environmental policy, and consumer protection, as well as energy and research policies; it spoke explicitly of the "constitutional charter" of the Community (*Parti Ecologiste, "Les Verts"* 294/83, 1986); it ruled in favor of compensation for those adversely affected by EU negligence (*Francovich* 6/90 and 9/90, 1992); in many cases the Court sanctioned the harmonization of member state social security programs to protect migrant workers and intra-EU immigrants; it struck down unequal pension-eligibility ages in the United (*Barber* 262/88, 1990); and the ECJ decided numerous cases furthering the single European market (primarily on the basis of the monumental *Cassis de Dijon* [120/78] decision). Previously, the most important ECJ cases dealt with interinstitutional relations: for example, ordering the Council to wait for reports from the European Parliament (EP) before enacting legislation (138/79, 1980) or deciding on the full extent of the EP's budgetary powers (joined cases 89, 104, 114–17, 125–9/85, 1988).

As pointed out in the supranationalist literature, while the ECJ cannot initiate action itself, it has significant power when asked to rule: it can order a member state to fulfill its obligations to other member states and individuals; it can void EU acts if they are not adopted according to procedures laid out by Community treaties; and it can set fines (unlimited in scope) for treaty or directive violation. Most frequently, member state courts ask the ECJ to rule on specific points of law, and the Council or Commission can seek the ECJ's opinion on international agreements. Thus, the ECJ and European law seem to function according to important criteria associated with high courts in both the traditional liberal *Rechtsstaat* and the twentieth-century *Sozialstaat* specifically: adherence to principles of legal supremacy, and the Court's role as arbiter of supremacy controversies; jurisdiction over the institutional relations of the other "branches" of EU governance; and the Court's role in steering the political economy of the Union.[22]

The normative vision of scholars with a generally optimistic view of the ECJ's power, albeit tempered of late, can be summed up as follows: the EU develops as a supranational legal order that may be appealed to by European citizens through local courts on issues initially economic but increasingly social and political. This process facilitates a normative interaction between, on the one hand, domestic individuals and groups and, on the other, a transnational order that protects the former through binding decisions against states and large-scale organizations. It also facilitates a mutual socialization of local, national, and continental jurists, refining the coherency, consistency, and power of ever more effective legal decisions.[23]

---

[22] I evaluate more extensively the ECJ and European law in terms of these two paradigms of the rule of law in "Supranational Challenges to the Rule of Law: The Case of the European Union," in David Dyzenhaus, ed., *Recrafting the Rule of Law* (Oxford: Hart, 1999).

[23] This is, of course, an oversimplification: even before the pessimistic turn in his more recent writings (e.g., Weiler, *The Constitution of Europe*, 99–101, 207, 258, 282, 296, 330), Weiler fully recognized that emerging ECJ legal supremacy in the institutionally formative years of the Community coincided with member state reassertion of power through the so-called Luxembourg Compromise: "Historically (and structurally) an equilibrium was established. On the one hand stood a strong constitutional integrative process that, in

Along these lines, then, according to Joseph Weiler, what decisively sets EU law apart from previously established international treaty law is not the principle of supremacy itself, but its reliable and effective implementation in Europe.[24] In traditional international law, treaty provisions often have equal status with domestic law, which may be superseded by subsequent national legislation. But EU law relates to member state law in the way that, for instance, federal law relates to the law of individual states in the United States, not as international law relates to U.S. federal law. European law is *definitively*, not *conditionally*, supreme over member state law.

According to Weiler, the ECJ is also a better guarantor of EU policy than the EC, which maintains links perhaps too intimate with member state bureaucracies. On the basis of treaty provisions, the Court sets out structural doctrine on the rules governing EU and member state relations, as well as material doctrine on the economic and social aspects of that relationship. Member states seek judicial remedy, and clarification on European law when necessary, and abide by it. For Weiler, these are factual, not simply normative, statements about ECJ power. When individuals appeal through national courts to European law, according to Weiler, even though member state courts make the final decision on these claims, requests by the latter for clarification by the ECJ through Article 177 of the Rome Treaty increasingly "Europeanize" national law.

Therefore, national actors interact with EU law through national courts more extensively than with any previous kind of international law, making it accessible to them and increasing their stake in its efficacy. National courts do not want to violate norms of professional courtesy among jurists by violating or ignoring ECJ rulings. Nor do they want to seem less progressive than more enthusiastic member states. EU law has given power to the lowest national courts, previously denied such authority by higher national courts. Indeed, EU law empowers national judiciaries as a whole vis-à-vis other national branches of government, thus encouraging them to further Europeanize as a way of empowering themselves. According to Weiler, national executives and legislatures do not behave antagonistically toward the ECJ because they see it as relatively neutral, because they are

radical mutation of the Treaty, linked the legal order of the Community with that of the Member States in a federal-like relationship. This was balanced by a relentless and equally strong process, also deviating radically from the Treaty, that transferred political and decision-making power into a confederal procedure controlled by the Member States acting jointly and severally." Weiler, *The Constitution of Europe*, 32, 35.

[24] See Joseph H. H. Weiler, "The Quiet Revolution," 510, and "The Transformation of Europe," *Yale Law Review* 100 (1991), 2403.

willing to sacrifice short-term for long-term gain, and because they have so much power in *making* the policy that the Court decides over in any case. Weiler claims that national courts, and to a lesser extent legislatures and executives, accept ECJ decisions partly because they are formulated in legally formalist terms, appearing objective and neutral. Thus, the ECJ is granted latitude by the national executives and legislatures, which they previously granted to national courts under the classical formulation of the separation of powers in the traditional *Rechtsstaat*.

An additional reason offered by supranationalists for the surprising success of the ECJ and EU law is that they fulfill the expectations of internationally inclined intellectuals who were disappointed by the Cold War–era United Nations. But, by the mid-1990s, Weiler was willing to admit that the brightness of the ECJ's future was being somewhat dimmed by a number of developments: an increasing backlog of cases that he predicted would cause irritation on the part of claimants, a general backlash against extensive judicial review, and increased interinstitutional rivalry within the EU itself. However, these are constraints that courts managed to overcome in the transition from the traditional *Rechtsstaat* to the *Sozialstaat* within nation-states and that the ECJ might be able to surmount within the EU. A more ominous development and, as borne out by Weiler's more recent essays, a more accurately predicted one, was the fact that majority voting in the Council of Ministers (the strongest representation of individual member state interests) means less overall consensus on policy, which limits the parameters of the Court's decisions. Like national courts, the ECJ must move more tentatively on issues where there is not clear public or elite consensus.[25] But Weiler's boldest intuition still shines through in the more "supranational" moments of *The Constitution of Europe*: the economic sphere of adjudication explicitly granted to the Court was already spilling over, and would increasingly do so, into social and political ones. The Court would continue to argue subtly that full economic integration couldn't be achieved without social spheres becoming integrated as well. After all, on this assumption, a fully common market cannot function properly without universally high levels of private and social insurance, environmental protection, medical benefits, worker compensation, and so on. Thus, the EU could become a supranational liberal, and even social, democracy through legal integration.[26]

---

[25] On this high court strategy in the U.S. national context, see Gerald N. Rosenberg, *The Hollow Hope: Can Courts Bring About Social Change?* (Chicago: University of Chicago Press, 1991).

[26] See Weiler, *The Constitution of Europe*, 58–9.

The work of other supranationalist scholars highlights trends that could outlive member state reaction to the expansion of the ECJ's jurisdiction. Anne-Marie Slaughter and Walter Mattli understand legal integration as a gradual penetration of EU law into the domestic law of its member states – a penetration not easily halted or reversed.[27] *Formal penetration* is achieved through the supranational legal acts from treaty law to European law and through the cases by which individuals appeal to EU law in member state courts. *Substantive penetration* is achieved through spillover from economic into social spheres (health, worker safety, welfare, education, and eventually political participation). For Slaughter and Mattli, law is the functional domain that circumvents the direct clash of political interests in Europe. European actors have found it in their interest to promote incremental expansion through *functional spillover* (different economic sectors can only be well integrated by action in spheres other than those directly involved, which in turn requires more action; and *political spillover*) economic integration encourages changes in expectations, values, and strategies of national interest groups at the supranational level. In this sense then, for Slaughter, Mattli, and Weiler, rather than being an ideologically resistant obstacle to the socialization of formal law in the European context, the ECJ is a wholeheartedly enthusiastic, if cautious, actor in the construction of a still unrealized supranational *Sozialstaat*.

Christian Joerges emphasizes the normative power of European law despite its lack of violent sanction and direct democratic legitimacy.[28] A burgeoning constitutionalization of Europe is nothing to be surprised by according to Joerges, as a common market necessarily requires a common constitution, whether written or conventional.[29] The ECJ speaks

---

[27] Burley [Slaughter] and Mattli, "Europe Before the Court," 41. See also Anne-Marie Slaughter Burley, "New Directions in Legal Research on the European Community," *Journal of Common Market Studies* 31, no. 3 (September 1993), 391; and on supranational legal issues more generally, Burley, "Regulating the World: Multilateralism, International Law and the Projection of the New Deal Regulatory State," in Ruggie, ed., *Multilateralism Matters*.

[28] Christian Joerges, "Taking the Law Seriously: On the Political Science and the Role of Law in the Process of European Integration," *European Law Journal* 2, no. 1 (1996), 105–35 at 105.

[29] In what seems to be a confirmation of Marxian charges that national constitutionalism was the mere product of the nationalization of markets in the eighteenth and nineteenth centuries, Joerges assumes that continental marketizing in the EU brings about continental constitutionalization. Whether such marketizing will have the same devastating economic effects on vast portions of the European populace as did the first two centuries of national marketizing in individual states before the establishment of the *Sozialstaat* is something to be addressed later.

"legalistically" to protect itself, as Slaughter, Mattli, and Weiler suggest, but it must be understood by, and be engaged with, political actors. After all, the terms of legal integration have a direct impact on political reality. Borrowing a conceptual trope from Michelle Everson,[30] Joerges explains how the legal integration process is simultaneously one of political disintegration as well: for instance, member states that rely on minimal environmental standards experience pressure to conform with higher ones; member states with high social welfare levels are somewhat disadvantaged competitively in an open market. As external standards change, internal regulations collapse and crumble. Joerges assumes an ongoing repetition of the development pattern of the national market/constitutional state at the continental level. Thus, he predicts the second coming of a legally enabled process of constitution building whereby macrolevel economic and political development proceeds at the expense of more obstructionist local institutions.

Tackling the most public challenge to European law and the ECJ in the history of integration, Joerges explores the ramifications of the October 1993 Maastricht Decision of the German High Court that struck a blow to legal integration.[31] The *Bundesverfassungsgericht* declared that (1) the EU is a state association suspended *between* a confederation and a statelike entity; (2) if the ECJ extends EU power itself, without a treaty amendment, such judgments will not have binding force in Germany; and (3) the German High Court defines a politically relevant "people" as a *Staatsvolk*, a state-people, making it nearly impossible to define democracy beyond the state. In other words, the German High Court seemed to roll back substantively the traditional *Rechtsstaat* status of the ECJ and virtually ruled out its development into a *Sozialstaat*. Law, as suggested by the etymological makeup of the word *Rechtsstaat*, does not exist without a state order, which the EU, by its own profession, is not. Moreover, Europeans cannot be considered a people or *Volk* without a state. The

---

[30] See Michelle Everson, *Laws in Conflict: A Rationally Integrated European Insurance Market?*, Ph.D. dissertation, European University Institute, Florence, 1993.

[31] The October 1993 Maastricht Decision of the German Constitutional Court was one of the most prominent manifestations of an emerging Euroskepticism and neo-nationalism at the time (*BVerfGE* 89, 155). Consult the responses to this decision by Weiler, Neil MacCormick, U. K. Preuß, and Dieter Grimm in the *European Law Journal* 1, no. 3 (November 1995). Joerges further elaborates on his criticisms of the decision in "The Law in the Process of Constitutionalising Europe," in Erik Oddvar Eriksen, John Erik Fossum, and Agustín José Menéndez, eds., *Constitution-Making and Democratic Legitimacy* (Oslo: ARENA, 2002), 18–38.

decision declares the ECJ to be an institution not *remotely* autonomous of other EU institutions and, by extension, of the member states.

As a result, according to the logic of the German High Court decision, neither EU law nor the ECJ can be understood in terms of traditional rule-of-law notions. In addition, in the invocation of the nationalist basis by which the individual European *Sozialstaats* were largely justified, the German Court undermines the possibility of a EU *Sozialstaat* on ethno-political grounds. While this is a potentially grave foreboding of the kinds of retrenchism faced by ECJ-driven supranational expansion of substantive rule of law in the European context in the future, Joerges argues that the decision did not have any immediate practical effect. The specter of nationalist judiciaries asserting themselves against the ECJ in the future is mitigated for ECJ-sanguine scholars like Joerges by the fact that the latter has had powerful allies in local courts that may serve as a domestic constituency against higher-level appellate and constitutional courts, as well as against the legislative and executive arms of the member states.

Alec Stone (now Stone Sweet) takes this argument furthest in what may be the most chauvinistic and unapologetic advancement of what might be called a "Eurocracy through jurocracy" strategy of supranationalism. Consistent with other supranationalist scholars, Stone Sweet credits the ECJ with negative integration through the dismantling of the barriers to the free movement of goods, people, services, and capital within Europe by encouraging states to *renounce* certain authority, and positive integration by creating new rules and institutions to regulate developments among states.[32] In a familiar way, Stone Sweet concentrates on two facets of legal power mentioned previously: the preliminary reference practice established by Article 177 of the Rome Treaty and the principle of supremacy established in the *Costa* case (6/64, 1964). However, further updating, expanding, and documenting the Slaughter, Mattli, and Weiler theses, Stone Sweet argues that the ECJ expands its power through appeals by individuals through national court references to the ECJ, and through spillover from narrow economic spheres to broader ones like gender equity, environmental protection, and taxation policy.[33]

---

[32] Alec Stone, "Governing with Judges: The New Constitutionalism," in Jack Hayward and Edward C. Page, eds., *Governing the New Europe* (Durham, NC: Duke University Press, 1995), 286.

[33] Alec Stone Sweet and Thomas L. Brunell, "Constructing a Supranational Constitution: Dispute Resolution and Governance in the European Community," *American Political Science Review* 92, no. 1 (March 1998), 63–82 at 72. See also Martin Shapiro and Alec Stone, "The New Constitutional Politics of Europe," *Comparative Political Studies* 26,

Intergovernmentalism, the thesis asserting that the ECJ is ultimately the agent of the member state governments, assumes a lowest common denominator of minimal integration as a result of unanimous or supermajoritarian voting in the Council of Ministers.[34] In other words, integration can be driven only as far as some of the member states less in favor of it will allow. But Stone Sweet suggests that litigation through national courts with appeals to European law *raises* this lowest common denominator by eliminating negative boundaries to integration and by addressing the lack of full compliance with European directives. He claims to demonstrate how EU law Europeanizes the least Euro-friendly states from within, thus changing their preferences in Council voting. Stone Sweet asserts that member state preferences do not in fact predict Court decisions (EC briefs, for instance, are a much better indicator), and that even in the most integration-unfriendly context, parliamentary sovereignty has been "swept aside" in areas of EU supremacy: even Tory governments have asked the British Parliament regularly to amend UK statutes to conform with EU law.[35] Stone Sweet believes that his thick thesis of integration through law has ramifications beyond the study of EU law and supposedly dispels much of the intergovernmentalist position in general.[36]

2. State Centrism – EU Law Constrained

According to many rational choice scholars and more state-centrist approaches to European law, the ECJ codifies the preferences of the major

---

no. 4 (January 1994), 397; and Stone, "What Is a Supranational Constitution?: An Essay in International Relations Theory," *Review of Politics* 56 (1994), 441.

[34] A position perhaps best represented by Moravcsik, *The Choice for Europe*.

[35] See Stone Sweet and Brunell, "Constructing a Supranational Constitution," 74–6.

[36] Contra Moravcsik, for instance, Stone Sweet boldly asserts that the member states did not control the forging of the Single European Act. See Stone Sweet and Brunell, "Constructing a Supranational Constitution," 76; and Moravcsik, "Negotiating the Single European Act: National Interests and Conventional Statecraft in the European Community," *International Organization* 45, no. 1 (Winter 1991), 19–56. Note also other work by Moravcsik, which is a somewhat odd target, as it has been rather careful to allow room for conceptions of ECJ autonomy: Moravcsik, "Preferences and Power in the European Community: A Liberal Intergovernmentalist Approach," *Journal of Common Market Studies* 31, no. 4 (December 1993), 473–524; "Integrating International and Domestic Theories of International Bargaining," in Peter B. Evans, Harold J. Jacobson, and Robert D. Putnam, eds., *Double-Edged Diplomacy: International Bargaining and Domestic Politics* (Berkeley: University of California Press, 1993); and "Why the European Community Strengthens the State: Domestic Politics and International Cooperation," paper prepared for the annual meeting of the American Political Association, New York, 1–4 September 1994.

member states into law to prevent hostile member state action against itself and to ensure compliance with its decisions.[37] Representatives of this approach acknowledge the singularity of the ECJ on the international scene, finding it more similar to the U.S. Supreme Court than other international judicial bodies, such as the International Court of Justice, or the NAFTA or WTO dispute panels. The Court functions more like a federal constitutional court than an arbitration body. Yet, the intergovernmentalists argue that the ECJ is neither nearly so autonomous nor so capable of generating the normative structure of the EU as the supranationalist and ECJ-friendly scholars suggest.

Intergovernmentalists trace the Court's strategic gauging of national governments' preference positions in the following way: where there is clear precedence for activism, the ECJ does not worry too much about member states' reactions. But in realms where the domestic cost of Court activism is high for member states, individual states will not comply, or the concerted action of the states through treaty revision will change the very terms by which the Court adjudicates. Both scenarios discourage ECJ activism: noncompliance embarrasses the Court, and circumvention emasculates it. In this framework, the Court is faced with the prospect of losing legitimacy in three ways: (1) by appearing to sacrifice consistent rule of law adjudication to the wills of the member states should its rulings always reinforce member state positions; (2) through the noncompliance of individual states should the ECJ rule against the latter in important cases; or (3) by a circumvention of its powers through treaty amendment under the same circumstances. Moreover, qualified majority voting in the Council of Ministers makes it easier to undermine the Court through secondary legislation that waters down its decisions, thus further deterring it from an activist agenda.

Geoffrey Garrett, in particular, argues that the ECJ will be most active on treaty measures where the collective action of member states is difficult (e.g., 1979 *Sheep Meat Cases* 232/78). In the history of pension cases that address gender inequality, on the other hand, the Court has backed off when faced with treaty circumvention and formulated open-ended decisions, giving it more room to maneuver in subsequent cases. As we observed in Chapter 4, open-ended decisions are one of the chief sources

---

[37] See G. Garrett, D. R. Keleman, and H. Schulz, "The European Court of Justice, National Governments, and Legal Integration in the European Union"; Garrett and Weingast, "Ideas, Interests and Institutions"; and Garrett, "International Cooperation and Institutional Choice."

of the supposed legal indeterminacy that arises when courts preside over socially complicated and politically controversial cases. As the argument goes in political analyses of courts more generally, they either fail to get the issues correct despite good faith, or they adjudicate in a deliberately vague manner so as not to rouse the ire of more powerful branches of government.[38]

The chief ramification of Garrett's arguments concerning ECJ conflict-avoidance is that the adjudication of EU law will remain exclusively confined to issues where there is member state consensus, that is, those related to an integrated market. Moreover, in those cases that the ECJ actually hears and decides, the latter's adjudication will be conducted under the apprehension that the Court's decisions will remain sufficiently muddy in the hope that the more political EU institutions may do with them as they see fit. This is a clear compromise of traditional *Rechtsstaat* standards of judicial independence and, on this basis, a threat to aspirations for the consolidation of a European *Sozialstaat*. The Court will certainly be discouraged from dealing with issues of substantive economic equality (such as disparity between pensions earned by the two genders within one state or varying degrees of social insurance among different member states). The priority of market "liberty" over social "equality" in supranational adjudication potentially sets back over a century of the rule of law in the European context. At the EU level, contra the expectations of supranationalist scholars, the *Sozialstaat* will have reverted to an even further scaled-back capitalist *Rechtsstaat*, since the ECJ would have even *less* autonomy than, for instance, U.S. courts in the nineteenth century.[39]

All of the students of European law treated in this chapter recognize a newly emerging juridical reality in the EU and new normative possibilities

---

[38] For recent formulations of this argument in various incarnations, see Richard Posner, *The Problem of Jurisprudence* (Cambridge, MA: Harvard University Press, 1990); Roberto M. Unger, *What Should Legal Analysis Be Like?* (London: Verso, 1996); Cass R. Sunstein, *Legal Reasoning and Political Conflict* (Oxford: Oxford University Press, 1996); Duncan Kennedy, *A Critique of Adjudication: fin de siècle* (Cambridge, MA: Harvard University Press, 1997); and Rogers M. Smith, "The Inherent Deceptiveness of Constitutional Discourse: A Diagnosis and Prescription," in Ian Shapiro and Robert Adams, eds., *Nomos XL: Integrity and Conscience* (New York: New York University Press, 1998), 218.

[39] Garrett himself does not draw such generally apocalyptic conclusions for social democracy in the EU; he asserts that globalization does not adversely affect, but rather, on the contrary, actually enhances, domestic social welfare policy in the European member states. See Geoffrey Garrett, "Global Markets and National Politics," *International Organization* 52, no. 4 (Fall 1998), 149–76.

concomitant with it.[40] From the perspective of the ECJ-sanguine supranationalist scholars (at least their work from the early 1990s), the likelihood
of a fully liberal or social democratic rule of law in Europe is exception-
ally good. The ability of European citizens to appeal to a court above the
governments of the nation-states in which they live – even if through local
courts – is a potential safeguard against nation-state violations of rights
or even an encouragement of those states to expand rights. The ECJ is a
supranational court with greater power to guarantee cosmopolitan norms
than international courts of human rights have been, since it is more intimately tied to domestic legal orders. The mutual interaction and socialization of jurists from all levels and countries of the EU that these scholars
point to as the source of an ever more norm-refining professional process
may guarantee a more coherent and effective international-federal order
than any that has ever existed before. On the other hand, these lawyers
might be forgiven for exaggerating the substantively progressive possibilities of expanded international discourse among jurists and generally
underestimating the inherent democratic deficiencies of such an outlook.[41]

The work of the "juro-skeptical" intergovernmentalists suggests that a
rule of law other than one confined exclusively to economic integration is
not likely to emerge in the near future. Moreover, given the lack of autonomy attributed to the Court in this literature, they raise serious questions
concerning the ECJ's ability to conduct even such a narrowly defined task
as strict common market making by standards of the traditional rule of
law. One of the ramifications of this perspective is that European law will
function like nineteenth-century federal law in the United States, regulating only the contemporary equivalent of property rights and free trade –
with all the business-friendly implications that this entails. But it may do
so without the consistent and good-faith laissez-faire perspective maintained by most jurists in the nineteenth century, a perspective that judicial
actors were able to maintain in practice by appeals to constitutional or

---

[40] See also Francis Snyder, "The Effectiveness of European Community Law: Institutions,
Processes, Tools and Techniques," *Modern Law Review* 56, no. 1 (January 1993), 19–54;
Nicholas Green, *The Legal Foundations of the Single European Market* (Oxford: Oxford
University Press, 1992); Neil MacCormick, "Beyond the Sovereign State," *Modern Law
Review* 56, no. 1 (January 1993), 1–18; and Karen J. Alter, *Establishing the Supremacy
of European Law: The Making of an International Rule of Law in Europe* (Oxford:
Oxford University Press, 2001).

[41] For an early criticism of jurocentrism from within the discipline itself, see Joseph H. H.
Weiler, "Eurocracy and Distrust: Some Questions Concerning the Role of the European
Court of Justice in the Protection of Fundamental Human Rights within the Legal Order
of the European Communities," *Washington Law Review* 61, no. 3 (1986), 110–74.

rule-of-law norms and the factual condition of their institutional independence.

This lack of ECJ autonomy in the juro-skeptic presentation implies that the Court will be unable to socialize surreptitiously European and domestic law in a progressive manner. To be sure, national courts have not, and do not, function free of institutional constraints,[42] but because the ECJ, while more entrenched in domestic orders than other international courts, nevertheless remains somewhat remote from national institutional structures, it seems to be especially vulnerable to such pressure from stronger institutions. In contrast to the inspiringly optimistic projections of the supranationalist literature, those that can be drawn from the ECJ-skeptical literature are bleak. If the governing principles of a juridical unit like the EU in fact merely pertain to the regulation of an economic free-trade zone, those principles will clearly be too thin to preserve the gains of liberal or social democracy associated with two or three centuries of expanding civil and social rights. This is especially so if the judicial arbiter of them, the ECJ, lacks the necessary autonomy to keep the other political institutions from enacting arbitrary and inconsistent policies – perhaps one of the few attributes of the laissez-faire judiciaries of the nineteenth century worthy of admiration.

The need for supranational legal protection in response to the expanding transnational power of economic and hence political actors would be, according to the Court-skeptical model, stymied by the still quasi-sovereign nation-states. The EU member states may have suffered some loss of sovereignty to the extent that they participate in the process of European integration as an attempt to compensate for economic losses that some would attribute to international developments related to economic globalization.[43] However, these states may still be sufficiently strong, and exceedingly jealous of what sovereignty they actually maintain, to be able to block the extension of social principles of justice from entering the adjudication processes of the ECJ. The fact that economic issues are the only ones to be adjudicated at a supranational level in Europe would not be so problematic if member states remain capable of commanding a monopoly on the legal protection and enforcement of social

---

[42] As classically depicted in Rosenberg, *The Hollow Hope*.

[43] See Paul Hirst and G. Thompson, *Globalisation in Question: The International Economy and the Possibilities of Governance* (Cambridge: Polity Press, 1996); Ash Amin and Nigel Thrift, eds., *Globalization, Institutions, and Regional Development in Europe* (Oxford: Oxford University Press, 1996); and Saskia Sassen, *Losing Control?: Sovereignty in an Age of Globalization* (New York: Columbia University Press, 1996).

rights domestically. If, however, they abdicate economic control at the domestic level to any significant extent in the future due to the pressures of globalization, one would expect them to abdicate social and political control as well. As we will see in the next section, scholars such as Streeck and Scharpf will argue whether this is actually the case. This scenario would leave standing no legal forum, national or Europe-wide, in which social issues are adjudicated decisively. This is the looming danger to the *Sozialstaat* at all levels of European governance should the ECJ-skeptical prognostications prove to be true.

While it is fashionable to indulge in Cassandra-like pronouncements concerning the demise of both the *Sozialstaat* and the rule of law as a result of the growing transnational mobility of capital, Streeck and Scharpf will raise this issue: in the gap between the European member states' declining ability to secure and advance principles of the *Sozialstaat* themselves (as a result of evaporating tax bases, increased environmental threats, anti-immigrant and minority-unfriendly policies, etc.) and their reluctance to fully accede these responsibilities to fora like the ECJ lies the abyss of the supranational democratic possibilities of European social democracy and the rule of law as theorized by Habermas. If the ECJ is to adjudicate exclusively on the basis of market-related rules, and merely hortatory appeals to principles associated with civil, social, and human rights, then the subtle distinction and interplay of economic adjudication and social adjudication in the Court-friendly spillover model would appear to be virtually ineffectual in the EU context.

But what if the object of investigation appropriate to an analysis of the future of democracy in the EU is neither a would-be *Sozialstaat* nor a more intricate intergovernmental treaty organization, as these two sets of literatures aver? What if the EU is a qualitatively different and new form of polity, one that would require adaptation of *Rechtsstaat* and *Sozialstaat* principles to decidedly non-*Rechtsstaat* and non-*Sozialstaat* institutions? What is the configuration of these new institutions, and how might democratic aspirations be realized within it? The next section on the *Sektoralstaat* attempts to answer these questions.

3. The European *Sektoralstaat* Model

I will address three principal issues in this section: (a) the extent to which the EU *Sektoralstaat* can be expected to adopt *Sozialstaat*-like, legally facilitated social regulation and redistribution; (b) the details of the microsegmented transnational policymaking that scholars have tried to capture with the terms infranationalism, comitology, associationalism, and so on, and its ramifications for legally facilitated democracy at the EU level; and (c) the likelihood of macrosectoral governance for various large-scale policy spheres to which only specific subsets of European member states will belong. Subsection (a) pushes the analysis of law in the EU beyond the supranationalist/intergovernmentalist debates, suggesting that the either/or posed in that debate concerning legal integration and social policy is a chimera. There will be neither a EU federal *Sozialstaat* nor a race to the bottom that hollows out the welfare states of the individual EU members. The present and future reality is to be found in a much more unclear middle. As we observed, Habermas places a heavy wager on the constitutionalist narrative expounded by Weiler and the supranationalists, and so he expects or at least hopes that a continental *Sozialstaat* will emerge from legal integration and an eventual constitutional debate/convention. Evidence suggests that, on the contrary, legal integration described by Weiler has undermined the possibility of high levels of social protection across the European polity in most areas – but, contrary to most intergovernmentalists, not all of them.

Subsection (b) focuses on the semiformal, semipublic, superspecialized policy-making practices across member state borders that seem to conform with Habermasian discourse-theoretical principles, while (c) focuses on the large-scale sectors to which different sets of member states will belong, separated by fairly strict regulative divides. These three topics show that the question of governance in the EU, and the possibility of democratizing it, is not just one of multilevel governance but one of multisegmented governance as well. In this vein, the *Sektoralstaat* is characterized by horizontal and vertical segmentation, both of which are qualitatively different than industrial relations, corporatist, Fordist, or iron-triangle policymaking in the *Sozialstaat*, most dramatically because the latter were supervised by constitutionally sanctioned judicial review and parliamentary oversight. As we will observe, there are so many different aspects of the EU *Sektoralstaat* – from different vantage points and in various policy fields – that it is alternately socially democratic, neoliberal, or new-agely postpolitical and therefore more multifaceted than the *Sozialstaat* ever was. One of the goals of this analysis, however, is to avoid retreating from normative-empirical investigation into the category of "complexity" as a result of this less than simple state of affairs.

(a) Legally Facilitated Race to the Bottom or Stroll to the Top?
Since the mid-1990s, evidence has emerged suggesting that legal integration in the EU has exacerbated a globalization-related decline in social protection at the member state level without, in turn, restoring something

similar at the EU level.[44] Whether or not the ECJ and EU law have successfully established a European *Rechtsstaat*, Fritz Scharpf argues that
they have undercut the *Sozialstaat* of individual EU member states and
have come just short of dooming any prospect for social democracy at
the European level. According to Scharpf, the "constitutionalization" of
competition law at the EU level has decreased market-correcting capacities at the national level; and the ECJ has helped to intensify "competition
among regulatory systems" that prevents member states from sustaining
market-correcting policies that were previously supported by democratic
majorities.[45] In the name of a continental common market, European law,
by prohibiting individual member states from protecting national industries, workforces, or regulatory practices, effectively dismantles market-
correcting institutions within those states. Consequently, countries that
have been forced to lower protection levels and open their own markets
ally with the EU to make other member states do the same.[46] In this scenario, European law effectively dismantles market-correcting institutions
within the member states that the Council of Ministers, as a result of near-
unanimity requirements, will block reconstruction of at the EU level. In
particular, Scharpf charges that ECJ decisions enforcing the supremacy
and direct-effect doctrines have undermined antitrust rules and enshrined
the "neo-liberal conceptual framework" of – contra the Franco-phobia
of many Euroskeptics – German specialists in competition law.[47] Even

---

[44] As a cautionary note, Fritz Scharpf suggests that the globalization issue is not so simple
as blaming the "usual suspects" for the economic problems of European countries since
the 1970s: the ubiquitous laments over "institutional rigidities, union power and the
burdens of the welfare state." See Scharpf, *Governing in Europe*, 124. These neo-liberal
explanations do not confront "critical structural factors," particularly concerning gender
demographics, such as the fact that unemployment figures are open to political manipulation, that they neglect the impact of women in the workforce, or the separate taxation of
spouses' incomes or the impact of day-care availability on the labor market. See Scharpf,
Governing in Europe, 125. This is not to mention the impact of changes in incarceration
rates on political economy; see Bruce Western and Katherine Beckett, "How Unregulated Is the U.S. Labor Market?: The Dynamics of Jobs and Jails, 1980–1995,"*American
Journal of Sociology* 104, no. 3 (January 1999), 1030–60. Scharpf is agnostic on the
competitiveness of the EU vis-à-vis worldwide capital mobility and globalization: "the
answer is likely to vary from one policy area to another, and it also depends very much
on assumptions about the probability of protectionist policies of the EU." See Scharpf,
Governing in Europe, 102, n. 12.

[45] See Scharpf, *Governing in Europe*, 2–3. Scharpf defines regulatory competition as member states vying "to influence the content and form of European regulations with a view
to minimizing their own adjustment costs." See Scharpf, ibid., 85.

[46] Ibid., 69, 85.

[47] Ibid., 53–4. Scharpf's criticisms of his own country's role in hollowing out the regulatory regimes of the member states stand in marked contrast to Larry Siedentop's

national parliamentary supermajorities cannot counteract these institutionalized business-friendly and neo-liberal biases within EU policy.[48]

Philippe Schmitter and Larry Siedentop also criticize the business-friendly orientation of the EU facilitated by the ECJ and EU law in Scharpf's analysis. Schmitter lists the many players who have been disadvantaged by business gains in the integration process: "policy takers" like workers, the unemployed, women, consumers, pensioners, and youth; participants in public interest or ideological movements such as environmentalists, free choicers, and peace activists; subnational units like regions, provinces, communes, and municipalities; and any and all transnational coalitions that draw upon these groups for support.[49] For his part, Siedentop is especially eloquent on the historical ramifications of an emerging "businessman's Europe": "are we simply making Europe safe for bankers, consultants and managers? Has the West seen off the communist challenge only to fall victim to an unelected elite, in its own way as arrogant and exploitative as the communist elite, though relying on a different rhetoric and managing in a different style?"[50]

But for all of Siedentop's powerful rhetoric against a hypercapitalist EU, he seems to lack the social-philosophical resources to propose a genuine solution. Running throughout *Democracy in Europe* is a philo-aristocratic narrative intended to provoke readers into thinking critically about the enlightened statesmanship required for an historic undertaking like European integration. But it is not, as Siedentop implies, so easy to separate a supposedly benevolent political elitism from a more base form of economic elitism. In fact, attempts to create the conditions from which political leadership can emerge may only further corrode the accomplishments of European social democracy already severely undermined by a form of economic elitism. Siedentop exhibits little sensitivity to the fact

Franco-phobic positions on EU administration: Siedentop remarks that "Brussels has in some respects become an appendage of Paris and of the French political elite." See Larry Siedentop, *Democracy in Europe* (New York: Columbia University Press, 2001), 113. Further, he pronounces that the French have been "taking over Europe" as a result of their "enormous advantage" in knowing "what they want," which is to contain Germany and protect agricultural policies that favor themselves (115). The force of these sentiments is not really mitigated by a statement professing admiration for French belief "in Europe as a cultural and a moral undertaking" (224). For a more elaborate discussion of these works, see my "Democratic Theory Confronts the European Union: Prospects for Constitutional and Social Democracy in a Supranational *Sektoralstaat*," *Political Theory* 34, no. 1 (February 2006), 121–31.

[48] See Scharpf, *Governing in Europe*, 54.
[49] See Schmitter, *How to Democratize the European Union*, 54.
[50] See Siedentop, *Democracy in Europe*, 34.

that in modern capitalist democracies the attempt to nurture enlightened political elites often fostered the emergence of unaccountable economic elites.[51] To be sure, Siedentop's patrician heroes – Montesquieu, Madison, and Tocqueville[52] – contributed profoundly to the theory and practice of prudent and constrained leadership in modern representative government. But they, and certainly their more recent conservative devotees, may have exaggerated the threats of bureaucratic centralization and expanding egalitarianism in a way that exacerbated the economic inequality to which the former were in large part responses. In this spirit, Siedentop views the history of class consciousness and class contention within European nation-states *not* as necessary preparation for the post–World War II social democratic consensus on the continent, but rather as the dangerous foundations of Bonapartism and fascism.[53] Thus, the portended demise of social democracy in a "businessman's Europe" is not nearly so serious a problem for Siedentop as is its deleterious implications for the development of his hoped-for enlightened political elite.

By contrast, for Scharpf, the Commission's and the ECJ's active elimination of nontariff barriers to the exchange of goods is deeply at odds with principles and practices undergirding the mixed economy characterizing most European *Sozialstaats*. Their efforts against violations of competition rules and against discrimination toward foreign competitors undermines political strategies that successfully combined market and interventionist approaches throughout the postwar era.[54] In particular, legal integration has rendered the mixed economy vulnerable to neoliberal attack in "service public" areas (*staatsnahe Sektoren*) as varied as "education, basic research, radio and TV, health care, old-age pensions, telecommunications, rail, air, and road transport, energy supply, banking, stock exchanges, and agriculture."[55] In situations where businesses do tolerate high protection levels, it is only on the condition that the cost of social regulation and redistribution is passed on to consumers – an outcome that Scharpf insists is neither fair nor economically optimal as long-term social policy. Equally disconcerting, the difficulty of taxing a rapidly mobile pan-European and transglobal business and capital sector

---

[51] This is one plausible interpretation of the formative years of the United States, an inspiration to Siedentop. See Gordon S. Wood, *The Creation of the American Republic, 1776–1787* (Chapel Hill: University of North Carolina Press, 1998).

[52] See Siedentop, *Democracy in Europe*, 3, 15, 21.

[53] Ibid., 17, 18, 20.

[54] See Scharpf, *Governing in Europe*, 58.

[55] Ibid., 59.

forces governments to tax immobile targets such as wages and consumption.[56] In Scharpf's estimation, just as the regulative burden should not and cannot fall on citizens, workers, and consumers disproportionately, redistributive costs ought not to be and cannot be borne by them as well.

The Commission has been more aggressive in using treaty provisions (e.g., Articles 89 II and 90 III TEC) to promote the liberalization of only certain public service areas (such as telecommunications, air transport and airport operations, road haulage, postal services, and the energy market), but the ECJ has been complicit in the general result that "no area of *service public* is now beyond the challenge of European competition law."[57] Scharpf discerns a resulting dynamic whereby trade liberalization within Europe enlists individual member states in the cause of carrying out such liberalization even further:

> Once a country has been forced to open its own markets unilaterally, it cannot have an interest in allowing other countries to maintain their protectionist practices. Hence governments that were the victims of successful legal action are likely to become political allies of the Commission when a general directive subjecting all member states to the same regime is subsequently proposed to the Council.[58]

Even attempts on the part of more socially progressive member states to raise the level of protection or regulation within the Union can be met with resistance, as sets of countries with diametrically opposed common interests will more than likely outvote such mavericks in the Council. As an example, Scharpf points to the success of more Euroskeptic countries in thwarting Danish, German, and Dutch attempts to strengthen European regulation of waste packaging.[59] Moreover, even if agreement is reached among members of the Council, it is difficult to ensure the actual implementation of EU policy once formally adopted by a grudging member state.[60]

---

[56] Ibid., 114.

[57] Ibid., 61. Scharpf points to the following examples: the German Labor Administration was successfully challenged by private placement services, as were the privileges of public radio and television, and public banks; so too, he predicts, will public health and education institutions be challenged in Scandinavia and Britain.

[58] Ibid., 69.

[59] Ibid., 72, n. 31. Scharpf explains the agenda-setting and compromise-facilitating power of the Commission in cases of member state disagreement in the Council, when some solution is preferred to the status quo; but he also shows that agreement is virtually impossible in circumstances where there are (1) sharp ideological commitments, (2) fundamental economic interests at stake, or (3) the likelihood of prohibitively expensive institutional change. Ibid., 77.

[60] Ibid., 103.

This is not to say that a uniform raising of social protection levels throughout the EU would be an unmitigated positive – something addressed in subsection (c) when I discuss the necessity of sectoral divisions among groups of member states. After all, full harmonization of social-welfare and environmental regulations at levels commensurate with, for instance, Denmark's policies would ruin countries with levels like those of, say, Portugal: as Scharpf shows, competitiveness would evaporate in the latter countries, or attempts to compensate with lower exchange rates would raise prices and impoverish their consumers.[61] Consumers, in general, have been bearing and could further bear even more of the costs of social regulations in these circumstances, if businesses agree to a raising of levels, but it bears repeating that this is neither fair nor economically optimal as a long-term policy. In any case, universal regulatory levels within Europe are made difficult and, as of now, undesirable by the varied ways that labor is organized and structured throughout the member states – strong versus weak unions; unions organized along party/ideological lines, by industry, or by skills; centralized versus decentralized wage bargaining; legalistic versus consensual collective bargaining; and so on.[62] Most problematically, these differences and others like them among the economies of the various member states are devastating to any hope for a tax revenue–based redistributive policy across the EU. The difficulty of taxing a variegated and ever-changing business and capital sector has forced governments to shift "ever larger shares of total revenues to taxes on immobile factors, in particular to taxes on wages and consumption."[63]

In the previous chapter, we observed Habermas adopt what Scharpf identifies as a supranational Keynesian position, which anticipates the pursuit and recovery "either through the policy choices of European institutions or through coordinated action among the member governments of the Union" of macroeconomic full-employment strategies abandoned at the state level.[64] But, in a manner that contravenes Habermas's expectations, he indicates that trends point in the opposite direction: institutional arrangements adopted in the Maastricht and Amsterdam treaties were designed precisely to *block* publicly managed full-employment policies.[65] Moreover, a tight central bank policy like the one presently pursued at the EU level is generally detrimental to the goal of full employment.

[61] Ibid., 79.
[62] Ibid., 82.
[63] Ibid., 114.
[64] Ibid., 114.
[65] Ibid., 115, n. 19.

So there is not much that a European Central Bank, "more independent than, and as committed to price stability as, the Bundesbank," could do for EU-wide employment through a European monetary policy.[66] Further endangering full employment, the "stability pact" entailed by the Amsterdam Treaty is committed to extend this kind of fiscal discipline into the indefinite future.[67] Ultimately, in Scharpf's analysis, a uniform *Sozialstaat* is impossible on an EU level because precisely the following spheres fall within the area where both supranational and national regulation capacity is low: social policy, industrial relations, macroeconomic employment policy, and taxes on mobile bases.[68]

A somewhat less bleak view of social democracy in an integrated Europe is offered by Wolfgang Streeck.[69] He suggests that there is room for limited substantive social policy at the EU level and specific opportunities for the preservation of social democratic practices within member states. According to Streeck, this regulation and redistribution depend on political pressure from informed and organized publics at the continental and national levels. But he concedes that EU policy, despite official rhetoric proclaiming the contrary, has been undermining the social citizenship necessary to exert such requisite pressure. Put bluntly, there is no substantive social citizenship in the EU beyond the formal civil right of workers who migrate to and from member states to enter into contractual relations across borders. And Streeck avers that recent EU efforts to appear progressive in the social sphere have actually favored management and ownership rather than labor. In particular, workplace participation rights, institutionalized by the 1994 Directive on European Works Councils (DEWC), are quite weak at the continental level and actually help to undermine strong social rights regimes at the national level.[70] Despite initial high expectations for social rights in Europe, Streeck argues that the latter were progressively weakened in a succession of policy arrangements over the history of the EC and EU.[71] In the transition from policies

---

[66] Ibid., 115. Carol Harlow describes how European Central Bank (ECB) advocates use the goal of price stability to ward off efforts to render the bank politically accountable through more procedural openness (e.g., the publication of board members' voting records, meeting minutes, and ECB inflation forecasts). See Harlow, *Accountability in the European Union* (Oxford: Oxford University Press, 2003), 48–9.

[67] See Scharpf, *Governing in Europe*, 116.

[68] Ibid., 117.

[69] Wolfgang Streeck, "Citizenship under Regime Competition: The Case of the 'European Works Councils,'" in Eder and Giesen, eds., *European Citizenship*, 122–56.

[70] Ibid., 128.

[71] Ibid., 131–2.

aimed at, successively, harmonization, incorporation, and coordination, Streeck traces the lowering of expectations from a supranational welfare state to mere voluntary compliance with social regulation on the part of management.

First off, *harmonization* aimed at a full-blown supranational welfare state by making industrial citizenship uniform across the Community; *incorporation* then treated the different national welfare systems as "building blocks" of varying levels of protection in a common European social system and shifted the emphasis from company law to labor law, placing more of the burden of proof on unions; and, presently, *coordination* entails the supranational regulation of national systems with a complete emphasis on labor law, voluntary agreement, and shunning legal-statutory protection of workers almost completely.[72] Harmonization was expected to culminate in a Europeanization of the German industrial citizenship model through union codetermination of decisions at the company level, worker council consultation, and co–decision making at the factory level.[73] But the German model was rejected for Europe as inflexible and as too inhibiting of the information-gathering and consultation methods by which companies purportedly address unpredictable developments and manage risk.[74] Streeck interprets the rise of the Community governance principle of "subsidiarity" alongside the move to the economic policy of incorporation in the 1980s as an effort to weaken substantive industrial rights.[75] In particular, he understands the fate of the "Vredeling directive" as indicative of this trend.[76]

Even the 1994 DEWC is only a modest policy statement that makes it obligatory for member states to ensure that nationally based companies that employ a significant number of employees in other EU countries negotiate with representatives of their entire European workforce, which would constitute a continentwide workforce information arrangement. Absent such an agreement, firms must establish a "European works council" with representatives from all their European plants, and member

---

[72] Ibid.

[73] Ibid., 132–3.

[74] Ibid., 134.

[75] Subsidiarity is the principle, formally adopted in 1992, that encourages decisions on European policy to be made at institutional levels operating as close to citizens as possible.

[76] Commissioner for Social Affairs Henk Vredeling issued a draft directive on information and consultation rights for workforces in 1980. But the directive was formally suspended by Council vote and a looming British veto in 1986. See Streeck, "Citizenship under Regime Competition," 135.

states must grant such councils a common minimum of legal rights that must be extended to nonnational employees as well.[77] But the directive is more company-friendly than *Sozialstaat*-style industrial relations, most significantly by underplaying worker/workplace participation and by overemphasizing voluntarism. Streeck reminds us of what we observed Weber concede in Chapter 3: in property relations, "voluntarism does not favor the weaker party."[78] Unfortunately, according to Streeck, due to ambiguity in DEWC stipulations over the authority of European versus state institutions on social issues, it has been possible for business and EU officials to parade the demise of worker participation rights as precisely the triumph of such rights: the option of firms to institute or not observe worker participation programs is celebrated as a victory for economic "freedom of choice":

Working out the details of the coexistence between national and supranational participation rights is left to national legislation and to the voluntarism of the marketplace. Here, too, what in fact was an admission of defeat by the unsolvable technical complexities and political dilemmas that follow from fragmentation of state capacity and citizenship is presented as an inventive practical application of the new creed of decentralization and "subsidiarity." Indeed even with respect to the substance of European rights, the directive goes out of its way to turn industrial citizenship, from an *institutional condition* of negotiations between employers and workforces, into their *result*. While it does not prevent firms from agreeing to councils with consultation or even co-determination rights, no firm has done so yet, and all known agreements have remained at or below the statutory minimum of participation rights.[79]

Thus, according to Scharpf, Streeck, and Schmitter, despite early aspirations and expectations of supranationalists like Weiler and, more recently, Habermas, legal integration has *not* facilitated social, let alone political, integration but rather economic (i.e., *market*) integration alone. This result is somewhat different from those predicted by intergovernmentalist scholars who emphasize the general weakness of the ECJ. On the contrary, the Court has been sufficiently strong to push market-promoting legal integration further than many forces in the member states would like. Therefore, like intergovernmentalist scholars, Scharpf shows that the ECJ is too weak to promote positive integration that would create substantive

---

[77] Ibid., 137.
[78] Ibid., 138, 142.
[79] Ibid., 140. As he continues, "unions have not been able to gain a single European works council agreement providing for participation rights above the legal minimum." Ibid., 145.

social policy, but that it is much stronger than intergovernmentalists recognize at promoting a neo-liberal, business-friendly, negatively integrated European market. (The Court has "negatively" integrated Europe by forbidding various kinds of trade barriers within member states.) Like intergovernmentalist scholars, however, Scharpf also shows that the ECJ is too *weak* to promote positive integration that would create a substantive European social policy. (The Court cannot order the construction of common, "positive" policies throughout the member states.) But how did the supranationalist scholars miss this development for so long?

Weiler and many of his supranationalist consociates are perhaps easy targets for the charge that their juridical naiveté is not attuned to the intricacies of power politics.[80] But Weiler in particular did draw attention to the dual legal/political or negative/positive paths, conceding that supranational constitutionalization is only one path toward integration, while intergovernmental state coordination on substantive matters is the other equally important path. Weiler is attentive to both supranational negative integration (through treaty compliance guarded and enforced by the Commission and the ECJ) and intergovernmental positive integration (through the near-unanimous agreement of the Council of Ministers, with the participation of the EP).[81] But probing a little more deeply into his work, the question arises as to whether he is sufficiently attuned to the intimate *interplay* of these two tracks, such that the story of European integration has not really been at any particular time the either/or of ECJ supranational supremacy versus member state supremacy that Weiler tells. Weiler's work scarcely reflects the fact that the Court's behavior at its most powerful has actually facilitated the more neo-liberal member state interests and therefore has not acted substantively supranational at all.[82]

To be sure, Weiler fairly masterly recounts the ebb and flow of supranational constitutionalization and the Court's seesaw ride for ascendancy over the Council and the member states: for example, silent ECJ ascendancy in the 1950s and its retreat from member state encroachment

---

[80] Weiler sets himself up for such criticisms by relying so extensively on a Kelsenian "pure theory" of law framework, translated into Teubnerian systems theory, according to which politics is merely an "external factor" in relationship to the "self-referentiality" of the European legal system. See Weiler, *The Constitution of Europe*, 15. Nor does he help himself with statements such as the following, which make Habermas look downright Machiavellian when it comes to political realism: "A state, in our Western democracies, cannot disobey its own courts." See Weiler, *The Constitution of Europe*, 28

[81] Ibid., 16; cf. 96, 319, and footnote 11 in this book. This is judiciously discussed by Scharpf in *Governing in Europe*, 50.

[82] See Weiler, *The Constitution of Europe*, 189.

in the 1960s. But Weiler adopts a triumphalist tone while recounting the expansion of *material* jurisdiction in the 1970s and 1980s, such that "constitutionally, no core of sovereign state powers was left beyond the reach of the Community."[83] Notwithstanding the setbacks in trying to help formulate a European industrial policy in this era, Weiler emphasizes how the ECJ Europeanized "ancillary issues," such as "environmental policy, consumer protection, energy, and research,"[84] and circumvented, in conjunction with the Commission, the Luxembourg Compromise through Article 235.[85] In only few moments of this account does Weiler even hint that Court-driven harmonization of an internal market was obviously neo-liberal in philosophy and effect.[86]

Generally, Weiler does not confront the fact that legal integration has not laid the groundwork for substantively social integration, but may in fact have made the latter impossible within the member states that then might coordinate a European-wide social policy or at least compile a menu of social policies that might have some vitality. Weiler remarks how use of Article 235 "opened up practically any realm of state activity to the Community, provided the governments of the Member States found accord among themselves."[87] The problem is that where there is such Community action and member state accord, a race to the bottom ensues that undermines the social conditions of substantive, positive integration in social policy. Contra Scharpf, for instance, Weiler interprets this process, if not its result, as a good thing:

A rigorous (and courageous [sic!]) jurisprudence of the Court of Justice seriously limited the ability of the Member States to adopt protectionist measures vis-à-vis each other. Indeed, it went further. The Court held that once the Community enacted measures regulating nontariff barriers to movement of goods, such measures would preempt any subsequently enacted Member State legislation that frustrated the design of the extant Community measures.[88]

But lacking social policy at the European level, policies that "protect" welfare state measures at the member state level are a necessity for the civic and social well-being of these countries! Weiler concedes that ECJ judicial review represents a "problematic" extension of jurisdiction into "areas of

---

[83] Ibid., 42–3.
[84] Ibid., 58.
[85] Ibid., 59.
[86] Here he refers to the legacy of the Cassis de Dijon case: Weiler, *The Constitution of Europe*, 189.
[87] Ibid., 60.
[88] Ibid., 67.

social regulation." But it is problematic for him on *formally* democratic grounds alone – that is, member state citizens should have some input into or oversight over this process. Weiler does not find it problematic on the *substantively* democratic grounds that ECJ adjudication is helping to exacerbate regulatory competition among member states that guts crucial aspects of their redistributive and regulatory institutions. Like Siedentop, then, Weiler seems fairly indifferent to the concrete means of securing the social bases necessary for meaningful political citizenship.[89]

Nevertheless, despite these shortcomings in Weiler's supranationalist vision of a EU *Rechtsstaat*, the usually subdued Scharpf suggests that things are not completely without hope. If the EU will not carry out regulation and redistribution as extensive and substantive as did the national *Sozialstaat*, neither will it completely abandon these functions or fully thwart the member states from continuing to do so themselves. For instance, notwithstanding criticisms of the Amsterdam treaty mentioned previously, Scharpf points to "unexploited opportunities" for increasing the problem-solving and market-correcting capacities in the treaty's commitment to coordinated employment strategies.[90] Moreover, he points out that there is fairly robust supranational capacity in other spheres, such as international trade negotiations, agriculture, and telecommunications, to improve the conditions of European workers and consumers. Also, a decline in problem-solving and market-correcting capacities is not completely generalizable across all spheres and sectors, according to Scharpf: policy areas "differ with regard to both the impact of the lowering of trade barriers associated with negative integration and ensuing regulatory competition on national solutions and the difficulties of [EU] positive integration."[91] Some national policy spheres are simply unaffected by negative integration and regulatory competition, and these spheres may continue to reflect, on the contrary, different indigenous policy preferences: for example, neo-liberalism in the United Kingdom, a red-green party alliance in Denmark, and a consensus-oriented grand coalition approach in the Netherlands or Austria.[92]

---

[89] In his more optimistic essays before the late 1990s, Weiler seems to assume that functional spillover from formal or negative integration to substantive or positive integration has already taken place and requires only conventional political access for national populaces. On the failure of functional-formal integration to spill over into substantive-positive integration, see Schmitter, *How to Democratize the European Union*, 88.

[90] See Scharpf, *Governing in Europe*, 4.

[91] Ibid., 83.

[92] Ibid., 90.

Echoing Habermas, even if tempered by the conclusions of his more sober empirical analysis, Scharpf holds out hope that, in the future, an informed political will aimed at the supranational level may possibly bring about regulation that eludes the coordination of member state interest in the Council. Governments, unions, and environmental groups that are frustrated at the national level by the downward economic pressures of regulatory competition will almost certainly attempt supranational reregulation that has previously proved unsuccessful. Also, business interests in high-regulation member states may seek to raise the uniform level of regulation throughout the EU to "level the playing field" at a high rather than a low standard.[93] Scharpf avers that efficiency concerns will encourage industrial associations and multinational firms to support EU-wide health, safety, and environmental standards for machine tools and office equipment beyond the level of existing national regulations – even if this impulse will not affect many environmental "process" regulations.[94] As a result, levels of protection may rise as countries are induced "to imitate foreign models of regulation or deregulation if information about the performance of national systems is spreading through transnational communication."[95] Leaving open a Habermasian door that his account of regulatory competition would have seemed to close, Scharpf emphasizes the concrete benefits of a continental civil society of free information exchange on socioeconomic issues. Perhaps emphasizing self-interest more than mutual understanding, Scharpf at least acknowledges that informed discussion and choice will progressively affect the political regulation of product quality within Europe when

[c]onsumers are *informed* of differences between national systems of regulations and.... that these differences affect the *utility* of the product for (self-interested) consumers ... stringent national regulations may become a competitive advantage

[93] Ibid., 109.

[94] Ibid., 110. Scharpf explains the difference between "product-related" and "process-related" regulations. Consumers prefer *products* that they know will not have deleterious effects on health or the environment and tend to reward producers who provide such goods and services even if they are more costly. Thus, high Europe-wide standards may obtain for product-related foodstuff regulations, consumer safety, work safety, and environmental regulations. Ibid., 107. On the other hand, since the negative effects incurred by the production process, whether pollution, danger to workers, low sick pay, or substandard wages, do not affect the quality of the products themselves, member states cannot count on enlightened or self-interested consumers to choose more expensive goods and services produced under more stringent process regulations. Ibid., 97. Consumers can ignore or remain oblivious to such ill effects resulting from the manufacture of items that they will not ignore with respect to their *consumption* or *use*.

[95] Ibid., 90; cf. 86.

for national firms.... [This] certificate effect will put pressure on other governments to upgrade their regulatory systems in order to protect their own industries
against foreign competitors whose products are *more attractive because they are
more highly regulated.*[96]

Thus, to summarize Scharpf's view: there is no possibility of Keynesian
full-employment policies on the EU level; product-related environmental,
health, and safety regulations may raise standards of protection; taxation
is intensely affected by transnational mobility, as are process-related environmental, health, and safety regulations, but the latter are susceptible to
pressure in the form of political will.[97] Hence, an educated, deliberatively
based popular will poses a quasi-Habermasian way back from any race to
the bottom. Scharpf warns against reading all constellations of European
political economy in terms of a symmetrical Prisoner's Dilemma game that
would portend a race to the bottom. The latter is relevant in situations
where each member state wants the benefit of access to larger markets
but seeks to persist in protectionist practices, and when the negative integration enforced by the Commission and adjudicated by the ECJ under
the treaties is unavoidable.[98]

So, prospects point to neither a race to the bottom, as globalization
pessimists and social democratic Euroskeptics predict, nor to the groundwork for a robust, full-scale EU *Sozialstaat,* as some supranationalists,
including Habermas, might have hoped. Looking ahead to the next section, which examines literatures that question whether labor issues are
relevant at all to the contemporary political economy of the EU, Wolfgang Streeck warns against forsaking the commitment to egalitarianism
inherent in the *Sozialstaat* project in the name of some illusory postsocial
and postpolitical configuration:

[W]orkplace participation may also be seen as an "industrial" issue of declining
significance in a "post-industrial" society in which, allegedly, consumer interests
take precedence over producer interests.... Since workplace participation regimes
regulate, or may precisely fail to regulate, the extent to which the organization
and intensity of work may be governed by market pressures, and since social
regulation of the "effort bargain" at the workplace may be anti-competitive, they
present a strong test for the ability of a polity to mediate the impact of competition
on social life.... A non-state regime of industrial citizenship rights that is forced
to rely heavily on national and managerial voluntarism must accept considerable

---

[96] Ibid., 93.
[97] Ibid., 101–2.
[98] Ibid., 104.

inequality, as it must allow participation to vary with firms' national origin and corporate strategy.[99]

Scholars focused on comitological, infranational, and associational processes in the EU will celebrate the inclusiveness of all parties most concerned with or affected by policies within a deliberative supranational policy-making process. Streeck's example of workplace participation will make us pause to question whether everyone is included to the same degree and with an equally effective voice.

(b) Comitology – Open, Public, and Equitable Deliberation?

There are two main approaches to rendering EU policymaking, depending on one's perspective, more legitimate, democratic, and/or progressive: the first, which we observed Habermas advocate in the previous chapter, would further empower the EP, while the second, which is the primary focus of this subsection, more or less circumvents the EP and emphasizes instead EU committee arrangements and the comitological, infranational, and/or associational policy-making process that is conducted through them.

The main problem for the first approach is the fact that the EP is no conventional parliament. Despite an incremental expansion in responsibilities over time, the EP remains a decidedly junior partner in a lawmaking process that is dominated by the Commission and the Council. The EP may suggest policy to the Commission, which is under no compunction to comply, despite the EP's formal budgetary, agenda, and censure powers over the Commission. The ECJ has been a powerful ally of the EP, sanctioning the latter's delay power over the Council through the requirement that the latter wait for EP approval of its policy implementation. But delay is not statute creation. Moreover, as Carol Harlow points out, the EP ensures virtually no public accountability of the Commission through its limited legislative capacities and only partial accountability through its formal appointment, budgetary, investigative, and financial influence over the Commission.[100]

---

[99] See Streeck, "Citizenship under Regime Competition," 148.

[100] See Harlow, *Accountability in the European Union*, 92. On the other hand, Christian Joerges suggests that the EP wields real power of oversight over EU policymaking, in particular the comitology: the EP, "by setting up committees of enquiry, can assuredly bring effective means of publicity to bear by calling on those involved in regulatory policy to reason." See Joerges, "'Deliberative Supranationalism' – Two Defences," *European Law Journal* 8, no. 1 (2002), 133–51 at 150.

Despite these limitations and changes, scholars such as Habermas envision an eventual expansion of EP power and transpose up to the European-level expectations concerning the traditional interaction of legislatures and civil societies within nation-states. In the recent essays discussed in the previous chapter, Habermas advocates the development of a transnational, European-wide, civil society via the proliferation of communication technologies within Europe. Through such communicative action, Habermas claims that an increasingly powerful EP can be made responsive to citizens of Europe and make law on that basis.[101] After all, the EP does *look* like a conventional legislature internally: MEPs are elected by universal suffrage, and institutional hierarchy, rules of procedure, and committee work are organized along traditional parliamentary lines. However, besides premature institutional presumptions about the development of the EP, Habermas does not address the literature on European telecommunications that does not necessarily support his expectations about a communicatively democratic continental public sphere.[102] Again, in Habermas's model, the EU will eventually approximate a continental version of a liberal-parliamentary democracy. But just as his expectations for European law were somewhat at odds with the empirical evidence on the ECJ, his aspirations for a European civil society/European public sphere/European parliament relationship are not especially well founded.[103] Discursively active transnational associations *are* impacting

---

[101] The following also consider the prospects for a European civil society: Shirley Williams, "Sovereignty and Accountability in the European Community," in Keohane and Hoffmann, eds., *The New European Community*; Teija Tiilikainen, "The Problem of Democracy in the European Union," in Allan Rosas and Esko Antola, eds., *A Citizens' Europe: In Search of a New Order* (London: Sage, 1995); and the essays contained in Eder and Giesen, eds., *European Citizenship*. In this literature, the strengthening of the EP is often recommended as the appropriate solution to any European "democratic deficit."

[102] See Stephen D. Krasner, "Global Communications and National Power: Life on the Pareto Frontier," *World Politics* 43 (1990–1); Hamid Mowlana, *Global Communication in Transition: The End of Diversity?* (London: Sage, 1992); and Wayne Sandholtz, "Institutional and Collective Action: The New Telecommunications in Western Europe," *World Politics* 45, no. 2 (January 1993).

[103] Note that there *is* room for EP influence, albeit limited, upon EU policymaking in present and future circumstances. George Tsebelis claims that the EP can affect European lawmaking by exercising a "conditional agenda setting power" in cases where its cooperation is procedurally required in policymaking. The treaty-established cooperation procedure works as follows: after the EP and the Council have contributed input to a Commission proposal, the EP undertakes a second reading of the proposal. With an absolute majority, it can make an amended proposal that, if adopted by the Commission, can be accepted by a qualified majority of the Council or amended with a unanimous vote by the same. A fairly large swath of policy falls under this "cooperative" category

EU policy, as we will see, but their institutional focus is not the EP, but rather the committee system organized under the Commission. Whether this new associationalism in Europe can approximate the achievements of national civil societies that Habermas brilliantly delineated in *Public Sphere* – especially with respect to legally facilitated self-government – is the pressing question.[104]

Circumventing the EP altogether, a recent wave of normative enthusiasm over the progressive possibilities of EU politics emphasizes instead EU committee arrangements and the comitological, infranational, and/or associational policy-making process that is conducted through them.[105] The optimistic literature on EU infranational policymaking, or "The Comitology,"[106] accepts almost as fact the obsolescence of twentieth-century-style, let alone nineteenth-century-style, parliamentary control over policy in today's thoroughly transnational Europe.[107] Since economic globalization and regional integration processes have undermined or at

---

of policymaking, between one-third and one-half of all procedures in fact. See George Tsebelis, "The Power of the European Parliament as a Conditional Agenda Setter," *American Political Science Review* 88, no. 1 (March 1994), 128, 135–6. Cf. Tsebelis, "Conditional Agenda Setting and Decision Making Inside the European Parliament," *Journal of Legislative Studies* 1(1995), 65–93.

[104] See Habermas, *The Structural Transformation of the Public Sphere: An Inquiry into a Category of Bourgeois Society* (1962), trans. Thomas Burger with Frederick Lawrence (Cambridge, MA: MIT Press, 1989).

[105] See especially Joshua Cohen and Charles F. Sabel, "Sovereignty and Solidarity in the EU and US," in *Governing Work and Welfare in a New Economy: European and American Experiments*, ed. Jonathan Zeitlin and David Trubek (Oxford: Oxford University Press, 2003), 345–75. See also Joshua Cohen and Joel Rogers, "Solidarity, Democracy, Association," in Wolfgang Streeck, ed., *Staat und Verbände* (Wiesbaden: Westdeutscher Verlag, 1998), 177–218.

[106] Comitology was established in 1987 and revised in 1999. See Francesca Bignami, "The Democratic Deficit in European Community Rulemaking: A Call for Notice and Comment In Comitology," *Harvard International Law Review* 40 (1999), 451–515; and Koen Lenaerts and Amaryllis Verhoeven, "Towards a Legal Framework for Executive Rulemaking in the EU?: The Contribution of the New Comitology Decision," *Common Market Law Review* 37 (2000), 645–86.

[107] See Svein S. Andersen and Thomas R. Burns, "The European Union and the Erosion of Parliamentary Democracy: A Study of Post-Parliamentary Governance," in Svein S. Andersen and Kjell A. Eliassen, eds., *The European Union: How Democratic Is It?* (London: Sage, 1995), 227–51; Andersen and Burns, *Societal Decision-Making: Democratic Challenges to State Technocracy* (Hampshire, U.K.: Dartmouth, 1992); Knill and Lenschow, "Modes of Regulation," 3, 7; Alexander Ballmann, "Infranationalism and the Community Governing Process" (Project IV/95/02, Directorate General for Research, European Parliament, 1996 [http://ww.iue.it/AEL/EP/fpp.html]); and Christian Joerges, "Bureaucratic Nightmare, Technocratic Regime and the Dream of Good Transnational Governance," in Joerges and Ellen Vos, eds., *EU Committees: Social Regulation, Law and Politics* (Oxford: Hart, 1999), 3–17.

least transformed parliamentary accountability, responsibility, and effectiveness vis-à-vis civil societies *within* nation-states, many argue that it would be hopelessly anachronistic to replay on a *continental* level a legislature–policy relationship that no longer works domestically. Infranational enthusiasts claim that the EU requires a form of "postparliamentary governance," since Euro-elections do not predictably determine the content of EU policy; the latter is in reality the result of a complex overlapping of regulative apparatuses rather than a system of legislature-centered inputs and outputs.[108] Less ecstatically, Weiler describes infranationalism as a "meso-level of norm creation and governance" in which mid-range European and national officials interact with various private and semipublic players (e.g., administrations, departments, private and public associations, and certain, mainly corporate, interest groups) within the European committee structure – hence the name "comitology."[109] While most observers agree that these Commission-supervised interactions do not constitute "government" per se, it remains an open question whether "governance" and "regulation" are also too strong a set of terms for the process. After all, the Commission's efforts, conducted through its committees or informal working groups, are largely taken up with "harmonization," or as Harlow describes it, merely the "building and controlling of networks."[110] It performs the latter function by funding, encouraging, and supervising projects developed by the multiple public and private actors previously mentioned.[111]

On one view, national interest is much less important than technical expertise in comitology, concerned as it is with "the miasma" of health and safety standards, the pan-European harmonization of telecommunications policy, international trade rules, and so on.[112] According to Weiler, infranationalism involves "transnational interest groups, governance without (State) government, [and] empowerment beyond national boundaries."[113] But member state representatives are present within the committees, purportedly to make up for the limited expertise of the Commission on the policy field at hand; they apply their knowledge and skills

---

[108] See Joerges, "'Deliberative Supranationalism,'" 150.
[109] See Weiler, *The Constitution of Europe*, 98, 273.
[110] See Harlow, *Accountability in the European Union*, 181.
[111] See also Karl-Heinz Ladeur, "Towards a Legal Theory of Supranationality – the Validity of the Network Concept," *European Law Journal* 3 (1997), 33–54.
[112] See Weiler, *The Constitution of Europe*, 272.
[113] Ibid., 285.

(and interests and biases?) to the development and drafting of policy.[114] On these grounds, Harlow argues that committee dominance biases comitology *toward* the member states, despite the process's transnational façade. She suggests that the Council cripples the Commission with a work overload that then forces dependence on this "help" from member state actors in the committees: the Commission is "increasingly dependent on staff seconded for short periods from national civil services and on short-term contracts concluded with the many 'experts' who cluster around the Commission in Brussels."[115] Furthermore, committee preeminence, and therefore member state power within it, is formally institutionalized by their effective veto over Commission measures and the fact that both their approval is required for Commission action and their requests for resubmission must be respected.[116]

Whether thoroughly transnational or secretly biased toward member state actors, comitology allows the Commission to oversee trans-European, interassociational negotiations and, especially in technical harmonization areas, steer "fundamental societal decisions" over risk and resource allocation.[117] Public-private European "networks" or "Euroquangos" develop in specialty spheres where interested parties effectively shape "the normative outcomes of the process."[118] Harlow observes that in this process the Commission "steers" but does not "row"; it is a "policy entrepreneur" that enlists "expert groups, advisory bodies, and networks" in its policymaking.[119] But in no sense can the Commission be said to *control* the process: Harlow argues that "in principle, it is the Commission which acts as agent in ensuring accountability; in practice, although Commission representatives participate in and work with policy networks, it is by no means clear that the Commission can supervise them."[120]

A skeptic might point out that, as we observed in Chapters 2 and 3, all of this is nothing new, since the most frequent criticisms of parliamentarism under an emerging and consolidating *Sozialstaat* in the early

---

[114] See Günther Schäfer, "Linking Member State and European Administrations – The Role of Committees and Comitology," in Mads Andenas and Alexander Turk, eds., *Delegated Legislation and the Role of the Committees in the EC* (The Hague: Kluwer, 2000), 3–24.

[115] See Harlow, *Accountability in the European Union*, 64; see also 67.

[116] See Ellen Vos, "EU Committees: The Evolution of Unforeseen Institutional Actors in European Product Regulation," in Joerges and Vos, eds., *EU Committees*, 19–47.

[117] See Weiler, *The Constitution of Europe*, 277.

[118] Ibid., 278.

[119] See Harlow, *Accountability in the European Union*, 63.

[120] Ibid., 63.

twentieth century prefigured this description of postparliamentary government and comitology. Critics argued either that private and semiprivate actors (corporations, interest groups of various kinds, technical experts, trade unions) gained unprecedented influence over legislation[121] or that an unaccountable and intrusive bureaucracy undermined the legitimacy of the *Sozialstaat* and the moral fiber of the societies it served. Following the latter neo-Tocquevillian line of thought, Siedentop understands EU policymaking as a replay of dangerous state-centralizing bureaucratization: "the increasingly important relations between Brussels and member states have worked to the advantage of bureaucratic power on both sides. As a result, democratic accountability in Europe is in danger of becoming perfunctory."[122]

Yet this fact, in and of itself, is not necessarily any more of a problem for democracy than was the influence of non-state actors or the expansion of bureaucratic authority in the early twentieth century. As Scharpf makes plain, output-oriented legitimacy, or government "for" rather than "by" the people, can be carried out with success by associative or corporatist means "through negotiated agreement and with legal force" on wages and working conditions.[123] From an input-oriented perspective, such arrangements were often criticized as violations of parliamentary sovereignty, yet they nevertheless satisfied the will of fairly large majorities of citizens even if the latter did not actively participate in formulating the specifics of such arrangements. This kind of input-oriented legitimacy that concerns Siedentop aside, the burning question is whether infranationalism and comitology can meet even output-oriented standards of democracy today.

After all, many EU observers claim that circumstances in the EU are unprecedented and find no corollary in the history of national state administration. Scholars such as Charles Sabel, Joshua Cohen, and Christian Joerges depict comitology as a more deliberative, public, accessible,

---

[121] See the classic critiques by Mosei Ostrogoski, Carl Schmitt, and Jürgen Habermas: Ostrogoski, *Democracy and the Organization of Political Parties* (1902) (New York: Haskell, 1970); Schmitt, *The Crisis of Parliamentary Democracy* (1926), trans. Ellen Kennedy (Cambridge, MA: MIT Press, 1985); and Habermas, *Structural Transformation of the Public Sphere*.

[122] See Siedentop, *Democracy in Europe*, 122. See also Larry A. Siedentop, *Past Masters: Tocqueville* (Oxford: Oxford University Press, 1994).

[123] See Scharpf, *Governing in Europe*, 16–17. Consult the literature that revives interest in consociationalism within the context of the EU: Anne Peters, "A Plea for a European Semi-Parliamentary and Semi-Consociational Democracy," *European Integration Online Papers* 7, no. 3 (2003) (http://eiop.or.at/eiop/texte/2003-003a.htm).

contestable, and revisable form of governance than anything that prevailed within *Sozialstaat* administrative practice. On this view, comitology provides those most interested in a particular policy a forum in which experts and counterexperts are institutionally enabled, and where debates by a genuinely engaged public creates a demos procedurally, rather than assuming that one exists before the fact.[124] For these reasons, many advocates of comitology suggest that the EU promises to become a different and better type of polity, not only in terms of political *level* – that is, not only because it is supranational – but in terms of political *kind* – that is, comitology makes the EU a qualitatively new and improved kind of regime. Again, since parliamentarians do not have the expertise to dictate policy to those with far greater knowledge of particular technical issues, and since they cannot control the unintended and undesirable consequences that will ensue should they attempt to do so, notions of participatory democracy must adapt to allow those with proper knowledge to do so themselves.

According to such analyses, the access and influence of contemporary semipublic/semiprivate entities have expanded and transformed as a result of the decidedly supranational and discursive quality of infranationalism. Moreover, this transnational access and influence elude even the limited kind of control exercised by constitutional norms, judicial review, and parliamentary oversight over semipublic/semiprivate actors under the *Sozialstaat*. Such observers claim that directly affected parties like contemporary semipublic groups and the European quangos or networks in which they operate now have the right to participate in, to determine, and not just to exert influence over policy- and lawmaking. In this novel scenario, the principles of neutrality, objectivity, and detachment are explicitly exchanged for those of interested access and technical precision. Indeed, the standing of participants in comitology seems to render the principle of "due process" somewhat tautological: whoever participates is whoever is most affected, and if the latter are present, then the process is correct.[125] Another long-standing liberal democratic principle, the insistence that the parties most interested in a policy *not* be the ones to make it (or at least that the most powerful ones not be the only ones to do so), is swapped by the pro-comitology literature for purportedly more informed, representative, and participatory policymaking.

---

[124] See Joerges, "'Deliberative Supranationalism,'" 148–9.
[125] A point made very well by Knill and Lenschow, "Modes of Regulation," 12.

Sabel and Cohen refer to this new political configuration in which European specialist and interest groups determine policy processes of immediate concern to themselves by the name "deliberative polyarchy."[126] Through this configuration, particular activists make specific policies with little need for appeal to a general public and perhaps even to general standards. But this empirical reality and the many positive normative evaluations of it create a curious situation for political debates in contemporary Europe: while the recognition claims of culturally, religiously, and ethnically particularist groups, such as Muslim immigrants, gain attention and criticism in academia and the press, those of particularist economic interest groups like the ones engaged in the comitology are either overlooked or, if noticed, perhaps too easily celebrated as progressive. Siedentop, for instance, insists that Islamic identity is rooted in principles of "equal submission" and practices of "involuntary association," rather than "equal liberty" and voluntary membership, and hence it is not necessarily compatible with universalist projects like "representative government."[127] Yet, as Yasemin Soysal demonstrates, cultural groups within Europe, including Turkish immigrants, make their claims in a language and according to a logic that are deeply universalist.[128] However, as advocates of infranationalism insist, such "universalism" may be passé as far as contemporary "economic identities" are concerned.

It is not as if infranationalist advocates completely dismiss universal standards and the overarching legal structure necessary to institutionalize them. As Joerges observes, "the legitimacy of [comitological] governance is to be measured by the *deliberative* quality of the decision processes organized in it; with the help of *law*, these qualities are to be guaranteed, and additionally to have their connections to both the institutions of the nation states and the EU ensured."[129] But exactly who is deliberating under

---

[126] See Sabel and Cohen, "Sovereignty and Solidarity in the EU and US," 346. See also Oliver Gerstenberg and Charles Sabel, "Directly-Deliberative Polyarchy: An Institutional Ideal for Europe?" in C. Joerges and R. Dehousse, eds., *Good Governance in Europe's Integrated Market* (Oxford: Oxford University Press, 2002), 289–341.

[127] See Siedentop, *Democracy in Europe*, 207–8, 148.

[128] See Yasemin Soysal, "Changing Boundaries of Participation in Europe Public Spheres: Reflections on Citizenship and Civil Societies," in Eder and Giesen, eds., *European Citizenship*, 159–79; as well as Soysal, *Limits of Citizenship: Migrants and Postnational Membership in Europe* (Chicago: University of Chicago Press, 1994). For a philosophical account of the negotiation of this particularist/universalist cultural dynamic in contemporary Europe, see Seyla Benhabib, *The Rights of Others: Aliens, Citizens, and Residents* (Cambridge: Cambridge University Press, 2003).

[129] Joerges, "'Deliberative Supranationalism,'" 143, emphases added.

comitology and by what means? Weiler, for instance, calls it "fanciful" to associate infranational deliberation with "Habermasian dialogue," as its advocates sometimes do, because infranationalism seeks "legitimation in results rather than process."[130] Moreover, are the laws coordinating comitology that Joerges invokes earlier sufficiently strong to make deliberation equitable and public?

Given the stridency of his criticisms, Weiler may be faulted for not working harder to conceptualize a more democratic way to constitutionalize infranationalism, but this charge does not diminish the force of his critique. According to Weiler, infranational technocratic practices "mask ideological choices which are not debated or subjected to public scrutiny"; access to them is reserved for "those privileged by the process"; they do not ensure "real equality of voice of those who actually do take part in the process"; judicial review of comitology has so far only focused on access and not outcome fairness; and infranational practices "are little affected by elections, changes in government," and so on.[131] Clearly resenting the disparity between, on the one hand, the severe criticism directed at his own theory of legally facilitated supranationalism in the last decade and, on the other, the low level of scrutiny presently devoted to comitology, Weiler exclaims:

Once there were those who worried about the supranational features of European integration. It is time to worry about infranationalism – a complex network of middle-level national administrators, Community administrators and an array of private bodies with unequal and unfair access to a process with huge social and economic consequences to everyday life – in matters of public safety, health, and all other dimensions of socio-economic regulation.[132]

In response to this demand for public accountability, some representatives of the infranational, associational, and comitological literature imply that changes in the territorial basis of affected interest representation justify a departure from traditional methods of oversight. Since not only member states, but also specific ministries, industries, and associations, now make themselves "present" in a more immediately felt way

---

[130] See Weiler, *The Constitution of Europe*, 284.

[131] Ibid., 284–5.

[132] Ibid., 349. Note Joerges's responses to Weiler's criticisms of infranationalism where he demonstrates that they are incompatible with Weiler's own analysis of European law: see Joerges, "The Law's Problems with the Governance of the European Market," in Joerges and Dehousse, eds., *Good Governance in Europe's Integrated Market*, 3–31; see also Joerges, "Rethinking European Law's Supremacy," Working Paper of the European University Institute, no. 12 (July 2005), 3–28.

than geographically defined populaces once did, something more complex than traditional constituency representation obtains in the EU. For Sabel and Cohen, a "public" within today's EU is even more variegated, overlapping, and free-forming than the social segments that made up the mass public of the national *Sozialstaat*: "A public is simply an open group of actors, nominally private or public, which constitutes itself as such in coming to address a common problem, and reconstitutes itself as efforts at problem solving redefine the task at hand. The polity is the public formed of these publics."[133] "Identity," according to this logic, is the concept that must be readapted to sociopolitical circumstances in the EU: identity is no longer determined by state, region, or class boundaries, but by membership in specialized technical associations and practices.[134] "Epistemic communities," not dynamic markets, self-interested member states, or unaccountable supranational institutions, actually drive EU governance on this view.[135]

But, as Weiler's criticisms cataloged previously make plain, comitology-sanguine scholars often speak of "organic identity" or "techno-identity" as if there are no ramifications for groups other than those involved in making a specific policy, or as if there is no hierarchy of access and effect among the ones that do participate. They sometimes discuss these "technical groups" as if the latter never compete for resources with, or as if there exists no overlap of affects among, different "techno-identities."[136] There is an obvious mutuality/interaction problem in a theory such as this that presupposes contemporary socioeconomic development as a process of subsystem differentiation of specialized spheres that are separated and discrete from each other. It simply does not account for how those spheres might be interrelated, integrated, or coordinated.[137] This leads to another shortcoming: many comitology proponents exhibit some serious myopia when it comes to asymmetries of power. As Philippe Schmitter explains,

---

[133] See Cohen and Sabel, "Sovereignty and Solidarity in the EU and US," 362.

[134] Sabel and Cohen claim provocatively that EU associationalism transforms "diversity and difference from an obstacle to cooperative investigation of possibilities into a means for accelerating and widening such enquiry." Ibid., 368.

[135] Joerges, "The Law in the Process of Constitutionalising Europe," in Erik Oddvar Eriksen, John Erik Fossum, and Agustín José Menéndez, eds., *Constitution-Making and Democratic Legitimacy* (Oslo: ARENA, 2002), 13–48 at 42, n. 88.

[136] Although Joerges emphasizes the necessity of deliberation and connections *among* technical spheres and with the public. See Joerges, "'Deliberative Supranationalism,'" 154–5.

[137] See the famous Habermas-Luhmann debates on this topic: Jürgen Habermas and Niklas Luhmann, *Theorie der Gesellschaft oder Sozialtechnologie* (Frankfurt a.M.: Suhrkamp, 1971). Andersen and Burns are guilty of the traditional coordination problem inherent in differentiation theories from Durkheim and Weber to Luhmann, which Habermas observed and criticized.

tyranny of the majority through state mechanisms may indeed be avoided in infranational arrangements, as proponents claim, but disproportionate influence by privileged minority interests still prevails and perhaps proliferates in these schemes: in the EU today, "policy outcomes become less predictable; majorities become more difficult to mobilize. The power of public coercion is blunted, *but so is the capacity of the state to overcome private exploitation.*"[138]

Schmitter notes that missing from the associational account of the "gradual and uneven accumulation of organizationally privileged access" within comitology is a general and systematic practice of "equalizing access to these rights and obligations for all the organized interests."[139] Advocates of supranationalism often claim that decentralized regulation spreads responsibility evenly among varied economic and societal actors, but they do not acknowledge how difficult this can make attempts to hold the major players accountable. In certain respects, infranationalism may be more participatory than previous forms of policymaking. But participation cannot be equitable and hence democratic without strong enforcement mechanisms, which are lacking here except in the small sphere where the Commission sets actual rules and guarantees their adherence.

One might expect that if there were to be losers in infranational policymaking, those who most need legal recourse in inequitable circumstance, it would be employees. They are the ones affected by policies who may not have the same deliberative access and input in the policymaking process. Unions are conspicuously absent from discussions of infranationalism and comitology, perhaps because the policy spheres involved are technical rather than industrial. Certainly, the picture of worker participation painted by Streeck earlier would give one cause to worry about the voice of both white- and blue-collar workers in the EU.[140] In general, Scharpf takes as an indication of a portending change in practice post-Amsterdam rhetoric regarding the "common concern" of employment policy to the whole EU, official warnings over the impact of regulatory competition on unemployment, and grave concern over low wages.[141]

---

[138] See Schmitter, *How to Democratize the European Union*, 36, emphasis added.
[139] Ibid., 35. See also John Coultrap, "From Parliamentarism to Pluralism: Models of Democracy and the European Union's Democratic Deficit," *Journal of Theoretical Politics* 11 (1999), 107–35.
[140] Sabel and Cohen are silent on worker participation but do emphasize how OMC-style practices have been effective in employment promotion. See Cohen and Sabel, "Sovereignty and Solidarity in the EU and US," 347.
[141] See Scharpf, *Governing in Europe*, 158–60, 163.

To their credit, Andersen and Burns, in particular, draw some conclusions that pose problems regarding infranational/comitological/associative governance: (i) They admit that there will be asymmetries of economic resources, technical expertise, organizational coherence, and fervency among groups participating in infranational policies. (ii) They wonder whether legal or administrative "police power" will be unnecessary in postparliamentary governance. But how can it not? Will decisions reached by "Euroquangos" be enforced by the good will of those involved simply because they know the most about particular issues? Compulsion will necessarily be factored into the equation, thus raising the inevitable question of the legitimacy of sanctions. (iii) The authors further admit that while no political configuration ever really has controlled unintended consequences, postparliamentary governance, in particular, is deficient in this sphere. On this topic, Andersen and Burns betray the fact that self-governing technical and interest groups in postparliamentary governance may not function so free of regulating general norms as they initially suggest. And while they concede that this scenario may look chaotic, (iv) it is not dangerous because the "disciplined anarchy" of EU institutions functions under presuppositions of democratic principles and a shared political culture. This seems to be a rather large begging of the question.

Along these lines, they ultimately *do* call for the further development of normative principles to regulate and hold accountable agents engaged in postparliamentary governance: a constitution of group organization; a postindividual concept of citizenship; and a redefinition of parliamentary power in a way that oversees organizational interaction. Apparently, the empirical developments that the authors describe are not simultaneously producing their own normative coordination methods "organically," as one might assume based on the major thrust of the overly cheerful account of many comitology advocates. Normatively informed and proactive policymaking is required to facilitate the development of postparliamentary governance as they conceive it. Their account initially seemed to suggest that the normative requirements of the novel historical situation that they describe were emerging along with empirical developments. Here, it becomes clear that normative support and effective practice are not developing as "organically" as they claimed after all. There are serious shortcomings to an empirical account that jettisons, or at least jeopardizes, for instance, equal protection, due process, individual rights, and the principle of prohibiting judgment in one's own case, and replaces them with a call for a constitution of "techno-identities."

Clearly, there are serious prima facie problems with the normative claims made for comitological governance by its adherents given a certain naiveté rampant in the associationalism literature on the supposedly new populism of EU governance.[142] Until proven otherwise, apropos of the earlier discussion of the "businessman's Europe," it would make sense to assume that the decisive figures in infranational, associational, and comitological policymaking are economic elites. New-age normative enthusiasm notwithstanding, these novel modes of governance make it possible for interested parties themselves to determine what regulatory forum will be used and which regulatory approach will be adopted so that it favors their interests, and they do so largely in the absence of public monitoring.[143] Who would be best situated to take advantage of this?

As we observed in Chapter 4, Habermas focuses on law as a way of addressing such asymmetries of power. Presumably, if the EP's parliamentary oversight capabilities are as yet immature, then substantive judicial review by the ECJ might ensure the requisite conformity with norms, encouragement of publicity, and to some extent accountability of officials reminiscent of social regulation under the *Sozialstaat*. Surprisingly, however, on this issue, the evaluative roles in the literature are somewhat reversed: the previously optimistic Weiler worries that judicial review over infranationalism will not become "substantive" but merely "procedural," and hence cannot be a means to ensure the full accountability of actors engaged in it.[144] The Court merely ensures that infranational actors abide by the rules – largely set up for themselves by themselves – in making policy, rather than judge those rules qua rules or the content of that policy.

On the other hand, the usually more juridically cautious Scharpf is willing to entertain the notion that the ECJ is starting to guard substantive political and social issues in its recent adjudication by limiting negative integration, especially in service public domains, and that this will impact policymaking throughout the EU.[145] Yet, Sabel and Cohen are fairly effusive in praising the ECJ's role in developing a new form of deliberatively

---

[142] Discussed quite well by Knill and Lenschow, "Modes of Regulation," 10.

[143] Ibid., 16.

[144] See Weiler, *The Constitution of Europe*, 276.

[145] See Scharpf, *Governing in Europe*, 165–6. In general, Scharpf observes that the ECJ has begun to weigh "the competing concerns of undistorted competition, on the one hand, and the distributional, cultural, or political goals allegedly served by, say, postal monopolies, subsidized theatres, or public television, on the other hand." See Scharpf, *Governing in Europe*, 167.

democratic constitutionalism by promoting more supranational public–
private partnerships, by requiring comitological deliberations to be transparent to the public, and by forcing parties to come up with concrete
solutions after consulting with affected interests.[146] Whether the Court
has been *effective* in bringing about the latter two results, especially, is
still very much an open question.[147]

As Weiler complains, infranational advocates often gesture to openness
in principle but do not concede that the issue is much more complicated:
"Transparency and access to documents are often invoked as a possible
remedy to this issue. But if you do not know what is going on, which
documents will you ask to see?"[148] Nevertheless, he himself recommends
the ubiquitous panacea of using the Internet to improve the publicity of
EU policymaking in this and other regards: Weiler argues that the EU's
"entire decision-making process" should be put on the Web under the
name "*Lexcalibur – The European Public Square.*"[149] But as Weiler's
own remarks suggest, it is one thing to make information available and
another to encourage and enable EU citizens to seek it out and critically
discuss it.

[146] See Cohen and Sabel, "Sovereignty and Solidarity in the EU and US," 347. Indeed,
as Harlow notes, the ECJ is moving toward "synoptic dialogue and hard-look process
review," which require institutions like the Commission to give reasons for decisions and
closely conform to procedural prescriptions. Harlow, *Accountability in the European
Union*, 162. Moreover, the as-yet nonbinding European Charter of Fundamental Rights
includes a right to good administration, and the rights to be heard and gain access
to one's file, and also affirms the duty of officials to give reasons and grant access
to EU institutions – rights that will eventually be adjudicated by the ECJ. Harlow,
Accountability in the European Union, 164.

[147] Sabel and Cohen preempt the obvious "access" criticism with a not so subtle jibe at
Habermas and his students: while Habermas's procedural deliberative democracy is
covertly or inadvertently elitist, Sabel and Cohen suggest, they seek to be explicit about
deliberation among expert elites in their deliberative polyarchical model. See Cohen
and Sabel, "Sovereignty and Solidarity in the EU and US," 368. While this charge may
apply to Habermas's idealization of the nineteenth-century bourgeois public sphere in
Public Sphere, it is a somewhat unfair characterization of Habermas's egalitarianly
reconstructed *Sozialstaat* model, explicated in his mature writings. See *The Theory of
Communicative Action, Vol. 1: Reason and the Rationalization of Society* (1981), trans.
T. McCarthy (Boston: Beacon Press, 1984); *The Theory of Communicative Action,
Vol. 2: Lifeworld and System: A Critique of Functionalist Reason* (1981), trans. T.
McCarthy (Boston: Beacon Press, 1987); and *Between Facts and Norms: Contributions
to a Discourse Theory of Law and Democracy* (1992), trans. William Rehg (Cambridge,
MA: MIT Press, 1996).

[148] See Weiler, *The Constitution of Europe*, 349; cf. Siedentop, *Democracy in Europe*,
121.

[149] See Weiler, *The Constitution of Europe*, 351.

Among the many schemes proposed by several of the authors discussed here, only one, that of Schmitter, seems powerful enough to galvanize requisite public attention on EU policy. In particular, he calls for the insertion of direct referenda into EU elections: "competition for yes and no votes would definitely increase public attention with regard to European issues in general and improve the *Öffentlichkeit* with which specific measures would be discussed and defended."[150] While this proposal may generate interest over broad policy measures, it seems, however, inappropriate to the policy minutiae of infranational governance, the site where transparency and publicity are most needed. Moreover, since the 1990s, public attention to general EU policy has tended to push the European public in a Euroskeptical direction. Perhaps recent recognition of the necessity of a common foreign policy to counter American unilateralism will be sufficient to generate pan-European solidarity on at least *one* major policy issue.[151] From this issue, at least, solidarity over and deliberation on other policy spheres may ensue.

(c) Multiple Policy Europes – Out of One, Many?

Many scholars of European integration resign themselves to the fact that a uniformly high level of political and social integration cannot be attained in the EU, at least without grave unintended consequences. In response, some seek to solidify varying levels of integration among different subsets of nation-states in separate policy spheres or sectors. The EU already practices a fairly flexible means of doing so: functioning in tandem with infranationalism, the "Open Method of Coordination" (OMC) leaves the style and pace of integration to individual member state actors, who adopt EU guidelines in piecemeal and voluntary fashion and then report back to EU authorities with recommendations for subsequent policy guidelines. More hypothetically, a few scholars promote the formation of blocs of member states, internally bound together by adherence to uniform regulatory and redistributive standards not adopted by other member state groupings.

Much in line with their evaluation of infranationalism, Sabel and Cohen deem OMC to be emblematic of a new form of enlightened,

---

[150] See Schmitter, *How to Democratize the European Union*, 36–7. On Europe-wide referenda, see: Edgar Grande, "Demokratische Legitimation und europäische Integration," *Leviathan* 24 (1996), 339–60; and Michael Zürn, "Über den Staat und die Demokratie im europäischen Mehrebenensystem," *Politische Vierteljahresschrift* 37 (1996), 27–55.

[151] This issue has served to bring two erstwhile rivals together: see Jacques Derrida and Jürgen Habermas, "Unsere Erneuerung. Nach dem Krieg: Die Wiedergeburt Europas," *Frankfurter Allgemeine Zeitung* 125 (May 31, 2003), 33–4.

educable, and persuadable technocracy: it is a process where local, regional, and European authorities require experts to revisit assumptions and consult with a wide range of affected parties to formulate the most effective policies serving the best interests of those most concerned with them.[152] The goal of this enlightened technocracy is mutual correction of policies by policymakers and policytakers, a correction process that so far necessarily excludes the wider European public. According to this model, local or lower-level actors "are given autonomy to experiment with their own solutions to broadly defined problems of public policy. In return they furnish higher-level units with rich information regarding their goals as well as the progress they are making towards achieving them."[153] Further, by encouraging states and actors to share information and experiences concerning "best practices" and by promoting "innovative approaches," recent treaty provisions promote a more "deliberative" approach to policymaking.[154] Many of the concerns raised over comitology in the previous section obviously apply in the case of OMC-style governance.

The making of micropolicy through comitology and OMC already exists across and within EU member state borders. But Schmitter and Scharpf draw our attention to a macro-policy-making arrangement that may allow the EU to compensate for the diminishing of problem-solving or market-correcting capacities within the member states attributable to globalization or even to integration itself. In such schemes, different member states will only sign on for certain levels of regulation or for particular policy arrangements, depending on policy sector. As Schmitter foresees the future of what he terms a European *consortio* or *condominio*: "instead of a single Europe with recognized and contiguous boundaries, there would be many Europes: a trading Europe, an energy Europe, an environmental Europe, a social welfare Europe, even a defense Europe, and so forth."[155] Scharpf goes one step further than Schmitter by supposing that for each of these policy sectors there will be *multiple* Europes of varying regulatory levels. Rather than an "in" and an "out" group of member states for each policy sphere, there will be several "in" groups of states. For our purposes here I will focus on the prospective social welfare and environmental "Europes."

---

[152] See Cohen and Sabel, "Sovereignty and Solidarity in the EU and US," 346–7, 350.
[153] Ibid., 365–6.
[154] See Scharpf, *Governing in Europe*, 159.
[155] See Schmitter, *How to Democratize the European Union*, 17–18.

As we observed Scharpf argue in subsection (a), welfare policy and certain environmental standards were rendered most vulnerable to integration-facilitated regulatory competition among member states. Furthermore, attempts to legislate higher protection levels in these spheres at the EU level are precisely those most likely to be blocked in the Council. But Scharpf adds that even if European member states could overcome regulatory competition and obstructionist votes by member states in the Council, there are structural obstacles to a coordinated European social welfare policy: in particular, stark differences among the member states' administrative practices, policy patterns, industrial relations protocols, and welfare institutions. He suggests that universal regulatory levels within Europe are made difficult and, as of now, undesirable by the varied ways that labor is organized and structured throughout the member states.[156] Moreover, there is a vast chasm between the service-intensive welfare-state model that prevails in the Scandinavian member states and the transfer-intensive model characteristic of the other continental states.[157] In addition, health care is publicly provided in Britain and Scandinavia but, on the continent, while publicly paid for, health care is privately provided.

There are two ways around these problems of will and coordination as they pertain to European social welfare: a minimal one that provides a common floor among member states and the more ambitious "multiple Europes" and "consortio" approach mentioned previously. With respect to the former, Scharpf recommends a floor on welfare expenditures that no member state, no matter what their style of social protection arrangements, can fall below.[158] Similarly, Schmitter proposes that the EU grant a "Euro-stipendium" to citizens who earn less than one-third of the average European income.[159] Schmitter predicts that such an effort would go a long way toward creating "euro-equality" and eliminating European

---

[156] Unions vary in strength in different countries: they may be organized along party/ideological lines, by industry, or by skills; they may engage in centralized or decentralized wage bargaining with management; and so on. See Scharpf, *Governing in Europe*, 82.

[157] The former is tax-based and obviously gendered, aiming at the replacement of lost services traditionally provided by mothers, wives, and daughters, while the latter, so-called "Bismarkian," model is wage-based and seeks to compensate male breadwinners in circumstances of injury, unemployment, and old age. Ibid., 80–1. Similarly, pension benefits break down differently between Scandinavian and continental regimes. Ibid., 82.

[158] Ibid., 175.

[159] See Schmitter, *How to Democratize the European Union*, 44–5.

poverty. According to Scharpf, his proposed welfare floor could be instituted rather easily given the commitment to social protection that he
assumes still prevails in member states. He notes that there is a correlation between wealth and welfare spending in Europe that exists nowhere
else in the OECD countries, a testament to a "latent consensus...[that]
the welfare state should increase in relative importance as member states
become more affluent."[160] This was certainly the case before the 1980s,
but why has not this consensus militated against the regulatory competition already plaguing EU countries that Scharpf laments elsewhere in his
book? Why has not it slowed the emergence of the businessman's Europe
that we observed both he and Schmitter criticize? In any case, Scharpf
suggests that such a welfare threshold "would limit the extent to which
countries could reduce overall expenditures on social transfers and services," even if it would leave them free "to pursue whatever structural or
institutional reforms they consider necessary above that purely quantitative threshold."[161]

As a more radical response to different styles and levels of social protection, Scharpf advocates a "differentiated integration" of multiple policy
Europes that can facilitate productive EU activity in policy areas of "high
problem-solving salience and divergent national interests."[162] Admittedly,
this would constitute a "structural transformation of European welfare
states," namely, a coordinated institutional reform of national welfare
states in accord with levels of development and institutional styles.[163] He
proposes that individual welfare states be grouped into institutional "families" sharing "specific historical roots, basic value orientations, solution
concepts, and administrative practices, and whose path-dependent evolution has required them to cope with similar difficulties in comparable
ways."[164] Thus, countries conforming with Scandinavian, continental,
and Anglo-Danish models can be grouped together as "family types" and
encouraged to harmonize their welfare modes and institutions. The reform
strategies internal to each family might mirror those that proved successful in the post–World War II *Sozialstaat* and that have been undermined
by regulatory competition in a negatively integrated EU: "a combination of employment-intensive forms of tax-financed basic income support
with health insurance systems and (funded) pension schemes that will be

---

[160] See Scharpf, *Governing in Europe*, 176, 179.
[161] Ibid., 179.
[162] Ibid., 169.
[163] Ibid., 180.
[164] Ibid., 182.

financed through individual contributions, part of which will be mandated by law, and subsidized for low-income groups."[165] Rather than a EU-wide depletion of social welfare in *every* member state, a "differentially integrated" EU will provide groupings of *Sozialstaat* families with varying, but aggregately higher, levels of protection.

Scharpf argues that another extremely vulnerable and highly contentious policy area, environmental regulation, can be advanced through differentiated regulation. He favors nonuniform standards for environmental process regulations and emission standards, resulting in a "two-tiered Europe."[166] Two separate levels of protection at two different levels of cost would both ensure better environmental protection throughout the EU and limit the disadvantages suffered by less efficient nationally based industries.[167] Such a scheme allows less developed countries to establish "common standards at lower levels of protection and cost that would still immunize them against the dangers of ruinous competition among themselves."[168] As with social welfare, sets of countries that establish separate but relatively high levels of more cost-effective environmental protection are preferable to an all-out pan-EU race to the bottom, where most member states would wind up with sub-par levels of regulation. This does, however, sacrifice the social democratic ideal of uniformly high levels of protection throughout a specific polity of coequal citizens.

It is not hard to see how this approach would work beyond these two high-salience policy sectors of welfare and the environment. But what about EU-wide common policies? How should decisions be made in the spheres that the whole Union still shares? How will the differences among families of member states, especially discrete sets comprised of member states with different population sizes, affect the *fairness* of decisions on common policies? As Schmitter puts it, the decision-making arrangement in the Council today poses problems such as veto power wielded by either overrepresented small countries or underrepresented large countries.[169] He puts forth an ingenious proposal to balance out states according to size, a proposal the EU should consider adopting in the new constitution. Schmitter proposes the principle of "proportionate proportionality," which would apply "the square root value, rather than the absolute value, of a country's citizenry or population as the basis for allocating

[165] Ibid., 181.
[166] Ibid., 171–2.
[167] Ibid., 174.
[168] Ibid., 174.
[169] See Schmitter, *How to Democratize the European Union*, 89.

weighted votes in the Council of Ministers and seats in the European Parliament."[170] This will still result in some overrepresentation of citizens in small states vis-à-vis those in larger ones. But it is a far better alternative than resorting to the other extreme that allows naked population numbers to determine voting weight. To Schmitter's mind, the latter alternative would tend toward either an imperial Euro-democracy dominated by Germany or an elitist Euro-directorate dominated by a Franco–German partnership.[171]

Once EU countries are weighted in this way, Schmitter recommends grouping them into three "colegii" or colleges based on the relative size of the member states: one group comprised of Germany, France, the United Kingdom, Italy, and Spain; a second including the Netherlands, Greece, Portugal, Belgium, and Sweden; and a third group to which Austria, Finland, Denmark, Ireland, and Luxembourg would belong.[172] In this arrangement, concurrent majorities could determine policy such that no individual member state or set of like-sized member states would be disadvantaged by population: Council decisions would require majorities in each of the three colleges, simple majorities for ordinary policy and qualified majorities for amendment or enlargement decisions.[173]

4. Democracy, the EU *Sektoralstaat*, and Further Questions

With the possible exception of Schmitter, and very much like Habermas, most democratic theorists evaluate the EU in terms of previous state forms associated with constitutional and social democracy. Moreover, they worry whether the EU will secure the rule of law and provide social protection as well as did, respectively, the *Rechtsstaat* and the *Sozialstaat*. On the other hand, many analysts of infranational policymaking and comitology discussed earlier champion the notion that the EU is a completely new kind of polity, one with little in common with previous state formations – except, somewhat conveniently, that it will purportedly better satisfy the normative aspirations of the earlier paradigms than did the latter themselves. If we abstract away from all of these depictions of the EU, we may indeed recognize the emergence of a new and distinct institutional form, perhaps more dramatic in its

---

[170] Ibid., 82.
[171] Ibid., 83.
[172] Ibid., 83.
[173] Ibid., 84.

novelty than even pro-comitology scholars envision, but one to which the constitutional- and social-democratic perspectives of some of the analyses discussed cannot be applied directly. If the EU is a qualitatively different and new form of polity, it may require the creative and flexible adaptation of *Rechtsstaat* and *Sozialstaat* principles to decidedly non-*Rechtsstaat* and non-*Sozialstaat* institutions and circumstances without simultaneously compromising those principles.

As we observed, the emerging European polity is characterized by microsectoral policymaking within and across state borders through comitology and the OMC; and it likely will undergo macrosectoral differentiation in the form of multiple policy Europes. Despite the fluidity and segmentation of policymaking in this arrangement, it still operates within the boundaries of a unit set apart from other polities and collections thereof. Hence, besides the vertical differentiation that has long been a part of EC/EU studies, most notably in analyses of "multilevel governance" that took traditional federal arrangements as their point of reference,[174] the EU will be horizontally divided into these micro- and macropolicy sectors. On this basis, and in keeping with the admittedly cumbersome practice of using ideal-typical German names for political configurations, I have thought it appropriate to call the EU a *Sektoralstaat*.

Building upon the work of the scholarship discussed in this chapter, and the analysis conducted here that judges it by general Habermasian normative standards, future research should evaluate the microsectoral, comitological aspect of the *Sektoralstaat* in light of the extraparliamentary, delegative practices, and extra-statutory policymaking that were tolerated within the *Rechtsstaat* and that especially characterized the functioning of the *Sozialstaat*.[175] As discussed in Chapters 2 and 3, following Weber, many critics claimed that the increased delegation of policymaking authority to judiciaries, bureaucratic agencies, and semipublic actors that accompanied the transition from the nineteenth-century *Rechtsstaat* to the twentieth-century *Sozialstaat* compromised the latter's democratic legitimacy. In order to evaluate the legitimacy of the *Sektoralstaat*, we need to know: does comitology merely replicate these practices such that accountability has been merely altered or only slightly

---

[174] See Ian Bache and Matthew Flinders, eds., *Multi-Level Governance* (Oxford: Oxford University Press, 2004); and Nick Bernard, *Multilevel Governance in The European Union* (New York: Aspen, 2004).

[175] See Andrew Moravcsik's analysis along these lines: "In Defense of the 'Democratic Deficit': Reassessing Legitimacy in the European Union," *Journal of Common Market Studies* 40, no. 4 (2002), 603–24.

diminished? In such a case, infranationalism or comitology would not spell a full-blown "legitimacy crisis" for the EU. Or, on the other hand, is comitology so much further removed from public/institutional oversight than were *Sozialstaat* delegative and corporatist practices that it pushes the legitimacy problem beyond the point of any reconciliation with traditional constitutional-democratic standards?

Alternately, research analyzing the macrosectoral side of the *Sektoralstaat* should compare the varying levels of regulation and redistribution that will obtain in the different policy Europes with nonuniform regulatory levels inherent in federal types of the national *Sozialstaat*. Will differences in environmental, consumer, and social protection among the various subsets of EU member states correspond with similar kinds of variation among component political units within federal systems such as the United States and the Federal Republic of Germany? The answer would help us understand the extent to which the much-lamented absence of a homogeneous "people" or "European demos" or "social solidarity" within the EU portends a novel political scenario, and, if this absence renders governance in the EU *Sektoralstaat* fundamentally incompatible with constitutional-democratic principles. If, as Scharpf and Schmitter suggest, the EU *Sektoralstaat* will permit individual member states to opt in or out of different energy, defense, welfare, environmental, and other subpolities, does this mean that the EU will be a "Union" that tolerates – in de jure and not just de facto manner – greater disparities of material welfare, economic liberty, and social protection among its component parts than any federal state permitted in the *Sozialstaat* era?[176]

---

[176] On the relationship of federal arrangements and social protection, see Paul Pierson, "Fragmented Welfare States: Federal Institutions and the Development of Social Policy," *Governance* 8, no. 4 (1995), 449–78; Pierson, ed., *The New Politics of the Welfare State* (Oxford: Oxford University Press, 2001); Harold L. Wilensky, *The Welfare State and Equality: Structural and Ideological Roots of Public Expenditures* (Berkeley: University of California Press, 1975); Evelyne Huber and John D. Stephens, *Development and the Crisis of the Welfare State: Parties and Policies in Global Markets* (Chicago: University of Chicago Press, 2001); and Duane Swank, *Global Capital, Political Institutions, and Policy Change in Developed Welfare States* (Cambridge: Cambridge University Press, 2002).

7

Conclusion

Habermas's Philosophy of History and Europe's Future

Much of the current literature normatively evaluating the EU is fixated on the "in" and "out" of emerging European citizenship: What will it mean to be European as the EU consolidates internally and enlarges outward? What will be the juridical status within EU member states and throughout the Union generally of residents and migrants originating from other member states and from non-EU nations?[1] In Chapter 5, we observed Habermas focus on the less fashionable but equally important issue of the EU's institutional form and internal workings: Whoever European citizens are, how and under what conditions will they govern or be governed? Will the EU constitutionally facilitate the political accountability and substantively ensure as much social welfare as European nation-states traditionally afforded their citizens? Will the EU reproduce supranationally the same institutions that ensured constitutional and social democracy on the nation-state level or will it at least establish similar ones? Drawing upon the example of Weber's efforts to answer commensurate questions amid a previous structural transformation, in this book I have accentuated the critical-historical limitations of Habermas's answers to such questions.

Yet, I do not intend my analysis of Habermas's reflections on the EU, or my own engagement with the EU democracy literature in the preceding two chapters, to imply that we ought *not* to be hopeful about the future of democratic practices in supranational institutions and therefore not

---

[1] Klaus Eder and Bernhard Giesen, eds., *European Citizenship: National Legacies and Transnational Projects* (Oxford: Oxford University Press, 2001) contains several first-rate contributions on this issue. See also Seyla Benhabib, *The Rights of Others: Aliens, Residents and Citizens* (Cambridge: Cambridge University Press, 2004).

work to attain them. I merely wish to emphasize the necessity of better attention to the historical suppositions undergirding attempts to theorize supranational democracy. In fact, on normative-empirical grounds, I would suggest that we should not place the bar for the possibility of supranational social democracy *too high*. The EU should not be held to normative standards that nation-states themselves did not and could not meet. The accomplishments of liberal and social democracy ought not to be exaggerated such that the EU can only come up hopelessly short by comparison. In particular, I think that it would be a mistake to forget the leftist critique of the national *Sozialstaat* that accused the latter of not going nearly far enough in redistributing wealth and of creating social pathologies and economic crises for which solutions were never sought, let alone found. These considerations ought not to be flushed away as we evaluate political responsiveness, accountability, participation, equality, and so on in supranational contexts. Notwithstanding Habermas's best intentions and efforts, democracy in a supranational age could never stand up to criteria derived from a democratic past that never existed. Furthermore, empirically informed normative analysis should resist the temptation to retreat from substantive investigation into the ubiquitous and too often insipid category of "complexity" simply because the *Sektoralstaat* appears at first blush to be more multifaceted and difficult to characterize than was the *Sozialstaat*.

Critics of democracy in the EU often adopt an ineffectuality thesis: the EU cannot be democratic in any serious sense because it cannot guarantee normative promises in the manner of democratic states. Such discussions frequently lament the EU's so-called democratic deficit. In other words, distant, supranational EU institutions make decisions affecting segments of Europe's population that are not directly sanctioned by those people through democratic channels. There is one obvious retort to this position: why have we forgotten the devastating critiques of the nation-state itself as an imperfectly effective guarantor of rights and executor of popular will? A rampant, all-too-easy, ex post facto valorization of the democratic successes of the mass party state pervades studies of transnational democracy. According to the standards often used to evaluate the European public sphere – opinion polls, EU leader recognition, voter turnout, and so on – virtually no nation-state would escape the criticism of having a democratic deficit. By standards used to measure traditional democratic accountability *within* nation-states, the decision-making apparatus of the EU is by no means so threatening to democratic accountability as some alarmists might have it.

The democratic deficit charge is likely to be leveled against any international body that seeks to secure or enforce universalist norms within nation-states. But we ought not to exaggerate the democratic successes of the nation-state such that the political accomplishments of cosmopolitan democratic efforts seem automatically wanting – as if there is or ever was a democratic equilibrium, let alone a *surplus*, in industrial-democratic states. The very standards presently used to reflect poorly on supranational institutions around the globe do not reflect very well on liberal or social democratic nation-states themselves. By criteria traditionally applied to nation-states, in fact, it might be said that there is no democratic deficit at all in the EU. To whatever extent so-called intergovernmentalists are correct in arguing that little policy is made at the EU level that is not in one way or another sanctioned by the executives of the member states, there is certainly some truth to this defense of the EU's democratic legitimacy. However, if one concedes that there were massive democratic deficits within postwar industrialized nation-states, then, yes, there is indeed a similar, perhaps worse, legitimacy problem in the EU. My provisional normative-institutional analysis of European law, comitology, and multiple policy Europes in Chapter 6 is intended to point the way toward more fine-grained evaluation of political practice and democratic possibilities beyond the state.

On the other hand, grand-scale proclamations, panglossian or pessimistic, are especially misplaced at this moment. The rigorous interrogation of democratic possibilities beyond the state is presently unavoidable; its ramifications should not be made more disturbing and aversive than sober reality already dictates. It is only after the most careful study that the following possibility can be confronted with the requisite perspective, maturity, and gravity: that the age of legally secured democratic government is over, and that the transition to a globalized age is even more of a drastic historical-structural rupture than was the transition from the *Rechtsstaat* to the *Sozialstaat*. Only then can we ponder whether the earlier transformation at least allowed for some continuity of and adaptation for principles and practices of self-government, political and economic liberty, socioeconomic equality, elite accountability, and so on, while the latest structural transformation of the state, quite simply, does not.

If the theoretical and practical stakes in ascertaining the institutional prerequisites for supranational democracy were not as high as this question suggests, it would be almost amusing to hear talk of the democratic deficit in the EU. Social and political theorists need to compare the respective democratic deficits of the nation-state and continental regimes like the EU without recourse to illusions about the former that encourage ineffectual analyses of the institutions constituting the latter. In the spirit of the critical theory of Habermas's *Public Sphere*, this means reviving and refining our notions of history and historical change as we approach and evaluate socioeconomic phenomena and political institution development in a supranational present and future.

I argued in Chapters 1 and 2 that, in order to fully understand Habermas's theoretical efforts in BFN and elsewhere, one must take into account the legal-sociological framework that he inherits from Max Weber, even if Habermas fundamentally reconstructed that framework. This is by no means a purely intellectual or cultural inheritance, for Weber's sociology of law played a crucial role in the historical drama that was the collapse of Germany's first effort at liberal and social democracy: the Weimar Republic. It is the ghost of this failure that has haunted virtually all of Habermas's theoretical endeavors, including BFN – perhaps even more so because of law's centrality to the work. As the legacy of Weber's work and the example of Weimar show, it is precisely qualitative historical transformation that can either provide the possibility for emancipatory social progress or else facilitate reactionary social regression.

I claimed that Habermas's textual and often subtextual desire to address those legal-theoretical problems that confronted Weber in a particular crisis of the state at the outset of the previous century significantly undermines his attempt to address contemporary sociopolitical concerns: a qualitatively different crisis of the state, and the role of law within it, at the twilight of the twentieth and the dawn of the twenty-first centuries. As I discussed in Chapter 3, the legal crisis with which Weber dealt was initiated in large part by the transition from a nineteenth-century noninterventionist-state model to a twentieth-century welfare-state one, and the present predicament of law and the state is increasingly generated by transnational phenomena associated with economic globalization and European integration. More importantly, the intellectual categories on which Habermas relies in dealing with the deficiencies of Weber's earlier approach merge fairly uniformly with Weber's own Kantian philosophical perspective, thus consummating the gradual shift from Hegel to Kant manifest in Habermas's work over the past twenty years. This philosophical shift impinges on Habermas's ability to account for historical change in his social theory of law and his attempt to apply the latter to contemporary conditions of globalization and constitution making in the EU. Habermas's adoption of a transhistorical notion of socioeconomic and political developments within modernity (rather than his earlier notion of a European modernity characterized by multiple discrete moments of transformation) encourages him to transpose some combination of the *Rechtsstaat* and *Sozialstaat* to the European level, rather than contemplate and engage the emergence of new social formations, such as, for instance, a continental *Sektoralstaat*.

As discussed in Chapters 1 and 4, Habermas's theoretical project in BFN can be understood ostensibly as an attempt to overcome the antinomy between the purely functional sociological focus on the "facticity" of state action and the purely normative focus on the "validity" claims of political or legal philosophy. And in response to the Weberian "historical" dilemma just described, Habermas undertakes a Hegelian synthesis in his attempt to merge the framework of the nineteenth-century formal rule of law with that of the twentieth-century "deformalized" or "materialized" law that emerges with the welfare state (while simultaneously purging each "paradigm" of its regressive characteristics). I suggested that Habermas's success in carrying out such a superficially Hegelian strategy while relying extensively on a Kantian historical orientation is severely compromised.

Throughout his recent work, including BFN, Habermas distances his own theory from the holistic and deterministic assumptions of what he labels "philosophies of history."[2] In an explicit reaction against the neo-Hegelianism of his formative work and to a large extent the "Western Marxist" tradition in which he developed intellectually, Habermas declares explicitly in BFN that his approach "does not need a philosophy of history to support it" (BFN 287). Unfortunately, however, Habermas now interprets Hegelian methodology almost exclusively in terms of a kind of crude totalism – that is, its supposed inability to appreciate the diversity within and complexity of modern societies. Yet, Habermas's extensive reliance on the neo-Kantian sociological assumptions of secularization-cum-societal rationalization and social differentiation results in a negative image of "totality," one in which history is equivalent to the perpetual expansion of complexity into the future.[3] As demonstrated in Chapter 2, this orientation also functions as a philosophy of history, a linear postulation of a future constituted ultimately by *more* of the present.

---

[2] See Jürgen Habermas, LC 2, 86–7, 115, 120; TCA2 136, 332, 378–9, 382, 397; and especially "Further Reflections on the Public Sphere" in Craig Calhoun, ed., *Habermas and the Public Sphere* (Cambridge, MA: MIT Press, 1989), 430, 435–6, 442–5.

[3] See Habermas, "Further Reflections on the Public Sphere," 445, 464.

In this way, Habermas renders inaccessible the aspect of his earlier Hegelian–Marxian methodology, put into practice so deftly in *Public Sphere*, that is ultimately indispensable for his emancipatory goals: sensitivity to historical specificity and qualitative social transformation. By avoiding the excesses to which Hegelian philosophies of history were prone in the past, Habermas seems to have banished from his thought the possibility of real, qualitative historical change, the locus where theoretical false oppositions like facticity and validity can be grounded and understood in practical reality. As I show in Chapter 5, when he gestures to the possibility of change reminiscent of a structural transformation and its normative implications in his writings on globalization and European integration, Habermas is incapable of reconciling these moments with the dominant theme of the essays: the historical continuity of markets and the nation-state in modernity.

Despite his criticisms of Hegelian philosophy of consciousness and historical theodicy, Habermas is in the end a Kantian Hegelian. In his mature work he is motivated to realize Kantian moral imperatives in a linear "transepochal philosophy of history." He believes that he has escaped the excesses associated with the latter phrase because he has not designated a universal or class-specific embodiment of consciousness. But the unreflective anointing of a particular subject of historical progress is only one unsatisfying aspect of an unreconstructed philosophy of history, or philosophy of consciousness. True, Habermas now attributes social change to the interaction of communicating individuals rather than competitive groups – there are no "world historical personages" in his theory.[4] But communication that remains ungrounded in social and economic institutions, in the manner that critical-rational discourse had been so well grounded in *Public Sphere*, cannot be legitimately identified as a motor of world history or historical changes any more than could "spirit" or "labor" in earlier, more orthodox philosophies of history.[5]

Toward the end of BFN, Habermas insists explicitly on the historical focus of his enterprise:

Because [democratic-constitutional] rights must be interpreted in various ways under changing social circumstances, the light they throw on this context is refracted into a spectrum of changing legal paradigms. Historical constitutions can be seen as so many ways of construing one and the same practice – the

---

[4] Ibid., 440.
[5] See Jürgen Habermas, *Theory and Practice*, trans. John Viertel (Boston: Beacon Press, 1973).

practice of self-determination on the part of free and equal legal subjects; but like every practice this too is situated in history. Those involved must start with their own current practice if they want to achieve clarity about what such a practice means in general. (BFN 386–7)

This is an explicit injunction to contextualize one's own moment and one's proposed activity within it as a basic step in the process of democratic practice. However, Habermas's own mode of analysis, an analysis that overaccentuates Kant at the expense of Hegel, ultimately forecloses the very emancipatory possibility that it aspires to open. The dilemma of historicizing emancipatory practice necessarily evokes the figure of Lukács, who, though ultimately succumbing to his own "philosophy of history," helped lay the social-theoretical foundations for the project of critical theory in which Habermas still claims to be engaged. Habermas had intended that his Kantian turn in the years leading up to the publication of TCA would serve as the second, more efficacious, appropriation of Weber in the tradition of critical theory. In the present context, however, one of the most enduringly relevant aspects of Lukács's first appropriation of Weber in *History and Class Consciousness* is his indictment of neo-Kantian, Weberian methodologies for their inability to grasp qualitative historical transfigurations.[6] As I have shown, in TCA and subsequent works like BFN, Habermas demonstrates that it is rather his own "critical theory" that has been appropriated by Weberian methodology and not vice versa, for his theoretical project succumbs to that sociohistorical myopia still characteristic of frameworks that posit modernity in terms of secularization, rationalization, or differentiation as opposed to a series of structural transformations of markets and the state.[7]

BFN, as Chapter 4 demonstrated, is an impressive attempt to resolve the dilemmas, normative and historical, bequeathed to Habermas by Weber's SL. The discourse theory of law effectively renourishes Weber's morally impoverished analytical approach and straightforwardly addresses the dilemma left by Weber's historical understanding of the *Rechtsstaat*'s demise. But because Habermas, for the most part, carries out this resolution with the assumption of a historical, social, economic, and political reality having grown merely more complex since Weber's day, Habermas's legal solution lacks full contemporary efficacy. His own

---

[6] See Georg Lukács, *History and Class Consciousness*, trans. Rodney Livingstone (Cambridge, MA: MIT Press, 1988), 144–5.

[7] As Habermas himself admits: see Habermas, "Further Reflections on the Public Sphere," 464.

somewhat mechanical attempt to update his theory in application, with only minor adjustment, to a supranational level in the EU lacks the historical sensibility of the author of *Public Sphere* and the heir, however skeptical or reluctant, of the author of *History and Class Consciousness*. These works delineated the relationship between the changing intellectual currents and transforming socioeconomic conditions at two different points in the emergence of the European *Sozialstaat*.[8]

Habermas's present project requires just such a radical interrogation of the European state model, a model undergoing changes typified by the relationship of European law to national welfare states, the transnational functioning of comitology, and the eventual emergence of multiple policy Europes. In light of precisely such developments must Habermas situate, and thus necessarily reconfigure, his discourse theory of law. A complexity theory of social differentiation, a traditional/posttraditional framework for understanding the origins of modernity, and a linear conception of historical change within modernity inhibit Habermas's attempt to formulate a coherent normative vision of European integration and prevent him from apprehending the EU *Sektoralstaat* as a historically novel social form. In order to do so more perspicaciously, the master and his many students could do worse than reappropriate the methodology that the young Habermas deployed to investigate the last structural transformation of the European state in *Public Sphere*.

Die Geschichte aber haben wir zu nehmen, wie sie ist; wir haben historisch, empirisch zu verfahren. (G. W. F. Hegel, *Die Vernunft in der Geschichte* [1837], ed. J. Hoffmeister [Hamburg: Meiner, 1955], 30)

---

[8] Unfortunately, Habermas consistently misrepresents the argument of *Public Sphere* and underestimates the theoretical-empirical achievement it represents. In "Further Reflections on the Public Sphere," for instance, he erroneously suggests that STPS confined the realization of a public sphere to the bourgeois era exclusively (442); he exaggerates by accusing the book of operating with an overly homogeneous notion of sociopolitical totality (443); he neglects to acknowledge that, unlike his own later work, STPS does not assume "background consensus" in "premodern societies" (444–5); and he forgets that the book's historical narrative of modernity is multiepochal and not simply reducible to a *Rechtsstaat–Sozialstaat* opposition (445, 452–3).

Index